THE
COMMUNIST MOVEMENT

FERNANDO CLAUDIN

THE
COMMUNIST MOVEMENT

FROM COMINTERN TO COMINFORM

✾

**PART ONE
THE CRISIS OF THE
COMMUNIST INTERNATIONAL**

Translated by Brian Pearce

**MONTHLY REVIEW PRESS
NEW YORK AND LONDON**

Originally published by Editions Ruedo Ibérico,
copyright © 1970 by Editions Ruedo Ibérico

Library of Congress Cataloging in Publication Data
Claudín, Fernando.
   The Communist movement.
   Translation of La crisis del movimiento comunista.
   Includes bibliographical references and index.
   1. Communism—History. I. Title.
HX40.C59813   335.43   74-25015
ISBN 0-85345-366-7

First Printing

Monthly Review Press
62 West 14th Street, New York, N.Y. 10011
21 Theobalds Road, London WC1X 8SL

Manufactured in the United States of America

To my daughters, Carmen and Tania

CONTENTS

Contents

NOTE TO THE FRENCH EDITION

For the French edition I have revised the Spanish text, making some changes which, in the main, concern points of detail, and are aimed at clarifying certain formulations and making some factual allusions more precise, or including new bibliographical references. The only change of substance is the merging of the last chapters of the two parts (the titles of which in the Spanish version are 'Notas finales' and 'Primer epilogo') into a single chapter – an epilogue – which concludes the book. In this new text I have discarded some questions which seem to me of secondary importance, while expanding my treatment of others to which I had not paid sufficient attention in the concluding chapters of the Spanish version.

F.C.

NOTE TO THE ENGLISH EDITION

The conscientious work done by Brian Pearce in producing the English translation to Part One has enabled me to correct some errors in the original text, and also some that occurred in the French version. I take this opportunity to thank him.

PREFACE

'It seems,' wrote Isaac Deutscher in 1950, in one of the articles collected in his book *Heretics and Renegades,* 'that the only dignified attitude the intellectual ex-Communist can take is to rise *au-dessus de la mêlée.*' At first sight this seems strange advice. Let us examine it more closely.

In these pages, written in 1950, Deutscher analyses the reflections on Communism published by certain writers – Arthur Koestler, Ignazio Silone, André Gide, Louis Fischer, Richard Wright and Stephen Spender – who had been either members or fellow-travellers of the party, and he comes very quickly to the conclusion that it would have been better if all of them had remained silent. It is obvious that Deutscher does not like the intellectuals who were expelled from the party, or at least not those who were expelled after 1929, that is, after the defeat of the left opposition. They find it too easy, he seems to be saying, to play the role of renegades, towards which all circumstances impel them – the objective conditions, the anathemas of the expulsion procedure, and the condescending sarcasm of those whose expulsion took place a little earlier.

Actually, one is always expelled at the wrong moment, either too late or too soon. Too late in relation to the objective facts about Stalinism, the USSR and the societies that have resulted from the expansion of Russia's sphere of influence in the world, facts that one has concealed from oneself over a long period, in the ideological haze surrounding the priorities of action and the tricks played by 'historical reason'. Too soon in relation to the possibilities of being understood and followed within the party itself, where one wages a battle in which one is always in the minority, a battle that is lost in advance. But this twofold lateness – delay in achieving awareness in relation to the objective density of the

1

course of events, and lagging behind by the bulk of the militants as compared with the advanced minorities who want to see a 'new course' adopted – does not result from a chance situation which could be disposed of by means of ridicule. It possesses the rigorousness, the rigorous characteristics, of a historical law applicable to all the periods and all the crises of Communism.

Isaac Deutscher, then, is mistrustful of the intellectuals with whom the Communist Party parts company, or who break with it. He advises them to engage no further in politics, but to remain above the battle: in short, to cease to be involved. Deutscher would doubtless have approved of the attitude taken up by Roger Vailland, with his abrupt switch from an alienating fideism to the agnosticism of a *grand seigneur*.

With that taste for historical analogies which has produced such great theoretical ravages among revolutionaries, Deutscher offers as an example to the ex-Communist intellectuals the attitudes taken in the past by such men as Jefferson, Goethe or Shelley. Why does he bring forward these startling names? Because, in his opinion, it is possible to establish a historical parallel between the Stalin epoch and the epoch of Napoleon. Accordingly, the ex-Communist intellectuals ought to copy Jefferson, Goethe and Shelley because the latter were able to appreciate that 'despite Napoleon's violence and frauds, the message of the French revolution survived to echo powerfully throughout the nineteenth century,' and so they never joined in that chorus of Liberals which played into the hands of the Holy Alliance.

It is, as we see, a curious historical comparison. *Has* the message of the October revolution continued to be spread, despite the 'violence and frauds' of Stalin? *Has* the 'Jacobin' essence of Leninism continued to make itself felt despite the Soviet 'Thermidor'? *Do* the intellectuals expelled from the Communist movement inevitably become renegades because the party is the embodiment of Historical Reason? Deutscher does not formulate these conclusions categorically, but he seems to be suggesting them, with a mixture of ideological illusion and despair which is highly characteristic of the period when he wrote his article.

Today, however, we live in a different period; and Fernando Claudin is not a writer who joined the Communist movement on the basis of the

People's Front platform of defence of culture and peace and then was expelled from it for the crime of petty-bourgeois humanism.

A leader of the Young Communists in Madrid and a student of architecture, Fernando Claudin abandoned, in or about 1933, all personal ambitions in order to become a functionary of the revolution. (The fact that the revolution has not functioned in accordance with the prescriptions of its functionaries is quite another matter.) Since that time, right down to his expulsion from the Communist Party of Spain in February 1965, his life has been merged with the life of the Communist movement, with the history of the Spanish revolution, its successes, setbacks and mistakes. The years of the bourgeois republic, the civil war, defeat and emigration, underground activity against Franco – all these episodes were experienced by Claudin in posts of central responsibility in the Communist Party machine.

It was at the end of 1963 that a discussion began in the Executive Committee of the Communist Party of Spain which went on until the spring of 1964 and ended with the expulsion of Claudin and some other leaders of the party. (A discussion? But is it possible to give the name 'discussion' to that repetitive and sterile confrontation of two monologues, that talk without any meeting of minds, which the very structures of 'democratic centralism', produced by thirty years of Stalinist practice, doomed irremediably to the choice, equally ineffective though for different reasons, between mechanical submission by the minority on the one hand, and faction work on the other?)

The essential questions involved in this clash had been maturing for years, ever since 1956. Sooner or later, a crisis was bound to break out at the top of the Spanish Communist Party machine. And yet the dates that define the beginning and the end of this process (in both senses of the word – historical and juridical) are not without significance. The year 1956 was not only the year of the Twentieth Congress, of the secret report 'attributed to' Khrushchev, it was also, and above all, the year in which all the centrifugal tendencies burst forth in the bloc of countries subject to Russian hegemony. Some of these, *nationalist* in character, were essentially negative, although inevitable, since they represented – and this is one of the historical problems illuminated by Claudin's analysis – the price to be paid for all the years of barbarous subjection of national revolutionary interests exclusively to those of Russian *raison d'état*. The other centrifugal tendencies, however, were of a *social* nature, and these were highly positive. Over the years, from Poland to Hungary to Czechoslovakia, and despite the crushing of them one after the other by the military intervention of the Russian state, these tendencies have put on the current agenda the need for new instruments of socialist democracy – the need for revolution, in fact, for the criticism of weapons, replacing the weapons of criticism. To be sure, the political expression assumed by these tendencies has often been a confused one, since the social forces that convey them are emerging from several decades of historical darkness, bureaucratic destruction of every initiative on the part of the masses, and collective depoliticization and demoralization, which have seemed to leave open no roads but those of individual 'salvation': careerism, technocratic cynicism, religiosity, etc.

On the other hand, 1956 was also a crucial year in Spain. It was a year of great mass struggles by workers and students, in the course of which a new correlation of class forces began to take shape, to some extent freed from the fancy dress and ideological over-determinations of the civil war. It was a year in which the system of political leadership inherited from the period of autarky began to enter into crisis. The very aims of Spanish capitalist economy started to change, under the pressure of objective requirements: the stage of extensive accumulation gave way to that of increase in the productivity of labour, of acquiring ability to compete in world markets. In other words, the driving-force of Spanish capitalist economy could no longer be the extraction of absolute surplus-value but, instead, must be the production of relative surplus-value – a clear sign that Spanish capitalism was approaching its 'modern' phase.

And yet, in 1963–4, when the crisis that had been maturing in the top leadership of the Spanish Communist Party reached breaking-point, none of the problems confronting the Communist movement, none of the questions of the strategy of the struggle in Spain, had been solved. On the contrary: the gulf between a subjectivist and triumphalist ideological view of reality and that reality itself had become steadily wider. At every level, in all fields, this was a period of retrogression.

In the USSR 'de-Stalinization' had not gone beyond the limits of a settlement of accounts between leading groups of the central political bureaucracy, a new distribution of roles within a system that remained intact in all essentials.

In Spain the very magnitude of the workers' struggles in 1962 served to demonstrate the definitive failure suffered by the strategy of the 'peaceful national strike'. These struggles showed the necessity for approaching in a radically new way the problems of the revolution in Spain – the character of this revolution, its immediate and long-term aims, its class alliances.

Expelled from the party in 1965, Fernando Claudin has not followed Isaac Deutscher's advice. He has not placed himself 'above the battle', he has not 'ceased to be involved'. He has not sought to emulate the distant example given by Jefferson, Shelley or Goethe, but rather that, nearer in time, of Deutscher himself. Like the latter, and however great the differences between them in style of work, method and political conclusions drawn, Fernando Claudin has set himself the aim of arriving at an overall understanding of the reason for the failure and degeneration of the Communist movement. Thereby he has, of course, put himself on trial and under interrogation. Is this not, indeed, the best way to get to know oneself and grasp the meaning of the story of one's own life – to master and comprehend the historical experience from which one has issued and which one has helped to make?

In the course of his work, Claudin has re-discovered the bracing properties of critical Marxism. In undertaking a historical analysis of the Communist International, Claudin does not apply himself to the reality of the Communist movement in order to find confirmation in it for his own suspicions and grudges or his theoretical intuitions. He studies this reality so as to make it unfold before us in its objective significance, its dialectical development. And it is this deployment of historical reality itself that gives Claudin's book its original formal structure, for it breaks through the narrow framework of chronological order so as to establish a dialectical order, with two planes which are complementary and contradictory: that of indispensable logical reconstruction, and that – dia-chronic–synchronic – of history itself. But are we not here faced precisely with the features distinctive of the Marxist method?

JORGE SEMPRUN

INTRODUCTION

The year 1956 marked for me, as for so many other Communists, the beginning of a break with a comfortable and optimistic view of our movement's situation and prospects. Until then its past and present, and even its future, had constituted no problem. Marx and Engels, Lenin and Stalin, the super-geniuses of mankind, had solved, on our behalf, all the basic unknowns. The road of the revolution was certainly longer and harder than we had expected when we were young, and it had described a broad curve, through the backward countries, which Marx had not foreseen, but it continued to appear to us both clear and sure. Socialism, already finally established over a sixth of the earth's surface, was beginning to be built, with the same success, in a number of other countries, whereas capitalism, in its death-agony, was floundering in the 'second stage' of the 'general crisis'. The victory of the great Chinese revolution heralded the collapse of imperialism's 'colonial rearguard'. In the rest of the world we Communists, individuals 'of a special mould', constituted the only conscious and organized revolutionary force. Possessed as we were of a scientific theory which had been verified a thousand times by practice, and supported as we were by the formidable power which had crushed the Hitlerite armies, it was beyond question that the future belonged to us. The defeats suffered in the past were due to 'objective conditions' and to 'betrayals by the Social Democrats', but our policy had always been right in essentials. With the Communist International gone from the scene, we still counted on the aid of a guide so wise and experienced as the party of Lenin and Stalin – aid that made up for the inadequacy of the other Communist parties, its disciples. In short, final victory on the world scale was guaranteed. It was only a matter of time, perseverance and effort.

The revelations of Khrushchev's 'secret report', and then the revolts of the workers and intellectuals of Hungary and Poland against the Stalinist system, destroyed at a stroke this whole view of things. And disturbing question-marks arose from its ruins. One there was, in particular, which embraced all the rest: what sort of Marxism was this of ours, with its two sides, theoretical and practical, which, instead of helping us to interpret reality, had hidden it from us and disguised it? In my own case, the answer to this fundamental question came to light through a long and painful settlement of accounts with twenty-five years of education in Stalinism, and through a series of conflicts within the leadership of the Communist Party of Spain, to which I had belonged since 1947. I was expelled from the party in 1965, at the same time as Frederico Sanchez, the youngest member of the leadership, whose evolution had been similar to mine. As popular wisdom has it, it's an ill wind that blows nobody any good, and this unavoidable occurrence gave me the time and the freedom of mind needed to search out, so far as my knowledge and experience allowed, the answer to the question I have set out above. That was how this book originated.

In the course of my work I came to a conclusion which had not been clear to me at the outset: the Communist movement – the Stalinist party, in both its national and its international dimensions, in the exercise of power as well as in its function as an instrument of struggle for power – had entered during the 1950s into a general and irreversible crisis. By its very nature it is incapable of transforming itself, of 'negating' itself in the Hegelian sense of the term. This does not, of course, rule out the possibility that more or less substantial sections of this movement may contribute to the creation of a new Marxist revolutionary vanguard, the need for which in our times is beyond any doubt. One must distinguish between the revolutionary subjectivity of very many Communists and the ideological and organizational system which makes it sterile.

I speak of a new *Marxist* revolutionary vanguard because in my opinion – and my work on this book has scattered the doubts that at one stage had troubled me on this score – it is not Marxism that has been shipwrecked historically, but, rather, a certain dogmatization and perversion of Marxist thought. Its critical and revolutionary essence, and many of its chief conceptions and theses, remain vital and relevant – on condition, naturally, that we agree to set Marx in his own period, and to continue his work taking due account of the period that we ourselves are in. This compels us to recognize the fact, among others, that the premises of Marxism's dogmatization and perversion lie in its very function as the *ideology* of the revolutionary movement. It was not accidental that Stalinism was not the first – any more, perhaps, than it will be the last – of these deformations. My research on the crisis of the Communist movement represents an attempt to use Marxism, conceived in this way, to make a critical analysis of the political theory and practice of Marxism since the October revolution.

The problem that is being tackled here is so vast and so complex that its elucidation can only be achieved by means of many contributions, in all branches of the social sciences. A good number of such contributions have already been made, but nevertheless the bulk of the work still remains to be done. The present book has no higher claim than to be one more such contribution. It is not a history of the movement, but an analysis of the principal factors and processes that have brought about the movement's crisis. This undoubtedly gives my analysis a 'negative' aspect. But if this 'negativity' can help even a little to open the way to new forms of the revolutionary movement, liberated, so far as possible, from the myths and errors of the past, then it will be, as I intend it to be, a dialectical, Marxist negativity.

Does it need saying that this book is not only a criticism of the Communist movement but also a self-criticism by the author? However, this last aspect is of no importance whatsoever.

December 1969

As in private life one distinguishes between what a man thinks and says of himself and what he really is and does, still more in historical struggles must one distinguish the phrases and fancies of the parties from their real organism and their real interests, their conception of themselves from their reality.

MARX

We must not conceal our mistakes from the enemy. Anyone who is afraid of this is no revolutionary.

LENIN

PART ONE:
THE CRISIS OF
THE COMMUNIST
INTERNATIONAL

I

THE DISSOLUTION

Departing from us, Comrade Lenin enjoined us to remain faithful to the principles of the Communist International. We vow to you, Comrade Lenin, that we shall not spare our lives to strengthen and extend the union of the working people of the whole world — the Communist International!

STALIN, 1924

THE LAST EPISODE OF A LONG CRISIS

On 10 June 1943 the Communist International ceased to exist as 'the directing centre of the international working-class movement'. This formulation signified that the national sections of the Communist International continued to exist, but were transformed into independent Communist parties, freed from 'their obligations arising from the statutes and resolutions of the Congresses of the Communist International'.[1] In the resolution of the Presidium of the Executive Committee of the Comintern announcing this historic decision, no other form of international tie between Communist parties was provided for, nor was the slightest allusion made to the possibility of one being established in the future. From being sections of 'a single world Communist Party', directed by an executive committee whose decisions were 'binding on all sections of the Communist International and must be promptly carried out',[2] the Communist parties became, overnight, national parties that were wholly independent and without any links between them – at least, if we keep to the letter of the official document that put an end to the Comintern's existence.

It was hard to reconcile such complete independence of the Communist parties with Marxist internationalism. The establishment of the

15

Third International, like that of its two predecessors, had been the logical consequence, on the plane of political *praxis*, of the theoretical principle enunciated by Marx in the statutes of the First International: 'The emancipation of the workers is not a local, nor a national, but an international problem.'[3] From the international scope of this task there followed the need for an organization of corresponding type. Its structures, functioning, programme, etc., would doubtless have to be modified, in the light of changes in historical conditions; but the Marxists had never questioned the need for proletarian internationalism to find embodiment in a concrete form of organization.

When the Franco–Prussian war and the defeat of the Commune, together with the internal struggle between Marxists and Bakuninists, brought about the crisis of the First International, Marx and Engels looked on its disappearance as merely temporary.[4] And when the majority of the leaders of the Second International gave up internationalist attitudes in order to enter into *union sacrée* with their respective national bourgeoisies during the war of 1914–18, Lenin described their conduct as treason, and at once proclaimed the necessity and urgency of creating a new International. One of the features that most sharply distinguished this new International from its predecessors was the absolute primacy accorded to the 'international' over the 'national'. From the very first moment it elevated to a principle the necessity for 'subordinating the interests of the movement in each country to the common interest of the international revolution'.[5] This principle was reaffirmed at each of its congresses. The triumph of 'the proletarian world revolution', it is stressed in the programme of the Comintern approved by the Sixth Congress (1928), 'compels the workers to unite closely in a single international army of the proletariat of all countries, irrespective of frontiers and of all differences of nationality, culture, language, race, sex, or occupation.'[6] The Comintern is the organizer and leader of this 'army', its general staff, with the historical mission of elaborating and implementing the overall strategy which defines and articulates the activity of the various national 'detachments' of the world army of the proletariat.[7]

Lenin and his followers considered, moreover, that the need for an international revolutionary organization, firmly centralized and disciplined, was especially imperative in wartime, when social contradictions become acute and the possibility of a revolutionary way out can become an immediate issue. The structures that the Comintern adopted were intended precisely to prevent a repetition of what had happened in 1914: the Third International would not collapse as the second had done when the moment of truth arrived. This was why the Sixth Congress of the Comintern called upon all its sections 'to give the struggle against war a more international character and to take preparatory measures for the international coordination of revolutionary action in order that they may be in a position at the required moment to carry out important international mass action against imperialist war'. And it laid down that 'the closest possible contact must be established between all the sections [of the Communist International] before the outbreak of war, and every means must be employed to maintain those contacts throughout the whole course of the war'.[8] The Seventh and last Congress of the Comintern (1935) confirmed the decisions of the Sixth as far as war was concerned, and reasserted the thesis of Lenin and Rosa Luxemburg which had been adopted by the Stuttgart Congress of the Second International: 'If nevertheless war breaks out, it is their duty to work for its speedy termination and to strive with all their might to utilize the economic and political crisis produced by the war to rouse the masses of the people and thereby hasten the downfall of capitalist class rule.'[9]

War came. The international proletariat was faced with a struggle the world-wide dimensions of which were without precedent in the history of the labour movement. This war, moreover – especially after the German attack on the USSR – did not fit into any of the patterns carefully set out by the Comintern, but presented fresh, original characteristics.[10] Looked at from the standpoint of the Comintern's principles and traditional postulates, this situation would seem to have enhanced the necessity for a centre to ensure strategical and tactical guidance of the world proletariat, both during the war and at the moment of victory. But it was precisely when 'the international army of the proletariat' was engaged in the hardest struggle against Fascist imperialism, and when the ulterior motives of the other sector of imperialism, which circumstances had made the USSR's momentary ally, were becoming clearly

defined, that the 'general staff' of the world revolution decided . . . to
dissolve itself.

What happened? Was it an act of betrayal, as the Trotskyists at once
declared? Or was it a measure that was 'proper and timely because it
facilitates the organization of the common onslaught of all freedom-
loving nations against the common enemy', as Stalin declared? Was it a
decision dictated by the Comintern's historical experience which had
revealed the inadequacy of its structures, as the Executive Committee of
the Comintern (the ECCI) itself declared?

As all have said who have studied the question critically, and as I
shall endeavour to show afresh, the Comintern was dissolved quite suddenly, in the spring of 1943, on Stalin's orders, so as to facilitate negotiations with Roosevelt and Churchill, whose aim was not merely to
secure Germany's defeat but also to ensure the partition of the world
among the 'Big Three'. The reality was concealed from the Communists
in the resolution of the Presidium of the ECCI – behind specious
arguments about the dissolution corresponding to the most fundamental interests of the international proletariat, being inspired by the
example that Marx had given, and so on. The resolution proclaimed that
the Comintern had succeeded historically, and gave a clean bill of
health to the Communist movement. Over a quarter of a century
later, the Communist Party of the Soviet Union is still putting
out the same deceptive explanation of what happened. And this is
equally true of almost all the other Communist parties, as could be
observed when the fiftieth anniversary of the formation of the
Comintern and the twenty-fifth anniversary of its dissolution came to
be celebrated.[11]

In reality, Stalin was able to get rid of the Comintern so expeditiously
because the latter had been gravely ill for a long time. Its inglorious
death, at a crossroads of world history, closed the final episode of a long
crisis, the premises of which has already begun to be created in Lenin's
time, when the actual course being taken by the capitalist world came
into contradiction with certain pre-suppositions, theoretical, political
and organizational, of the Communist International. The history of the
Third International is the story of its inability to overcome this contradiction by means of a self-reform that would have made it capable of

interpreting reality correctly and acting effectively upon this reality so as to transform it in a revolutionary way.

However, what is of interest in the dissolution of the Comintern is not confined to the fact that it expresses in concentrated fashion the ultimate phase of the crisis of that institution. This event contains, at the same time, the premises of the subsequent crisis of the world Communist movement, of that movement whose birth certificate was written in the death certificate of the Comintern. The dissolution in fact, failed to eliminate the factors that determined the crisis: it merely shifted them forward, either in other forms or else without any change at all, into the new stage of the Communist movement. The crisis of the latter, which forms the principal subject of my investigation, cannot be understood without a thoroughgoing examination of these factors. In other words, an analysis of the crisis of the Comintern is indispensable if one is to make intelligible the present crisis of the Communist movement. This is why I have devoted the first part of my book to a study of the crisis of the Communist International. I begin by analysing the dissolution because knowledge of the eventual point of arrival helps one to understand the process. Study of the latter will then enable us to come back to the dissolution of the Comintern equipped with awareness of all the implications that it involved for the subsequent development of the Communist movement.

The official version of the dissolution of the Comintern is contained in three documents which I have reproduced in full[12] because of their relative brevity and because of the repeated references I shall make to them. These documents, the only sources at our disposal, are: the resolution of the Presidium of the Executive Committee of the Communist International, 15 May 1943; the statement issued by the same body on 9 June; and the declaration made by Stalin on 28 May of the same year. The discussions that may have taken place within the Presidium, the views expressed by other Communist leaders, the specific terms of Stalin's intervention in the matter, the precise facts of the inner connection between the dissolution of the Comintern and the strategic and diplomatic problems confronting the government of the USSR at that moment – all these are questions the answers to which still remain locked in the secrecy of the Soviet archives. In investigating this, as with many other problems of the Comintern, we come up against the notorious difficulty that even Togliatti pointed out in 1959: the sources 'are now difficult of access, scattered in different places, in publications that it is almost impossible to obtain in the West. Even in the Soviet Union re-publication of the documents essential for a historical study has hardly begun. And one cannot but add that in addition to the material difficulties, there are others which are related to the *substance* of the themes that a history of the Comintern would have to deal with.'[13] The 'even' of this discreet criticism by Togliatti of the Soviet leaders should be replaced by 'especially', in order to come closer to the truth. For, at the time when Togliatti wrote those lines – and this is still truer for the following years – many more documents of the Communist International had been re-published in the West than in the Soviet Union.[14] Furthermore, Marxist criticism has need not merely of re-publication of documents that were public when they originally appeared, but also of access to the internal documents of the Comintern. Naturally, where the history of a revolutionary organization is concerned, a great deal of its activity is clandestine and certain aspects cannot be made public even a long time after the events. But, on the one hand, the Comintern's activities took place between twenty-five and fifty years ago, and, on the other, the 'substance' that Togliatti mentions does not essentially consist of matters connected with 'conspiratorial technique': it is above all political in character, and relates to the internal struggles of the Soviet Communist Party and the Comintern, the methods used in this struggle, the connections between the activity of the Comintern and Soviet foreign policy, and so on. It is obvious that this state of affairs is a real scandal from the standpoint of the interests, theoretical and political, of the revolutionary struggle. It constitutes, very concretely, a barrier to critical utilization of the rich experience embodied in the twenty-five years of the Comintern's existence. In the inaugural address of the First International, Marx called upon the workers to 'master the mysteries' of international politics. He certainly never suspected that it would prove so hard for Marxists, in the course of time, to master the 'mysteries' of their own organization. Despite these difficulties, analysis of the accessible documents does provide us with significant pointers to the immediate cause of the dissolution – Stalin's *raison d'état* – and also shows that the dissolution gave expression, as I have already said, to the historical crisis of the Comintern.

THE IRONY OF HISTORY

It is well known that questions of 'procedure' are sometimes revealing, especially in politics. At first sight, the procedure followed for the dissolution of the Comintern (see the resolution, point 7 and the statement) was as democratic as the circumstances allowed. It was of course impossible to convene a congress, which would have been obligatory under the Statutes for a matter of such importance: but the Presidium, 'anxious' not to decide on its own, did submit the question to consideration by the sections. Thirty-one affirmative replies came back to it, including those of 'all the most important sections'. No objection would be raised. What more could be required under wartime conditions?

And yet, if we look more closely at this consultation, matters appear in a different light. In the first place, the Presidium's statement shows that the dissolution was approved by only a minority of the sections. According to the last congress of the Comintern, the latter embraced sixty-six sections.[15] Thus, thirty-five parties, over half of the total, were not 'able to send in their decisions'. Among these were nearly all the parties of the colonial and dependent countries of Asia and Africa. Since, according to the statement by the Presidium, 'the most important sections' had sent in their views, this means that, for the leaders of the International, none of the Communist parties of Asia, apart from the Chinese and Syrian Communist Parties, belonged to this category – a significant fact, which for the moment I merely mention.

Furthermore, among the thirty-one sections which gave their opinion there were fourteen (apart from the Soviet one) which were operating illegally at that time, in the Fascist countries or those countries occupied by the forces of the latter, and separated from Moscow by the warfronts. Is it conceivable that these parties should have been able to reply within a few days to the Presidium's request? Their 'reply' is accounted for, in almost every case, by the fact that certain leading cadres of these sections of the Comintern were living as refugees in Moscow. It was they, no doubt, who gave approval to the dissolution, in the names of their respective parties.

Another significant fact is this: the resolution of 15 May was published immediately (this was why the Reuter correspondent in Moscow was able to refer, in his interview with Stalin, to the 'very favourable' British comment on it); on 28 May Stalin's declaration appeared, speaking of the dissolution as an accomplished fact. Thus, before the Presidium had been able to collect a decent number of representative 'yes' votes, the dissolution was put before the whole world as a matter already decided. The consulting of the sections was only an artifice serving to hide the way it was done.

This obviously shows that the dissolution of the Comintern was an *urgent* matter. Imperative reasons rendered it impossible to wait. Yet at the same time it would have seemed going too far to dissolve it by mere decree. The solution found was to hide the decree behind the parody of a consultation.

Why was it so urgent for the Comintern to disappear? After the Soviet victory at Stalingrad and the defeat of the Axis in North Africa there was clear prospect of victory for the anti-Fascist alliance. What reasons stood in the way of waiting until the end of the year, when the parties might examine at their respective congresses such an important question as the dissolution of their international organization? The resolution of the Presidium does not say. Its fundamental argument is that the Comintern's experience had proved that it was impossible to lead the movement from a single international centre. Even if this argument be accepted as valid – I shall consider this point later – it still does not justify the urgency of the dissolution. If the alleged impossibility really existed, it would have sufficed to 'freeze' the working of the leading organs of the Comintern until a congress could take a decision.

The true key to this urgency shows through, however, in the declaration made by Stalin: 'The dissolution of the Comintern is proper and timely because it facilitates the organization of the common onslaught of all freedom-loving nations against the common enemy . . . [It] is perfectly timely – because it is exactly now . . . that it is necessary to organize the common onslaught of freedom-loving countries,' because it will result in 'a further strengthening of the United Front of the Allies'.

The precise meaning of these formulations is well explained in the book by William Z. Foster, *A History of the Three Internationals*. Foster, chairman of the Communist Party of the USA until his death, was from 1935 onwards a member of the Presidium of the Executive Committee of the Communist International, and was always well known for his total identification with the attitudes taken by the Soviet leaders. His book corresponds completely to the schemas of Stalinist history-writing: but it is just because of this that the following passage is so interesting:

It is *significant* that the historic decision was taken right at the *most crucial moment* of the fight to establish the second front. This front was very greatly needed for a quick and decisive victory; but the Western reactionaries (who also believed Goebbels' lies about the Comintern) were blocking it. *Undoubtedly the favourable impression all over the bourgeois world made by the dissolution of the Comintern helped very decisively to break this deadly log-jam.* It was only a few months later (in November-December 1943) that there was held the famous Teheran conference, at which the date for the second front was finally decided.[16]

The 'deadly log-jam' referred to was this. The Comintern had not formally discarded its programme of 'world revolution'; left lying dormant during the Popular Front period, it was brandished once more by the Comintern during the period of the Soviet–German pact, and in the direction, moreover, of just those capitalist states that were soon afterwards to become the Soviet Union's allies. The 'bourgeois world' continued to take this programme seriously. Thus, the *New York Times* wrote on 14 February 1943: 'Swiftly, inexorably, the Russian armies continue to drive toward the west.' Their victories

foreshadow the collapse of the 'New Order' which Hitler started to impose on the world. But as the Red Armies plunge forward, they are also raising many questions in many minds as to what other order they have written on their banners ... And these questions carry the danger that they will provide a fertile ground for the latest Nazi propaganda with which Hitler hopes to escape the consequences of defeat — the propaganda which raises the bogy of a Bolshevist domination of Europe, in an effort to scare the world, divide the United Nations and therewith pave the way for a compromise peace.

In order to win the war, the Soviet army had to advance and destroy the Hitlerite army. But fear of revolutionary consequences from the defeat of Germany might break up the anti-Hitler coalition. It was therefore necessary to break the 'deadly log-jam' by defining clearly, and in a way acceptable to all the interested parties, the aims of an Allied victory. And, of course, the prospect of revolution in Europe was not acceptable to the USSR's capitalist allies.

So far, no document has come to light to prove that Roosevelt and Churchill officially called upon Stalin to do away with the Comintern. But this demand shows through like a watermark in certain articles published in the most responsible organs of the bourgeois press and certain public statements by front-rank official personages. For example, the same *New York Times* wrote on 20 December 1942 that it was 'because of the subversive and, in the result, suicidal activities of a Communist International guided by the Trotskyist ideology of the proletarian world revolution' that Hitler 'could . . . raise an issue which frightened many Germans into his camp and won a following for similar crusaders elsewhere, including the United States'. And the Vice-President of the United States, Henry Wallace, speaking about future relations between the USSR and the Western allies, declared on 8 March 1943 that 'World War No. 3 . . . would be inevitable if Russia should again embrace the Trotskyist idea of fomenting world-wide revolution'.[17] As will be shown in the chapter devoted to examining Stalin's strategy during the war, he yielded to the blackmail of his 'allies' not so much through fear of a separate peace as because the renouncing of any intention of 'fomenting world-wide revolution' was the necessary condition for a far-reaching agreement, based on a share-out of 'spheres of influence', with American imperialism. And this was one of the essential aims of Stalin's policy. Coming to an agreement about the second front, especially about its location, amounted to taking a decisive step towards the 'share-out' of the continent of Europe. This was why Stalin could not refrain from eliminating that unknown factor which gave rise to hesitation on the part of the 'bourgeois world'.

The reasons why it was urgent to dissolve the Comintern thus appear plain enough. Even if there were also other reasons for doing it, the moment chosen was entirely determined by the urgent need to give 'guarantees' to the capitalist states so far as the political objectives of the USSR were concerned. With the problem arising in this way, it is conceivable that Stalin could not wait for a Comintern congress to meet, nor even for the Communist leading group in each country to be consulted (which would not have been out of the question, given the 'technical' resources available to the Comintern, but which would have meant a lapse of time amounting to several months). In the last analysis, anyhow, the decisive element in settling what it was desired to settle was not what the Communists thought but what Roosevelt and Churchill thought – the attitude of the 'bourgeois world', as Foster puts it.

Let us note in passing – without stopping to dwell on details that would take us too far from our subject – that the dissolution of the Comintern seems to have been 'synchronized' with a number of measures which all pointed in the same direction. Not long afterwards, Stalin received Metropolitan Sergius, head of the Russian Orthodox Church, and announced, at the end of a long and friendly interview, his decision to restore the Holy Synod. At the same time, the *Internationale* was abolished as the official anthem of the Soviet state, and replaced by a song in praise of Great Russia. And on 10 May, five days before the date that appears at the foot of the resolution dissolving the Comintern, a Pan-Slav congress was held in Moscow, under the chairmanship of Dimitrov – symbolic 'changing of the guard'!

But could the dissolution of the Comintern prove really sufficient to make fear of revolution vanish from among the allies of the USSR? According to Stalin, this measure would mean a 'strengthening of the united front of the allies' and would facilitate, 'exactly now', the organization of the 'common onslaught', for it exposed the 'lie' that Moscow interfered in the affairs of other nations so as to 'Bolshevize' them, as well as the 'calumny' that the Communist parties were acting 'not in the interests of their people but on orders from outside'. The Nazis and the 'adversaries of Communism within the labour movement', said Stalin, represented the Comintern as being the instrument of this interference, and so its dissolution would finally put an end to these calumnies.

The dictionary tells us that a calumny is a false accusation, brought forward out of malice in order to do harm. If accusing the Comintern of meddling in the affairs of other countries was a calumny, then this must mean that the Comintern did not actually involve itself in the problems of the different countries and did not give orders to the various Communist parties. If that was so, then dissolving it made no substantial change, at any rate for well-informed persons. This gesture could possess only propaganda value, aimed at ignorant people who mistook calumnies for the truth. Was it possible to include in this category the leaders of world capitalism, men like Roosevelt and Churchill? What was at stake was setting up the political premises for an agreement that would decide the fate of the world for an entire epoch. Could the dissolution of the Comintern exercise an important – even decisive, according to Foster – influence in this great diplomatic process if, in fact, it changed nothing and amounted merely to 'abolishing' something that did not exist?

Stalin calmly reduced twenty-five years of history to nothing but a 'calumny'. The statutes, the programme, the resolutions of the Comintern proclaimed that the Comintern existed, and its Executive Committee operated continuously with a very specific aim: to lead the revolutionary struggle in every country, through the corresponding national section, and to coordinate these national struggles on the international scale, in a world strategy of the socialist revolution. The bourgeoisie of every country and international capitalism had always made use of Comintern theory and practice in order to charge the Communists with being under Moscow's orders, and so forth. Lenin and the Communists had not answered these charges by denying the facts but by refuting the reactionary interpretation that was put upon them. The undeniable intervention of the Comintern in the internal affairs of each country, they declared, was in conformity with the interests of its proletariat; the 'national' aspect of the struggle had to be subordinated to the 'international' aspect; the Soviet state had a duty to help the revolutionary struggle in every country – an obvious form of interference in 'internal affairs', etc. Moreover, the various Communist parties and the Comintern itself acknowledged openly that the CPSU was the 'leading party' of the Comintern. Besides, the very resolution of the Presidium which dissolved the Comintern provided a categorical denial of the 'calumny' thesis. By stating that the Comintern was dissolving itself in order to put an end to the method of 'solving the problems facing the movement in each separate country' from an 'international centre', it admitted that the Comintern *had* interfered in the internal affairs of each country. The dissolution of the Comintern thus put an end not to a 'calumny' but to a *reality*, to what it had really been, with all its successes and mistakes. That was why this measure could facilitate the negotiations between Stalin, Roosevelt and Churchill.

Why did Stalin resort to the subterfuge of talking about 'calumny'? Perhaps he saw in this a way of concealing from the Communists and from the working masses the profound significance of the concession he was making to the leaders of world capitalism. Presented like this, the dissolution could be interpreted – it was indeed in this way that the Communists generally understood it – as a *ruse de guerre*. The transformation of Stalin (now, moreover, haloed with the glory of the battle of Stalingrad) into a holy figure, a process that the Comintern had systematically promoted, made it very difficult for the Communists to read the declaration of 28 May in a critical spirit.[18]

Stalin did not merely bury a 'calumny', he sought to reassure the Allies that it would never recur. The Communist parties, he told them in effect, were no longer an internationally organized force; from now on they would confine themselves to action within a strictly national framework. This was certainly the significance of the resolution's strange silence on the possibility of international links, of any sort, between Communist parties. But neither the dissolution of the Comintern nor the tacit promise not to re-establish it in a different form was adequate for the experienced politicians of imperialism. For them it was obvious that a connection did continue to exist, however clandestine its functioning – namely, the link between each Communist party and the Soviet centre. Unless the Communist parties were to be dissolved – too much to hope for, however great Stalin's goodwill – what was essential for the bourgeois rulers was to know in what direction Moscow's influence would be exercised. In short, what would the policy of the Communist parties be in the final phase of the war and the post-war period? Were they going to 'strive with all their might to utilize the economic and political crisis produced by the war to rouse the masses of the people and thereby hasten the downfall of capitalist class rule', as the last Comintern congress had urged? It is in the reply given to this question that there lies the fundamental concession granted by Stalin to the allies. The resolution of the Presidium does not, in fact, confine itself to dissolving the International. It also defines an orientation capable of satisfying the capitalist states that were members of the anti-Hitlerite coalition: not because it constituted an infallible guarantee against revolution – the Communist parties themselves had no power to offer such a guarantee, even had they wished – but because it allowed the bourgeois parties a wide field of manoeuvre in which to ward off any danger. Events were to show that they knew how to make intelligent use of this facility.

Anti-Fascist alliance 'without difference of party or religion' (point 4 of the resolution) – that was the generic expression covering the tactics which the Comintern, in departing from the scene, recommended to the Communist parties and to the proletariat at large. This very general formulation could cover a variety of very different contents. As is known, the first manifestation of the policy of anti-Fascist unity was the People's Fronts. Then, however, it explicitly included a prospect of revolutionary deepening of the struggle, inspired by the Leninist strategy of transforming the bourgeois-democratic revolution into the socialist revolution. At the same time as the People's Front policy was adopted, the Seventh Congress, as had been pointed out, reaffirmed the Comintern's traditional orientation – to take advantage of the crisis that a new world war must produce in order to attack the very foundations of capitalism. In the resolution of the Presidium, not only is silence maintained on these prospects, but also tactical directives are supplied which are clearly intended to keep the anti-Fascist struggle within the bounds of bourgeois democracy. As regards the states allied with the USSR, it is declared that 'the sacred duty' of the Communists 'consists in aiding by every means the military efforts of the governments of these countries', each party 'working within the framework of its own country'. There is not even any advice to maintain a critical attitude towards these 'military efforts', which, in a number of cases, left a great deal to be desired. As regards the countries of the Hitlerite bloc, the tasks of the Communists, says the statement, consist in contributing to the defeat and downfall of the 'governments responsible' for the war. No reference is made to German and Italian monopoly capitalism, chief promoter of the aggressive policy of these countries (see resolution, point 4). In short, the prospect of transformation of the anti-Fascist struggle into the socialist revolution was tacitly dropped. It may be objected that this prospect could have survived in the secret intentions harboured by the Communist parties. Even if this were so, however, the problem is not essentially altered. Revolution is prepared only by way of *open* ideological and political activity, in which objectives, methods, and so on, are formulated clearly.

The rigorous correlation between the political last-will-and-testament of the Comintern and the requirements of the negotiations between the USSR and its allies (as these were conceived by the Soviet leaders) is shown in another feature of the resolution: it contains not the slightest allusion to the struggle for national liberation of the peoples of the colonies and semi-colonies. Some of these were at that very time striving to profit by the difficulties of Anglo–French imperialism (and also those of Dutch imperialism, etc.) to break the chains of colonial subjection. The Comintern remains prudently silent on this struggle so as not to upset the allies of the USSR. Others, like the revolutionary Chinese people, were participating in a war of liberation against Japanese imperialism, which was itself at war with the USA, the USSR's ally. The consideration just mentioned could therefore not apply where the USA was concerned. But the Soviet Union had signed in 1941 a pact of neutrality and non-aggression with Japan which was to remain in force until, when Japan was practically beaten, the USSR declared war against her so as to make sure of occupying some strategic positions in the Far East. In order not to disturb the Soviet–Japanese pact, the resolution of 1943 kept silence about the great revolutionary struggle being led by the Communist Party of China.

And this entire orientation which the Comintern prescribed for the Communist parties at the moment of its disappearance from history – an orientation which included, and not just as an established fact of the moment but as something to be respected in the post-war period, the maintenance in its integrity of the chief nucleus of imperialist capitalism – this orientation was presented, in the resolution of the Presidium and in Stalin's declaration, as providing 'assurance of the friendship of nations based on their equality', and as capable of 'clearing the way to the future organization of a companionship of nations based upon their equality'. Thus, the topmost leaders of the Communist movement were spreading among the masses the illusion that equality and fraternity between nations were compatible with the survival of the principal imperialist states: the illusion that these states, by virtue merely of being at war with their capitalist rivals alongside the Soviet Union, really intended to build an ideal world. The leaders of capitalism were to show themselves able to profit by this additional allowance of moral credit granted to them by the leaders of Communism, just as they were to profit skilfully from the margin of manoeuvre that was allowed them by the restriction of the aims of the Communist parties to the framework of bourgeois democracy.

It is not out of place to stress the fact that the implicit-explicit appeal made by the resolution of 1943 for the anti-Fascist struggle not to be taken beyond limits acceptable to the capitalist powers occurred at the moment when the offensive phase of the war had begun for the anti-Hitlerite coalition. This phase was marked not only by offensives on the military fronts but also by powerful advances on the part of the resistance in the occupied countries and the reinforcement within the resistance of the most radical tendencies. This was a phase in which the danger of a *renversement des alliances* was present – though the overall political setting made this less and less likely – but also one in which a new force was growing that was rich in revolutionary potentiality.

I shall come back to this question in the second part of my study. For the time being I will confine myself to the following observation. No objective research has yet been done on the Second World War that takes account of all the complexity of the correlation and dynamics of the military, social and political factors in this phase of the great drama. One therefore cannot brush aside the hypothesis that the resolution of 1943 did in fact correspond to a realistic appreciation of this correlation of forces, of the dangers present and the actual possibilities opening before the revolutionary vanguards. Even if this were so, however, the resolution would still appear as absolutely opportunist, owing to the deceptive manner in which the concessions granted to 'anti-Fascist' imperialism were presented, and the illusions that the policy of the Communist parties, inspired by this life, put about among the masses of the people. These were deceptions and illusions that could only aid the leaders of the 'free world' in the task of cheating their peoples.

To be sure, the 'capitalist allies' paid something too. In order to secure victory over their rivals in exploiting the world they had to contribute to the victory of the state born of the October revolution. The second great share-out of 'spheres of influence' to be effected in the twentieth century – begun at the Teheran Conference with the decision about where the second front was to be opened; defined more closely during the Stalin–Churchill conversation of October 1944; and finally consecrated at Yalta and Potsdam – meant that the victorious capitalist states recognized the Soviet *glacis* in Eastern Europe.[19] This *glacis* implied the establishment, in the east and south-east of Europe, of régimes that gave full and absolute guarantees to the Soviet Union, something that was hardly compatible with the retention of capitalist structures. The revolution – a certain revolution – that had been ruled out by the testament of the Comintern would be re-introduced so far as these particular countries were concerned, under the pretext of *raison d'état*.[20]

When we take a close look at the matter, we must admit that the tribute paid by the imperialist states to the 'working-class' ally that circumstances had given them, although not negligible in so far as it strengthened their great 'socialist' competitor, was not exorbitant, either, from the standpoint of the interests of these states. In exchange for the crushing of their capitalist rivals and for guarantees against revolution in the industrially developed West of Europe, as also in the strategically important Mediterranean zone, they 'accepted' the strengthening of the Soviet state and the abolition of capitalism in the most backward part of Europe. But it must not be forgotten that the capitalist system was emerging from a period in which it had experienced the most serious economic crisis and the most terrible armed conflict in its entire history up to that time. Nor must it be forgotten that, while saving Western Europe and the great capitalist state in the Far East, capitalism was also strengthening itself in a spectacular way in the USA.

Events took it upon themselves to show that the guarantees given by Stalin to his allies, that the anti-Fascist struggle would not go too far in the direction of revolution, did indeed operate effectively in those places where they were supposed to. In France and Italy, during the last phase of the war and the immediate post-war period, the politico-social balance of forces was undoubtedly more unfavourable to the bourgeoisie than it was in most of the countries of Eastern Europe. The Communist parties enjoyed enormous influence and a substantial left-wing tendency existed among the Social Democrats. But these parties knew how to take prudent account of the 'external factor'. In Greece, where the internal situation was plainly revolutionary, the Communist party did not observe the same prudence, and was crushed. Now, the 'external factor' consisted not only of the will to *intervention* on the part of the Anglo–American forces, as official Communist history maintains, but also of the will to *non-intervention* on the part of the Soviet forces. The same was true, inversely, where the countries of the Soviet *glacis* were concerned. The 'external factor' was the compromise agreed to between the three principals, Stalin, Roosevelt and Churchill, with only one true God between them – *raison d'état*. Thanks to this compromise, the revolution did not develop beyond the stage of potentiality in France and Italy, was crushed in Greece, and was unable to raise its head in Spain, but eventually imposed itself throughout the countries of Eastern Europe.

The Comintern was both abolished and utilized in order to achieve this compromise. *Abolished* so as to demonstrate, by means of so spectacular a gesture, that the Soviet leaders renounced any intention of 'stimulating' the revolution in the vital centres of their allies; *utilized* so as to give positive form to this renunciation, preparing the Communists and the European proletariat, politically and ideologically, to accept this compromise. The resolution of May 1943 was at one and the same time the death-certificate of the past and the document destined to serve as guide in the present and the immediate future.

For this was the irony of history: established in 1919 'to organize joint action by the proletariat of the different countries which pursue the one goal: the overthrow of capitalism, the establishment of the dictatorship of the proletariat and of an international Soviet republic ...'[21]

32

the Comintern resolved to dissolve itself in 1943 so as to facilitate 'joint action' by the first Soviet state and the capitalist states which had organized armed intervention in order to crush it in its cradle. Born with a programme of world revolution in the near future, it died twenty-five years later postulating a prospect of brotherly collaboration between the Soviet state and the capitalist states.

AN ADMISSION OF BANKRUPTCY

As could have been expected from the style that had prevailed in the Comintern for a long time before the dissolution, the document of the Presidium carefully avoided any explicit reference to the fact that the measure adopted was due to the urgent requirements of the negotiations between Stalin and the allies. Its entire argument rested on the thesis that the dissolution was dictated by the historical experience of the International. The fact that this argument served to hide from the Communists the aspect which I have just analysed does not mean that it lacked any substance or importance. The argument was based, as we have seen, upon the view that the Comintern's activity had itself shown that it was not possible for the working-class movement in every country to be led from an international centre. The resolution depicted a process whereby an ever-wider gap opened between the Comintern – as the *form* of international organization and method of direction – and the needs of the working-class movement (see resolution, point 3). The schema of this process was as follows:

(1) A 'first stage', the duration of which was not defined, in which the Comintern was the organization that corresponded to the needs of the movement. In this period apparently, 'solving the problems facing the movement in each separate country' was possible from an 'international centre'.

(2) A 'final stage' in which this method came up against 'insurmountable obstacles', and in which the Comintern even became 'a drag on the further strengthening of the national working-class parties'. It was not made clear exactly when this 'final stage' began, but that date placed some time 'long before the war'. Togliatti, a signatory of the resolution of 1943, declared in 1959 that from 1934 onwards, at latest, 'it became

33

impossible and even absurd to think of being able to carry out a real task of leadership from a single centre'.[22]

Unless we are to suppose that a sudden metamorphosis took place in the Comintern, from being an organization appropriate to the needs of the working-class movement into an obstacle to it, we must assume that between the 'first stage' and the 'final stage' there was an 'intermediate stage' during which the inadequacy was already present, even if it had not yet attained the dimensions of absurdity. In short, the resolution of 1943 recognized, even if it did not say this explicitly, that, as a matter of fact, *during the greater part of the history of the Comintern, the latter was not the type of international organization that the working-class movement needed to have.*

It is true that this admission of bankruptcy related exclusively to the Comintern as a method of leadership, an international structure: the resolution of 1943 made not the slightest critical allusion to the theoretical and political work of the International. If, however, one looks at the question in a Marxist way, is it possible to conceive that the unsuitability of the method and the organizational structures can have had no negative influence on the political resolutions and the theoretical constructions?

The argument used by the Presidium of the ECCI in order to make clear the failure of the mechanism based on the international ultra-centralization of the movement is consistent and coherent. It starts, indeed, from an unquestionable fact, the principal aspects of which it enumerates: 'the deep differences of the historic paths of development of various countries, the differences in their character and even contradictions in their social orders, the differences in the level and tempo of their economic and political development, the differences, finally, in the degree of consciousness and organization of the workers'. From this unquestionable fact it deduces something else no less unquestionable, namely, the existence of 'different problems facing the working class of the various countries'. And from these two unquestionable facts it draws a corollary: the impossibility of settling the problems of the labour movement of each separate country from any international centre whatsoever. The validity of this corollary has been confirmed, the resolution stresses, by the Comintern's entire practical experience (see the resolution, point 3).

And yet this experience 'convincingly showed', says the resolution, that the form of organization chosen by the First Congress of the Comintern in order to unite the workers was a form that 'answered the conditions of the first stages of the working-class movement'. How is this thesis to be linked with the preceding argument? Was there not in these 'first stages' a deep diversity in the historical paths and the social and political orders, were there no contrasts in the level of consciousness and organization of the working-class movement? It is enough to glance at the spectacle presented by Europe and the world on the morrow of the war of 1914–18 to appreciate that those features were as obviously apparent then as in the subsequent periods of the Comintern. What are involved here are generic features that are to be found in absolutely any period of the working-class movement, and the common basis of which is well known, namely: the existence of *nations*. All the arguments used by the Presidium to justify the dissolution amount to admitting that the Comintern was shipwrecked on the fact of nationality. And this was, indeed, one of the essential causes of its crisis. Since its creation, with its '21 Conditions',[23] its ultra-centralism, its draconic subordination of the periphery to the centre, of the base to the summit, the Comintern ignored in practice, in its own internal life, the fact of national differences. Thereby it made difficulties for itself when it came to taking account of this fact in the outside world, despite its theoretical theses and political declarations recognizing the right of nations to self-determination. However, the fact of nationality is not among those that allow themselves to be overlooked easily. The last twenty years, from the 'Yugoslav crisis' to the 'Czechoslovak crisis' – by way of the Hungarian, Polish, Romanian, Albanian, Chinese, etc., crises – have recorded the history of the open *revanche* of the fact of nationality in the Communist movement. Before then there was the stage of 'underground' *revanche*, gradually sapping the Communist International. I shall return several times in the course of my analysis to this fundamental factor in the Comintern crisis, a factor that made itself felt at every level – theoretical, political, organizational.

The thesis according to which the form of organization of the Comintern *corresponded*, in its 'first stages', to the needs of the revolutionary movement was not supported by any proofs in the resolution of 1943.

On the contrary, all the arguments intended to show that the other periods saw a growing contradiction between this form of organization and the needs of the movement can be applied perfectly well, as I have shown, to the 'first stages'. It is impossible not to think that the attempt to exclude this initial period was dictated by a subjective motive, namely, to save the face before history of the creation of the Comintern, an event inseparably linked with the name of Lenin.

In the 'first stages' there was indeed a 'correspondence', but not that which was indicated in the resolution. The Comintern's ultra-centralized structure, its methods of leadership, 'corresponded' not to the real needs of the working-class movement but to a certain theoretical conception of the course to be followed by the world revolution, and to the tactical and organizational requirements of this course: the conception held by Lenin and the Bolshevik nucleus (a conception which Lenin began to re-consider in the last period of his life). The contradiction between the Comintern's organizational structures and the 'needs of the working-class movement' was only the concretization on the practical level of the contradiction between the theoretical conception of the course of the world revolution as a sort of tremendous civil war on the international scale, and the actual course taken by events in the world. To sum up, it can be said that the Comintern crisis was due not merely to its organizational structures: it was also a theoretical and political crisis.

It is significant, in this connection, that at the time when they dissolved the Comintern and drew up its historical balance-sheet, the leaders were unable to record any revolutionary victory to its credit. They had to confine themselves to four 'positive' generalizations, each of which serves to disguise the alarming negative side of the balance. 'The historic role of the Communist International,' says the resolution of 1943, '... consisted in upholding the principles of Marxism from vulgarization and distortion by the opportunist elements in the working-class movement, in helping to promote the consolidation in a number of countries of the vanguard of the foremost workers in real working-class parties, and in helping them to mobilize the workers for the defence of their economic and political interests and for the struggle against Fascism and the war the latter was preparing and for support of the Soviet

Union as the chief bulwark against Fascism.'[24] No mention is made of the fact that the great majority of the working class of the capitalist countries was still, twenty-five years after the creation of the Comintern, under the influence of reformism, and that, in the principal fortress of capitalism, the influence of Marxism upon the proletariat was practically nil.[25] Nothing is said of the fact that, in most of the advanced capitalist countries, the Communist parties were a political factor of little weight or none at all; that, where they had played a role of importance, they had suffered severe defeats, and that the strongest of them, the 'model' party in the capitalist world, had proved incapable of effectively resisting Fascism. The resolution also avoids dealing with a fundamental fact: in the quarter-century of the Comintern's existence, capitalism had undergone the gravest economic crisis in its history, followed soon after by the Second World War, and yet the Comintern had been incapable in any country of finding a revolutionary way out of the great economic crisis, and at the moment of its dissolution, when the war was already moving towards the defeat of Fascism, it was bequeathing to the Communist parties the prospect of re-establishing or defending bourgeois democracy. The resolution was silent on the defeat of the Chinese revolution of 1926–7 and the general weakness of the Comintern in the colonial countries, the defeat of the Spanish revolution, the frustration of the People's Front in France, and so on.

No Communist party can guarantee the proletariat a path without defeats or setbacks; but what is one to think of a 'Marxist' party that reviews its own history as though the defeats and setbacks in which it had played the major part had never taken place? The sombre picture sketched above, contrasting with the note of self-satisfaction sounded in the resolution of 1943, is attributable not only to subjective factors, to the Comintern's mistakes and shortcomings. Powerful objective factors played their part, helping to explain to a large extent why capitalism was able not only to survive these hard tests but even to strengthen itself in a whole series of essential secrets. But it must not be forgotten, first, that in the dialectic of the objective and the subjective, what is subjective becomes objective fact, and *vice versa*; and, secondly, that one of the Comintern's chief weaknesses consisted, precisely, in its inability to take account theoretically of these objective factors and to work out, on that basis, the appropriate forms of action. (I will limit myself to mentioning here – intending to deal more thoroughly with them in later chapters – two closely connected problems: the influence of Social Democracy in the working-class movement, the objective roots of this, etc.; and the problem of capitalism in its monopoly phase, or, more precisely, its phase of transition to state capitalism, which began between the two world wars.)

Defeats and setbacks are tribute that the revolutionary struggle cannot avoid paying in order eventually to attain victory; but this tribute is fruitful only when the revolutionary party is able to assimilate critically the experience of its defeats and the mistakes it has made. What was worst in the way the Comintern was wound up was that it turned the page without subjecting the experience accumulated to a rigorous critique. And this it did at a moment when a new epoch of radical world-wide change in every sphere was opening, when fresh millions of revolutionaries were going into action, and when the success of their action depended to a large extent upon Marxist assimilation of past experience.

The war could not provide any justification for failing to undertake this task, at least in its most urgent aspects (not to mention the fact that even when the war was over it was not attempted, either). If the Communist parties were really the revolutionary vanguard, the Communists could not be regarded as mere anti-Fascist soldiers or officers; they should have been called upon to work out, even while engaged in the struggle, revolutionary strategy and tactics that could utilize to the utmost, in each country and internationally, the possibilities offered by the profound crisis of the capitalist system and the revolutionary wave that was begining to rise. From this standpoint, experiences like those of the Spanish civil war and the People's Front in France, which had revealed the dead-ends into which the tactic of anti-Fascist unity could lead, possessed inestimable value in the situation in which the Communist parties were going to find themselves in the last phase of the war and after the war was over. Furthermore, in the conditions of anti-Fascist war on the European scale, when the outcome of the struggle in each country depended less than ever on the mere *internal* relation of forces, coordination of activity between the different Communist parties was obviously called for. The resolution of 1943 ran directly counter to these two requirements.

In the first place, it laid down a uniform line for all the parties, instead of calling upon them to work out on their own initiatives the policies that would best correspond to the concrete peculiarities of each country. In other words, the International dissolved itself declaring that the method of leading the revolutionary movement of every country from an international centre had proved historically bankrupt, while at the same time making use of this very method.

Secondly, this line was derived above all from the requirements of negotiations between the 'Big Three' of the anti-Hitlerite coalition, a fact that could not but accentuate to the maximum the right-wing tendencies that had shown themselves in the period of the People's Front policy.

Thirdly, the Comintern was dissolved without any consideration being given to the problem of new types of link between the Communist parties. The failure of the form of international organization represented by the Comintern was tacitly presented as proof that *no* form of international organization of the revolutionary movement ought to exist. In a situation that clearly called for close coordination of the activities of the Communist parties, the resolution of 1943 imposed on each of them a limitation of their activity strictly to the national framework.

In practice, as we know, each country had to restrict itself to the limits of its own country – but to do this in close relationship with the superior guidance of the Soviet Union. Actually, the Comintern's methods survived its departure. Not merely did it, at the moment of death, lay down once again a uniform line for all the Communist parties; henceforth, the role of the ECCI, as go-between for the CPSU in running the Comintern, was taken over directly, even though not openly, by the Political Bureau of the Soviet party.[26] Under these conditions, not merely the general formulation of the line laid down by the resolution of 1943, but also its concrete application would be subject to adjustment, at a moment's notice, to the needs of the USSR's high politico-military strategy. In the second part of this volume we shall see in detail the consequences this dependence entailed for the Communist movement that succeeded the Comintern.

In the subsequent chapters of this first part I propose to back up the opinion, formulated above, that underlying the liquidation of the Comintern at a turning-point of world history was the reaching of a critical moment in a long crisis that had begun already in the earliest years of the International. And I shall start by looking at the commencement and course of this crisis on the plane of the conceptions that served as the theoretical foundation for the Comintern's political activity and organic structures.

APPENDIX TO CHAPTER 1

TEXT OF THE RESOLUTION OF THE PRESIDIUM OF THE ECCI (15 MAY 1943)[27]

1. The historic role of the Communist International, which was founded in 1919 as a result of the political collapse of the great majority of old, pre-war working-class parties, consisted in upholding the principles of Marxism from vulgarization and distortion by the opportunist elements in the working-class movement, in helping to promote the consolidation in a number of countries of the vanguard of the foremost workers in real working-class parties, and in helping them to mobilize the workers for the defence of their economic and political interests and for support of the Soviet Union as the chief bulwark against Fascism.

2. The Communist International from the first exposed the real meaning of the 'Anti-Comintern Pact', as a weapon for the preparation of war by the Hitlerites. Long before the war, it ceaselessly and tirelessly exposed the vicious, subversive work carried on in other countries by the Hitlerites who masked it by their screams about the so-called interference of the Communist International in the internal affairs of these states.

3. But long before the war it became more and more clear that, with the increasing complications in the internal and international relations of the various countries, any sort of international centre would encounter insuperable obstacles in solving the problems facing the movement in each separate country. The deep differences of the historic paths of

development of various countries, the differences in their character and even contradictions in their social orders, the differences in the level and tempo of their economic and political development, the differences, finally, in the degree of consciousness and organization of the workers, conditioned the different problems facing the working class of the various countries.

The whole development of events in the last quarter of a century, and the experience accumulated by the Communist International, convincingly showed that the organizational form of uniting the workers chosen by the first congress of the Communist International answered the conditions of the first stage of the revival of the working-class movement but has been outgrown by the growth of this movement and by the complications of its problems in separate countries, and has even become a drag on the further strengthening of the national working-class parties.

4. The world war that the Hitlerites have let loose has still further sharpened the differences in the situation of the separate countries, and has placed a deep dividing line between those countries which fell under the Hitlerite tyranny and those freedom-loving peoples who have united in a powerful anti-Hitlerite coalition.

In the countries of the Hitlerite bloc the fundamental task of the working class, the toilers and all honest people consists in giving all help for the defeat of this bloc, by sabotage of the Hitlerite military machine from within, and by helping to overthrow the governments who are guilty of the war. In the countries of the anti-Hitlerite coalition, the sacred duty of the widest masses of the people, and in the first place of the foremost workers, consists in aiding by every means the military efforts of the governments of these countries aimed at the speediest defeat of the Hitlerite bloc and the assurance of the friendship of nations based on their equality.

At the same time the fact must not be lost sight of that separate countries which are members of the anti-Hitlerite coalition have their own particular problems. For example, in countries occupied by the Hitlerites which have lost their state independence, the basic task of the foremost workers and of the wide masses of the people consists in promoting armed struggle, developing into a national war of liberation against Hitlerite Germany.

At the same time, the war of liberation of the freedom-loving peoples against the Hitlerite tyranny, which has brought into movement the masses of the people, uniting them without difference of party or religion in the ranks of a powerful anti-Hitlerite coalition, has demonstrated with still greater clearness that the general national upsurge and mobilization of the people for the speediest victory over the enemy can be best of all and most fruitfully carried out by the vanguard of the working-class movement of each separate country, working within the framework of its own country.

5. Already the Seventh Congress of the Communist International, meeting in 1935, taking into account the changes that had taken place both in the international situation and in the working-class movement that demand great flexibility and independence of its sections in deciding the problems confronting them, emphasized the necessity for the Executive Committee of the Communist International, in deciding all questions of the working-class movement arising from the concrete conditions and peculiarities of each country, to make a rule of avoiding interference in the internal organizational affairs of the Communist Parties.

These same considerations guided the Communist International in considering the resolution of the Communist Party of the U S A of November 1940, on its withdrawal from the ranks of the Communist International.

6. Guided by the judgement of the founders of Marxism–Leninism, Communists have never been supporters of the conservation of organizational forms that have outlived themselves. They have always subordinated forms of organization of the working-class movement and the methods of working of such organizations to the fundamental political interest of the working-class movement as a whole, to the peculiarities of the concrete historical situation and to the problems immediately resulting from this situation. They remember the example of the great Marx, who united the foremost workers in the ranks of the Working Men's International Association, and, when the First International had fulfilled its historical task, laying the foundations for the development of

the working-class parties in the countries of Europe and America, and, as a result of the matured situation creating national working-class parties, dissolved the First International inasmuch as this form of parties, dissolved the First International inasmuch as this form of organization already no longer corresponded to the demands confronting it.

7. In consideration of the above, and taking into account the growth and political maturity of the Communist parties and their leading cadres in the separate countries, and also having in view the fact that during the present war some sections have raised the question of the dissolution of the Communist International as the directing centre of the international working-class movement.

The Presidium of the Executive Committee of the Communist International, in the circumstances of the world war not being able to convene a congress of the Communist International, puts forward the following proposal for ratification by the sections of the Communist International.

The Communist International, as the directing centre of the international working-class movement, is to be dissolved, thus freeing the sections of the Communist International from their obligations arising from the statutes and resolutions of the congresses of the Communist International.

The Presidium of the Executive Committee of the Communist International calls on all supporters of the Communist International to concentrate their energies on wholehearted support of and active participation in the war of liberation of the peoples and states of the anti-Hitlerite coalition for the speediest defeat of the deadly enemy of the working class and toilers – German Fascism and its associates and vassals.

The Presidium of the Executive Committee of the Communist International (signed): G. Dimitrov, M. Ercoli, W. Florin, K. Gottwald, V. Kolarov, J. Koplenig, O. Kuusinen, D. Manuilsky, A. Marty, W. Pieck, M. Thorez, A. Zhdanov.

The following representatives of Communist Parties also append their signatures to the present resolution: Bianco (Italy), Dolores Ibarruri (Spain), Lehtinen (Finland), Ana Pauker (Romania), Matyas Rakosi (Hungary).

STATEMENT OF THE PRESIDIUM OF ECCI ON THE DISSOLUTION OF THE COMMUNIST INTERNATIONAL
(9 JUNE 1943)

At its last meeting on 8 June 1943, the Presidium of the Executive Committee of the Communist International considered the decisions received from its sections in connection with its proposals of 15 May 1943 on the dissolution of the Communist International, and decided the following:

1. That the proposal on the dissolution of the Communist International has been approved by: the Communist Parties of Australia, Austria, the Argentine, Belgium, Bulgaria, Great Britain, Hungary, Germany, Ireland, Spain, Italy, Canada; the United Socialist Party of Catalonia; the Communist Parties of China and Colombia; the Revolutionary Communist Union of Cuba; the Communist Party of Mexico; the Workers' Party of Poland; the Communist Parties of Romania, Syria, the Soviet Union, Uruguay, Finland, France, Czechoslovakia, Chile, Switzerland, Sweden, Yugoslavia, the Union of South Africa; and the Communist International of Youth (which is incorporated in the Communist International with the full rights of a section).

2. That not one of the existing sections of the Communist International sent in any objection to the proposal of the Presidium of the EC.

In view of all this the Presidium of the Executive Committee of the Communist International declares:

1. That the proposal for the dissolution of the Communist International has been unanimously approved by all sections able to send in their decisions, including all the most important sections.

2. It considers that, as from 10 June 1943, the Executive Committee of the Communist International, the Presidium and Secretariat of the Executive Committee, as well as the International Control Commission, have been dissolved.

3. It entrusts to a committee composed of Dimitrov (as Chairman), Manuilsky, Ercoli and Pieck to carry out the winding up of the affairs of the organs, apparatus and property of the Communist International.

(Signed) on behalf of the Presidium of the ECCI: Dimitrov.

The Dissolution

Question: British comment on the decision to dissolve the Comintern
has been very favourable. What is the Soviet view of this matter and of
its bearing on future international relations?

Answer: The dissolution of the Communist International is proper and
timely because it facilitates the organization of the common onslaught of
all freedom-loving nations against the common enemy – Hitlerism. The
dissolution of the Communist International is proper because:

(a) It exposes the lie of the Hitlerites to the effect that 'Moscow' allegedly intends to intervene in the life of other nations and to 'Bolshevize'
them. From now on an end is put to this lie.

(b) It exposes the calumny of the adversaries of Communism within the
labour movement to the effect that Communist parties in various countries are allegedly acting not in the interests of their people but on orders
from outside. From now on an end is also put to this calumny.

(c) It facilitates the work of patriots of all countries for uniting the
progressive forces of their respective countries, regardless of party or
religious faith, into a single camp of national liberation – for unfolding
the struggle against Fascism.

(d) It facilitates the work of patriots of all countries for uniting all
freedom-loving peoples into a single international camp for the fight
against the menace of world domination by Hitlerism, thus clearing the
way for the future organization of a companionship of nations based
upon their equality.

I think that all these circumstances taken together will result in a
further strengthening of the United Front of the allies and other united
nations in their fight for victory over Hitlerite tyranny. I feel that the
dissolution of the Communist International is perfectly timely – because
it is exactly now, when the Fascist beast is exerting its last strength, that
it is necessary to organize the common onslaught of freedom-loving
countries to finish off this beast and to deliver the people from Fascist
oppression.

2

THE CRISIS OF THEORY

No social order is ever destroyed before all the productive forces for which it is sufficient have been developed, and new superior relations of production never replace older ones before the material conditions for their existence have matured within the womb of the old society.

MARX

LENIN'S THEORETICAL SCHEMA

For Lenin, as for Marx and Engels, the socialist revolution was essentially a *world* revolution, even if it was not possible for the working class to take power simultaneously in every country, or even, except in unusual circumstances, in several countries at once.[1] This world-wide nature of the socialist revolution followed, for Marx, from the very nature of modern productive forces, which makes capitalism a world system, an economic system that tends towards the integration of human society on the planetary scale. *A fortiori*, socialism, being the product, in the last analysis, of a transition of the productive forces to a still higher level, cannot really exist otherwise than as a world system. Hence the necessity for the revolution to win through in the *advanced* countries 'when a great social revolution shall have mastered the results of the bourgeois epoch, the market of the world and the modern powers of production, and subjected them to the common control of the most advanced peoples, then only', Marx emphasized, 'will human progress cease to resemble that hideous pagan idol, who would not drink the nectar but from the skulls of the slain.'[2]

The version according to which Lenin revised Marx on this point, by establishing theoretically that it was possible to build socialism in one

46

country taken separately, does not correspond to historical truth: it was manufactured by Stalin in order to furnish the support of authoritative arguments to his own theses on the question. The present Soviet leaders have 'developed' these theses so far as to proclaim the possibility of building *Communism* in the USSR even if capitalism continues to dominate a considerable proportion of the world's productive forces.[3]

Stalin's manipulation of Lenin's ideas on this subject was facilitated by the very widespread confusion between two concepts which are commonly formulated in the same terms: the concept of the socialist revolution as a *social* revolution, as the socialist transformation of economic and social structures and of political and cultural superstructures; and the concept of the socialist revolution as a *political* revolution, marked with the distinctive feature of the capture of power by the working class. The first content of the concept 'socialist revolution' *wholly* includes the second: every social revolution, whether socialist or bourgeois, includes as a necessary stage a political revolution, the taking of power by a new class. The second content, however, includes the first only *partly*: every political revolution – unless it is merely a *coup d'état* that transfers power from one group to another within the same ruling stratum – has a more or less developed social content; and this is all the more so when the political revolution in question is the one implied by the capture of power by the working class. But this politico-social content is only the first stone of a building the construction of which is subject to laws and conditions different from those that made it possible to lay that first stone. In order to distinguish between the two contents of the concept 'revolution', Lenin brought in the expressions 'revolution in the broad sense' and 'revolution in the narrow sense', and these I shall make use of from now on.[4]

The difference of content between the socialist revolution in the broad sense and the socialist revolution in the narrow sense includes, among other fundamental aspects, a difference of space and time. In the first case, the space is world-wide and the time covers an entire epoch of history; in the second, the space is national (or, more precisely, country-wide) and the time is reduced to a brief period of history. When Marx and Engels speak of the possibility of a victory of the socialist revolution in some particular country, taken separately, they are employing the concept in its narrow sense. They do not contemplate the hypothesis that this victory may remain isolated, within a nationally confined space, for a long period. This problem was thrown up by practice itself, when the proletarian revolution was crushed everywhere except in Russia, in the years following the war of 1914–18, while Soviet power became consolidated. The failure of Marxists, from Marx to Lenin, to consider this eventuality was due to the fact that their theoretical conception of the socialist revolution as necessarily a world revolution caused them to rule out any such possibility.[5]

Starting from this conception of theirs, the assumption made by Marx and Engels about how the socialist revolution would develop concretely went as follows. This revolution would cover a whole period of history and would be a long process, not an act – a process in which structural transformations affecting politics, culture and so on would follow one another and overlap on a world-wide scale; but the *beginning* of this process, the essential condition for it to start, was a victory of the revolution (in its narrow sense) in the economically most advanced countries. And although Marx and Engels never supposed that this victory could occur *simultaneously* in all those countries, they nevertheless saw it as a succession of socialist political revolutions following each other closely and being closely dependent on each other. As we shall see, Lenin did not depart in essentials from this overall conception.

Owing to the changes that took place in the situation in Europe in the 1840s and in the second half of the nineteenth century, Marx and Engels put forward a series of more precise prognostications regarding the way the revolutionary process would begin. While keeping to their central thesis, namely that the *socialist* revolution would begin in the most advanced countries, they considered the possibility that *other* types of revolution – bourgeois-democratic, national-liberation, etc. – which might break out in the backward countries of Europe could serve as a prelude to the socialist revolutions in the advanced countries, eventually becoming merged with these in a single revolutionary process. In the 1840s they thought that the German revolution might play this role; in the last quarter of the nineteenth century they transferred their hopes on to Russia.[6] Echoing Marx, Kautsky wrote in 1902 that 'the centre of revolutionary thought and revolutionary action is shifting more and more to the Slavs', and he saw in the Russian revolution, the warning-signs of which were already undeniably visible, 'the storm that will break the ice of reaction and irresistibly bring with it a new and happy spring for the nations'.[7]

During the revolution of 1905–7 Lenin reflected upon the dialectical interdependence between the Russian revolution and the socialist revolution which, as he saw it, in common with Kautsky and other 'orthodox' theoreticians of the Second International, had matured in Europe. The way in which Lenin understood this interdependence is of capital importance for appreciating the attitudes he took up in 1917 and after October. Not only did he consider that 'the Russian political revolution' would be made 'the prelude to the socialist revolution in Europe',[8] he also thought that the fate of the Russian revolution depended on its nature as a 'prelude', that is, on its being followed by a socialist revolution in the West. This was the conclusion to which Lenin was led from his starting-point in an analysis of the revolutionary process in Russia. As this process went deeper, he thought in 1905, the liberal bourgeoisie and the well-to-do peasants, and even a section of the middle peasants, would go over to counter-revolutionary positions. A new crisis would break out, in which the proletariat, while defending the democratic gains won in the first phase of the revolution, would now put forward the socialist revolution as its immediate aim. In this new phase, had it come to that, wrote Lenin, defeat would have 'been as inevitable as the defeat of the German revolutionary party in 1849–50, or the French proletariat in 1871, *had the European socialist proletariat* not come to the assistance of the Russian proletariat'. Given this aid, however, 'the Russian proletariat can win a second victory. The cause is no longer hopeless. The second victory will be the *socialist revolution in Europe*. The European workers will show us "how to do it" and then together with them we shall bring about the socialist revolution.'[9] In order to be able to see with such assurance this prospect before the Russian revolution, Lenin *needed* to have confidence in the revolutionary maturity of the proletariat in the West. This predisposition on his part accounts, perhaps, for the optimism characteristic of the views he expressed in this period: 'The *masses* of workers in Germany, as well as in other countries, are becoming welded ever more strongly into *an army of revolution*, and this

49

army will deploy its forces in the not far distant future – for the revolution is gaining momentum both in Germany and in other countries.'[10] Or: 'Only the blind can fail to see that socialism is now growing apace among the working class in Britain, that socialism is *once again* becoming a mass movement in that country, that social revolution is approaching in Great Britain.'[11] Or again: 'This figure [the circulation of the weekly *Appeal to Reason*] ... shows more clearly than long arguments the kind of revolution that is approaching in America.'[12]

After 1905 Lenin also included in his overall vision of the revolution 'the awakening of Asia'.

> Following the 1905 movement in Russia, the democratic revolution spread to the whole of Asia – to Turkey, Persia, China. Ferment is growing in British India. A significant development is the spread of the revolutionary democratic movement to the Dutch East Indies ... World capitalism and the 1905 movement in Russia have finally aroused Asia ... The awakening of Asia and the beginning of the struggle for power of the advanced proletariat of Europe are a symbol of the new phase in world history that began early this century.[13]

The Russian revolution was no longer the 'prelude' to the revolution in the West alone but also to the revolution in the East.

Lenin, as a revolutionary leader in what was 'in very many and very essential respects ... undoubtedly an Asian country and, what is more, one of the most benighted, medieval and shamefully backward of Asian countries', understood better than the Marxists of advanced capitalist Europe the meaning and the implications of the 'awakening of Asia' – though without getting free of the 'Eurocentrist' standpoint that was as typical of the Second International as it had been of Marx and Engels. Referring to the Chinese revolution led by Sun Yat-sen, Lenin asks:

> Does that mean, then, that the materialist West has hopelessly decayed and that light shines only from the mystic, religious East? No, quite the opposite. It means that the East has definitely taken the Western path, that new *hundreds of millions* of people will from now on share in the struggle for the ideals which the West has already worked out for itself. What has decayed is the Western bourgeoisie, which is already confronted by its gravedigger, the proletariat. But in Asia there is *still* a bourgeoisie capable

of championing sincere, militant, consistent democracy, a worthy comrade of France's great men of the Enlightenment and great leaders of the close of the eighteenth century.

Regarding as 'altogether reactionary' the dream according to which 'capitalism can be "prevented" in China and that a "social revolution" there will be made easier by the country's backwardness, and so on', Lenin compares Sun Yat-sen's programme to that of Russia's Narodniks. The Chinese revolution, in Lenin's view, will be bourgeois-agrarian in type, and a long period will have to elapse before the question of abolishing bourgeois production-relations arises.[14]

Thus, before the war of 1914, Lenin had determined the essential elements of his strategic schema of the world revolution, in which the Russian revolution constituted the prelude and the link between the socialist revolution in the West and the bourgeois-democratic revolution in the East. This theoretical construct of his linked together *three* types of revolution: directly socialist revolutions in the advanced capitalist countries (Western Europe and the USA); the Russian bourgeois-democratic revolution, which, taking place in a situation where a relatively large and concentrated proletariat was present, could proceed without any interruption, given the help of the victorious proletariat of Europe, to develop into the socialist revolution; and the revolutions in the East, where, as there was practically no proletariat, a protracted phase of capitalism *sui generis* would be necessary. The essential agent in the grand combination of revolutionary forces foreseen by Lenin continued to be the proletariat of the advanced capitalist countries. They it was who would have to show the others 'how to do it'. On them it depended whether the Russian revolution would be able to unfold fully, to the end, and whether the Oriental revolutions, once the proletariat had developed in those countries, would in their turn be able to go forward to socialism. And, as we have already seen, Lenin had no doubt that the Western proletariat possessed this revolutionary capacity. His conception of the world revolution thus remained in essentials that of Marx and Engels, though perceived from the angle of the Russian revolution.[15]

Until he wrote his famous 'April Theses', Lenin did not think that the Russian working-class could take power before the working-class of the

West. The change of outlook he then revealed was supported by Trotsky but resisted by some well-known Bolshevik leaders who clung to the party's traditional line, according to which conditions in Russia did not permit the proletarian revolution to start there before it had begun in capitalist Europe. Lenin's new attitude was not inspired solely by the unprecedented situation of 'dual power' created after the February revolution; it was also based on conviction that revolution was imminent on the European and the world scale, and that the taking of power by the Russian proletariat would merely be the first act in this European and world-wide revolution. Lenin maintained, in defiance of his adversaries: 'The Russian revolution of February–March 1917 was the beginning of the transformation of the imperialist war into civil war. This revolution took the *first* step towards ending the war; but it requires a *second* step, namely, the transfer of state power to the proletariat, to make the end of the war a *certainty*. This will be the beginning of a "break-through" on a world-wide scale, a break-through in the front of capitalist interests.'[16] And he asserted that 'the proletariat, as represented by its class-conscious vanguard, stands *for* ... the development of a world workers' revolution, a revolution which is clearly developing also in Germany, and *for* terminating the war by means of *such* a revolution ... The world situation is growing more and more involved. The *only way out* is a world workers' revolution ...'[17] When, on 23 October 1917, the Bolshevik Central Committee met and took the historic decision to prepare for armed insurrection, the resolution which explained why the moment was opportune stressed that the socialist revolution was growing throughout Europe and there was danger of a separate peace being signed between the imperialist powers with the aim of crushing the Russian revolution before the European socialist revolution could come into play.[18]

Lenin's confidence regarding the imminence of the world revolution was organically connected with the analysis of imperialism that he had made in 1915–16, basing himself on the researches of Hobson, Hilferding and others, as well as on Bukharin's study of the subject. His conclusion, so far as the connection between imperialism and the revolution is concerned, can be summed up in these expressions he uses: 'imperialism is the eve of the socialist revolution', it is 'moribund capitalism'.[19] Today, after fifty years of capitalism's 'death-agony', some Soviet theoreticians – inspired, apparently, by the pious desire to safeguard Lenin's infallibility – claim that by 'moribund' Lenin only meant to say that imperialism was capitalism 'in transition'.[20] But all Lenin's writings of this period show that he was using this expression in its strictest and most ordinary sense.

The October victory looked like the first great confirmation of Lenin's schema: the world front had been broken through, and broken through where the 'April Theses' had foreseen that this would happen. Moreover, the terrible situation in which the Russian revolution found itself in 1918, compelled to accept the Treaty of Brest-Litovsk, seemed to confirm another forecast of Lenin's: the Russian revolution was doomed unless it spread to the West.[21] In November of the same year the German revolution (which, at first sight, presented a pattern suggestively similar to the Russian revolution of February 1917: overthrow of the monarchy, workers' councils, reformist hegemony in the government, opposition down below) came on the scene to provide brilliant final confirmation, apparently, of Lenin's assumptions. The real world seemed to be conforming to the world-as-thought with almost Hegelian rigour.

As soon as he received the first news of the German crisis, Lenin sent orders to Sverdlov, chairman of the Executive Committee of the Soviets. 'The international revolution,' he wrote, 'has come so close in *one week* that it has to be reckoned with as an event of the *next few days*,' and he urged Sverdlov to organize aid for the German workers, including 'military aid'. 'We must have *by the spring* an army of three millions to help the international workers' revolution.'[22] Lenin was more than ever convinced that the hour of the 'final struggle' had sounded; but there was a cloud darkening this horizon: 'Europe's greatest misfortune and danger is that it has *no* revolutionary party.'[23] And without a revolutionary party the revolution could not win.

This attitude of Lenin's may seem incongruous if we look at it in the light of a version of his thought that is very often found among some 'Marxologists' and 'Leninologists', according to whom Leninism owed more to Blanqui than to Marx. If the revolution is the work of a conscious minority, organized and determined – which was Lenin's theory, according to this version – how could Lenin see the revolution taking place while at the same time noting the absence of a revolutionary party? Who, then, had 'organized' this revolution? Actually, Lenin's conception of the revolution does not differ from that of Marx and Engels, for whom the social phenomenon called revolution is comparable to natural phenomena, in so far as it does not depend on the will, taken in isolation, of individuals, classes and parties; revolution is the independent *result* of all of these separate wills, the product of their contradictory inter-action, of the extremely complex articulation of economic, political, social, cultural and other factors, even if, 'in the last analysis', the deter-mining element in this diachronic–synchronic totality is the dialectic of the economic structures. This is perhaps why all revolutions up to the present have begun for apparently fortuitous reasons and why the de-velopment of each of them has displayed very original features as com-pared with its predecessors. Freely exaggerating the similarity between revolution and natural phenomena, Engels wrote in a letter to Marx on 13 February 1851 (*after*, that is, Marx's conception of revolution had reached the mature stage expressed in the *Manifesto*, and had undergone the test of 1848): 'A revolution is a pure natural phenomenon which takes place more under the influence of physical laws than under that of the laws which govern the development of society in normal times. Or, more precisely, these laws acquire in times of revolution a much more physical character: the material force of necessity is manifested more intensely. And inasmuch as one comes forward as the representative of a party one will be swept into this maelstrom of natural inevitability.'[24] In 1918 Lenin considered that the 'maelstrom' was present there and then, drawing the entire world into itself, and that all that was needed was a party capable of inserting itself into this maelstrom as the con-scious representative of 'natural inevitability'.

Lenin's vision of the march of the world revolution at the time of the German revolution of November 1918 can be summarized like this:

(1) The contradictions of the imperialist system have brought about – through their outcome, the world war – the complete maturing of the objective premises (on the plane of economic structures and of social forces alike) for the international socialist revolution;

(2) The revolution has begun where the concentration of these contradictions involves the biggest explosive charge (where oppression by the Tsarist autocracy is combined with the contradictions between capitalist and pre-capitalist structures, with the ruin caused by the war, the oppression of the non-Russian nationalities, and so on) and where, at the same time, a political agent exists which has been trained and prepared on the theoretical, political and organizational planes, namely, the Bolshevik party;

(3) In inevitable obedience to the international character of the contradictions that have engendered it, the revolution is beginning to spread into the advanced capitalist countries of Europe. Victory on *this* terrain will be decisive for the world revolution. The Russian revolution will be reinforced, the proletariat of North America will follow Europe's example, and the liberation movement that has begun in the colonies will see its triumph assured;

(4) In Europe, however, the conscious and organized agent, the revolutionary party of the Bolshevik type, is missing. Unless such a party is created, the fate of the world revolution is in danger.

The operational conclusion that emerges from this schema is obvious. The revolutionary party must at all costs be created, on the European and the world scale; and this must be done before the favourable objective situation changes. The Bolshevik leaders were engaged in a dramatic race against time. At a not very representative gathering, and ignoring the contrary opinion expressed by the Spartacists (the revolutionary group of greatest importance after the Bolsheviks, at that time), the Communist International, the 'world party of revolution', was founded in March 1919.[25]

In closing this First Congress of the Comintern Lenin said: 'The victory of the proletarian revolution on a world scale is assured. The founding of an international Soviet republic is on the way.' And, the same day, at a meeting of the foreign delegates with leaders of the Bolshevik party, he assured those present that they would live to see world-wide victory: 'The comrades present in this hall saw the founding of the first Soviet republic; now they see the founding of the Third,

Communist International, and they will all see the founding of the World Federative Republic of Soviets.'[26] A year and a half later, when the Second Congress of the Comintern met, Lenin's forecasts had been sadly rebuffed by reality, but it was still possible to suppose that the world revolution was 'there'. True, the Hungarian Soviet revolution had been crushed, together with the ephemeral Workers' Republic in Bavaria, and the German revolution had moved on to the rails of the very bourgeois-democratic Weimar Constitution. Nevertheless, the situation continued to be highly unstable in Germany and throughout Central Europe, as also in the Balkans, Italy and Spain – and, above all, the Red Army was at the gates of Warsaw.[27] These last hopes were to collapse very soon. When the Third Congress of the Comintern met, in the summer of 1921, it had begun very clearly to appear that the 'final struggle' would have to be postponed. The real world was separating itself from the world-as-thought. Something had cracked in Lenin's theoretical schema, and this 'something' could not but have serious consequences for the tool that had been created precisely to serve this schema, namely, the Communist International.[28]

MORIBUND CAPITALISM?

The defeat suffered by the attempts made at proletarian revolution in Western Europe after the war of 1914–18 was due to a highly complex set of factors and circumstances; but from this diversity it is possible to select one incontestable fact which was of fundamental importance, namely, that the majority of the European working class, even where the crisis went farthest, as in Germany, continued to follow their traditional political and trade-union organizations and not the new revolutionary party.[29] In one way or another this was acknowledged in all the analyses made by Lenin and the Comintern, when they alleged that the basic factor in the defeat was 'betrayal' by the reformist leaders. This explanation calls out for another to be given: why did the workers follow these 'traitor' leaders?

The confidence Lenin showed in the victorious advance of the world revolution contains an assumption that is implicit even when it is not clearly expressed: the proletariat of the West will soon turn their backs on the opportunist leaders and come over to the side of the revolutionary party when this takes the field. This was the meaning of his statements, quoted above, at the end of the inaugural congress of the Comintern. Obviously, without this presupposition Lenin's theses on international revolution in the near future would have been mere phrase-mongering: and nobody was more hostile than Lenin to the 'revolutionary phrase'. Of course Lenin did not imagine that the working class would go over to revolutionary positions automatically, through the mere effect of objective conditions. But he did think that the working masses would be won for the positions of the Bolshevik party very quickly, once this party had been launched, even if it were very much in the minority to start with.[30] The same phenomenon that had occurred in Russia between February and October would be repeated elsewhere.

Where this question was concerned, indeed, Lenin transferred to the European and even the world process of events the pattern that had been followed by the February-to-October process in Russia. Referring to the German revolution, he wrote: 'Once again it is here revealed that the general course of the proletarian revolution is the same throughout the world. First the spontaneous formation of Soviets, then their spread and development, and then the appearance of the practical problem: Soviets, or National Assembly, or Constituent Assembly, or the bourgeois parliamentary system; utter confusion among the leaders, and finally – the proletarian revolution.' Lenin puts on the same plane the German 'Independent Socialists' and the Russian Mensheviks, the struggle for the leadership of the workers' councils in Germany and that which had taken place for the leadership of the Soviets in Russia.[31] He draws a parallel between the repression of the Spartacists in January 1919 and the 'July days' of 1917 in Russia: 'We know from experience how quickly such "victories" of the bourgeoisie and their henchmen cure the people of their illusions about bourgeois democracy, "universal suffrage", and so forth.'[32] In short, the German 'November' was identified with the Russian 'February', and just as the Bolsheviks, from being a mere minority in February, had within a few months won the support of the proletariat and peasantry of Russia, so the Spartacists, from being a small minority in November 1918, would win the support of the masses in order to lead them to the German 'October', and would do this even more quickly than had happened in Russia: 'The German revolution is developing in the same way as ours, but at a faster pace.'[33] Lenin's genius did not escape the temptation that lies in wait for all victorious revolutionary leaders, namely, that of making 'their' revolution the model to which all subsequent revolutions must conform. But what it is interesting to note here in this transposition of the Russian model is Lenin's grave underestimation of the influence of reformist politics and the reformist mentality among the proletariat of the advanced countries. I do not mean to say that Lenin underestimated the wide *extent* of the reformist phenomenon, but rather its *depth*, the firm roots that it possessed in the working-class masses of the West.

This underestimation of the penetration of reformism into the Western proletariat was a symptom of theoretical shortcomings that were to have an effect on the political plane in the way that the new revolutionary party was created, the way its structures and mode of working were conceived and its tasks worked out. The root of these shortcomings can be found, it seems to me, in Lenin's analysis of capitalism in its monopoly phase. As I have mentioned already, Lenin, like Rosa Luxemburg, and like Kautsky in his first period, saw world capitalism in the monopoly, imperialist stage as having reached a terminal situation.[34] The world war, which led Kautsky to make a politico-doctrinal revision in which a penetrating understanding of the new structural phenomena of capitalism provided a foundation for opportunist political conclusions, had for Lenin the effect, on the contrary, of strengthening his belief. When analysing the contradictions of the system, Lenin tends to make much of their destructive side and little of their driving power – the role played by these contradictions as a factor in dynamizing and adapting the capitalist mechanism and transforming its structures. He appreciates accurately the process of capitalist concentration, the specific weight acquired by state monopoly capitalism in the system as a whole, the acceleration of this process owing to the war; but, for Lenin, all these structural changes result invariably in a linear intensification of the contradictions, a cumulative aggravation, which leads inevitably to the conclusion that the situation is hopeless – even if he elsewhere wrote that there can be no situation in which there is no way out for the bourgeoisie. He points out, very correctly, that the advanced degree to which production has become socialized creates the most favourable material foundations for the transition to socialism; he notes that this process provides capitalism with certain mechanisms of regulation and planning – but he underestimates the effect that these new instruments can have in reducing, within certain limits and in certain phases, the destructive role played by the system's contradictions. The economic and trade-union conquests won by the working class in the decades preceding the war are seen by Lenin almost exclusively as achievements that thrust capitalism helplessly towards the edge of its grave. He thus fails to see that, at the same time, they illustrate the capacity possessed by advanced capitalism to digest some of these changes and to use them as factors in 'rationalizing' its economic mechanism, while simultaneously increasing its capacity to alienate. This type of analysis leads him to describe monopoly capitalism not merely as *transitional* (alluding to the high degree of socialization of production) but also as *moribund*. It is this type of analysis that causes him to consider that a rapid radicalization process is going on amid the European proletariat, profoundly undermining the influence of the reformist leaders. The 'betrayal' by these leaders during the war and the disasters that this has brought upon the masses must bring to completion, provided only a revolutionary group of the Bolshevik type is present to do the work of enlightenment, the split which is bound to occur between the leaders and the masses.

Lenin sees the economic basis of reformism in the labour movement almost exclusively in colonial exploitation. As Stuart R. Schram and Hélène Carrère d'Encausse point out, the idea 'that colonization would make it possible to improve the lot of the European workers and thus to delay social revolution in Europe was a belief shared, at the beginning of the twentieth century, by all those who had thought about the problem, whether they were socialists like Kautsky, Hilferding or Rosa Luxemburg, liberals like Hobson, or partisans of imperialism like Cecil Rhodes, who saw in the colonies a means for avoiding civil war'.[35] Lenin concurs in this explanation of opportunism in the working-class movement, but considers that, in the continental countries that joined in the colonial share-out only late in the day, the 'corruption' of the workers affects only a small minority, which he calls the 'labour aristocracy'; while, as regards Britain, he considers that the phenomenon is on the decline, since she has lost her colonial monopoly. No doubt colonial exploitation has been (and still is, in its neo-colonialist form) an ideological as well as an economic basis for reformism. But it has become clear today that reformism is also nourished by structural transformations in capitalism that are connected with the development of the productive forces. In Lenin's day this aspect was particularly well perceived by the Bernsteinian revisionists, who were anxious to find all possible motives, true or false, to justify their renouncement of revolution.[36]

A problem of sociological viewpoint also enters into Lenin's subjectivism in appreciating the degree to which the Western proletariat had reached revolutionary maturity. Whereas he sees with perfect clarity the dialectical mediations between the contradictions at the level of economic structures and those at the level of politico-social forces *in the case of Russian society*, in which he was deeply rooted and which he had analysed thoroughly in a long process of theory and practice, he sees these same mediations in a rather abstract and simplified way when what is involved is Western society, which he knows only from the outside, as an observer, despite his years of exile there. It is above all the *cultural* universe in which the Western proletariat is immersed that escapes him: for example, to take two aspects which profoundly affect its political behaviour, the Western proletariat's deep attachment to national and democratic values. The nation and democracy were, historically, products of capitalism, but they were also conquests won by the working masses. The 'betrayal' of the principle of internationalism by the Social Democratic leaders expressed perfectly (while also stimulating) the attachment to the national principle that was a feature of the working people's consciousness. And when the German Social Democrats invoked 'defence' of parliamentary democracy against Tsarist autocracy, or the French Socialists invoked 'defence' of the gains of the Great Revolution against Prussian militarism, they were echoing sentiments that were deeply rooted in the masses. The great trade-union tradition of the European proletariat – absent in Russia – is another element with which Lenin's analysis does not sufficiently reckon, when he proclaims world-wide extension of the Russian Soviets as the form to be assumed by the mass movement.

Account must be taken, finally, of the special psychological inclination of Lenin and the other Bolshevik leaders that followed from their theoretical conception of the interdependence between the Russian revolution and the revolution in the West. It was necessary for the Russian revolution that the European revolution should not 'miss its appointment'. This *necessity* could not but affect in a negative way the scientific rigour shown when analysing the revolutionary potential of the European proletariat.

It is this psychological inclination that explains, perhaps, why, when studying the revolutionary situation in Europe after November 1918, Lenin did not accord the importance it deserved to the change in the role being played by the question of *peace*. In Russia, this had been the key question that had rallied the majority of the people round the Bolsheviks: the proletarian revolution meant making peace. In Germany and the other European countries, once the Armistice had been signed, it was revolution that represented for the masses a return to war – in the form of civil war and foreign intervention. And the masses wanted peace, above all.

To sum up: the divorce, revealed by practice, between Lenin's ideas about the proletariat of the industrialized capitalist countries and the actual behaviour of this proletariat shows up (as well as the psychological aspect that has been mentioned) the absence, in Marxist theory, of an answer to certain political and theoretical problems concerning the road to revolution in these types of society. And this is perfectly comprehensible if we keep in mind a fundamental circumstance, namely, that there was no precedent for revolutions of this kind.

If Lenin was able to work out the theory of the Russian revolution, with its original combination of bourgeois-democratic and socialist tasks, and make his rigorous analysis of the behaviour in it of classes and social groups, parties and political institutions, forms of struggle and so on, this was because the Russian revolution, as a 'natural phenomenon', to use Engels' expression, had been a *fact* since 1905. It was this that provided the materials that enabled the theoretical work to be done. If there are no 'materials' of this order available, the entire works of Marx and Engels are inadequate for building the theory of the revolution in a given society.

When he elaborates his overall theory of the socialist revolution as a world revolution, Lenin suffers from this lack of 'materials' where advanced capitalism is concerned, and also, to a smaller extent, where the colonial liberation movement is concerned. (In the latter case, he reckons with the experience of the first revolutions of this kind, which began after 1905, but the geographical remoteness of which made it hard to grasp directly in their extreme originality.) In practice, Lenin adopted without critical revision the ideas of the left or centrist-orthodox theoreticians of the Second International as regards the 'maturing' of the revolution in the advanced countries. But this certificate of maturity was in contradiction with the reality of the reformist process – the process of 'integration', as we should say nowadays – that was going forward in those countries. The supposed 'maturing' was based on general formulas of Marxism and not on a concrete analysis of the real process. Hence the fact that the struggle against reformism was abstract in content, and proved ineffectual on the political and ideological plane. It started out from a metaphysical conception of the readiness of the proletariat for revolution, even if the actual conduct of the proletariat seemed to give this the lie. The reformist bureaucracy, trade-union and political, which dominated the labour movement was seen by the left as a foreign body in relation to the proletariat. When the first major economic crisis struck – and, *a fortiori*, in a crisis like the war – the split between them would take place and the revolutionary 'essence' of the proletariat would manifest itself in full strength. However, the war proved exactly the opposite: it revealed the strength and the depth of the reformist phenomenon. This depth was itself only an aspect, though a fundamental one, of a larger reality, namely, that the revolution had *not* yet 'matured' in advanced capitalist society. It was only knocking at the door. The 'general crisis' of capitalism was beginning, but this was to be much more complex than Lenin had foreseen. It was very hard to imagine that several decades would pass before the socialist revolution presented itself in the principal capitalist countries. Lenin was even less able to imagine – though a shade of doubt does appear in his last writings – that the 'general crisis' of capitalism would be accompanied by a 'general crisis' of Marxist thought. And yet the premises that made this second crisis possible, even if not inevitable, had already been given.

LENIN'S LAST QUESTIONINGS

The overthrow of bourgeois power in a state covering a sixth of the earth's surface certainly constituted a historic international victory of the revolutionary movement inspired by Marxism. But the world context in which this victory had been won, the 'resistance' put up by capitalism in the advanced countries, the notable strengthening of capitalism in some key areas (North America, Japan), the *national* framework within which the socialist revolution was still confined – in a backward country, to boot – called in question some essential aspects of the theoretical conception of the process of world revolution that had been worked out by Marx, Engels and Lenin. It was not easy, however, in the setting of 1921, when Lenin saw clearly that the revolutionary drive in Europe had been checked, to penetrate the profound significance of this new reality. On the one hand, the importance of the revolutionary victory won in Russia and the impression made by the presence of the first proletarian state in history were sufficiently dazzling to hide the contradictions between the new situation and the traditional theoretical schemas. On the other, it was easy, at first, to reconcile this new situation with the old schemas: all that was needed was to look upon what was happening as a momentary interruption in the expected process of the world revolution. The curtain would not be long in rising on the second act. This was the solution found for the problem by the leaders of the Bolshevik Party and of the Comintern. Trotsky formulates it very clearly in presenting the principal report ('The World Economic Crisis and the New Tasks of the Comintern') to the Third World Congress, on 23 June 1921: 'Only now do we see and feel that we are not immediately close to our final aim, to the conquest of power on the world scale, to the world revolution. We told ourselves back in 1919 that it was a question of months, but now we say that it is perhaps a question of several years. Exactly how long, we do not know, but we know that development is proceeding in that direction, and that during this period we have become much stronger throughout the world.'[37]

The 'theses on tactics' voted by the Congress declare that 'the world revolution . . . will require a fairly long period of revolutionary struggle', but consider that 'what may be expected is not the waning of the star of the world revolution, not the ebb of its waves, but, on the contrary, the aggravation of social antagonism and social struggles, and the transition to open civil war'.[38]

The theses of this Congress acknowledge a fact of primary importance: 'The variety in the degree of acuteness reached by contradictions in different countries, the variety in their social structure and in the obstacles to be surmounted, the high level of organization of the bourgeoisie in the highly developed capitalist countries of west Europe and North America, *meant* that the world war did not issue immediately in the victory of the world revolution.'[39]

But the Congress did not try to ascertain why in 1919, and even in 1920, immediate victory was thought to be possible despite the existence of reasons which 'meant' ruling out that possibility. The theses explain the behaviour of the proletariat by the attitude of the 'powerful Social Democratic labour organizations and parties', but at the time when the congress met these parties and trade unions had recovered their former strength and even increased it. How was this fact, together with the high degree of organization of capitalism, to be reconciled with the prospect, which was held out as probable in those theses, of an immediate sharpening of social struggles? These ambiguities – which reveal the presence of theoretical uncertainties – are to be seen in all the documents of the congress. The old schema of the world revolution's progress is retained, with the new phenomena stuck on to it:

(1) The imperialist system is moving towards another world war, which will give rise to a new great revolutionary crisis. The principal contradictions that will provoke the war this time are the ones between the USA and Britain, on the one hand, and the USA and Japan, on the other.

(2) The initial revolutionary break-through will take place this time, as it did before, in that country where the concentration of contradictions, internal and external, creates the biggest explosive charge. Germany, defeated in the First World War, much weakened economically, oppressed by the Treaty of Versailles, and possessing a Communist Party that is the strongest section of the Comintern after the Russian party, is seen as a likely candidate to play the role that Russia played in 1917.

(3) After this break-through the revolution will spread to the other links in the capitalist system – the advanced countries and the colonies. This time, the revolutionary wave will be able to count from the start on the support of a proletarian state, of a military force ready to come to the aid of the international proletariat. Conserving and strengthening this citadel is therefore a matter of fundamental importance for the world revolution, and the congress says so. But the *principal* factor in the world revolution continues to be, for the Bolshevik leaders and for the Comintern, the proletariat of the advanced capitalist countries.

In order to ensure that the schema was both coherent and credible, two big unknowns had to be eliminated, the first of these being the behaviour to be expected from the European proletariat, given past experience. The Third Congress theses recognize, but only to reject it at once, the possibility that European capitalism may re-establish itself, with the working class agreeing to work under conditions worse than those that prevailed before the war. The reformist trade unions and parties, the theses ('on the international situation and the tasks of the Comintern') observe, are trying to urge the workers in this direction, 'but the European proletariat is not ready to sacrifice itself. It demands an improvement in its lot, which is at present *absolutely* incompatible with the *objective* possibilities of capitalism.'[40] By coming up against this 'absolute imcompatibility' the economic struggle of the working class would be transformed – so the congress forecast – into a revolutionary struggle, which would be provided with the appropriate political leadership by the sections of the Comintern. This prospect was based on two assumptions: the first, a new *terminal situation* of European capitalism, in which it would be incapable of satisfying economic demands that would imply a real improvement in the material situation of the working class as compared with pre-war; and, the second, connected with the first, that the reformist organizations would not take up the struggles for these economic improvements, thus losing their influence over the working class. Both of these assumptions were soon to be disproved by events.

The second unknown was no less important. The Third Congress recognized that, while European capitalism had come weakened out of the war, American capitalism, on the contrary, had been considerably strengthened, and 'the centre of gravity of world economy has shifted from Europe to America'.[41] In order to triumph on the world scale, the revolution would therefore have to spread to the United States. The Congress theses 'deal with' this unknown by means of the following argument:

While in Europe the concentration of property has been based on general impoverishment, in the United States both this concentration and the greater acuteness of class antagonisms have reached an extreme degree on the basis of a feverish expansion of wealth. The sudden changes in the economic situation because of the general uncertainties of the world market give to the class struggle in America an extremely tense and revolutionary character. A period of capitalist expansion unprecedented in history is bound to be followed by an unusual outburst of revolutionary struggle.[42]

As regards the national liberation movement in the colonies, the prospect seemed clear. Since the October revolution the importance of this 'front' of the world revolution had grown steadily, fully confirming Lenin's forecasts on the subject. The documents and the practical activity of the Comintern pay genuine attention to it – but this 'front' is always subordinated to the 'main front', namely, the advanced capitalist countries.

The Fourth and Fifth Congresses of the Comintern (in 1922 and 1924) made no important change in the general schema of the progress of the world revolution as conceived by the Third Congress. Soon after the Fifth Congress, recognition was to be introduced that a phase of 'relative stabilization' of capitalism had begun – a phase which was expected to be short-lived, and to be followed by a fresh great revolutionary break-through.

The first questionings of the relevance of this now already classical schema of world revolution, and of the optimism to which it testified, came from its principal author himself. In Lenin's last writings, and especially in his last article (February 1923), doubt and disquiet show through regarding the fate of the Russian revolution and of the world revolution. We hear for the first time a pessimistic note sounded in relation to the revolutionary possibilities in the advanced capitalist countries. Lenin looks for a way out in three main directions: the struggle of the oppressed peoples of Asia, exploitation of inter-imperialist contradictions and rapid industrialization of Soviet Russia. The prospect of the triumph of the world revolution has become blurred, in an uncertain view of the future. The propositions of this article[43] can be summed up thus:

(1) Lenin sees the whole world as embraced by the orbit of the world revolution and as divided into two camps: on one side the victorious and prosperous capitalist countries of the West and the East (Japan); on the other, the colonial and semi-colonial countries, Soviet Russia and the European countries defeated in the war. The main axis of development of the world revolution runs through the struggle between these two camps.

(2) The panorama offered by the camp of the oppressed is not at all a cheering one. The revolution has conquered in Russia, but the country lies in ruins, and petty production predominates. Germany can face up to her conquerors only with difficulty, for 'all the capitalist powers of what is called the West are pecking at her and preventing her from rising. On the other hand, the entire East, with its hundreds of millions of exploited working people, reduced to the last degree of human suffering, has been forced into a position where its physical and material strength cannot possibly be compared with the physical, material and military strength of any of the much smaller West-European states.'

(3) As regards the victorious capitalist states, Lenin considers that they are in a position, thanks to their exploitation of the colonies and the defeated European countries, to grant concessions to the exploited classes such as may hold back the revolutionary movement.

(4) In face of this setting for the world revolution, Lenin becomes extremely prudent concerning its prospects: 'The outcome of the struggle as a whole can be forecast only because in the long run capitalism itself is educating and training the vast majority of the population of the globe for the struggle. In the last analysis, the outcome of the struggle will be determined by the fact that Russia, India, China, etc., account for the overwhelming majority that has been drawn into the struggle for

emancipation with extraordinary rapidity ...' On the horizon of the world's history, Lenin sees approaching 'military conflict between the counter-revolutionary imperialist West and the revolutionary and nationalist East, between the most civilized countries of the world and the Orientally backward countries which, however, comprise the majority ...' In order that it may 'ensure our existence until' this occurs, however, 'this majority must become civilized'. And, referring specifically to Russia, he goes on to say: 'We, too, lack enough civilization to enable us to pass straight on to socialism, although we do have the political requisites for it.' ('Civilization' here means, for Lenin, industrialization and cultural development of the Western type. This is why, in another part of his article, he says that the people of the East have finally entered upon development along 'the general European capitalist lines'.)

If we compare this schema of Lenin's with the previous ones, we clearly perceive a shift in the role and relationship of the world revolutionary forces. The Western proletariat, as a revolutionary force, has moved down, for a certain period, to the second place. And the oppressed masses of what today we call the 'third world', together with the 'oriental' Soviet state, have moved up to the first place. At the same time, in order that this new force, which is rising 'with extraordinary rapidity', into the struggle for its own emancipation, may prove victorious, time is needed, sufficient time. The problem of 'gaining time' is in the forefront of Lenin's preoccupations.

Drawing from this analysis the conclusions that relate to the Russian revolution, Lenin says that the central problem is that of ensuring its survival until the armed confrontation takes place between the imperialist West and the revolutionary and nationalist East. The line he recommends in order to succeed in this task is as follows: inside Russia, to ensure leadership of the peasant masses by the working class and to carry out a policy of far-reaching economy so as to concentrate resources for industrializing the country; in international policy, to profit from the contradictions between the imperialist states, so as to avoid a clash with them. In short, gain time while actively preparing for the day when, on the one hand, the conflicts between the imperialist states and the aggravation of their 'internal contradictions', and, on the other, the

strengthening of the Soviet republic and of the national liberation movement of the oppressed peoples brings about a balance of forces on the
international scale that is favourable to the world revolution.

It is useless to speculate on the theoretical and political 'extensions'
that this beginning of a revision might have led to in Lenin's activity if
death had not taken him off prematurely. We find some of the ideas
outlined here in the conceptions of Mao Tse-tung and, in general, in
those strategies that see the masses of the 'third world' as the protagonist
of the world revolution. Others served as compass for Stalin's strategy,
especially as regards the principle of keeping the Soviet State out of the
conflicts between the imperialist states, and exploiting to this end the
contradictions between them. Here we find, too, the idea of according
priority to the economic and military strengthening of the Soviet state as
a part of the development of world revolutionary forces – an idea that is
not expressed with clarity by Lenin, but can easily be deduced from his
last writings.

Some analysts of Leninism have concluded, somewhat precipitately,
that these ideas of Lenin's implied a radical revision of Marx's conception of the socialist revolution. For Marx the specifically capitalist
contradictions are the mainspring of the socialist revolution, and the
optimum 'maturing' of this revolution occurs in advanced capitalism,
whereas, for Lenin, the conditions for the socialist revolution are to be
found, it is said, rather in 'backwardness'. According to Alfred G.
Meyer, Lenin substituted 'the dialectics of backwardness', as driving
force of the revolution, for the Marxian dialectics based on a high degree
of development of the productive forces.[44] This conclusion drawn by
Meyer and others results from two confusions. When Lenin refers to the
revolutions of the East he does not mean *socialist* revolutions, but bourgeois-democratic revolutions that will have to go a long way before they
become transformed into socialist ones. The second confusion is the one
I have already remarked upon: that between revolution in the broad
sense and revolution in the narrow sense. Before the October revolution
and right down to the end of his life, Lenin always maintained that
revolution in the narrow sense – and initially bourgeois-democratic in
character – is easier in the underdeveloped countries, but that the transition to socialism will present grave difficulties in these countries. On

the other hand, in his view, in the advanced capitalist countries the revolution in the narrow sense (the taking of power by the proletariat) is more difficult, whereas the building of socialism will be easier. At no stage did Lenin revise Marx's essential thesis. In February 1922 he wrote: 'We have always urged and reiterated the elementary truth of Marxism – that the joint efforts of the workers of several advanced countries are needed for the victory of socialism.'[45] What Lenin was beginning to revise, in fact, in the article summarized above, was his conception of the concrete course of development to be followed by the world revolution: in the first place by extending it in time, replacing the near-at-hand prospect by a very long-term one, and in the second by noting the need for a new 'prelude' to the decisive stage (which for Lenin is still the revolution in the advanced capitalist countries), namely, the bourgeois-democratic revolution in the oppressed countries of the East.

We may presume that, for a theoretical mind like Lenin's, the doubts and misgivings that appear in his last writings would have led to a deeper study of the new phenomena of capitalism and imperialism, of the revolutionary awakening of the 'backward' countries, of the behaviour of the proletariat in the 'advanced' countries, and so on. We may think that such a study would have induced him to revise the Comintern's strategy and tactics and also, perhaps, the very conception of its structures and working. It was not by accident, doubtless, that, at the Fourth Congress of the Comintern (November 1922), referring to the resolution on the structure, methods and activity of the Communist parties which had been adopted by the Third Congress, Lenin said: 'The resolution is an excellent one, but it is almost entirely Russian, that is to say, everything in it is based on Russian conditions ... I have the impression that we made a big mistake with this resolution, namely, that we blocked our own road to further success.'[46] It is no less significant that Lenin's main recommendation to the Communists, both of the Soviet Union and of other countries, at this congress, was that they should *study*. 'I think that after five years of the Russian revolution the most important thing for all of us, Russian and foreign comrades alike, is to sit down and study ... We must take advantage of every moment of respite from fighting, from war, to study, and to study *from scratch*.'[47]

70

This amounted to saying that there were some very important questions still to be cleared up. This was why Lenin also advised that no decision be adopted on the Comintern draft programme, but that it be studied more carefully, among other reasons because 'we have given scarcely any thought to possible retreat, and to preparations for it'.[48]

STALIN AS REVISIONIST: COMPLETE SOCIALISM IN A SINGLE COUNTRY

The problem of the world revolution – its course, its articulation, the role of the Russian revolution, defining the appropriate strategy – had formed the theoretical basis of the struggle within the Bolshevik leading group at the time of the 'April Theses', at the time of the October insurrection, and at the time of Brest–Litovsk. This problem re-emerged when the defeat suffered by the attempts at revolution made in Western Europe created a new situation which objectively necessitated revising the former schemas.

In the years that followed Lenin's death, the problem presented itself in the form of a discussion about whether it was possible or not for socialism to be completely victorious in one country taken separately. At the Fourth Congress of the Comintern, the last in which Lenin participated, a resolution on 'five years of the Russian revolution' was approved which reaffirmed the traditional Marxist thesis: 'The Fourth World Congress reminds the proletarians of all countries that the proletarian revolution can never triumph completely within a single country; rather must it triumph internationally, as world revolution.'[49] In May Stalin was still entirely faithful to this view: 'To overthrow the bourgeoisie,' he wrote, 'the efforts of one country are sufficient; this is proved by the history of our revolution. For the final victory of socialism, for the organization of socialist production, the efforts of one country, particularly of a peasant country like Russia, are insufficient; for that, the efforts of the proletarians of several advanced countries are required.'[50] From the end of 1924 onwards however, in the context of the fight against the Trotskyist opposition, Stalin began to revise the theory of the international character of the socialist revolution and to put forward as a possibility the idea that socialism might be fully achieved

71

within the framework of one country. In his article 'October and the Tactics of the Russian Communists' (December 1924) he starts by attributing to 'the opportunists of all countries' the view that 'the proletarian revolution can begin ... only in industrially developed countries', naturally including Trotsky among these 'opportunists'.[51] But this had been the view of Marx and Engels, and of Lenin too, down to his 'April Theses' of 1917. Unless Marx, Engels and Lenin are to be regarded as opportunists, Stalin is coolly falsifying history. A little later, Stalin attributes to Trotsky the idea that the revolution in the advanced countries must begin 'simultaneously' – though he cannot quote a single line from Trotsky to support this allegation. Once the Manichean manipulation has been accomplished, so as not only to facilitate the attack on Trotsky but also to conceal the fact that this attack is actually aimed against Marx, Engels and Lenin, Stalin concludes: 'There can be no doubt that the universal theory of a simultaneous victory of the revolution in the principal countries of Europe, the theory that the victory of socialism in one country is impossible, has proved to be an artificial and untenable theory. The seven years' history of the proletarian revolution in Russia speaks not for but against this theory.'[52] After manufacturing out of nothing at all an absurd theory about the revolution beginning simultaneously in several countries, Stalin demolishes this theory brilliantly ... with the history of the seven years of Soviet Russia's existence. But that history did not testify either for or against Stalin's new thesis: it merely attested empirically a certain fact – namely, that proletarian power had maintained itself in Russia for seven years despite the defeat of the attempts at revolution in the West – a fact which proved neither the possibility of building complete socialism in Russia nor the invulnerability of the Soviet state if faced by renewed capitalist intervention. In order to assert the first of these propositions Stalin could do no better than quote just a few lines taken from Lenin's works (the latest edition of which fills forty-five volumes) – lines that, moreover, he interprets very freely.[53] Where the second proposition was concerned, he did not even try to find such backing, and was therefore obliged to make a super-subtle distinction between 'the possibility of building a complete socialist society in a single country' – which he describes as an 'indisputable truth' – and a 'full guarantee against the restoration of the old order', which, he says, requires the victory of the revolution in several advanced countries, in other words the victory of the revolution on the world scale.[54]

Stalin does not trouble to prove this 'indisputable truth' either empirically or theoretically. In order to equip it with an empirical foundation he would have had to point to a socialist system completely accomplished in a national framework, something that obviously did not exist in 1924. To prove it theoretically he would have had to show the error in Marx's view that the productive forces upon which socialism can be built must dominate world economy and imply a *socialist* international division of labour. Stalin does not refute this view, which Lenin had never challenged; he merely 'ignores' it.

As regards the problem of the 'full guarantee against the restoration of the old order', Trotsky answers very soundly: if it be agreed that socialism can be completely built in the USSR, it is wrong to suppose that a 'full guarantee against the restoration of the old order' would require the victory of the revolution in several advanced countries, for in that case the military and economic strength of the USSR would be such that restoration would be for all practical purposes ruled out. One might conceive, in such a situation, an intervention by the USSR against the capitalist world, but would this be needed? The *reality* of such a socialist society would strike the death-blow at world capitalism and almost render world proletarian revolution unnecessary. 'This is why,' Trotsky adds prophetically, 'the whole Stalinist conception actually leads to the liquidation of the Communist International. And indeed, what would be its historical significance if the fate of socialism is to be decided by the highest possible authority – the State Planning Commission of the USSR? In that case, the task of the Comintern ... would be to protect the construction of socialism from intervention, that is, in essence, to play the role of frontier patrols.'[55]

The *deus ex machina* of Stalin's theory of national socialism is the famous 'law of the uneven development of capitalism'. The logic employed is simple. Given that capitalism develops unevenly, revolution will also take place unevenly, first in one country, then in another, or several others and so on. In each case, the 'break' in the 'imperialist chain' will occur where the link is weakest (naturally – the chain will not break where its links are strongest). Once the revolution has been victorious in a certain country, uneven development enables it to hold out against the capitalist states – by working to aggravate the contradictions that exist among these – and to carry through the building of socialism, and so forth. Uneven development thus solves all theoretical difficulties. Unfortunately for Stalin's logic, uneven development is also one of the sources of the general crises of the capitalist system, of world wars, etc. These crises tend to 'even out', to a certain extent and in certain periods, the revolutionary movement, and to link together more closely the revolutionary movements of different countries (as happened in the two world wars and in the culminating period of the crisis of the colonial system). One cannot, therefore, rule out, merely by empirically observing that development is uneven, the possibility of a situation in which, as Marx assumed, the socialist revolution would take the form of a chain reaction in a series of advanced capitalist countries. Nor does the law of uneven development explain why the 'revolutionary break-through' has not so far occurred in the advanced capitalist countries, which remains one of the major problems for the Marxist theory of revolution. Finally, this 'law' does not in the least invalidate Marx's thesis about the necessarily *world-wide* character of the productive forces of socialism, and so cannot establish theoretically the possibility or 'complete construction' of socialism in a single country. Stalin's methodological error is that he uses this 'law' in a metaphysical way, isolating it from the other tendencies in world economy and world politics, such as the increase by geometrical progression in economic, technical, social, etc., internationalization. In the metaphysical way in which Stalin employs it, this 'law' is good for everything and for nothing.

With the defeat of Trotskyism in the Soviet Union and in the Communist parties of all countries, the theory of socialism in a single country became the official doctrine of the Comintern. It underlies the conception of the world revolution that is given in the programme of the Comintern approved by its Sixth Congress (1928). Among the main elements in this conception, let me recall the following:

Unevenness of economic and political development is an absolute law of capitalism, and is even more marked in the imperialist epoch. Hence

74

the international proletarian revolution cannot be conceived as a single act taking place everywhere simultaneously. The victory of socialism is therefore possible at first only in a few capitalist countries, or even in one . . .[56]

And the course of the international revolution will be like this:

The transition from the world dictatorship of imperialism to the world dictatorship of the proletariat covers a long period of proletarian struggles, defeats and victories, a period of the continuing crisis of capitalism and the maturing of socialist revolutions . . . a period of national wars and colonial revolts . . .; a period when capitalist and socialist socio-economic systems exist side by side within world economy, in 'peaceful' relationships as well as in armed conflict; a period of the formation of a union of socialist soviet states, a period of the wars of imperialist states against them, a period when the union between these states and the colonial peoples becomes close and closer, etc.

This course taken by the world revolution is dominated by 'a new basic contradiction which emerged from the first round of imperialist wars, epochal in its scope and significance – the contradiction between the Soviet Union and the capitalist world'.[57] The USSR, says the programme, has become 'the leading force of the world revolutionary movement', 'the base of the international movement of all oppressed classes, the centre of the international revolution, the most significant factor in world history'. Consequently, since 'the Soviet Union is the true fatherland of the proletariat, the strongest pillar of its achievements, and the principal factor in its emancipation throughout the world, this obliges the international proletariat to forward the success of socialist construction in the Soviet Union and to defend the country of proletarian dictatorship by every means against the attacks of the capitalist powers.' The class struggle in each country and the national liberation struggle of the peoples oppressed by imperialism are still important factors in the world revolution, but the *essential* factor is the building of socialism in the USSR – hence the idea of 'the leadership exercised over the whole world revolutionary movement by the proletarian dictatorship in the USSR'.[58]

This series of formulations reveals the whole significance for practical politics of Stalin's conception of the world revolutionary movement. Down to Lenin's death, and even down to the Fifth Congress of the Comintern, held soon after that event, although a very important role was allotted to consolidating the dictatorship of the proletariat in the USSR, as the first political, economic and military state-base of the world revolution, nevertheless this role remained subordinate to the struggle being waged by the proletariat in the advanced countries. This was the logical conclusion to draw from the idea of Marx and Lenin, according to which socialist society could not be fully realized except on the basis of a victory of the revolution in the economically most advanced areas of the world. Neither the Russian revolution nor the revolutions of the peoples oppressed by imperialism could serve, despite their immense importance, as more than 'preludes' to the *decisive* step by the world revolution, namely, its triumph in imperialism's vital centres. From the moment that it is accepted that complete construction of socialism is possible in a country of the size, population and potential resources of the USSR, the entire prospect of the world revolution is altered. It must not be forgotten that when this doctrine was introduced the Comintern still upheld that capitalism was moribund, incapable of entering a new and higher phase of development of its productive forces, even if one admitted the possibility of periods of 'relative' stabilization or growth. These two processes, going in opposite directions, were expected to produce, after a certain lapse of time (which was thought of as comparatively short: Stalin spoke in 1931[59] of overtaking the advanced capitalist countries in ten years), a radical change in the picture of world economy. The Soviet zone would increasingly become the advanced zone, while the capitalist zone was doomed to irreversible decline, 'decay', until the hour of revolution struck. This twofold process could have no other outcome than the solution of 'this new fundamental' contradiction in favour of the USSR. *This* would be the decisive victory of socialism on the world scale. Naturally, any revolutions which might occur in other countries while this process was going on would contribute to its success, by weakening capitalism and bringing the ultimate outcome nearer – but such revolutions no longer constituted an absolutely indispensable condition for this outcome.

From the moment when the building of socialism in the USSR was seen as the essential, determining factor of the world revolution, all other revolutionary movements were reduced objectively to a subordinate role, and it was from that angle that they had to be regarded in the Comintern's strategy and tactics. It is worth recalling that the principle of 'subordinating' particular interests of the revolutionary movement to its common interests had been adopted by the Comintern from the very start. The Sixth Congress reaffirmed it with vigour: 'In order that revolutionary work and activities may be coordinated and given appropriate guidance, the international proletariat requires international class discipline ... [which] must be expressed in the subordination of local and particular interests to the common and enduring interests of the movement...'[60] This amounts to recognizing that, despite an essential community of interest between all the components of the world revolutionary movement, transient contradictions may appear which necessitate a hierarchizing of interests, priorities, options, etc. Immediately the building of socialism in the USSR had been defined as the essential, determining factor in the world revolution, it became *ipso facto* the representative of the 'common and enduring interests' of the revolutionary movement. All the rest – 'local and particular' – would have to be subordinated to it. As, however, a frank expression of this subordination lent itself to attacks by the enemy – to his 'calumnies', as Stalin was to say in 1943 – it was convenient to deny it. Everything done by the USSR in its internal and external policies was declared to be absolutely and permanently identical with the interests of the revolutionary struggle, considered internationally or in any part of the world. There could be no contradiction between the former and the latter. Any claim that there *could* became sacrilege for Communists. The subordination recognized had to be denied in order that it might be effective.

The theory of socialism in one country, having become the theoretical foundation for Comintern strategy, signified, in the last analysis, that the world revolution, in all of its phases and episodes, was to be subordinated to the requirements of building socialism in the USSR. Let us be clear about this. *Revolution*, wherever it really appears, does not bow to any authority or theory. What was made to bow was the political and theoretical activity of the Comintern, of its national sections. The

Comintern's ultra-centralized structures, with its all-powerful Executive Committee at the top of the pyramid, itself supervised by the Soviet party leadership, constituted the ideal mechanism for ensuring this subordination in practice.

Trotsky was, as is well known, Stalin's chief theoretical adversary in connection with the problem that concerns us here. Trotsky's importance in criticizing the phenomena of bureaucratic and nationalistic degeneration of the Russian revolution is now obvious to anyone who does not shut his eyes to historical truth. His analysis of certain problems of the revolutionary movement in a number of countries (especially in Germany in the period preceding the victory of the Nazis) is also of great value. On the matter of the concept of the world revolution, however, Trotsky does not go beyond the old schemas of Marx and Lenin, merely attaching to them the label 'permanent revolution'. In the chief work that he wrote on this subject, three basic aspects of his problematic can be distinguished: 'The question of passing from the democratic revolution to the socialist revolution' (the historical origin of the theory, where his chief disagreements with Lenin are concentrated); 'the characterization of the socialist revolution itself' (which contains no innovations as compared with Marx and Lenin); and 'the international character of the socialist revolution'.[61] Trotsky's principal thesis on this third point is formulated as follows: 'The completion of the socialist revolution within national limits is unthinkable . . . The socialist revolution begins on the national arena, it unfolds on the international arena, and is completed on the world arena. Thus, the socialist revolution becomes a permanent revolution in a newer and broader sense of the word; it attains completion only in the final victory of the new society on our entire planet.'[62] Trotsky does not solve the problem that really arises – that of the discontinuity of this 'permanent' process, of the alternation within it of revolutions-in-the-narrow-sense together with non-revolutionary, evolutionary phases. Historical practice had begun to show that the 'permanence' of the revolutionary process throughout the great 'epoch of social revolution' was demonstrating itself – by denying itself. As Gramsci observed, the theory of permanent revolution 'is nothing but a generic forecast presented as a dogma, and which demolishes itself by not in fact coming true'.[63]

When the Trotskyist conception of the world revolution comes down from the level of abstraction to that of concrete analysis of the world situation and prospects, we see repeated the schemas that had been worked out by Lenin and by Trotsky himself in the period of the First World War. The defeats that followed that first great crisis of capitalism, the fidelity of the majority of the proletariat to Social Democracy, the proof given by capitalism of its capacity to recover (or, what comes to the same thing, but expresses better the essence of the problem, its power to re-structure itself, both politically and economically, through its great crises) – all this taught Trotsky very little. He explains all these phenomena by means of the old concept of 'betrayal' by Social Democracy, to which he now adds that of 'betrayal' by the Comintern. In his *Transitional Programme* (1938)[64] he writes: 'Mankind's productive forces *stagnate*': even if in 'the historically privileged countries' (USA, Britain, France, etc.) 'the bourgeoisie can still for a certain period permit itself the luxury of democracy', this is done 'at the expense of national *accumulation*'. In this 'epoch of decaying capitalism', 'there can be no question of systematic social reforms and the raising of the masses' living standards'.

The New Deal represents but a special form of political perplexity ... The objective prerequisites for the proletarian revolution have not only 'ripened'; they have begun to get somewhat rotten ... All now depends on the proletariat, i.e., *chiefly* on its revolutionary vanguard. The historical crisis of mankind is *reduced* to the crisis of the revolutionary leadership.

The answer to the problem is – the Fourth International.

The orientation of the masses is determined firstly by the objective conditions of decaying capitalism and secondly by the treacherous policies of the old workers' organizations. Of these factors the first, of course, is the decisive one: the laws of history are stronger than the bureaucratic apparatus. No matter how the methods of the social betrayers differ – from the 'social' legislation of Blum to the judicial frame-ups of Stalin – they will never succeed in breaking the revolutionary will of the proletariat. As time goes on, their desperate efforts to hold back the wheel of history will demonstrate more clearly to the masses that the crisis of the proletarian leadership, having become the crisis in mankind's culture, can be resolved only by the Fourth International.

This is why Trotsky is so optimistic, not only as regards the future but even as regards the most immediate future.

The danger of war and a defeat of the Soviet Union is a reality, but the revolution is also a reality. If the revolution does not prevent war, then war will help the revolution. Second births are commonly easier than first. In the new war, it will not be necessary to wait a whole two years and a half for the first insurrection. Once it is begun, moreover, the revolution will not this time stop half-way.[65]

We seem to hear an echo of the Lenin of 1914–17, with just this 'little' difference that there are now two 'traitor' Internationals and that the problem is to be solved by the Fourth. And yet, in 1938, historical experience had been considerably enlarged, and, if no account were taken of this, and the right answer found to the new problems that had arisen, any attempt at reconstructing the revolutionary leadership must be vain. Why this sinister historical recidivism on the part of the Internationals, this recurrence of their 'betrayal'? Could it be explained by the leaders of the Second having 'sold' themselves to the bourgeoisie and those of the Third to Stalin? How was the influence of these leaders over the different sections of the proletariat to be explained, if the latter indeed possessed a 'revolutionary will', as Trotsky alleged? Why, if the 'laws of history' were stronger than the bureaucratic apparatus, had they not smashed the apparatus of the Second International, which had been in existence for half a century already, and why had they not prevented the establishment of that of the Third? Could all these phenomena be accounted for if one took account *only* of the highest levels of the political superstructures? Was it not necessary to take up afresh the task of analysing the whole social body as the indispensable condition for working out revolutionary strategy and tactics? Was it not necessary, finally, to examine *what* that capitalism was, and *what* that proletariat was, which had emerged from the First World War? Today we know that the problem, or at least one essential aspect of the problem, did indeed lie there: that the New Deal and the restructuring of monopoly capitalism carried out under Fascism embodied the first elements of the transition to a new phase of capitalism – state monopoly capitalism – and that this process implied fundamental structural changes in the proletariat, changes that began precisely at that time. To this should be added the new problems created by the building of socialism in the USSR and by the national liberation movement in the colonies and dependent countries, to which no answer is to be found in the Communist documents of the period, except at an empirical level and almost exclusively with regard to the tactics to be adopted. This was the case, for example, with the problem of the alliance with the peasantry, which constituted the central problem of the building of socialism in the USSR and of the struggle for liberation in the countries oppressed by imperialism. Rarely do we find sociological studies of this peasantry, of its actual structures and its cultural world.

In short, the crisis affected not only revolutionary leadership, in the narrow sense of strategic and tactical leadership, but also revolutionary theory – the capacity of this theory to analyse reality so as to transform it. What matters is, of course, not just to note this phenomenon, which it is easy enough to do from our present standpoint in history, but to explain it. Why this paralysis of Marxism? Needless to say, I do not claim to give a satisfactory answer to this question here: though directly connected with the purpose of my book, it is a task which goes a long way beyond that. In the section I devote later on to studying the crisis of the Comintern in its organizational aspects and in its political activity, I point to fragmentary elements *contributing* to an explanation of this theoretical paralysis, which, in turn and as it developed, had a negative effect on political activity and promoted organizational rigidity. At the end of this chapter, I shall put forward some hypotheses regarding the most general, and in my view most fundamental, causes of the theoretical crisis of the Comintern. First of all, however, I must conclude my analysis of the Stalin–Trotsky polemic on the problem of the world revolution and of the consequences that Stalin's ideas had for the Comintern.

As we have already seen, Stalin subordinates the entire process of world revolution to the building of socialism in the USSR, whereas Trotsky makes it depend on the victory of the socialist revolution in Europe in the immediate future. On this victory, according to him, even

the fate of the Soviet Union itself depends. 'Only the European proletariat, implacably opposing its bourgeoisie . . . can protect the Soviet
Union from destruction.'[66] Trotsky's extreme 'Eurocentrism' clashes
inflexibly with the no less extreme 'Russocentrism' of Stalin.

In the ardour of his polemic against Stalin's 'Russocentrism', Trotsky
falls into a major contradiction. On the one hand, he sees capitalism as
being in an extremely acute state of crisis, economically helpless and
torn by insurmountable inter-imperialist contradictions; but, on the
other, he considers that, in the event of a world war, defeat of the
USSR is inevitable, at any rate unless the European revolution inter-
venes, and this whether the USSR finds itself alone against the capitalist states or whether Stalin's strategy of allying with one imperialist
group against another proves successful. Defeat is inevitable for the
USSR in the first case, writes Trotsky in 1936, because 'in a technical,
economic and military sense, imperialism is incomparably more
strong'.[67] In the second case it is inevitable because, when the war has
reached a certain point, 'imperialist antagonisms will always find a
compromise in order to block the military victory of the Soviet
Union'.[68] The only way to prevent this compromise would be for the
USSR to make decisive concessions where its social order is concerned,
in other words to accept a restoration of capitalism.[69] Accordingly,
Trotsky concludes, 'without the interference of [European] revolution,
the social bases of the Soviet Union must be crushed, not only in the case
of defeat, but also in the case of victory'.[70]

Here Trotsky falls into a methodological error which is frequent with
him, that of seeing only as absolute the antagonisms between classes,
both on the national and on the international scale, and underestimating
the mediations, which are often extremely complex, that intervene. In
the present instance he regards it as inevitable that the class antagonisms
between the capitalist states and the 'workers' state' should take precedence over the inter-capitalist antagonisms as soon as the working of
the latter may facilitate victory for the 'workers' state' in a war. Practice
has shown that, in the concrete historical situation of the Second World
War, it was possible for inter-imperialist rivalries to predominate,
within certain limits, over class contradictions both national and international. Stalin's skill consisted in operating within these limits, *without*

making the absolute concessions which, in Trotsky's view, were un-avoidable. Instead of making concessions at the expense of the foundations of the Soviet social order, Stalin made them at the expense of the revolutionary struggle in the capitalist countries. In the period of the Soviet–German pact, this brutal realism gave a sinister look to Soviet policy. In the second phase of the war, brought about by Hitler's historic mistake in attacking the Soviet Union, Stalin's policy coincided with the real and vital interests of great masses, of entire peoples. But the revolutionary struggle for socialism in the capitalist countries was thrust back to second or even third place. It was not the European revolution that decided the fate of the Soviet Union, but the Soviet Union that decided the fate of the European revolution.

The result did not prove that socialism could be completely built in the USSR without a victory of the revolution in the vital centres of imperialism, but it did bring out very forcibly what the real basis was that gave substance to Stalin's ideas: the *relative* autonomy of the Soviet revolution in relation to the world revolution. The inter-war period had already provided an empirical demonstration of this autonomy, and the Second World War gave further backing to this demonstration.

The theory of the socialist revolution worked out by Marx and Engels did not allow of such autonomy, except as regards the improbability of a *simultaneous* conquest of power by the working class in all the advanced capitalist countries (the countries where this conquest *had* to begin). Once the revolution had begun in one of these vital centres of the capitalist system, thought Marx and Engels, it could not fail to spread, without any break in continuity, to the other vital centres – otherwise it would perish. The Russian revolution revealed two new facts: that the conquest of power by the proletariat might not begin in the vital centres of capitalism (as Lenin had perceived already in April 1917), and that this revolution could maintain and consolidate itself even if the socialist revolution should be delayed in the advanced capitalist countries for a period that it was hard to define (the Bolshevik leaders thought at first that it would be short, but later – as in Lenin's last reflections – they contemplated the possibility that it might be a fairly long one).

The conception of 'socialism in one country' was only an empirical generalization of the second of these facts – giving it, however, an absolute significance, as constituting sufficient proof of the possibility of building complete socialism in the USSR regardless of whether the revolution had triumphed or not in the advanced capitalist countries. Actually, this second fact proved only that the building of socialism could be *begun*, and that it was possible to make progress in this direction. As I have pointed out, provision of theoretical grounds for the 'leap' made by Stalin (with Bukharin's help) necessitated at the very least showing that the socialist socio-economic formation in its fully developed state was compatible with a regional framework – that it did not require, as an indispensable condition, a world-wide structure, which was what Marx had assumed. This was done neither by Stalin nor by Bukharin. All their arguments tend to show that a socialist reconstruction of agriculture is compatible with maintaining the alliance between workers and peasants, the political foundation of the Soviet regime.[71] For his part, Trotsky does not reject this possibility; but he maintains, and rightly, that this does not solve the other problem. This is the strong side of Trotsky's position. Its weak side is that it underestimates the relative autonomy of the Russian revolution, in relation to the process of world revolution. Whereas Stalin makes this autonomy absolute, Trotsky reduces it to its most modest expression.

The relative autonomy of the Russian revolution, in relation to the world revolutionary process going on outside the USSR, implied the relative autonomy of the revolutions that were in gestation, both in the West and in the East, in relation to the Russian revolution. Conscious recognition, with theoretical understanding, of this reciprocal autonomy and of its relative nature, its limits (determined in each case by a concrete situation) would have been extremely fruitful for the revolutionary movement, for the Comintern itself. It would have opened the way for theoretical, political and organizational autonomy of the Communist parties and for a new structure of their international organization. It would have made possible presentation of the major problem of 'defence of the USSR' not in terms of unconditional acceptance of the Soviet model – in respect both of the path followed to the taking of power and of that followed in building socialism – and in connection with the external policy of the Soviet party, but in terms of mutual collaboration and support, without reciprocal criticism being ruled out: in terms that would have corresponded, moreover, to the specific conditions in which each Communist party had to operate.

But Stalin's conception held within it a paradox. While in one way it recognized ('objectively', as Magri says[72]) the existence of this relative autonomy, at the same time it denied this: on the one hand, by carrying it to extremes – that is, by not recognizing its *relative* character – where the autonomy of Soviet socialism in relation to the world revolution was concerned; and on the other, by reducing it to zero, denying it in practice, as regards the autonomy of the revolutionary movement in the capitalist world in relation to the Russian revolution.

Magri is doubtless right when he says that this 'paradox' is not to be explained exclusively by the theoretical mistakes or weaknesses of the Bolshevik leadership; the extremely difficult objective conditions in which the Soviet experience was proceeding must also be taken into account. The different aspects of the problem overlap and condition each other, and it is only through a close and objective historical analysis that it will be possible to determine the weight of each element in the successive phases of the Soviet regime. In the present state of research one can do no more than formulate broad, approximate hypotheses. The intense political struggle that developed within the party, the Soviets and the trade unions during the first years of the Soviet regime; the sharp attitude taken up by Lenin on the eve of his death, in opposition to bureaucratism and Great-Russian nationalism, and to theoretical complacency; Trotsky's line after 1923, and that of Bukharin (which must be differentiated from Stalin's even during the period of their 'alliance') – all this shows clearly that the path and the means chosen by Stalin did not constitute an inevitable choice, but were the result of the defeat suffered by other tendencies and options. And this was a defeat that was not inflicted on the level of theory, for Stalin's faction never managed to give its actions a Marxist theoretical basis, but on the level of political and organizational activity. The prospect of building a complete socialist society 'in one country' was not a scientifically worked-out aim but a myth that was lifted up before the Soviet people in order to justify the immense sacrifices that were required of them. This was why it did not help to mould the masses into a conscious subject, critical and demanding in relation to what it had itself created historically, but, on the contrary, cultivated in them an uncritical and conformist attitude, and made of them an object easy to manipulate.

Like all myths that appear in response to demands of reality which have not been resolved scientifically, the myth of the complete building of socialism, to be achieved as the result of a few five-year plans, played an effective instrumental role – arousing illusions, kindling faith, facilitating mobilization of the masses and suppression of every critical attitude. When, however, the stages laid down had been accomplished and the time came to announce that socialism had now been built, the myth began to disintegrate. Faith gradually gave way to scepticism, generous feelings to cynicism, political ebullience to political indifference. In order to keep the myth going it was necessary to resort to terror. Problems were becoming more complicated every day, their quantitative aspect was giving way to a qualitative one, but the level of theoretical capacity to deal with these problems fell lower and lower: the ideas in circulation were poorer and poorer, and brains were increasingly atrophied by terror and, especially, by the habit of never thinking for themselves. The Soviet Union was plunged into war when this process had hardly begun, when only a minority had started to become aware of the myth – and had paid dear for its clearsightedness. Patriotic feelings than came to the rescue of the myth, and the great victory of 1945 gave it fresh vigour; but not for long. The gigantic industrial, technical and cultural 'leap forward' that Russia had made was unquestionable (except that, in the cultural field, the quantitative leap was expressed, as regards quality, largely in the development of a mass culture that was conformist, petty-bourgeois, and merely instrumental in character). But was this *socialism*? The Twentieth Congress gave the answer: socialism did not yet exist in the USSR. During the thirty years of Stalin's rule there had been a bureaucratic and police autocracy, not a proletarian democracy. And without proletarian democracy how could one speak of genuine possession of the means of production by the working masses? But I do not intend to tackle here the crucial problem of the nature of the social system that has been established in the USSR. This will be done in another part of the book.

Let us return to the Comintern. At the time of the Sixth Congress

(1928) Stalin's myth was approaching its zenith. Very few were the Communists outside the Soviet Union who cast doubt on Stalin's conception of 'socialism in one country' and the absolute priority accorded to the Soviet revolution in the process of world revolution.[73] The Bolshevik opposition to Stalinism inside the USSR found itself tragically isolated in the international Communist movement. The latter did not insist on the autonomy which was expressed objectively, even though in distorted fashion, in the idea of 'socialism in one country', but unconditionally submitted to every interpretation given by Stalin of the higher interests of the USSR. It was not, of course, out of the question that, at one moment or another and to a greater or lesser degree, this interpretation might actually coincide with the interests of the world revolutionary movement. Whether this was so however, remained something that the Communist movement could not decide, since it had no means of analysing and checking the decisions taken by the Soviet leaders. At the same time the Communist movement was obliged to submit to all these decisions, from the moment when safeguarding the construction of socialism in the USSR was consecrated as the key problem for the world revolution. The Comintern and, consequently, the Communist parties had to determine their strategy and tactics primarily in relation to Soviet policy. If the Kuomintang was regarded by Moscow as a reliable ally of the USSR, then the Chinese Communists had to come to terms with it. If the German Social Democrats turned away from the spirit of Rapallo, the German Communists had to 'concentrate their fire' on the German Social Democrats. If Léon Blum showed a positive attitude towards the USSR, the French Communists had to take care not to oppose him, even when he was sacrificing the Spanish Republic and smothering the great struggles of the French proletariat in 1936. If Largo Caballero failed to follow Soviet 'advice', the Spanish Communists had to get rid of him in favour of Negrin, who had a better grasp of the needs of Soviet foreign policy. If safeguarding the pact with Hitler's Germany in 1939–41 necessitated that the Communists of all countries cease to treat Fascism as their main enemy, those Communists must not hesitate to call black what they had called white the day before. And if the Comintern constituted an obstacle to a better understanding with Roosevelt and Churchill, the Communists of the whole world must hail its dissolution – together with the moment and the way in which this was effected – as the ideal and only solution to the problem of the impossibility, proved by historical experience (as the Comintern resolution claimed), of leading the working-class movement of every country from an international centre. History thus confirmed the definition given by Trotsky in 1936:

> At the present time, the Communist International is a completely submissive apparatus in the service of Soviet foreign policy, ready at any time for any zigzag whatsoever.[74]

The possibility that this 'submissive apparatus' might become an embarrassment for Soviet foreign policy was objectively created as soon as the supreme purpose of the Comintern had been recognized as being to safeguard the building of socialism in the USSR. True, in so far as the principal capitalist states accepted the 'accomplished fact' of the Russian revolution, and concentrated all their efforts on preventing *new* 'facts' of the same order, there were increased possibilities for establishing 'peaceful co-existence' with the capitalist world, or, if the worst should come to the worst, for alliance with one group within that world against another. But the bourgeoisie is a class with a practical, prosaic outlook, brought up to believe in the principle of 'fair exchange'. It was therefore to be expected that, in exchange for 'help' in the building of socialism – by trading, by renouncing (though never finally) armed intervention and so on – it should want to be given 'something'. Bukharin expressed the situation very well in his report to the Fifteenth Congress of the CPSU at the end of 1927: 'Chamberlain tells us: "We have no objection to doing business with you, but be so good as to close down the Comintern!"' Bukharin added that it had become difficult to attack the USSR directly: the capitalists now winked at it – but they asked it to close down the Comintern. And he revealed that the Independent Labour Party had sent a letter asking whether the Second and Third Internationals could not be merged.[75]

In the epoch of the Sixth Congress these siren songs were treated with disdain. After overcoming the Trotskyist opposition, Stalin found himself suddenly faced with a serious economic and social situation in the USSR. The building of socialism 'at a snail's pace', as Bukharin had put it, leaving too much freedom to the kulaks, suffered a dramatic crisis in the supply of foodstuffs in the first months of 1928. Stalin then made a 180-degree turn, and crushed the opposition offered by the Bukharinite wing of the Party, using the methods that had already proved their efficacy when the Trotskyists were put down. From the 'snail's pace' Stalin switched to the gallop, from excessive consideration for the kulaks to ruthless liquidation of them overnight. As, however, a large section of the middle peasants – in other words the majority of the peasantry – and even some of the poor peasants as well, were under the influence of the kulaks, the repression launched against the latter fell, and with unheard-of violence, upon tens of millions of peasants in the USSR. This forced collectivization accompanied the first five-year plan, which demanded real 'heroism in labour' from the mass of the workers. Stalin had adopted, in fact, part of the Trotskyist programme, and Preobrazhensky's plan of 'socialist primitive accumulation', but had speeded up the pace of it, in accordance with the delay and with the empirical way in which he had made this 'turn'. The 'turn' gave rise to severe inner tensions in the party and in Soviet society. At the same time Stalin was observing with anxiety the policies of Britain and France, and especially the activity of 'perfidious Albion'. He thought that a new anti-Soviet intervention was being planned. It was this set of circumstances that determined the ultra-left direction then taken by Stalin's policy, both internally and in the Comintern. This was no time for liquidating the Comintern but, on the contrary, for utilizing it against the 'right' opposition in the Bolshevik party, and also for hurling it into a furious offensive against the Social Democrats and the Catholic Centre Party in Germany, against the Socialists and Radicals in France, and against the Labour Party in Britain – all of those being seen as the most dangerous potential accomplices in an Anglo-French war of intervention. It was the time of 'social Fascism' and 'class against class'.

Hitler's victory changed the European scene, causing Soviet policy to veer towards seeking alliance with the 'democratic' capitalist states. The latter did not dismiss the possibility of such alliances, even though they entertained mental reservations. But it was precisely in these countries that, after the smashing of the German Communist Party, the most important sections of the Comintern were to be found – in France and

Czechoslovakia especially and, from 1934 onwards, in Spain too, where the Communist Party was beginning to play an important political role in the young Republic established in 1931. A period was thus opening in which the Comintern, and the programme approved by the Sixth Congress, was to become an embarrassment for Soviet foreign policy. In the eyes of the international bourgeosie, the Comintern embodied world revolution. The fact that the latter figured in the Sixth Congress programme with the building of socialism in the USSR as its centre merely confirmed the leaders of capitalism in their notion that the Comintern was under Moscow's direct control – the instrument used by Stalin in order to interfere in the domestic affairs of other countries. The 'request' made by Austen Chamberlain to which Bukharin had referred in 1927 now became more pressing. It is significant that the Seventh and last Congress of the Comintern did not meet until seven years after the Sixth, despite the statutes providing for an interval of only two years between congresses. It is also significant that the very words 'Communist International' almost completely vanished from Stalin's speeches, articles and political reports after 1933. Unless I have missed something, he alluded to the Comintern only twice thereafter: in his report to the Eighteenth Congress of the CPSU, in March 1939, when he waxed ironical about those who 'look for Comintern "hotbeds" in the deserts of Mongolia, in the mountains of Abyssinia, or in the wilds of Spanish Morocco', and in 1943, when he said that the dissolution had put an end to a 'calumny'.

The Seventh Congress met in July 1935. The first noticeable innovation was that the principal personages were no longer Russian, as they had been at all the previous congresses.[76] Dimitrov delivered the main report, and Ercoli (Togliatti) the one next in importance. The Soviet Party was represented by Manuilsky, a secondary figure among the Soviet leaders. Thorez appeared in the forefront: Stalin remained in the wings. The congress focused its attention on the problems of struggle against Fascism and war. The policies of 'workers' united front' and 'people's front' clearly tended towards an alliance with the Socialist parties (described not long before as 'social Fascists') and the democratic and liberal section of the bourgeoisie. From a formal standpoint, this strategy seemed to be subordinated to an overall prospect of struggle against capitalism, but the emphasis was laid on immediate aims: defence (or recovery) of bourgeois-democratic freedoms, in face of the Fascist threat, fight against the danger of war, support for the collective security policy of the USSR. It is noteworthy that even the very words 'world revolution' made not a single appearance in Dimitrov's lengthy report.

This final congress of the Comintern revealed certain tendencies to renovation then appearing among the Communist parties, which were seeking to rid themselves of meaningless schemas and sectarian traditions; at the same time, however, it was the least theoretical congress ever held by the Comintern – the transition to what Dimitrov called 'a new tactical orientation'[77] was effected without any critical analysis of the past. Thus, the crisis of the Marxist theory of world revolution was 'resolved' by renouncing, in practice, any *explicit* theory of world revolution.

CAUSES OF THE PARALYSIS OF THEORY

We have seen that the Leninist theory of the course of the world revolution made necessary a 'world party', strongly centralized on a global scale, with a semi-military discipline and rigorous ideological unity. As we have also seen, the urgency of creating this party was due to Lenin's view that the objective conditions had arrived for the world revolution to be victorious ('moribund' capitalism, and a very high revolutionary level of the Western proletariat). All that was lacking was a party capable of putting itself at the head of the irresistible revolutionary process. We have seen, too, that this conception of Lenin's was refuted, both in its general theoretical aspect and in its conjunctural aspect, by the actual march of history. The crisis of theory thus opened was not recognized as such, but remained, in fact, subjacent all through the internal struggle that went on in the Bolshevik Party leadership and in the Comintern. Stalin 'resolved' the problem by means of an empirical revision of the theory of world revolution, propounded by Marx and Lenin: as a result of this revision, the victory of the revolution in the industrialized part of the world ceased to be a necessary condition for building socialist society, which could now be fully constructed within the national limits of the USSR. Nevertheless, Stalin's revision still retained the conception of a 'moribund' capitalism which had reached the end of its historical evolution and was incapable of allowing for any substantial new development of the productive forces. The coming victory of the world revolution was inexorably determined in advance by the junction of these two processes: 'building socialism' in the USSR (with, consequently, ascent of the productive forces to a higher level, without precedent under capitalism), and 'decay' of capitalism, becoming ever more acute. The key factor became the 'building of socialism in the USSR', whereas the Western proletariat, and along with it the peoples of the colonies and semi-colonies, saw themselves relegated to the role of auxiliary factors. In this way the Comintern's total subordination to Soviet policy was given theoretical justification. This was the essence of Stalin's theory of the world revolution, which was taken over by the Comintern. A victim of its own logic, the theory was itself set aside when the security of the USSR, as seen by Stalin, required that this be done. And, to conclude, one day it became opportune, by virtue of this same requirement, to put an end to the Comintern, the 'world party' conceived by Lenin.

In Chapter 3 I shall examine more closely the way in which the Leninist conception of the world revolution concretely determined the structure and working of the Comintern and how the bureaucratic centralism resulting from this became increasingly a brake on the theoretical and political activity of the Comintern. Before taking up these subjects, however, let me close the present chapter with some brief thoughts on the most general causes of the progressive sclerosis of Marxist thinking in the Comintern.

The Bolsheviks, said Rosa Luxemburg in her essay on the Russian revolution, 'by their determined revolutionary stand, their exemplary strength in action, and their unbreakable loyalty to international socialism ... have contributed whatever could possibly be contributed under such devilishly hard conditions'. But she added, prophetically: 'The danger begins only when they make a virtue of necessity and want to freeze into a complete theoretical system all the tactics forced upon them by these fatal circumstances, and want to recommend them to the international proletariat as a model of socialist tactics.'[78] The danger did indeed begin there. For, on the one hand, the Russian revolutionary theoreticians yielded to the temptation to make a virtue of necessity, and, on the other, the admiration and enthusiasm with which the Russian revolution filled the revolutionaries of all countries predisposed them to accept its message uncritically. This development was favoured by the fact that the 'theoretical forces' formed in the Second International had (with rare exceptions such as Rosa Luxemburg, Mehring and some others of less importance) all deserted the camp of revolution. Their critique of the Russian revolution, from reformist or liberal positions, contributed to reinforcing still further, for the revolutionaries of the capitalist world, the authority of the Bolshevik conceptions.[79]

At the moment when critical thinking was most necessary, the October revolution introduced *theoretical complacency*. Everything seemed to have been settled, in principle – the paths of the revolution, the tactics to be used, the model for the party – when in reality everything had become more problematical than at any previous moment in the history of the labour movement. This was so in the West, where the revolution had been beaten and the bulk of the proletariat turned a deaf ear to revolutionary Marxism, and in the East, where the revolution was awakening in a setting that Marxism had hardly yet explored. It was so even in Russia, where the proletarian revolution was isolated, encircled internationally by the capitalist world and bogged down internally in the peasant and petty-bourgeois marsh. Unlike Marx, however, the heralds of the October revolution proclaimed to the revolutionaries of all countries: 'Behold the truth, and bow down before it!' This doctrinaire attitude could not but encourage sectarianism and authoritarianism, favouring the dogmatization of Marxism in its Bolshevik version and leading to underestimation of the national originality of other countries – those of advanced capitalism as well as those oppressed by imperialism.

Lenin himself, though he often emphasized the need to avoid copying Russian experience in a mechanical way, wrote in '*Left-Wing' Communism, An Infantile Disorder* (and he repeated this in other places): 'Not merely several but all the primary features of our revolution, and many of its secondary features, are of international significance.' And even though he stressed that, when the revolution had triumphed in an advanced country, Russia would then become a backward country, from the socialist standpoint, he added: 'At the present moment in history, however, it is the Russian model that reveals to *all* countries something – and something highly significant – of their near and inevitable future.' In the conclusion to this famous lesson in tactics, Lenin reiterated the need to take into account 'the *concrete features* which this struggle assumes and must inevitably assume in each country, in conformity with the specific character of its economics, politics, culture and national composition (Ireland, etc.), its colonies, religious divisions, and so on and so forth'.[80] It was a matter, however, of taking these 'concrete features' into account in order to *apply* a theoretical and political set of ideas regarded as having already been worked out and tested by historical experience, so far as its essential components and 'principles' were concerned. To those inherited from Marx some new elements were added: soviets constitute the universal form of the dictatorship of the proletariat; the party of the Bolshevik type is the universal model of the Marxist revolutionary party; etc. At no stage was it suggested that the diversity of national realities and the new world reality might require a new Marxist analysis in depth capable of bringing forward new revolutionary theories. There seemed to be no notion at all that events, instead of *fully* confirming the theory of the revolution inherited from Marx and Engels, enriched by Lenin's contributions, had called in question some essential aspects of this theory.

The mental attitude of the Bolsheviks, which was transmitted through the Comintern to the non-Russian Communists, could be summed up as follows: the October revolution had made it possible to *complete* the Marxist theory of the revolution with regard to questions on which, owing to their lack of concrete experience, the two great masters had not been able to get far enough. For example: the contradictions of imperialism, the form of the dictatorship of the proletariat, problems of strategy and tactics, the type of party, etc. What still remained problematical thenceforth was not the theory of the revolution as such, but only its particular interpretation in relation to the specific conditions prevailing in each country. On a more general theoretical plane, the October victory was seen as irrefutable proof of the absolutely scientific character of Marxism. 'It is therefore clear,' wrote Bukharin in his *Historical*

Materialism, 'That Marxists have a perfect right to regard proletarian science as true and to demand that it be generally recognized.'[81]

The depository of this 'true science' in the world outside the Soviet Union was the Comintern. But the Comintern concentrated its attention – since the basic questions of the theory of the revolution were seen as having been settled – on strategic, tactical and organizational forms of action. Philosophical, economic, historical and sociological investigations were of only secondary interest. Political schemes became increasingly detached from the social sciences and, in general, from the cultural milieu in which they were to be applied. In the Comintern's discussions on the colonial problem, for example, the categories remained, baldly: 'proletariat', 'peasantry', 'national bourgeoisie', etc., without ever, or only rarely, taking into account the cultural universe characteristic of those countries, so radically different from that of the West.

The contradiction between theoretical positions and actual development began to find symptomatic reflection in the passionate discussions on tactical problems that dominated the first congresses of the Comintern. No one, however, formulated clearly the idea that there was a crisis of theory.[82] After Lenin's death, as though in an attempt to overcome all doubts and misgiving, the tendency to 'theoretical complacency' and the dogmatization of Marxism rapidly intensified. One must not hesitate to defend the Marxist 'dogma', wrote *Bolshevik*, the theoretical journal of the Soviet party: 'Only by fulfilling this task without deviation will it be possible to keep unspotted the flag of the theory of the proletarian revolution, the flag of the Marxist "dogma". It is quite pointless to be afraid of this word. The fight against "dogmatic" Marxism has always been an activity of reformists far remote from Marxism, such as Bernstein. All that is best in the working-class movement has always fought for the "dogma" of Marxism.'[83] The dogma (without quotation-marks) was, needless to say, Leninism. History repeated itself. After Lenin's death the young Third International was making the same mistake as that made by the Second after the death of Marx and Engels, when it 'canonized' their doctrine.

In 1924 Zinoviev recalled that the first people to speak of 'Leninism' were, in 1903, the adversaries of the Bolsheviks, when they sought to 'counterpose Lenin's ideas to Marx's principles'. 'Lenin,' Zinoviev adds, 'would undoubtedly have been against the use of the term, for reasons obvious to all who knew his modesty. But we, his contemporaries and disciples, *must* [Zinoviev's own emphasis] speak of Leninism now, just as the continuators of Marx's work spoke of Marxism ... and as the supporters of Darwin spoke of Darwinism.'[84] Leninism, Zinoviev went on, 'is the Marxist understanding and explanation of the *new* historical phases of the evolution of society, the *new* experience of the world working-class movement (and of the revolutionary movement in general), of everything that has emerged *since* Marx.' Lenin could not have been Lenin without Marx, Zinoviev acknowledges, but it was necessary to declare that '*now, there can be no revolutionary Marxism apart from Leninism*'.[85] Here, Zinoviev is only repeating what Stalin had been the first to proclaim, in April 1924, in his lectures on Leninism. For the moment, Stalin's formulations coexisted with those of Zinoviev, Bukharin, etc. Soon afterwards, they were to become the only orthodox definitions of Leninism, and every militant in the Comintern would have to know them by heart. Indeed, after the crushing of the Trotskyist and Bukharininist oppositions, there was to be a transition from *Leninism*, the only valid Marxism 'of the epoch of imperialism and proletarian revolution', to *Stalinism*, the only valid Leninism of the epoch of imperialism, proletarian revolution and ... socialism in one country. After a *Marx ad usum Lenini* came a *Lenin ad usum Stalini*. And the oppositions that rose up against the second made the mistake of remaining enclosed within the first.

This process of dogmatization and continual shrinking of the theoretical foundations of the Comintern was clearly reflected in the Communist parties. Those which, when they were formed, lacked any national heritage of theory (such as, for example, the Spanish one) vegetated in a routine-ridden activism; those which possessed such a heritage (like the German and Italian ones) were unable to cultivate it: the theoretical work of Rosa Luxemburg was doomed to ostracism, as was, later, that of Gramsci. In his report on the Comintern delivered to the Fifteenth Congress of the CPSU (December 1927), Bukharin alluded to the theoretical weakness of the Communist parties in general, and of their leading circles in particular, as constituting one of the Comintern's main shortcomings. He emphasized how few intellectuals there were in these leading groups, noting that 'the series of crises which we witnessed in our Communist parties, since the time when the revolutionary wave subsided, affected first of all the intellectual upper stratum'. With a careful choice of words, he mentioned that this misfortune had not left the Soviet party untouched. The leaders of the USSR, he observed 'are overburdened with general work and cannot give enough attention to the theoretical work'. And this weakening in theoretical work through the Comintern was taking place at a time when 'the situation now is much more complicated and much greater demands are made on the executive than before', as regards theoretical leadership.[86]

Bukharin was one of the few leaders of the Comintern who, during the 1920s, began to think about fundamental problems connected with the structure of capitalism, the changes taking place in the working class, the colonial question and so on. 'The concentration and centralization of economic life,' he said in the report already quoted, 'is advancing with seven-league boots. We might even affirm that there is taking place a "trustification of the state power itself", i.e., that the state of power of the bourgeoisie is becoming more and more dependent on the great and powerful capitalist concerns or combinations of concerns . . . This is not an altogether new phenomenon, though I must admit that as long as capitalism has existed these processes have never developed so far as is now the case, a fact which appears to me to be of great significance.' After analysing different forms assumed by this process, in Germany, Italy, Japan and Austria, he concluded: 'Thus we have on the one hand a growth of the differences among the various capitalist states. On the other hand we see the further process of an *organization* of capitalist forces within the countries expressed in a tendency towards state capitalism.' Examining the situation of the working class, he mentioned, among other things, the structural changes observable in the industrial wage-earning class in Germany; the percentage of office-workers among them had increased from 11·1 per cent in 1907 to 36·5 per cent in 1925–6. And he noted that these changes made it easier for the capitalists to integrate part of the working class, operating through this office-worker stratum. He pointed to the increasing role of the trade unions in effecting this integration – although this did not mean that there were no more strikes.[87] All these observations, and especially the ones referring to the process of 'organization' going on within capitalism, were to be entered in the file of evidence that was used to condemn Bukharin not long afterwards. (Actually, Stalin began his preparations against Bukharin as early as this period of the Fifteenth Party Congress.) He was to be accused, for instance, of adopting Hilferding's views, despite the criticisms that Bukharin expressly formulated regarding the reformist conclusions drawn by Hilferding from his scientific observations. In the same report Bukharin commented that the Comintern had only a very general notion of the colonial problem. The Chinese revolution, he said, had made it possible to perceive this weakness: 'The entire complication of the social class entanglement, the great difficulty of the tasks connected with the conduct of such a tremendous colonial revolution, only faced us quite recently in grim reality.'[88] In each concrete case, Bukharin emphasized, it was necessary to analyse the class structures. The Comintern's theses on the colonial question provided it with only a very general basis.

All these incitements to tackle the new problematic presented by world development were to be swept aside during the struggle against 'the right-wing deviation as the main enemy'. Even so, neither the prestige-backing that the October revolution had brought to the dogmatization of Leninism as Marxism's last word, nor the repressive and administrative mechanism of the Comintern, is sufficient to account for the progressive paralysis that overcame revolutionary Marxist thinking in the capitalist world between the wars. During this same period, within the framework of the Comintern, the Chinese revolutionary intelligentsia did begin to break out of the schemas manufactured by the Comintern centre in Moscow and really to follow the Bolshevik example. They took the first step towards the elaboration of a revolutionary theory of the Chinese revolution, just as the Bolshevik intellectuals had done when they created an original theory of the Russian revolution.[89] But the Chinese Communists not only had the Comintern, they also had *a revolution under way*, just as the Bolsheviks had not only had Marx and the Second International but also the revolution taking place in Russia. It is therefore legitimate to wonder if it was not a deeper-lying reality – the objective immaturity of the socialist revolution in the countries of advanced capitalism – that conditioned the paralysis of theoretical thinking among the revolutionary Marxists of the West, even if the factors that have been mentioned did contribute strongly to aggravating it, or can account for it as, specifically, a state of 'paralysis'.

It is not my intention, of course, to claim that the productive forces of advanced capitalism did not already constitute, in the period of which I write, an adequate material basis for the socialist transformation of society. I refer to the immaturity of the *revolution*, which is a very different matter, despite the frequent confusion made between these two problems. If we start from Marx's theoretical theses on the objective maturing of the socialist revolution, taking the concept of revolution in its broad sense and not in the narrow sense of the capture of power by the working class (or by a party claiming to represent it), then it is not enough for this maturity to have arrived that productive forces should exist that can sustain a new social order. It must also be the case that capitalism is incapable of developing *new* productive forces. If, at certain moments of their lives, Marx and Engels foresaw the victory of the socialist revolution in Europe, this was because they thought that capitalism had reached this *terminal situation*. We see that conviction expressed already in the *Manifesto*. Lenin made a similar appreciation regarding capitalism as transformed into the imperialist system. The Comintern's leaders took this over as it stood, and built upon it all their strategic and tactical plans. As we have seen, the thesis of 'socialism in one country' is justified as a new theory of the world revolution in so far as it presupposes, besides the *prospect* of building socialism in the USSR, the *reality* of the stagnation and decay of capitalism, now incapable, as Trotsky was to say – in complete agreement on *this* point with his implacable adversary – of any new development of the productive forces. However, the two world wars and the world economic crisis of 1929 proved to be not the expression of capitalism's arrival at the terminal situation mentioned, but essential means for transforming it structurally, and giving it a new capacity to expand the productive forces. Monstrous means, to be sure, but the monstrous is a moral category, not an economic one. The two world wars, in particular, furnished a most striking illustration of the infernal logic of capitalism, of that logic in which, as Marx put it, 'progress' resembles the pagan idol who will not drink the nectar otherwise than from the skulls of his victims. If we were to approach the problem exclusively from the 'moral' standpoint, it would be hard to understand how mankind, faced with such obvious monstrosities, has not yet put an end to capitalism. This, however, would be to forget that a system that is capable of developing the productive forces also 'develops' its own 'moral' justifications (in the case of capitalism – patriotism, nationalism, racism, individualism and many other 'isms'). The reformist ideology, secreted organically by the system's capacity to develop the productive forces, holds a place of honour among capitalism's moral as well as political justifications. Would Fascism have been able to exert such attraction upon millions of petty-bourgeois, peasants and workers between the two world wars, constituting one of the most monstrous forms of ideological justification of capitalism, if there had not been, behind the demagogy of Mussolini or Hitler, the capacity of German and Italian monopoly capitalism to restructure the system for a new development of the productive forces?

No terminal situation seems to have yet to have occurred for capitalism, in the sense of incapacity to develop the productive forces. And the theoretical problem of whether such a situation is now foreseeable, and what processes might lead to it, remains open. But the objective immaturity of the revolution (in the broad sense) under the advanced capitalism of today does not in the least signify that between the two world wars, and at the end of the second of these, no situations were presented that were propitious for 'a bold stroke' by the revolutionary party (as Lenin sometimes spoke of the October assault) that could have put an end to the monstrous logic of capitalist development in one or another of the industrial countries.

Nevertheless, there must be an underlying connection between this objective immaturity and the theoretical and political immaturity hitherto demonstrated by the revolutionary vanguards formed under advanced capitalism, when it is a matter of profiting by situations propitious to revolution (in the narrow sense).

The first 'immaturity' represents a considerable barrier – operating through a very complex series of justifications, such as those already mentioned and many others as well – across the road by which *current social consciousness* can arrive at a root-and-branch condemnation of the system. And *theoretical consciousness*, which can arise only in the intellectual strata, suffers from the absence of this pressing stimulant. When society is really in a situation of *general crisis* (I include among the components of such a situation an incapacity of the socio-economic mechanism to continue developing the productive forces without changing its own nature), this is not only reflected, in a more or less confused way, in ordinary social consciousness: the 'theory-producing' stratum is affected by it, too, in its own social existence as well as in the values and conceptions that have until then made up its cultural universe. It is not only the experience of society as a whole but its own most immediate experience that impels this stratum to find a revolutionary theory appropriate to the prevailing crisis. This is what happened in the societies of Russia and China, as it had happened already in the society of Germany in the middle of the nineteenth century, without our needing to go any farther back in history. (Let us not forget that Marx and Engels, as *revolutionary* theoreticians, were above all products of the general crisis of German society in the middle of the nineteenth century and of the theoretical consciousness of this crisis. Analysis should be undertaken to determine how far Marx's 'German standpoint' affected the scientific analyses in *Capital*, leading him to draw excessively hasty conclusions about the maturity of the revolution in the advanced capitalist countries of the nineteenth century, just as Lenin's 'Russian standpoint' led *him* to draw similar conclusions regarding the capitalism of the first years of the twentieth century.) However, as we know, the terminal situations of *these* societies did not result from the contradictions inherent in capitalist structures, but from the contradictions between the latter and *pre*-capitalist structures. It was on this basis that the objective premise of the revolution (in the broad sense) theorized by Marx became a reality; namely, the incapacity of the existing socio-economic system to cope with new productive forces.

For the problem that concerns us here we have no need to dwell on the well-known reasons why the Russian and Chinese revolutions did not remain within the 'bourgeois framework' but became transformed into proletarian revolutions. What is of greatest interest here is to bring out the fact that elaboration of the theory of revolution in the advanced capitalist countries has up to now lacked the powerful 'stimulant' that was enjoyed by both the Russian and Chinese revolutions. What has been absent is that 'general crisis' which official Marxism sees as having been present since the First World War, and which has been said to have now entered into its 'third stage' – but which has not yet expressed itself in what should have been its main feature, namely, incapacity of the capitalist mechanism to develop the productive forces. Such development is a fact, and it is going forward at a rate never previously seen.

But recognition that this handicap exists for the theory of the revolution in the advanced capitalist countries does not mean acceptance that no such theory is possible. This may be the necessary first step in a theoretical effort to open new prospects for revolutionary transformation of the societies of advanced capitalism, on the basis of a more rigorous knowledge of these societies. In any case, the first condition for arriving at such a theory is that all the schemas and 'principles' that social practice has shown to be erroneous shall be reconsidered, along with the methods and institutional structures that have contributed to preventing the discovery of error. The Comintern's theoretical paralysis may be explicable 'in the final instance' by the objective immaturity of the revolution in advanced capitalist society, but, even so, we must concern ourselves above all with those other 'instances' that contributed to accentuating and aggravating the effects of the 'final' one.

3

MONOLITHICITY

The functioning of a given party furnishes discriminating criteria: when a party is progressive it functions 'democratically' (in accordance with democratic centralism), when it is regressive it functions 'bureaucratically' (in the sense of bureaucratic centralism). The party in this second case is purely executive, not deliberative: it is then technically a police organization and its name of 'political party' is pure mythological metaphor.

GRAMSCI

THE SOVIET MODEL TRANSPLANTED

The triumph of reformism in nearly all the parties of the Second International undoubtedly put the need to create a Marxist party of a new type on the order of the day during the period of the First World War. But there was more than one way of tackling this task, and Marxists contemporary with Lenin were aware of the choice of approaches. Many elements on the left of the Socialist parties considered that it was not necessary, and would even be very harmful, to treat as essential, from the outset, the carrying through of a *split* in the labour movement, especially in the trade-union field. A political and ideological fight against reformism could be begun within the organized labour movement, basing oneself on the experiences of the war and the October revolution as well as on the revolutionary struggles of the post-war years. Other revolutionary Marxists, despite their agreement with Lenin on the immediate need to set up new parties, thought that a Communist International could be formed only when these parties had really struck root in their respective national soils. This was the attitude taken by Eberlein, representing the German Spartacists, when the question was discussed at the meeting that was to transform itself into the First Congress of the Comintern. 'The need for a Communist International,' he said, 'is absolutely obvious, but founding it now would be premature. The Communist International should be definitively established only when, in the course of the revolutionary mass movement gripping nearly all the countries of Europe, Communist parties have sprung up.'[1] Eberlein was expressing the view of Rosa Luxemburg, which was inspired not only by concern for realism but also by fear lest the Comintern adhere rigidly to the Bolshevik party model. But the enormous authority that the October victory had conferred upon Lenin got the better of the hesitations of both groups. In the end, the Comintern and its national sections conformed in every way to the conception held by the Bolshevik leaders not only of the march of the world revolution but also of the type of party that was needed. As regards the first point we have already looked, in the previous chapter, at the general features of Lenin's conception, from which there logically followed the urgent need to create the Comintern, the 'world party' of the revolution. In order, however, to appreciate how this conception was to determine the structures and working of the Comintern, it is not enough to take account of its general content: one has to come down to more concrete levels. For the Bolsheviks, as for many revolutionaries of other countries, the Russian revolution had shown in a detailed and precise way that which Marxist theory of the revolution had only been able to forecast in broad outline – the inner mechanism of the revolutionary process, the forms of struggle, the relationship of one to another among these, and so on. In the Russian revolution almost every imaginable form of struggle had been combined, from political propaganda and agitation to armed insurrection and civil war, and including political strikes and demonstrations, as well as wars between the new revolutionary state and the bourgeois states. Parliamentary and trade-union activity also figured in this many-faceted experience, though only to a limited extent. The decisive forms of struggle in the Russian revolution were extra-parliamentary, and the role played by the trade unions was an extremely modest one. One of the most important characteristics of the combination of all these forms of struggle, over a period of twelve years (1905–17), was the sudden transitions that took place from one form to another, together with the overlapping of a whole series of them, which object-ively demanded of the revolutionary party that it be capable of rapidly altering its tactics, moving flexibly from one form of activity to another.

The Russian scene had also displayed combined operations between the army of the revolutionary state and the internal revolutionary forces (political groups and guerrillas) of counter-revolutionary states. It must not be forgotten that, thanks to the German invasion, before and after the signing of the peace of Brest-Litovsk, and, subsequently, to the intervention by the Entente, a number of nation states arose on the huge territory of the former Tsarist empire – states that were headed by bourgeois parties or by Mensheviks, Socialist-Revolutionaries and other opponents of Bolshevism – in the Ukraine, the Caucasus, the Baltic region, etc. Lenin's order in October 1918 that an army of three million men be formed, to come to the aid of the international revo-lution, like, later, the Red Army's offensive against Warsaw in the summer of 1920, resulted from this experience of combining different methods of struggle which had been developed within the Russian empire. It needs to be kept in mind, too, that before becoming a 'union', in which the national independence of the component units actually disappeared, the Russian revolution assumed the constitutional form of a 'federation' of national Soviet states, in which Lenin and the Comin-tern saw the prototype of a world-wide federal republic of Soviets.

The Bolshevik party had taken shape under the conditions of a large multinational state. It was the single international party of the Russian, Ukrainian, Georgian, Polish, Finnish and other revolutionaries working within that state – in fact, a little 'International' in itself. Inside the party, nationality did not count, formally speaking: in practice, however, contradictions between 'national' and 'international' factors often mani-fested themselves, and Russian hegemony was latent.

The circumstances in which this type of party had to maintain its cohesion and effectiveness – illegality, repression, the situation of the proletariat as a minority in a peasant and petty-bourgeois milieu, cen-trifugal tendencies derived from national oppression, etc. – account very largely for the semi-military features of its structure and mode of oper-ation. The years of civil war were to intensify these features, giving rise to habits and methods that left deep traces on the subsequent life of the party. The eventual establishment of Stalin's system cannot be understood except against this background.

Generalization of this Russian model in an empirical way led to the world revolution being conceived as a gigantic revolutionary war embracing all the forms of struggle that have been mentioned – as a joint operation by the different national detachments of the international army of the proletariat, necessitating a central general staff, akin to that which the Bolsheviks had provided for the Russian revolution. The military terminology that we find in Comintern documents is merely the linguistic expression of this manner of conceiving the world revolution, its forms of organization and leadership and its strategic and tactical demands.

Just as the Bolshevik party had organized *joint action* by the proletarians of the different nationalities of the Russian empire in order to establish the Russian Federal Soviet Republic, so the Comintern came into being, as the first article of its Statutes declared, in order to organize joint action by the proletariat of the various countries, with the aim of establishing a World Federal Soviet Republic – and as we have seen in the preceding chapter, with this not a distant aim, but the practical task of the moment.

Just as the Bolshevik party had been the single party of the revolutionaries of every nationality in the Russian empire, so the Comintern was organized as the 'one world party' of the revolutionaries of all lands. Its permanent leading organ, the Executive Committee, was endowed with extraordinary powers. Its directives had immediate 'force of law' for all the national sections. It could expel members of groups or members belonging to any country, or entire national sections, it could change the leadership of a national section, even against the will of the majority of its members, and so on. Under these conditions, the national leaderships held in practice merely the power that was delegated to them by the Executive Committee of the Comintern. From top to bottom, an iron discipline and a most rigorous centralization were established, for, 'in the present epoch of acute civil war, the Communist Party will be able to fulfil its duty only if its organization is as centralized as possible, if iron discipline prevails, and if the party centre, upheld by the confidence of the party membership, has strength and authority and is equipped with the most comprehensible powers'.[2] The 'comprehensive powers' were always understood to be held in descending order: each committee was omnipotent in relation to those below it and impotent in relation to those above it.

The way in which the Comintern was set up had a marked effect on the characteristics that it assumed from the very start. Taking for granted that the world revolution was irresistibly on the march, that the masses were in movement, and that everything depended on the formation of a vanguard that would be uncompromising in its attitude to reformism and centrism, the Comintern adopted draconian measures from the outset to ensure the purity of the new parties. This was the aim of the '21 Conditions', a model of sectarianism and bureaucratic method in the history of the working-class movement.[3] As the introduction states, the purpose of the '21 Conditions' was to prevent the entry into the Comintern of groups and parties that 'have not in fact become Communist'. The criterion for recognizing those that had already 'in fact become Communist' was complete and unconditional acceptance of the '21 Conditions'. These points synthesized the conception of the party that has been set out above, and insisted upon the immediate purging of groups and parties wishing to join the Comintern, so as to ensure that all posts in the party press, in trade unions, parliamentary groups, cooperatives and municipalities, not to mention the leading organs of the party, were held exclusively by 'reliable Communists who have proved their devotion to the cause of the proletariat', with all 'reformists and centrists' of every stripe eliminated. An immediate and total break had to be made with all centrist and reformist organizations, both political parties and trade unions. The reformist trade-union International, which at that stage embraced the majority of the organized workers in the West (nearly 20 million members), was described as a yellow organization which the parties belonging to the Comintern had to 'wage an unyielding struggle against,' spreading within the unions the slogan of a break with this International.

On the one hand the '21 Conditions' signified in practice that the Communists were organizing a split in the labour movement, and were doing this, moreover, in a mechanical way and not through a political and ideological process that would have enabled the working people to convince themselves that it was necessary. On the other hand, they signified the introduction into the sections of the Comintern, and into any new parties that might join it, of a mechanism of internal purging based on a distinction between 'reliable and proved' Communists and those who were infected with the reformist or centrist virus – at a stage when the majority of both categories were only just taking their first step towards Communism!

A large number of socialists and trade-unionists who wanted to join the Comintern because they were in sympathy with the Russian revolution and shared, generally speaking, the revolutionary objectives of the new International nevertheless disagreed with it on certain points, especially where structure and methods of work were concerned. Above all they regarded the policy of splitting the labour movement as wrong, particularly in the trade-union field. The '21 Conditions' shut the doors of the Comintern to all these elements, who included many of the best cadres of the movement, inspired by sincere revolutionary feeling. At the same time, numerous elements who had no connection with the masses, and for whom it was therefore easier to declare war on the traditional organizations, were able to stand forth as 'good Communists' by the mere fact of showing neophytes' zeal in relation to the new catechism. Under the influence of the '21 Conditions', and in general of the methods adopted by the Comintern in its struggle against reformism and centrism, a sectarian and dogmatic spirit began from the very beginning to clear a way for itself in the Communist parties, disguised under a revolutionary verbalism that concealed its remoteness from reality. Members thought they were applying the 'Bolshevik model' when, in fact, they were utterly denying the spirit of the Bolshevik party that had made the October revolution and established the Soviet state.

That party had been formed during a long and complicated process, through a political and ideological struggle against the Mensheviks and the socialist revolutionaries, carried on in close connection with the real problems of the social and political world of Russia. It had been formed by going through the experience of the 1905 revolution, of the counter-revolution that followed, and then of the new revolutionary upsurge; by operating in illegality and in the Duma, in Soviets dominated by the

Mensheviks and socialist revolutionaries and in Soviets dominated by the Bolsheviks themselves; in the fire of political strikes, insurrection and civil war. This experience, without parallel at that time in the history of the revolutionary movement, had brought about the selection of a nucleus of intellectuals and workers who were able to take advantage of an exceptional situation in order to seize power.

What was now proposed was to create chemically pure Bolshevik parties overnight, and to do this on the basis of a working class which had for decades been trained in the reformist spirit, in parliamentary and trade-union activity – a working class which, in its great majority, had supported the 'traitor' leaders in entering into *union sacrée* with their respective bourgeoisies. In so far as this working class possessed some recent revolutionary experiences – mainly in the strike field – these offered characteristics that differed from those of the Russian movement. For example, the trade unions played a far more important part in the West than they had played in Tsarist Russia. How did it come about that Lenin, fully aware as he was of the complexity of the process that had forged the Bolshevik party (as he himself stresses in *'Left-Wing' Communism, An Infantile Disorder*), could have adopted the method symbolized by the '21 Conditions'? I can suggest no other answer than that put forward in the previous chapter to account for Lenin's optimism regarding the imminence of the world revolution.

Until the Third Congress, the '21 Conditions' seemed to be the 'Open, Sesame' of the Comintern for winning the working masses and forming exemplary Communist parties. Expel the reformist wing from your party without delay, Lenin told the Italian delegates to the Third Congress, and 'the masses of workers will follow us'.[4] Practice immediately showed that such expectations were out of true with the reality of the European countries, even those where the revolutionary crisis had gone farthest. The break with reformism thus effected resulted in a break with the mass of the workers. Except in rare cases the Communist parties remained confined to minority sections, sometimes tiny ones, of the proletariat.[5] And, what was worse, they appeared, in the eyes of the workers who had stayed loyal to their organizations, as splitters responsible for the division in the ranks of the working class. Their historical mission was – to use the military jargon that was favoured – to

conquer for the Comintern's ideas the international army of the proletariat, in order to transform it into the army of the revolution. But they
began by putting themselves outside the main bulk of this army, leaving
it in the hands of the reformist leaders and providing the latter with
splendid arguments for charging the Communists with splitting, sectarianism, unconditional submission to an alien and remote centre that
took no heed of national realities, and so forth. Only the deep sympathy
that the Russian revolution inspired in the working-class masses, even
those grouped in the reformist organizations, palliated a little the negative effects which this way of 'breaking with reformism' brought upon
the Communist parties and the Comintern.

When the attempts at revolution failed everywhere outside Russia,
the words and attitudes of the Socialist and trade-union leaders became
especially convincing to the majority of the workers: what matters now,
they said, is to improve our economic situation, enforce the eight-hour
day, achieve reforms and so on. And the workers knew from experience
that, in this field, their traditional organizations had secured good
results.

The Comintern tried to remedy the situation with its tactic called 'the
united front', inspired above all by *Left-Wing' Communism*. As, however, this turn was purely tactical in character, without any strategic
consideration apart from recognition that the conjuncture had changed,
with an ebb in the revolutionary tide, and as it was not accompanied by
any fundamental analysis of the problems of capitalism, the roots of
reformism, etc., it encountered incomprehension among many Comintern members. Their reaction is easily understood, since the Communist
parties, which had only just been formed in the spirit of a thoroughgoing
breach with the reformist 'traitors', were now being called upon to establish a common front with these same 'traitors'.[6] Thus, this first 'big turn'
by the Comintern at once multiplied its internal conflicts and led to the
widespread appearance of 'left-wing Communists', for whom the
'united-front' tactic, putting partial aims in the forefront (in place of the
direct overthrow of capitalism), with utilization of parliament, etc.,
seemed to be a return to reformism, a betrayal of the revolution and of
Comintern principles.

Furthermore, while the ebbing of the revolutionary wave was certainly a fact on the European scale, it showed great diversity as between different countries. In Germany, for example, the situation continued confused. The attempt at insurrection organized by the Communist Party in March 1921 had doubtless been an adventure, but all the same one could not rule out the prospect of serious political crises, as was shown by the events of 1923. The situation was equally uncertain in some other countries, such as Poland and Bulgaria. In prescribing a 'general retreat' to all its sections the Comintern's policy came into conflict with national diversity, just as had happened with the line of the 'general offensive' in 1919–20. The consequences could not be other than harmful, especially where newly created, inexperienced parties were concerned. Thus, and contrary to what was claimed in the resolution of 1943, already in this 'first stage' the guidance of Communist policy in every country from an international centre possessed of full powers, together with the method used to establish these parties, came into sharp conflict with the needs of the revolutionary struggle in each country.

As early as this epoch, too, the 'Russian viewpoint' greatly influenced Comintern policy, even though it was not imposed by the methods that Stalin was to use later on. Just as the line of an offensive at all costs, in 1919–20, had been largely inspired by the idea that the survival of the October revolution depended on its rapid extension to the West, so the universal retreat decreed by the Comintern in 1921 was strongly influenced by the appearance, in the international situation surrounding the Russian revolution, of a new, unhoped-for possibility, namely, peaceful coexistence and economic relations with the capitalist states. In the meantime Russia's internal situation had gravely worsened: the economic and social crisis, reflected in workers' strikes, the peasant boy-cott and, above all, the Kronstadt revolt, dictated a withdrawal that would ensure that the party did not become cut off from the masses – and so the New Economic Policy was introduced. There can be no doubt that the two circumstances mentioned, one international and the other national, had considerable influence on the outlook of the Bolshevik leaders where the problems of the revolutionary movement outside Russia were concerned. And it was they who were the Comintern's actual leaders – not so much, for the moment, because of the way the

Comintern worked as because of the great prestige they enjoyed among the world's proletariat.

ULTRA-CENTRALISM AND RUSSIFICATION

Hardly had it been set up than the mechanism conceived for the purpose of leading and coordinating great revolutionary struggles on a world scale was obliged to apply itself to directing activity which became increasingly bound up with concrete situations, and, in the end, increasingly reformist, as the great revolutionary prospects faded. From a far-away centre installed in the beleaguered fortress of 'socialism in a single country', decisions were promulgated on all the details of the political situation in every country, the tactics to be followed were laid down, and party leaders confirmed or replaced in accordance with their willingness to apply the policy prescribed by the ECCI.

The contradiction between this system of leadership and the demands of national reality in each country was reflected in the constant conflicts that arose between the all-powerful Executive Committee and the general staffs of the national sections, in the internal crises of the sections, and in the stagnation or even the actual decline of most of the parties. Between 1921 and 1931 the membership of the Comintern (apart from the Soviet party) was steadily reduced.

1921	1922	1924	1928	1931
887,745	779,102	648,090	445,300	328,716

On the world plane, the Comintern was an essentially European organization. In 1924 the distribution of its membership between the continents was as follows: Europe 659,090, America 19,500, Asia 6,350, Oceania 2,250, Africa 1,100. In Europe, four-fifths of the figure given were accounted for by four countries: Germany, Czechoslovakia, France and Yugoslavia (1924 figures) – which means that, in the majority of the countries of Europe, the Communist parties were very small and had very slight influence. This was true also of the USA.[7]

To be sure, so marked a decline cannot be attributed exclusively to the political and organizational effects of the contradictions between the Comintern system of leadership and the demands of national reality in each country; it was partly due to objective conditions. The post-war revolutionary wave was followed, in several countries, by the establishment of reactionary dictatorships which severely persecuted the Communist parties. It would, all the same, be quite wrong to underestimate the first-mentioned factor. Besides, the reactionary dictatorships were established in the most backward countries of Europe, in the south and south-east, and in Poland. In the advanced capitalist countries the Communist parties were legal; but they became bogged down, and their membership, outside Germany, Czechoslovakia and France, remained very small.

Theoretically, the need to adapt the policy and methods of operation of each party to the national peculiarities of its country seemed obvious to the leaders of the Comintern, and all their documents spoke of it. The campaign for the 'Bolshevization' of the parties, which was carried on in the years immediately following Lenin's death, included this demand among its principal slogans. But the Comintern's very structure, the way it was actually run, came into radical contradiction – as was eventually to be recognized in the resolution dissolving it – with this need to adapt the working of the parties to their respective national realities.

Between the Second and Sixth Congresses the statutes of the Comintern were amended in such a way as to strengthen still further centralism and the powers of the Executive Committee. The statutes approved at the Second Congress (1920) laid it down that the instructions of the ECCI were binding on all the national sections, and that 'the Executive Committee of the Communist International has the right to demand that parties belonging to the International shall expel groups or persons who offend against international discipline, and it also has the right to expel from the Communist International those parties which violate decisions of the world congress'. The Fifth Congress (1924) emphasized that the directives of the Executive Committee were 'imperative' and must be applied 'immediately'. The ECCI had the power 'to annul or to amend decisions of both the central organs and the congresses of the sections, and to take decisions which the central organs are obliged to carry out'. It could expel parties, groups or individuals from the International for transgressing not only the decisions of world congresses but also those of the Executive Committee. Furthermore, the

ECCI and its Presidium were empowered to 'send plenipotentiary delegates to the individual sections', persons who would 'receive instructions from the ECCI and are responsible to it for their actions'. They 'must be admitted to all meetings and sessions of the central organs and the local organizations of the sections to which they are sent by the ECCI'. At congresses, conferences and meetings of the section 'they may, in the interests of the consistent execution of ECCI directives, put forward opinions differing from those of the central committee of the section concerned at congresses, conferences or meetings.' The report of the statutes commission at the Sixth Congress (1928), though acknowledging that it was 'absolutely impossible for the ECCI to carry out its leading role directly from Moscow',[8] put forward no real scheme for decentralization. A number of 'bureaux' were set up within the leading centre itself, to help the ECCI in conducting the struggle in certain regions of the world (Western Europe, South Africa, the East, etc.). This meant considerably strengthening the bureaucratic apparatus at the disposal of the Executive Committee. The latter was also given by the Sixth Congress the right to send to the national sections not only 'delegates' but also 'instructors'. Instead of being loosened, the Gordian knot of the ultra-centralistic structure of the Comintern was drawn still tighter.

It was becoming ever harder, moreover, for the initiative in correcting this constitutional fault of the Comintern to come from the lower levels, which were in direct contact with national realities. As the mechanism of the Comintern kept on working, it promoted a process of selection within the active nucleus of each national Communist party in favour of those elements that were readiest to submit to the will of the centre in Moscow. Whoever showed too much critical spirit found himself removed from posts of responsibility. Innovatory initiatives stood no hope of success unless they came from above. But the docility of the lower levels made it difficult to see from above what the new problems were, to grasp in good time the changes that were under way. Increasingly, as conformism became more widespread in the national and local organizations, the information and reports they sent up to the ECCI tended to reflect back to the latter its own view of things. The same phenomenon occurred at congresses, the delegates to which were the product of the selection process already mentioned. 'Monolithicity' became established in practice before it was proclaimed as a principle, and, once consecrated as a principle, this accentuated the 'monolithic' character of praxis. Gradually, at every level of the Comintern, from the party cells up to the Executive Committee itself, and including the leaderships of the national sections, political and theoretical discussions (the latter becoming ever less frequent) degenerated into a kind of ritual, by means of which the truth emanating from on high, from the supreme depository of truth, was passed on to those down below. In so far as this ritual act could still be called discussion, its function was purely operational: the task was merely to discover the best way of putting into effect, in a given situation, the 'line' thus received.

The distorting effect of this mechanism was intensified still further by the increasing weight of the interests of the Soviet state in the Comintern policy. Without repeating what has already been said on this point, or anticipating what will be shown later in detail in connection with some of the Comintern's most important experiences, it is proper to stress that the premises for the transforming it into an appendage of the Soviet state were present from the first day of its creation, even if this transformation was not inevitable. Thanks to the enormous theoretical and political authority they enjoyed in the eyes of the Communists of other countries, the Bolshevik leaders filled the chief posts of responsibility in the ECCI and thus had at their disposal the extraordinary powers possessed by the latter. The ECCI was housed in Moscow, and the technical and financial resources of its apparatus were dependent mainly on the Soviet state. The role played by the Russian party in the Third International has often been compared to that played by the German party in the Second. But this analogy is valid only in a very general way. The Social Democratic Party of Germany was indeed the 'centre' of the international Socialist movement, on the theoretical and political plane; but it had no effective power of decision. Besides, in those days, no Socialist leader would have tolerated the wielding of such power. In 1906 Kautsky wrote an article on the driving forces of the Russian revolution, with which Lenin expressed full agreement. In a preface written for the Russian edition of this article, Lenin emphasized Kautsky's merits and said that the revolutionaries of all countries had need of the help of the movement's 'authorities'; but he added at once: 'Important though this authority is in widening the horizon of the fighters, it would be impermissible in the workers' party to claim that the practical and concrete questions of its immediate policy can be solved by those standing a long way off. The collective spirit of the progressive class-conscious workers immediately engaged in the struggle in each country will always remain the highest authority on all such questions.'[9]

Nevertheless, the Comintern took upon itself this 'impermissible' role – and, through the ECCI, the Soviet party. So long as the Bolshevik leaders remained faithful to the theoretical schema of the world revolution that had been held by Marx and Lenin, the Russian revolution was seen as a factor subordinated to the world revolution, and this helped to endow Comintern policy with an international outlook – although, even at this stage, the 'impermissible' role produced negative effects in relation to a whole series of aspects of the political activity and internal life of the national sections. But the theory of 'socialism in a single country' led, as we have seen, to the security of the Soviet state being treated as the matter of highest concern for the world revolution, and, consequently, to the interests of the movement in every country being subordinated to the *raison d'état* of the Soviet Union. From that time on, the requirements of the Soviet government's foreign policy weighed even more heavily in the scales when the Comintern made decisions on strategy and tactics, and also increasingly dominated the Comintern's internal life. The same happened with the internal problems of the Russian party: the struggle against Trotskyism, Bukharinism, etc., poisoned the whole life of the Comintern, provoking crises and splits in the various sections that were not justified by their respective national realities, and weakening the revolutionary movement in each country and also internationally. In 1926 Gramsci wrote a prophetic letter to the Central Committee of the CPSU, in which he said: 'Today you risk destroying your own handiwork, you are degrading and may even annul completely the leading position which the CPSU acquired under the direction of Lenin. It seems to us that your passionate absorption in Russian questions is making you lose sight of the international implications of these questions, and is causing you to forget that your duty as Russian militants can and must be fulfilled only with reference to the interests of the international working class.'[10] Stalin followed the directly opposite path, enclosing the interests of the international proletariat firmly within the framework of 'Russian questions'.

THE ITINERARY OF MONOLITHICITY

As we have seen, the Leninist conception of the structure and functioning of the revolutionary party, which served as the model for the Comintern, was a highly distinctive product of the Russian revolution. It corresponded to the type of difficulty that the proletarian revolution had to overcome in a backward country where the overwhelming majority of the people were peasants and where there were no democratic traditions or institutions. This conception, however, as Rosa Luxemburg saw very clearly, bore within it a tendency towards authoritarianism, the dictatorship of the leader, the establishment of bureaucratic uniformity – towards what can be summed up in the word 'monolithicity'.[11]

This tendency was countered, though, until the last years of Lenin's life, by other powerful factors. In the first place, there was the vigour, depth and richness of the Russian revolutionary process, which set its mark on the Bolshevik party. It was a process that formed revolutionary intellectuals of resolute character, with a sharply critical spirit, who were heirs to a philosophical and political tradition which prepared them to assimilate Marxism in a way that was appropriate to Russian reality. The history of the Bolshevik group records continual conflicts, controversies and debates revealing the permanent tension between the tendencies to ultra-centralism and military discipline on the one hand, and the party's intense theoretical and political life on the other. Lenin's unusual personality, in which a will to scientific rigour was combined in remarkable fashion with a will to effectiveness in struggle, contributed in no small degree to maintaining this dynamic tension within unity. Freedom of discussion, of tendencies and even of factions was also retained during the civil war period, when the Comintern was founded. In the Comintern, the risk of 'monolithicity' inherent in its mechanism was countered by the spirit of criticism and free discussion that emanated from the Bolshevik party and which was also characteristic of the left-wing sections of the European Socialist parties that joined it. The tendency to 'monolithicity' began to predominate in the Bolshevik party, as in the Comintern, with the beginning of the constructive phase of the Russian revolution. Under the pressure of grave social and economic problems, the internal struggle in the party reached unprecedented intensity. Lenin tried to resolve it by following, in essentials, the Marxist method – through open and unlimited discussion, in the party and in the soviets. Eventually, however – driven to this, no doubt, by the seriousness of the situation – he resorted to a measure without precedent in the history of the party, namely, a formal ban on factions. Lenin's speeches at the Party Congress at which this measure was adopted (the Tenth, in 1921) show that he saw it as something temporary, dictated by circumstances, and not to be elevated to the status of a principle, as was done later by Stalin.[12] But the first step towards this 'principle' had been taken. The next step followed during the struggle against the Trotskyist opposition. The ban on factions was followed by a ban on tendencies, and at last came the turn of ideas themselves, in so far as, however individual, they might cast doubt on the policies and conceptions of Stalin. 'Nowadays, as we know,' wrote Trotsky in 1929, commenting with bitter irony on the situation at which the Comintern had arrived, 'all ideas and actions of man are divided into two categories: absolutely correct ones, that is, those that comprise the "general line", and absolutely false ones, that is, deviations from this line. This, of course, does not prevent what is absolutely correct today from being declared absolutely false tomorrow.'[13]

One of the gravest manifestations of this practice was the elimination from the publications of the parties of any opinion differing from the official criteria. In the previous period, despite the Comintern's centralistic and authoritarian regime, it had been possible to set forth opposing views in the press and other publications of the International. This became an increasingly rare occurrence after the Sixth Congress. In the Comintern, as in the Soviet state, a regime of censorship was installed to which might well have been applied the criticism of the Prussian censorship made by the young Marx, or Engels's angry reaction in 1891 against the leaders of the German Social Democratic Party, who were claiming the right to censor *Die Neue Zeit,* the Party's theoretical organ, edited by Kautsky: 'It is in fact a brilliant idea,' exclaimed Engels, scandalized, 'to put German socialist science, after its liberation from Bismarck's Socialist Law, under a new Socialist Law to be manufactured and carried out by the Social Democratic Party authorities themselves.'[14] The 'brilliant idea' of the German Social Democratic bureaucrats was put into practice to perfection by Stalin's bureaucracy, both in Soviet society and in the Communist international organization.

Soviet historians generally look upon the Third International as the most correct embodiment of Marx's conception of what a revolutionary International ought to be. Nothing is farther from the truth. As regards, for example, the method by which the International which he led might succeed in working out a common theoretical platform, Marx declared:

Since the various sections of working men in the same country, and the working classes in different countries, are placed under different circumstances and have attained to different degrees of development, it seems almost necessary that the theoretical notions, which reflect the real movement, should also diverge. The community of action, however, called into life by the International Working Men's Association, the exchange of ideas facilitated by the public organs of the different national sections, and the direct debates at the General Congresses, are sure by and by to engender a common theoretical programme. Consequently, it belongs not to the functions of the General Council to subject the programme of the Alliance to a critical examination. We have not to inquire whether, yes or no, it be a true scientific expression of the working-class movement. All we have to ask is whether its *general tendency* does not run against the *general tendency* of the International Working Men's Association, viz. the complete emancipation of the working class.

'The general tendency' referred to here means, as the context shows, recognition of the principle of class struggles. Elsewhere Marx states:

The International Rules ... speak only of simple 'workers' societies', all following the same goal and accepting the same programme, which presents a general outline of the proletarian movement, while leaving its theoretical elaboration to be guided by the needs of the practical struggle and the exchange of ideas in the sections, unrestrictedly admitting all shades of socialist convictions in their organs and congresses.[15]

It may be objected – and is habitually objected by the school of historians mentioned, in order to be able to claim that there was 'continuity in difference' – that the conditions under which the Third International was born and in which it had to work were different from those of the First or Second. Indeed they were, but not in a way that affected the profound reasons determining the methods recommended by Marx. The diversity of conditions in which the different sections of the working class lived, the need for theoretical elaboration to start from the demands of the practical struggle, and to take the exchanging of ideas as its principle, with free expression in the publications of all the sections – these were governing factors that were just as absolute, from the methodological standpoint, in the epoch of the Third International as in those of the Second or the First. What is involved is, in fact, the basic condition needed for the working-out of a revolutionary theory and policy that are not dogmatic but correspond to the demands of the actual movement.

In absolute contradiction to the conception that Marx and Engels held of what a revolutionary party ought to be, on the national and international planes alike, the Comintern increasingly introduced, following Stalin's inspiration, a bureaucratic conception of the party's work, and of its unity – not merely political and organizational but also theoretical. Unity was identified with unanimity, monolithicity. 'This unanimity,' said Trotsky,

is represented as a sign of the particular strength of the party. When and where has there yet been in the history of the revolutionary movement such dumb 'monolithism'? ... The whole history of Bolshevism is the history of intense internal struggle through which the party gained its viewpoints and hammered out its methods. The chronicle of the year 1917, the greatest year in the history of the party, is full of intense internal struggles, as is also the history of the first five years after the conquest of power; despite this – not one split, not one major expulsion for political motives ... Whence then this terrible 'monolithism' of today, this destructive unanimity, which transforms each turn of the unfortunate leaders into absolute law for a gigantic party? 'No discussions!' Because, as *Rote Fahne* explains, 'in this situation we need deeds not speeches.' Repulsive hypocrisy! The party must accomplish 'deeds' but renounce participating in discussing them beforehand.[16]

Trotsky is here referring to the German party, but his arguments are valid for any and everyone of the sections of the Comintern, and for the Comintern as a whole. He was right in pointing out that this 'terrible "monolithism" ' did not exist in the past in the Bolshevik party, down to Lenin's death. But he did not see that certain premises for it already existed at that time, and that was why he clung dogmatically to that past period, which for him embodied what the party ought to be.

'Discord arising in a party, and seeming to be a misfortune for it, is on the contrary a sign of its good fortune,' said Hegel. In order to appreciate this truth, however, it is necessary to start from a dialectical conception of what a party is, and the fundamental fault of Stalin's conception was precisely the abandonment of this dialectic. From Stalin's standpoint, the contradictions inherent in the development of the party had to be resolved by measures of an administrative, bureaucratic character. And in order that these 'solutions' might triumph, 'party unity' had to be elevated into a myth. The myth, in this case, consisted in making 'party unity' the highest good, which must be protected 'like the apple of one's eye'. The ideological justification was simple and certain to be effective, for it appealed to common sense: can the party, engaged in a hard fight against a powerful enemy, be victorious unless it possesses 'iron discipline'? Must one not, therefore, sacrifice for the sake of unity any political or theoretical discussion that might arouse difference of opinion? For these may become tendencies, tendencies may become factions, and factions may lead to splits ... This evil must be nipped in the bud. It is not enough for the minority to accept the will of the majority. There must be no minority. If it so happens that divergences appear, it is not good enough to bow to the opinion of the majority (which, once the mechanism is set going, always becomes the faithful echo of the leadership): it is necessary to *think* like the majority. This is how monolithic perfection is arrived at. All differences vanish not only as regards action but also as regards thought. This is, reduced to essentials, the ideological and organizational schema that was brought into force in the Comintern during the 1930s. Its logic tended to establish the idea that the principal virtue of a revolutionary, called upon to change the world, and allegedly upholding the most advanced of social ideologies, was *not to think.*

After Hitler's accession to power, the threat of Fascism and war, the danger of aggression against the Soviet Union, furnished powerful arguments in support of the metaphysics of 'monolithicity'. 'Anyone who tries to break the iron unity of our ranks by any kind of factionalism will be made to feel what is meant by the Bolshevik discipline that Lenin and Stalin have always taught us,' Dimitrov threatened in his closing speech at the Seventh Congress of the Comintern.

'Let this be a warning to those few elements in individual parties who think they can take advantage of the difficulties of their party, the wounds of defeat or the blows of the raging enemy, to carry out their factional plans, and to further their own group interests. The party is above everything else! To guard the Bolshevik unity of the party as the apple of one's eye is *the first and highest law of Bolshevism!*'[17] The warning given and the methods its execution implied become fully comprehensible if we observe that Dimitrov himself gave as an example of the way in which unity must be guarded, not only in the party but in the working-class movement in general, the 'merciless struggle against the enemies of the people, Trotskyite–Bukharinite spies, diversionists and agents of Fascism', which, in that same period, was being carried through in the Soviet Union.[18] Terror and lies became the exemplary method for guarding the 'monolithic unity' of the Communist movement, and even that of the working-class movement in general.

The dialectic of the real movement was to take ever more cruel revenge for the metaphysics of monolithicity. Its first victim was to be the Comintern itself. The period when monolithicity was fully enthroned coincided, paradoxically enough, with the period when the Comintern became a hindrance for Stalin and the Communist parties. First, as we have seen, because it got in the way of diplomatic agreements between the Soviet state and the 'democratic' capitalist powers in face of the danger of Hitlerite aggression. Secondly, because it was politically embarrassing, on the national plane, to the alliance between the Communist parties and the Social Democrats and the anti-Fascist sections of the bourgeoisie. Thirdly, because the appearance on the scene of the first two factors removed the ideological postulates which had hitherto prevented *acknowledgement* of a third, historically the most important, namely, the impossibility of leading the revolutionary movement in every country by means of a system that was ultra-centralized on the world scale. It was for this reason, and not because no contradictions had existed previously, that the Comintern leaders became aware of this impossibility during the 1930s, as Togliatti was later to admit. In other words, a certain institutional, structural, determined form of monolithicity had proved bankrupt: it had come into contradiction with the *national factor* – both the Russian national factor and the national factor in every other country. As emerges from what has already been said, however, this contradiction differed in character depending on whether what was involved was the Russian national factor, to which the Comintern remained subordinate, or the other national factors, in relation to which it was an instrument of subordination. The first aspect was certainly the decisive one in its suppression, the second being only complementary. This was why its dissolution was to give only partial satisfaction to the non-Russian national factors in the revolutionary movement. They would continue to be subordinated to the interests of the Soviet state, owing to the retention of Stalin's system of monolithicity *in other forms*.

If the impossibility of leading the Communist movement in every country from an international centre became clear to the leaders of the Comintern from the early 1930s, and if, moreover, its very existence became an embarrassment for the new foreign policy of the Soviet Union after Hitler's accession to power, why was its dissolution not contemplated at that stage? According to the testimony of William Z. Foster, the idea *was* actually being considered in the leading circles of the Comintern on the eve of the Seventh Congress.

One of the most basic elements tending to render the Comintern obsolete 'in its existing form' was the coming forth actively of the Soviet Union in the mid-thirties as the world champion of the people. Prior to this time the USSR was largely on the defensive, and the Comintern led the world fight. But the burning menace of Fascism and war, against which the Soviet Union stepped forward on the world arena as the basic opponent, gave that country a world political leadership of the anti-Fascist forces. This was clearly expressed in Manuilsky's report to the Seventh Congress, when he said that because of the victory of socialism in the USSR and because of its fight against Fascism and war, 'it had become the centre of attraction and the rallying point for all peoples, countries, and even governments which are interested in the preservation of international peace'. Already therefore, on the eve of the Seventh Congress, at the supreme height of Comintern activity, discussions were had at which it was indicated that the new, active world role of the Soviet Union, as the great champion of peace and democracy, tended to render obsolete the world political leadership of the Communist International.[19]

This passage shows us not only that in 1935 dissolution of the International was on the agenda but that the aim of this dissolution – besides answering to the current needs of Soviet foreign policy – was not to do away with *any and every international centre* of the Communist movement, but to leave in being, freed from the mediating institution that was compromising it, the centre that had already long been undertaking the real leadership of the Communist movement, namely, *the Soviet centre.*

And yet Stalin and the Comintern leaders did not decide in 1935 to dissolve it. One day the Soviet archives will show us the precise motives that led them to put off this operation. Meanwhile we can only guess. Perhaps a preparatory phase was thought to be useful, during the 'new tactical orientation', in order to use the Comintern's apparatus to overcome any resistance to it that might be manifested in some of the national sections. Certain passages in Dimitrov's report, such as the one I have quoted, lead one to this assumption. It may be that the Soviet leaders feared that if they were to give up programmatic positions that were strongly rooted in the Communist parties, this, along with the effect of the frightful purges and 'trials' in Moscow against the Bolshevik 'Old Guard', might lead many Communists to interpret the dissolution of the Comintern as the total liquidation of everything that the international revolutionary movement created by Lenin had stood for. Perhaps they were also afraid of provoking a crisis that would facilitate the efforts of Trotsky and his supporters to form a Fourth International.[20] Another hypothesis is also plausible. In face of the threatening storm, Stalin was not playing one card alone in his foreign policy. At no stage did he rule out the possibility of achieving a *modus vivendi* with Hitler's Germany, such as he had achieved with the Italy of Mussolini. Alliance with the capitalist states that were rivals of the Third Reich constituted only one of the possible alternatives, nothing more. In the public statements made by Stalin in the period between Hitler's accession to power and the Second World War he obviously manipulated these two cards of his with extreme prudence. So long as neither of the alternatives had actually been realized, the Comintern might continue to serve as a useful instrument of 'pressure' on the international gaming-table. In short, at the time of the Seventh Congress, it was already a hindrance to Soviet foreign policy without, however, having lost all operational value. It was not yet a definitive hindrance. It was to become that in 1943.

4

THE CRISIS OF POLICY

Never put too much trust in the stupidity of your opponents.

TALLEYRAND

Our tactical and strategical methods (if we take them on an international scale) still lag behind the excellent strategy of the bourgeoisie, which has learned from the example of Russia and will not let itself be 'taken by surprise'.

LENIN

The contradictions that appeared from the beginning of the Comintern, between the theory of the world revolution which provided its theoretical foundation and the realities of historical development, between its ultra-centralized structure and national diversity, between its growing subordination to Soviet policy and the needs of the revolutionary movement, on both the national and international planes – these contradictions, which we have looked at in the previous chapters, could not but have (combining in a variety of ways, depending on concrete situations) a negative effect on the political activity of the Comintern and of each of its sections. It was at the level of policy that the crisis of the Comintern found general expression.

In analysing this aspect of the Comintern's activity I shall focus attention on certain experiences which, in my view, had a decisive effect on its destinies and which have also had repercussions on the subsequent course of the Communist movement. What is lost in length by proceeding in this way will probably be gained in depth.

I propose to study Comintern policy from its creation until the beginning of the 1930s in terms of the German experience. I shall then examine the policy of the People's Front, analysing its two main experiences, in France and Spain. Thirdly I shall consider, though only briefly, the Comintern's colonial policy with special reference to its Chinese policy. Lastly, I shall deal with its final period, that of the Soviet–German Pact and the initial stage of the anti-Hitlerite coalition.

THE GERMAN EXPERIENCE

The Greatest Disaster Suffered by the Comintern

'The foremost place among the Comintern sections in capitalist countries has been, and is, taken by the German Communist Party. It is one of the best organized Communist parties, the largest numerically, with deep roots in the working class, and the leader of the broad masses.'[1] This was the view taken by the leaders of the Comintern in 1930, when the German Communist Party (KPD) had 124,000 members and 4,500,000 voters. From that time until Hitler's accession to power, the party's strength grew steadily. In 1932 it had 200,000 members and 6,000,000 voters. The latter figure, added to the number of voters for the Social Democratic Party (SPD), exceeded by 1,500,000 the voters for the Nazi Party, whose influence began noticeably to decline during the final months of 1932.[2] Yet, in January 1933, Hindenburg gave power to the Nazis. In March, Hitler dissolved the KPD by decree, confiscated its property, occupied its premises, expelled its 100 deputies from the Reichstag, and began imprisoning its members *en masse*. Soon afterwards he did the same with the Social Democratic Party. The working class put up no resistance. The model party of the Comintern vanished from the scene as an effective political force. It was the greatest disaster in the Comintern's history, the one that was to have the most serious and lasting consequences for the subsequent course of the revolutionary movement in Europe.

The collapse of the KPD not only enabled Hitlerite imperialism to launch the Second World War, it also contributed very largely to the fact that the great world crisis of capitalism did not result in a socialist revolution in Europe. When, in 1943, the defeat of Nazism appeared on the horizon, and in all the countries of Europe, including Fascist Italy, popular and revolutionary forces began to rise up, Communism continued to be practically non-existent as a political factor in Germany. And yet it had had ten years in which to reorganize its forces, and was to dispose of two years more in which to try and act in the phase of the retreat and ultimate downfall of the Third Reich. Even so, it did not raise its head. In 1968, thirty-five years after its suppression, the German Communist Party has not yet succeeded in recovering substantial influence among the proletariat of capitalist Germany. This is sufficient to show how important was the defeat suffered in 1933.

A month and a half after Hitler's accession to power, Trotsky wrote: 'The criminal role of the Social Democracy requires no commentary: the Comintern was created fourteen years ago precisely in order to snatch the proletariat from the demoralizing influence of the Social Democracy. If it has not succeeded up to now, if the German proletariat found itself impotent, disarmed, and paralysed at the moment of its greatest historic test, the direct and immediate blame falls upon the leadership of the post-Leninist Comintern. That is the first conclusion which ought to be drawn immediately.'[3] It was a judgement that was too sharp and oversimplified – a fault often to be found in Trotsky – but which contained a large element of truth.

Two and a half years later, Dimitrov was implicitly to admit that Trotsky had been right, though without openly recognizing the grave responsibility borne by the ECCI – which would have implied direct responsibility on the part of Stalin. In his report to the Seventh Congress of the Comintern, Dimitrov made explicit criticism of the mistakes committed by the KPD, while keeping silent on the responsibility borne by the ECCI for these mistakes. After saying that, in general, 'in our ranks there was an impermissible underestimation of the Fascist danger', he went on:

Our comrades in Germany for a long time failed fully to reckon with the wounded national sentiments and the indignation of the masses against the Versailles Treaty; they treated as of little account the waverings of the peasantry and petty-bourgeoisie; they were late in drawing up their programme of social and national emancipation, and when they did put it forward they were unable to adapt it to the concrete demands and to the level of the masses.

There was shown 'a narrow sectarian attitude in formulating and solving the immediate political tasks of the party'. The KPD continued to 'concentrate their fire' against the Weimar Republic when 'the Fascists were organizing and arming hundreds of thousands of storm-troopers against the working class'.[4] But this list of errors, which is far from being exhaustive, failed to answer the question that was essential from the Marxist standpoint: why had the KPD made mistakes of such importance? The victory of Fascism, said Dimitrov, had not been inevitable in Germany, the working class could have prevented it, but for that purpose it 'should have achieved a united anti-Fascist proletarian front, and forced the Social Democratic leaders to put a stop to their campaign against the Communists and to accept the repeated proposals of the Communist Party for united action against Fascism'.[5] In reality – a fact that Dimitrov kept silent about – the KPD did not approach the national leadership of the Social Democratic Party and the trade unions, to propose joint action, until the very last months before Hitler took power, and then only in a form that made it difficult to reach agreement. It was for the KPD above all a matter of 'unmasking' the Social Democratic leaders, an attitude that actually favoured the manoeuvres of the latter.[6] Down to the summer of 1932, as a French Communist historian observes, 'the unity of action which was proposed seemed sometimes to mean that the workers were to leave the Social Democratic Party and join the KPD'.[7] And, what was worse, for several years the leaders of the KPD described the Social Democratic Party, as such, as 'social Fascist'.[8] How could the Social Democratic workers 'force their leaders to put a stop to their campaign against the Communists' if the Communists did not put a stop to *their* campaign against the 'social Fascist' leaders? How could they force their leaders to accept proposals that were non-existent until the very eve of the catastrophe, and that were regarded as unacceptable by the Social Democratic workers themselves? How could the German working class show maturity when its own vanguard party was showing immaturity, as Dimitrov reveals? 'Under no circumstances,' said Lenin in 1922, 'shall we thrust the blame for the mistakes of our Communists upon the proletarian masses . . .'[9]

As we shall see later on, in the section of this chapter devoted to the People's Fronts, the Seventh Congress of the Comintern formulated this new tactic without carrying out any critical examination of the previous experience. And it omitted to do this, among other reasons, because such an examination would have meant coming to the same conclusions as Trotsky – that 'direct and immediate blame' fell upon the leadership of the Comintern, and in particular upon Stalin, for the disaster suffered by the German Communist Party.

For many years, indeed, the KPD had not taken a single step without strictly obeying the orders of the ECCI. The KPD was not only the largest section of the Comintern after the Soviet party, it was also the section that was most closely and directly subjected to 'aid' by the ECCI, or, more precisely, by the Soviet leaders of the International. This 'special' position held by the German section in the Comintern was due to Germany's very special position both in the Comintern's general strategy and in the Soviet Union's foreign policy.

Until the Nazi victory, Germany figured in the Comintern strategy as the most likely place for the next revolutionary break-through in the imperialist system. For the fate of the October revolution it was vital that this expectation should be realized. But Germany was also, after Rapallo, the capitalist state with which the Soviet Republic maintained truly 'most-favoured' relations. Half of the USSR's foreign trade was carried on with Germany. German industry and German technicians (their number has been calculated at 5,000) contributed to the industrialization, and even directly to the armament, of the young workers' republic. In return (and in addition to the profits obtained by the German capitalists), the Soviet government allowed the military engineers of the Reich to perfect on Soviet territory types of weapon that were forbidden to Germany by the Treaty of Versailles. *De facto* collaboration was established between the Reichswehr and the Red Army.[10] Not only were the two economies complementary: the military and diplomatic interests of Soviet Russia and defeated Germany were in perfect harmony in that period.

The Bolshevik leaders of the new International and the new state thus found themselves confronted by two tasks that were hard to reconcile: on the one hand, they had to organize a revolution against the German state, as the first priority in the strategy of the world revolution; on the other, they had to safeguard the alliance with the German state (for there was indeed a *de facto* alliance, although the Treaty of Rapallo did not spell this out explicitly), as the first priority in the foreign policy of the Soviet Republic. Each of these two tasks was sufficiently important for the leaders of the Soviet party to supervise the German party very closely – and the difficulty in reconciling them required that this supervision be made even closer.

Premature Insurrections and Premonitory Expulsions

In 1919–20 the problem before the Soviet leaders was not yet so complicated. Their political will was wholly directed towards a single aim, the victory of the revolution in Germany. On that, they thought, depended the fate of the revolution in Russia. The reasons – belonging to the realms of theory, of information (inadequate knowledge of Western reality), and of psychology – that account for Lenin's optimistic view of the German revolution have already been mentioned. This view may also explain why he did not draw the necessary conclusions from the premature attempts at insurrection made by the Spartacist group (which had already become the Communist Party) in January–May 1919. And yet it was the burden of this tragic experience that was to weigh heavily upon the subsequent development of the party and of the political situation in Germany. The party emerged from it beheaded and drained of blood, having lost the best members of its leading group: a theoretician of Rosa Luxemburg's stature; Karl Liebknecht, its most popular leader; other able cadres like Leo Jogisches and Eugen Leviné; and hundreds of cadres of middle rank. But what the experience proved was no less serious, namely, that the great majority of the German proletariat were firmly controlled, politically and ideologically, by Social Democracy. Without changing that central reality, what possibility of proletarian revolution could there be in Germany?

It is worth stressing a fact that is not very well known. Liebknecht and Luxemburg regarded as premature the Berlin insurrection of January, and Leviné the establishment of the Soviet Republic of Bavaria in April. They were aware that the revolutionary vanguard could not rely on support from the masses, and that the bourgeoisie, aided by the Social Democratic leaders, was engaged in provoking the Communists and the revolutionary workers to hurl themselves into armed struggle under unfavourable circumstances.[11] But they were overwhelmed by the most radical element in the proletariat and in their own party, whose enthusiastic determination to follow 'the Russian example', and indignation against the policy of the Social Democratic leaders, matched their inexperience of revolutionary struggle. The decades of comfortable reformist practice had produced this twofold result: on the one hand, loyalty of the masses to the party under whose leadership substantial economic and political reforms had been won, and which was now promising, as the party in power, to carry out 'socialization' under conditions of democracy and legality; on the other hand, the extremism of a minority that was not content with reforms – a republic, a constituent assembly, the eight-hour day, recognition of workers' councils in the enterprises – but aspired to immediate capture of power, 'as in Russia'.

The new leadership of the Party, formed during the second half of 1919, with Paul Levi at its head, tried to work out a policy that started from this reality, but at the same time it behaved in a sectarian way towards the 'ultra-left', which was unshakably hostile to any participation in elections or in the reformist trade unions. The chief leaders of this tendency were expelled in February 1920 and formed the Communist Workers' Party (KAPD), taking nearly half the party members with them. The Paul Levi leadership, which was joined by Klara Zetkin, who broke with the 'Independents',[12] strove to assimilate the lesson in tactics given by Lenin in *'Left-Wing' Communism, An Infantile Disorder*. But the idea that the Soviet Comintern leaders still held regarding the maturity of the world revolution – which meant, above all, the maturity of the German revolution – was not such as to make easier the task of the KPD leadership in correcting 'leftism' within the Party. The Second Congress of the Comintern, as we have seen in Chapter 2, considered that 'the hour of decision' was approaching and that 'soon' the working class would have to 'go into battle, arms in hand'. In March 1921 the Comintern representatives in Germany encouraged the leaders of the KPD – who no longer included the Levi–Zetkin group, for reasons that will be seen later – to reply with armed insurrection to the government's latest provocation.[13] The defeat suffered was complete, and its consequences grave. Of the 360,000 members which the party had at the end of 1920 (after the merger with the bulk of the 'Independents'), it retained only half at the end of 1921. Once more, proof had been given that the majority of the working class followed the Social Democratic Party in a disciplined way. The new fact was that a considerable section of the party did not, this time, support the adventuristic line of the national leadership and the Comintern (the ECCI at first approved of the 'March action', although later, under Lenin's influence, it was to criticize it).

Not long before the 'March action', as this episode was thenceforth to be called in the documents of the Comintern, Levi, Zetkin and others among the top party leaders had opposed the Comintern on the '21 Conditions'. Finding themselves in the minority in the Central Committee of the KPD, they resigned from their posts. The new leadership, in which the chief figures were Brandler and Thalheimer, though most of them did not belong to the 'Leftist' wing, were more docile in their attitude to the Comintern representatives, and threw the party into the insurrectional movement of March 1921. The Levi–Zetkin group voiced its disapproval of this action, and Levi published a pamphlet making a thorough criticism not only of the tactics of the German party leadership but also of the methods of the Comintern. He was expelled at once, and the epithets of 'renegade', 'traitor', etc., flung after him.

Coming after the passivity of the Polish proletariat in face of the Red Army's drive towards Warsaw in the summer of 1920, and the retreat of the Italian labour movement before the spectacular offensive of Mussolini's Fascists in the winter of 1920–21, the attitude taken up by the German proletariat towards the insurrectionary attempt in March revealed a general setback of the revolutionary movement in Europe. This fact was recognized by the Third Congress of the Comintern, which altered its diagnosis of the immediate prospects for the world revolution. As Lenin said, one had to go over from 'assaults' to 'sieges'. In this context the Third Congress came to the conclusion that the 'March action' had been a mistake, and its analysis coincided essentially with Levi's critique. Nevertheless, the Congress ratified the expulsion of Levi, justifying it for reasons of discipline (publication of a pamphlet without authorization from the party leadership) and also on the grounds that this critique ought to have been made within the party and not under the eyes of the enemy. At the same time, the Congress demanded of the opposition in the German party (that is, Levi's supporters – meaning Klara Zetkin and many others) that they immediately dissolve 'any factional organization', stating that 'any factionalism' constituted 'the greatest danger for the entire movement'.[14]

In the course of the lively history of the Bolshevik party, Lenin, Trotsky, Zinoviev and the other Russian Marxists who were now at the head of the Comintern had often acted in the same way as Levi and the German 'opposition' of 1921.[15] Lenin had said many times that revolutionaries should not conceal their mistakes from the enemy. Now, however, they applied different rules – those which had just been imposed in the Russian party. The latter's Tenth Congress had approved the famous resolution forbidding factions, and the party was in full 'retreat' (the transition to NEP). 'During a retreat,' Lenin was to say later, referring to the period that opened with the Tenth Congress, 'discipline . . . is a hundred times more necessary . . . Anyone who introduced an undertone of panic or insubordination would have doomed the revolution to defeat.'[16] What might be justified by the dramatic conjuncture in which the Russian revolution found itself was made to apply to the German party, as to the other sections of the Comintern, which were in a very different situation – not in power, only recently formed and seeking their way forward, which required, above all, complete freedom of discussion, internal struggle, etc. Imposition of the Bolshevik model of 1921 meant negation of the Bolshevik model of 1903–21.

The 'Levi case', the first of its kind in the history of the Comintern, acquires premonitory significance in the light of the circumstances and when looked at with our historical perspective. So long as Lenin was alive the method was not yet converted into a system; under Stalin, however, it was to be carried to its logical consequences.

A Changed Viewpoint: Revolution in Germany Becomes a Danger to NEP Russia

In 1923 a situation arose in Germany that was particularly propitious for testing the tactic, recently formulated by the Fourth Congress of the

Comintern (December 1922), of Communist participation in 'workers' governments' along with left-wing Social Democrats. The occupation of the Ruhr by French troops and the policy of 'passive' national resistance proclaimed by the Cuno government in reply thereto, with the disastrous collapse of the Mark caused by this policy, resulted in an economic and political crisis that tended to develop into a revolutionary one.[17]

In the first months of 1923 the Soviet leaders did not dramatize the situation in Germany: quite the contrary. A British journalist asked Trotsky this question: if the French had marched into the Ruhr in 1919, Moscow would have seen that as a revolutionary crisis; why did it now see the matter in a different light? Trotsky's reply reflected perfectly the new viewpoint of the Bolshevik leaders since Rapallo and under the conditions of NEP. A new war in Europe, he said, would be contrary to the aims of socialism. A Europe 'exhausted and drained of blood' and reduced to 'ruins' might mean 'a most severe lowering of European culture over a long period and, accordingly, not the approach but, on the contrary, the postponement of revolutionary perspectives'.[18] At the enlarged plenum of the ECCI in June 1923 the policy of the KPD, which was following a line of united action with the Social Democratic left in order to prepare the conditions for a possible revolutionary outcome – without, however, taking the view that the revolution had 'arrived' – was examined and approved without any essential modifications. However, Zinoviev, the President of the Comintern – who in October 1917 had considered the situation unripe for armed insurrection in Russia – decided, when the general strike broke out in Berlin in August 1923 (basing himself on press reports received in Moscow), that power was now within reach in Germany. Trotsky, too, allowed himself to be carried away by this fever. Lenin was already out of action, and Stalin was not yet in control of the Comintern. The latter did, though, send a letter to Zinoviev and Bukharin setting out his views:

Should the Communists at the present stage try to seize power without the Social Democrats? Are they sufficiently ripe for that? That, in my opinion, is the question. When we seized power, we had in Russia such resources in reserve as (a) the promise of peace; (b) the slogan: the land to the peasants; (c) the support of the great majority of the working class;

and (d) the sympathy of the peasantry. At the moment the German Communists have nothing of the kind. They have, of course, a Soviet country as neighbour, which we did not have; but what can we offer them? ... Should the government in Germany topple over now, in a manner of speaking, and the Communists were to seize hold of it, they would end up in a crash. That, in the 'best' case .While at worst, they will be smashed to smithereens and thrown away back ... In my opinion the Germans should be restrained and not spurred on.[19]

His was the same viewpoint as Trotsky's, shown in the latter's reply to the British journalist, but held to more consistently: Stalin did not allow himself to be impressed by the general strike in Berlin.

The German crisis undoubtedly confronted the Soviet Republic with a dramatic choice. If the crisis resulted in a civil war, the Entente powers would certainly intervene in support of the German bourgeoisie and generals. The Soviet state could not refrain from going to the help of their brother proletarians in Germany. This would mean war again, and war with the economy in ruins and the peasant masses unsure, if not hostile, in their attitude to the Soviet power. A few months earlier, Lenin had said to the Ninth Congress of Soviets: 'We have before us a highly unstable equilibrium, but one that is, nevertheless, certain, obvious, indisputable. I do not know whether this is for long, and I do not think that anyone can know. That is why, for our part, we must display the utmost caution ... We must remember that we are always a hair's breadth away from invasion.' And after dwelling on the sufferings that the world war and then the civil war had inflicted on the workers and peasants of Russia, and on the incredible calamities endured, he declared: 'We are ready to make the greatest concessions and sacrifices, in order to preserve the peace for which we have paid such a high price.'[20]

From another angle, victory of the revolution in Germany had been the great dream of Lenin and all the Bolsheviks since 1917 – the real consecration of the triumph of the Russian revolution, its final consolidation, the path to victory for the revolution on the scale of Europe, of the whole world ... Suddenly, two years after they had seen this hope grow distant, here it was, apparently, drawing near again. What was to be done? Were the German Communists to be held back or to be spurred on? It is pointless to speculate on what Lenin's attitude would have been in this situation. To judge by his last writings it would seem that Stalin's attitude was closer to the 'caution' that Lenin advised than was the fever that had taken hold of Zinoviev and Trotsky. Nevertheless, the spirit of his reasoning would probably have been substantially different from that of Stalin, whose letter reveals, indeed, an outlook in which we can already perceive some of the elements that were later on to inspire his conception of the revolutionary movement outside Russia.

(a) *Mechanical transposition of the premises that enabled the Bolsheviks to take power, making them the criterion for judging whether it is possible to take power in other countries.* It was certainly the case that the German Communists did not 'have available' the banner of peace; but the invasion of the Ruhr had handed them the banner of struggle for national independence against the oppression of the Treaty of Versailles, with the possibility of using this against the ruling classes, who were taking the line of capitulation. It was true that the German peasants were not revolutionary; but at that moment they were in deep crisis, and, besides, the peasant factor was far from possessing the same importance in industrial Germany as in agricultural Russia. It was true that the majority of the working class were still under the influence of the Social Democrats; but precisely in those months an important tendency favourable to the Communist Party began to appear among the Social Democratic workers. Stalin was probably right in thinking that the situation was not ripe for an immediate seizure of power. (Radek and most of the German leaders held the same view.)[21] But the possibility of a deepening of the crisis could not be denied, and this, accompanied by an intelligent policy on the part of the KPD, might have created conditions favourable to a revolutionary outcome. (As we have seen already, Lenin himself was influenced by the tendency to follow the 'Russian model' when he analysed the German revolution of 1918: though he did this only where the forms and phases of its development were concerned – he did not equate the role of the peasants in industrial Germany with the role they had played in agricultural Russia. In any case, this precedent had already revealed one of the chief dangers lying in wait for the Comintern owing to the hegemony of the Bolsheviks in its leadership, namely, the habit of seeing the problems of the revolutionary movement, in West and East alike, in accordance with the Russian viewpoint.)

(*b*) *Lack of confidence in the revolutionary capacity of non-Russian Communists.* In assuming the possibility that the power of the bourgeoisie might 'topple over' and so fall into the hands of the German Communists, Stalin denied them the capacity to do what the Bolsheviks had done – use their possession of state power to dominate the adverse factors implicit in the exceptional situation that had enabled them to conquer it. He saw their ending up in a 'crash' as inevitable.

(*c*) *Complete subordination of the problem to the situation of the Soviet state.* 'What can we offer them?' Not: what can revolution in Germany offer to the revolutionary struggle in Europe, and vice versa? To what extent could a German revolution have revolutionized the whole European situation, and the situation in Russia itself? Even if the revolutionary wave of 1919–20 had ebbed, the situation in a number of countries was highly unstable. Bulgaria was practically in a state of civil war, and in September the Communist Party hurled itself into armed insurrection; in October a general strike took place in Poland, with an insurrection in Cracow; the Italian labour movement had not yet been crushed by Fascism; in several countries solidarity was being shown with the German workers against the intervention of French imperialism. Owing to the historical significance of the German labour movement, and the economic and political importance of Germany, a socialist revolution in that country must produce a much greater echo than the Russian revolution in the proletariat of Europe and America. The whole situation could be changed. But Stalin preferred to stick to the old peasant adage: a bird in the hand is worth two in the bush.

Trotsky shared Stalin's concern regarding the risks that a deepening of the German crisis would entail for the Soviet state, but in the end it was a wider outlook that predominated with him. His mistake, and that of Zinoviev and other Comintern leaders, consisted, no doubt, in seeing as ripe certain conditions which were still only potential, and in imposing their view on the German Communist leaders. In mid-September the ECCI summoned them to Moscow, where agreement was reached on immediate preparation for armed insurrection. It was also decided that the party should enter the left-wing Social-Democrat governments of Saxony and Thuringia, the calculation being that this would facilitate the launching of armed insurrection throughout Germany. The leaders of the Communist organization in Saxony were opposed to entering the government, and Brandler, the principal leader of the KPD, had doubts, but he bowed to the will of the ECCI.[22] Trotsky, who always showed feeling for grand historical effects, proposed that the date of the insurrection be fixed for some time between 7 and 9 November, the anniversaries, respectively, of the Russian October revolution of 1917 and the German revolution of 1918. In the end it was thought wiser to let the Germans themselves fix the precise dates of their insurrection.[23]

The insurrection was eventually arranged for the first week in October. But the central government took the initiative, sending 60,000 troops into Saxony. Brandler put forward the party's plan (to declare a general strike and organize armed resistance) at the conference of factory workers' councils of Saxony, but the majority of the worker delegates, who were left-wing Social Democrats, rejected the Communist proposals. Faced with this situation, the leaders of the KPD suspended the order for the armed rising: this took place, nevertheless, in Hamburg, where the countermanding order came too late. Several hundred Communists fought bravely for three days against the army and the police without receiving any active support from the proletarian masses of the city. The Reichswehr disarmed the workers' militias that the party had set up in Saxony and Thuringia, and the Communists were ejected from the two provincial governments.

The October events were described by the Comintern as a defeat for the KPD. This is a highly questionable view, since the party's influence increased among the masses, as was shown in the elections of May 1924 (when nearly 4,000,000 electors voted Communist). Moreover, what was even more important, the party had succeeded, for the first time since its creation, in establishing united-front relations with the left wing of the Social Democrats. The result could not be described as a 'defeat' except on the assumption that all the conditions had been present for the taking of power, an assumption that is far from confirmed by historical investigation.[24] The Hamburg rising itself showed that, while a certain radicalization of the German proletariat had indeed taken place, they were nevertheless not ready to hurl themselves into armed struggle. In reality, the decision of Brandler and Thalheimer, called 'treason' in the official historiography of the Comintern, probably saved the German party from another crushing defeat such as it had suffered in March 1921.

The 'October defeat' was to provide the subject for bitter argument in the KPD and in the Comintern during the months that followed. In accordance with a method that was beginning to become a tradition, the ECCI unloaded all responsibility on to the national leaders, blaming the policy they had followed in the preceding period for the miscarriage allegedly suffered by the German revolution. In reality, after Levi's expulsion, the leaders of the KPD had kept strictly to the orders received from the Comintern.[25] The first and last independent act performed by this leadership was to call off the order for insurrection when they realized that the party was going to remain isolated again, as in 1919 and 1921. At the Fifth Congress of the Comintern, in June–July 1924, Klara Zetkin declared, without anyone being able to prove her wrong: 'We are told here about Brandlerism and Radekism, regardless of the fact that until quite recently Radek was one of the most ardent champions of the left wing ... The policy of the former Central Committee was endorsed by the Executive [of the Comintern] until the October defeat. Therefore, if the German party is indeed guilty of any sin, the Executive is equally guilty, because it has not acted with the utmost vigour against the opportunist policy.' And she added that, by refusing battle under those conditions, Brandler 'rendered great service to the party'.[26]

What need for a theory of the German revolution if Stalin and the 'Leninist policy' are there?

The assumption that the events of October 1923 constituted a 'defeat' served as pretext for liquidating one of the tendencies in the KPD which, in the eyes of the ECCI, presented two serious faults: in the first place, while it was true that in the period 1921–3 the KPD had faithfully carried out the united-front policy of the Comintern, the logic of this policy had caused it to take increasingly into consideration the actual situation in Germany, which clashed with the method by which the Comintern was led; and, secondly, the Brandler–Thalheimer leadership had shown too much sympathy for the groups which, in the Russian party, were defending inner-party democracy.[27]

In the 'left' of the Germany party as well there was a strong tendency opposed to unconditional subordination to Moscow's orders, but the leaders of the 'left' took advantage of the condemnation of 'Brandlerism' to strike a compromise with the ECCI. In exchange for their cooperation with the all-powerful Executive Committee in the struggle against the Brandler–Thalheimer group, the leaders of the 'left' secured the ECCI's help in winning a majority in the leadership of the KPD. This happened despite the fact that the 'left' was in disagreement with the Comintern on tactical questions, that is, on the united-front policy, as a result of which it had been subjected to severe criticism by Lenin at the Third Congress of the Comintern. The campaign for 'Bolshevization' of the Communist parties which began in 1924 was expressed in the German party, as in the others, by a strengthening of bureaucratic centralism and a rejection of national realities. This process went forward, in its first phase, under the sign of struggle against the 'rights', who at that moment were the chief contenders for greater autonomy in relation to the ECCI and greater democracy within the parties. In a declaration signed by Brandler, Thalheimer and Radek in March 1925 it was stated that true Bolshevization

demands the most careful adaption to the peculiarities of the development of each country, that Bolshevization may be achieved only through free discussion in the organizations, by a regime of party democracy rendering possible the selection of the party leadership from among the most experienced comrades ... The development of the Western European Communist Movement calls for a synthesis of the leading elements which became crystallized in the battle of ideas against Social Democracy while they were still in the latter and which later, breaking with the Social Democracy, established the Communist Party – and the young elements which came to Communism in the battles of 1919 and later.

For this reason they declared that 'it is necessary to reinstate in the party more than fifty proletarians – the founders of the Communist Party of Germany'.[28] At the same meeting of the ECCI at which this declaration was published, Klara Zetkin said: 'I must decidedly protest against the presence of a powerful tendency in the German Party to call all the old Spartacus [members] "right-wing" and accuse the Central Committee of not having fought resolutely enough against this tendency.' She went on to affirm that 'the proletariat does not recognize any unity of action without freedom of discussion and criticism. In our Organization Statutes the same is said in substance. I believe that the interests of the party require that just the critical elements in the party be allowed to speak ... It is primarily a question as to whether in the future expulsion and disciplinary measures of a mechanical nature should be continued as before.'[29]

The future was to answer 'yes' to the question put by the old militant with so much service behind her. Expulsions and disciplinary measures were to be not merely continued but intensified, and they were, in the succeeding period, to be directed mainly against the 'left'. The victory won by the latter was, indeed, only a pyrrhic one. It coincided with the beginning of the duel between Stalin and Trotsky, and the majority of the leading group of the German 'left' supported Trotsky's line. Around Thälmann (who had belonged to the 'left') a so-called 'centrist' group was formed which, with Stalin's support, succeeded in taking control of the German party leadership at the end of 1925.[30] The offensive against the German 'left' was carried through in full synchronization with the great battle against the Trotsky–Zinoviev opposition in the Russian party. Between 1926 and 1928 hundreds of working-class militants, experienced officials and valuable intellectuals were eliminated from leading posts or even expelled from the party. In 1928–9, at the time of Stalin's offensive against the 'right' in the Russian party (Bukharin and his supporters), political elimination of the survivors of 'Brandlerism' was carried out in the German party – in particular the removal of Brandler and Thalheimer themselves. At that period – in other words, the period when the decisive phase of Germany's political evolution was opening, leading to the victory of Hitler – the KPD was deprived of nearly all of its original leading groups, which had come from Spartacism, on the one hand, and the left of the Independent Social

Democratic Party, on the other. After 1928 Thälmann became the absolute master of the party, as the unconditional executor of Stalin's policy. In that same year the Central Committee of the KPD had decided to remove Thälmann from the party's General Secretaryship, but Stalin had obliged the Presidium of the ECCI to veto this decision.[31]

To appreciate the full significance of the amputation suffered by the KPD, account must be taken of the fact that the 'left' and the 'right' in the German party, despite their differences on tactical and strategic questions, had in common from the party's beginnings a more or less explicit desire to decide the party's policy and implement it independently of outside control. They declined to be mere executants of the orders of the international centre dominated by the Soviet party. Rosa Luxemburg's report on the programme, at the party's foundation congress, set forth a strategic conception of the course of the German revolution that was very different from the Bolshevik conception. The imprint of this differentiation is to be seen in documents of 1919 and 1920.[32] Differences also appeared regarding the internal working of the party, and regarding the relation between the party and the masses, both in the phase of struggle under capitalism and after the taking of power. Rosa Luxemburg stood for real democracy, in the party and in the new social order. The original leading group of the party, despite their disagreements on tactical questions, were all soaked in the theoretical heritage of Luxemburgism. And this heritage became ever more valuable as experience of the evolution of the Soviet regime and the German party confirmed some of Rosa's criticisms and forebodings. It was not accidental that Levi, after his expulsion, proceeded immediately to republish her complete writings.

Despite the fact that Rosa Luxemburg's theoretical and political work, like that of Marx, Engels and Lenin, presented certain aspects that were contradicted by experience of social practice, it is clear that this work, carried out in close connection with German reality, with the reality of the German labour movement, constituted a valuable contribution to the building of a distinct theory of the German revolution. Critical account ought also to have been taken of the views of the theoreticans of the Social Democratic 'centre' and 'right', such as Kautsky,

Hilferding, Bernstein, etc., even if only to obtain a better understanding of the roots of reformism in the German proletariat and the specific characteristics of German capitalism. But all this theoretical heritage was thrown overboard after the first years of the existence of the German party, when transplantation took place, in a more and more sweeping way, of the Soviet model of socialism and of the party, with unconditional application of the tactical and strategic theses of the ECCI.

The Communist Party of the country where Marxism was born, the revolutionary party of the German workers, of whom Engels wrote that 'they belong to the most theoretical people of Europe; and they have retained that sense of theory . . .',[33] presented in 1928, when Stalin succeeded in establishing his control over the German Communists, a spectacle of the most deplorable theoretical sterility. The party's intellectual nucleus had been decimated and practically destroyed. It was in 1926 that Stalin gave the signal for sweeping away any remaining survivors. In a speech in the German Commission at the Sixth Enlarged Plenum of the ECCI he said:

We hear the voices of certain intellectuals asserting that the Central Committee of the German Communist Party is weak, that its leadership is feeble, that the work is adversely affected by the absence of intellectual forces in the Central Committee, that the Central Committee does not exist, and so forth. That is all untrue, comrades. I consider such talk as the antics of intellectuals, unworthy of Communists ... It is said that theoretical knowledge is not a strong point with the present Central Committee. What of it? If the policy is correct, theoretical knowledge will come in due course. Knowledge is something acquirable; if you haven't got it today, you may get it tomorrow. But a correct policy, such as the Central Committee of the German Communist Party is now pursuing, is not so easily mastered by certain conceited intellectuals. The strength of the present Central Committee lies in the fact that it is pursuing a correct Leninist policy, and that is something which the puny intellectuals who pride themselves on their 'knowledge' refuse to recognize ... Comrade Thälmann, use the services of these intellectuals if they really want to serve the cause of the working class, or send them to the devil if they are determined to command at all costs.[34]

And, indeed, those intellectuals who remained in the KPD were 'sent to the devil', not exactly because they wanted to 'command at all costs' or were unwilling to 'serve the cause of the working class', but because, in their stubborn way, they would not give up their baneful habit of thinking. Freed by the infallible leader from the boring necessity of basing its activity upon 'theoretical knowledge', the Central Committee of the KPD continued to apply the 'correct Leninist policy' which led it to the catastrophe of 1933. The starting point of this policy was the revision effected by the Fifth Congress of the Comintern of the tactics that had been followed in the preceding period.

When they condemned Brandler's policy, the ECCI were actually challenging the policy of the workers' united front as this had been conceived by Lenin and formulated by the Comintern at the Enlarged Plenums of the Executive Committee in December 1921 and February 1922, and at the Fourth Congress, in December 1922. The ECCI gave this policy a sectarian twist, which was formalized at the Fifth Congress, in June–July 1924. In order to appreciate what this revision meant for the KPD in particular, we must pause to examine, even if only briefly, the significance of this policy. Another reason for doing so is that the policy of the proletarian united front, in its 1921–3 version, was to provide a precedent when the Comintern made its change of line in 1934–5.

A United Front under Capitalism and a Single Party under Socialism

The united-front tactic was originally conceived as a defensive policy, based on the following circumstances: the ebb of the revolutionary movement in most of the capitalist countries; the capitalist counter-offensive against the standard of living of the masses and their economic and political gains; and the split in the working class, the majority of which continued to belong to the reformist parties and unions. In these conditions the struggle for power receded as an immediate prospect, whereas the working class was faced with the urgent necessity of counterposing a united front to the offensive of the employers and the state. Several reformist organizations shared this point of view. The so-called Two-and-a-half International, which brought together some

entire socialist parties along with fragments of certain others which refused to choose between the Second and the Third, took up as an urgent
task the re-establishment of working-class unity.[35]

In its first theses on the workers' united front, approved by the
plenum of the ECCI in December 1921, the Comintern proposed
agreements between political and trade-union organizations of all tendencies including agreements on the international plane: 'While the
Communist International puts forward the slogan of the workers' united
front and permits agreements between the various sections of the International and the parties and unions of the Second and Two-and-a-half
Internationals, it can itself obviously not reject similar understandings
at the international level', the theses declare.[36] At the beginning of 1922
the Two-and-a-half International addressed the other Internationals,
proposing that they hold a meeting of their top leaderships to discuss the
bases for possible joint action. The proposal was accepted and the conference took place in Berlin on 2–5 April 1922.

The conference of the three Internationals, as it was subsequently
known, was one of the important events of 1922. For the first (and last)
time since 1914 the highest representatives of the three great sections
resulting from the split in the old Social Democratic movement found
themselves face to face engaged in studying the possibilities of arranging
for at least a minimum of joint action. At this confrontation some of the
chief ambiguities and contradictions in the tactic of the workers' united
front adopted by the Comintern were revealed – those that were to be
fully demonstrated in the period following 1934.[37]

For the Comintern the united-front policy was not merely a means of
resisting the capitalist offensive more effectively. It was thought that
this policy would enable the Communist parties to tighten their links
with the masses, influence the latter towards a revolutionary policy,
detach them from reformist control and prepare them for offensive
battles in the future. In the theses adopted by the Fourth Congress it was
foreseen that, in a revolutionary or pre-revolutionary situation, the
workers' united front could lead to the formation of 'workers' governments' in which Communists, left-wing Socialists and other advanced
groups would participate, or 'workers' and peasants' governments' in
which, alongside representatives of the working class, there would be

representatives of the radicalized middle strata, especially the peasantry. According to these theses, governments of this type would not yet constitute an expression of the dictatorship of the proletariat, but might be able to prepare the way for its arrival, covering a certain transitional stage between the dictatorship of the bourgeoisie and the dictatorship of the proletariat. At the same time it was affirmed that 'the complete dictatorship of the proletariat is represented only by the real workers' government ... which consists of Communists'.[38] In other words, any other tendency in the working-class movement, however radical, could accompany the Communists only along part of the road leading to 'the complete dictatorship of the proletariat', and must in the end give place to exclusive leadership by the Communist Party. It was the pattern that had in fact been followed in Russia. To the allies of today it was proposed that they collaborate in creating conditions that would enable them to be eliminated tomorrow as a political force.

The proposals that the Communist parties and the Comintern would put to the reformist parties and unions, in order to arrive at agreements for joint action, would be 'useful', from the standpoint just explained, *whether they were rejected or accepted*. In the former case the reformists would be exposed at once. In the latter, the proposals would lead to the same result later, in one or other phase of the movement, since these leaders did not really intend to protect the workers' interests in a consistent way, and the Communists would in due course be able to denounce their hesitations or betrayals. These forecasts were based on two assumptions that have already been mentioned, but which it will be useful to recall in the Comintern's own words: (*a*) 'Not only is capitalism in decay incapable of ensuring the workers decent living conditions', so that 'the workers who fight for partial demands will be *automatically* forced into a struggle against the entire bourgeoisie and their state apparatus', but (*b*) 'the Social Democrats, the reformists of all countries, are proving every day that they do not want to wage any struggle *even for the most modest demands* put forward in their own programme'.[39] If, nevertheless, they sometimes accept the Communists' proposals for joint action they do this under constraint, forced by pressure from the masses, among whom the capitalist offensive has aroused 'a spontaneous striving towards unity which literally cannot be restrained', and because 'the "democratic" and reformist illusions which, after the end of the imperialist slaughter, were reborn among the workers (the better-off workers on the one hand, and the most backward and politically inexperienced on the other) are fading before they reached full bloom'.[40]

These assumptions were soon shown to be mistaken. Not long after the united-front tactic had been formulated there began a phase of economic development in the capitalist world which the Comintern called the phase of 'relative stabilization'. The reformist parties and unions were once again of service to the working class in obtaining certain economic satisfactions, which were compatible with the system. Except in very special cases, 'minimum' demands did not prove to be the ideal lever for separating the masses from the reformists. The Comintern's conception of the situation capitalism was in prevented it from seeing that reformism was rooted not only in the policy followed by the reformist leaders but also in the very nature of the demands being put forward, which were capable of being 'digested' by capital, and even of functioning as a 'stimulant' to its technical development.

The harsh accusations that the Communists hurled at the reformist leaders did not greatly contribute to rational explanation of the problems arising, or to convincing the workers who were imbued with 'democratic and reformist illusions'. They did, however, provide the reformist leaders with some excellent polemical arguments. 'An appeal is made for union,' said Vandervelde at the conference of the three Internationals,

for the realization of the united front, but no secret is made of the intention to stifle us and poison us after embracing us . . . Whilst we are being told, for example, that men like Jouhaux, Merrheim and Henderson, Vandervelde or Longuet, are serving the interests of the bourgeoisie, it is, to say the least of it, strange that these men should be invited to take part in the defence of proletarian interests . . . We are social traitors, social patriots; we are yellow, we are supporters of the bourgeoisie, Zinoviev has even said that I have committed crimes; and in spite of all this you consider that it would be useful to meet us in conference.

The logic of this reasoning was doubtless more comprehensible to the masses in the reformist organizations than the logic of the Comintern synthesized in Radek's reply to Vandervelde: 'You came to this conference because you had to; you were the instruments of world reaction, and now, whether you want it or not, you must be the instruments of the struggle for the interests of the proletariat.'

The proletariat's answer was this: between 1921 and 1928 the number of Communists in the capitalist countries fell by half, from nearly 900,000 to about 450,000, whereas the number of Social Democrats doubled (from about three million to more than six).

At the conference of the three Internationals one of the chief inner contradictions of the united-front policy was revealed with particular acuteness – the contradiction between the content of this policy in the capitalist countries and the political process that was developing during the same period inside the USSR. The socialist leaders skilfully exploited the 'paradox' of the situation: while the Comintern, led by the Bolsheviks, was calling for a united front of all socialist tendencies in the capitalist world, so as to defend the standard of living of the masses, democracy and the Russian revolution, in the Soviet world the Bolsheviks were repressing these same tendencies, depriving them of all their rights in the political and trade-union fields.[41] Similarly, they exploited the fact that, although the right of self-determination for all peoples had always been one of the essential points of the Bolshevik programme, the peoples of the periphery of the former Russian empire found themselves in practice unable to exercise this right. They made particularly vigorous play with the case of Georgia, which country had recently been invaded and occupied by the Red Army, despite the popular support enjoyed by the country's Menshevik government.[42]

The Comintern's representatives at the conference replied by applying the well-known principle according to which the best defence is attack: they set out, once more, the long list of surrenders and betrayals by Social Democracy of the cause of revolution during and after the world war. But two wrongs do not make a right. For the imperialists, more or less directly helped by the Social Democrat leaders, to trample on democracy and the rights of people to determine their own destiny was in accordance with the nature of these political forces and, at least so far as the imperialists were concerned, it seemed to the mass of the working people perfectly logical. But for the socialist revolution to attack proletarian democracy and not to respect the right of self-determination was in contradiction with the nature of the Bolshevik party, as it had defined itself. The Bolshevik representatives remained wholly on the defensive on this subject at the conference. Radek, who was allotted the tenor role, avoided giving any explanation, and Bukharin remained altogether silent.[43] The conference made plain that the 'united front' is a double-edged weapon: while, in some circumstances – when the struggle between proletariat and bourgeoisie becomes acute – it can help to set the masses against the reformist leaders, in others it can help the latter to reach the masses under Communist influence, through their critique of those aspects of the Russian revolution that infringe workers' democracy.

Drawing the lesson that seemed to him to emerge from the conference, Lenin wrote: 'Once again, the bourgeoisie, in the persons of their diplomats, have outwitted the representatives of the Communist International.' 'In my opinion,' he wrote in the same article, 'our representatives were wrong in agreeing to the following two conditions: first, that the Soviet government should not apply the death penalty in the case of the forty-seven Socialist-Revolutionaries; second, that the Soviet government should permit representatives of the three Internationals to be present at the trial.' The Comintern delegation had indeed made these two concessions, and also another which Lenin does not mention: the setting-up of a commission of the three Internationals to study the problem of Georgia. His silence on this point is significant, for it was at this period precisely that Lenin began to show concern at the 'Great-Russian chauvinist' methods employed by Stalin in Georgia. In a note written in December 1922 he sharply warned the party about the danger of displaying 'imperialist attitudes towards oppressed nationalities, thus undermining all our principled sincerity, all our principled defence of the struggle against imperialism'.[44] Lenin considered that the Comintern delegation made a mistake in granting the concession mentioned, because 'we got nothing in return'. Nevertheless, thanks to these concessions, the conference did register the first positive result in united action by the proletariat in the capitalist world. To start with, a permanent committee of the three Internationals was set up, with the task of preparing an international workers' conference to which the trade-union organizations would also be invited. Then, agreement was reached on holding workers' demonstrations on 20 April or 1 May with the following slogans: for the eight-hour day, against unemployment, for united action by the workers against the capitalist offensive, for the Russian revolution, for aid to famine-stricken Russia, for resumption of political and economic relations by all states with Soviet Russia, for re-establishment of the workers' united front in every country and in the International. It was doubtless in the light of these positive results that Lenin said: 'The mistake that Comrades Radek, Bukharin and the others made is not a grave one . . . It would be an incomparably greater mistake to reject all terms, or all payment for admission to these fairly well-guarded and barred premises where the representatives of the bourgeoisie are influencing the workers' (meaning the Social Democratic movement).[45]

Considering this view expressed by Lenin it is not easy to understand why the ECCI decided soon afterwards to withdraw from the committee set up by the conference and interrupt the process that had begun. Was it in order to avoid new open talks on the international level, in which the internal problems of the Russian revolution would be discussed? The Comintern's official explanation was that the leaders of the other Internationals did not sincerely mean to implement the agreements arrived at in Berlin. But they could have formed that view before the conference even met. Why, then, was it held at all? And, since, in spite of everything, *some* positive agreements had been reached, why not put to the test the 'sincerity' of those who had undertaken to implement them? Anyway, the Fourth Congress of the Comintern, which met at the end of 1922, no longer laid stress on achieving the united front on the international scale.

Apart from this implicit correction, the policy of the workers' united front underwent no modifications until the 'October defeat' in Germany. The Fourth Congress spoke out strongly against the Fascist danger and declared in its theses that 'it is one of the most important tasks of the Communist parties to organize resistance to international Fascism, to lead the entire working class in the struggle against the Fascist thugs, and to make vigorous use in this field also of the united-front tactics . . .' The menace of Fascism, it was pointed out, was directed not only against the proletariat but 'against the very foundations of bourgeois democracy'.[46]

Social Democracy = Social Fascism = Main Enemy

This tactical conception was revised at the Fifth Congress of the Comintern, as a result, as we have seen, of the supposed failure of the workers' united-front policy applied by Brandler during the events of 1923. Instead of using this experience to analyse thoroughly the range of problems presented by German capitalism and the German labour movement, the Comintern 'settled' the question by sticking the label 'right-wing opportunism' on the Comintern united-front policy in its Leninist version, and making a sectarian retreat that was to have baneful consequences for the entire Communist movement, and for the German party in particular. It was not, of course, German matters alone that determined this retreat: the contradictions in the united-front policy which have already been mentioned, and the impossibility of overcoming them without a fundamental revision of the tie-up between the Comintern and Soviet policy, together with the structure of the Comintern, certainly told in the same direction.

The Fifth Congress began by blurring the contradiction between Fascism and bourgeois democracy which the Fourth Congress had strongly emphasized. In its theses we read: 'As bourgeois society continues to decay, all bourgeois parties, particularly Social Democracy, take on a more or less Fascist character ... Fascism and Social Democracy are the two sides of the same instrument of capitalist dictatorship. In the fight against Fascism, therefore, Social Democracy can never be a reliable ally of the fighting proletariat.'[47] And Zinoviev: 'The Fascists are the right hand, and the Social Democrats the left hand of the bourgeoisie. The most important factor in all this is – that the Social Democratic party has been converted into a wing of Fascism.' As proof of this assertion he mentioned that in France the Socialist Party had agreed to joint lists with bourgeois parties for election purposes.[48] Zinoviev lumped them all together – Fascism, Social Democracy, French Radicals, German Catholic Centre, etc.

Whereas the Fourth Congress had sounded the alarm regarding the Fascist danger, the Fifth looked upon it as having practically disappeared: 'Because of its internal contradictions, Fascism, after its victory, becomes politically bankrupt (Italy) ... Where, without having won formal victory, it is forced openly to support and defend the bourgeois regime (as in Germany), it gets into a similar state of crisis.'[49]

The united-front tactic was reduced by the Fifth Congress to being 'only a method of agitation and revolutionary mobilization of the masses over a period'. Any possibility of reaching agreements with the Socialist parties was practically brushed aside. The united front was to be applied almost exclusively 'from below', and 'talks' with the Socialist leaders were to be undertaken with the sole aim of 'unmasking' them. The Congress categorically rejected the eventuality of 'workers' governments' formed as a result of an agreement between Communist and Socialist parties.[50]

After the Fifth Congress the united-front policy became a monotonous appeal to rank-and-file Socialists only, invariably accompanied by denunciation of the Socialist leaders, without any restraint on the insulting epithets employed. Yet this impotent sectarianism did not prevent Stalin, with his proverbial pragmatism, from applying the united front, when the interests of Soviet policy made this seem advisable, in an extremely 'broad' way – as happened in the case of the Anglo–Russian Trade-Union Committee, which the British reformist leaders were able to use with great skill in order to maintain their authority in face of the radicalization of the British labour movement in 1925–6.[51]

Soon after the Fifth Congress, Stalin 'deepened' the formulations of Zinoviev on Social Democracy and Fascism. 'Fascism,' he said,

is the bourgeoisie's fighting organization that relies on the *active* support of Social Democracy. Social Democracy is objectively *the moderate wing of Fascism* . . . These organizations do not negate but supplement each other. They are not antipodes, they are *twins*. *Fascism is an informal political bloc of these two chief organizations*; a bloc which arose in the circumstances of the post-war crisis of imperialism; and which is intended for combating the proletarian revolution. The bourgeoisie cannot retain power without such a bloc. It would therefore be a mistake to think that 'pacifism' signifies the liquidation of Fascism. In the present situation, '*pacifism' is the strengthening of Fascism* with its moderate, Social Democratic wing pushed into the forefront.

Stalin meant by 'pacifism', as he explained in the same passage, 'the advent to power, direct or indirect, of the parties of the Second International', 'the pacifist-democratic rule of Herriot and MacDonald'.[52] (Soon after these lines were written, representatives of Stalin and of MacDonald – in the sense of British reformism – came together to form the Anglo-Russian Trade-Union Committee.)

Vulgarly distorting Lenin's policy in the different stages of the Russian revolution, Stalin formulated in 1924 'the fundamental strategic rule of Leninism', according to which the Communist Party must always strike the main blow against the intermediate parties. In reality, Lenin's idea was to crush the resistance of the main enemy, while paralysing and neutralizing the instability of the hesitating intermediate forces.[53] Stalin's 'fundamental rule' was to become a strategical dogma for the Communist parties down to the turn of 1934–5. An example of how it was applied is seen in the tactics of the KPD in the presidential elections of 1925. Ruth Fischer and Maslov, spokesmen of the 'left' in the party leadership, proposed that a candidate be put forward jointly with the Social Democrats to oppose Hindenburg, a typical representative of German militarism and nationalism. Thälmann, however, with Stalin's backing, insisted on a separate Communist candidature – Thälmann himself. Hindenburg was elected with a majority cf less than a million votes over the candidates of the Social Democrats and the Catholic Centre. Thälmann had received nearly two million votes.[54]

One cannot rule out the possibility that Stalin's attitude over the presidential elections was also determined, or at least influenced, by pragmatic considerations other than the dogma of the 'fundamental strategic rule' It was at this time that France and Britain were carrying through, on the initiative of the 'demo-pacifists' (the left-wing bloc in France, the Labourites in Britain), a policy of rapprochement with Germany that was to lead to the Treaty of Locarno (October 1925). The Catholic Centre Party, which headed the central government of Germany, and the Social Democrats, who ruled in Prussia, supported the idea of a security pact with yesterday's enemies – an idea in which Stalin clearly perceived an anti-Soviet tendency. By its own logic the foreign policy of the USSR was interested in widening the gap between the Weimar Republic and the Entente powers rather than narrowing it. And it is significant that Stalin interpreted the election of the nationalist Hindenburg as a symptom of Germany's will to resist the powers that stood behind the Treaty of Versailles.[55] Did the concern of Soviet policy to undermine what has been called the 'spirit of Locarno' affect the attitude taken by the KPD in the presidential elections of 1925? This is a question that it will not be possible to answer until Soviet historians have freedom of research. One can, at any rate, note an 'objective' coincidence between the tactics of the KPD and the game being played by Soviet diplomacy. And it is quite possible that throughout the following years, right down to Hitler's accession to power, this factor may have continued to have a bearing on the tactics of the German Communist leaders in relation to the Social Democrats and to Brüning's party.

At the end of 1927 Stalin's hard fight against the left-wing opposition in the Russian party and the Comintern was crowned with victory. As we saw in Chapter 2, this victory coincided with a grave economic situation in the USSR which compelled Stalin to make a sharp turn, and put into effect some fundamental features of the opposition's programme. He then came into conflict with Bukharin, who, since 1926 (when Zinoviev joined forces with Trotsky), had stood at the head of the Comintern. The new struggle that opened in the party was to have, like its predecessors, profound repercussions in the Comintern.

One of the arguments used by Stalin at the Fifteenth Congress of the CPSU (December 1927) to justify the need for speeding up the pace of industrialization was that the capitalist world had entered a new stage, one of the chief features of which was an aggravation of the danger of intervention against the USSR. This thesis was in its turn based on the idea that 'capitalist stabilization' was breaking down and Europe 'entering a new phase of revolutionary upsurge'. Bukharin opposed this view, considering that, for the time being, there was no new element to be observed in capitalist stabilization.[56] The Ninth Plenum of the ECCI (February 1928) endorsed Stalin's views, though the concrete data on which its analysis of the political and economic situation of the capitalist world was based offered no serious grounds for such conclusions. On the contrary, capitalism was then at the zenith of the rising curve it had traced since 1924. It was legitimate to expect, on the basis of a Marxist analysis, that this upward movement would, eventually, lead to a new cyclical crisis; but it was also clear that, for the moment, there were no changes pointing in that direction. So far as the labour movement was concerned, this showed two main characteristics: increase in reformist illusions about economic development, and weakness of the Communist parties. In 1926 the British labour movement had suffered one of the most grievous blows in its history. The same year had seen Pilsudski's accession to power in Poland and, in Italy, the prohibition of all non-Fascist parties and organizations. To assert, in these circumstances, that Europe was 'obviously' entering a new phase of revolutionary upsurge and that a 'third period' had begun, as the ECCI did and the Sixth Congress confirmed, was clearly a most subjective appreciation of the position.[57]

But Stalin's subjectivism had its reasons. Bukharin's line in the Comintern differed substantially from Zinoviev's revolutionary verbiage and also from the schemas of Stalin which have just been mentioned. Bukharin's analysis of the condition of capitalism has already been referred to, in Chapter 2. As regards the policy of the Communist parties, Bukharin tried to correct the sectarian version of the united-front tactic that predominated after the Fifth Congress. He also advocated greater participation by non-Russian Communists in the ECCI. And these attitudes of his met with response in the leading circles of some of the parties (especially the Italian party) and in factions within others, as in the case of the German Brandlerists. The battle against Bukharin in the Russian party involved a risk of evoking resistance in the Comintern. Stalin needed, as during his fight against the Left opposition, to wage an offensive simultaneously in the Russian party and in the Comintern. Stalin's views, set out above, were destined to serve this purpose, following a simple 'logical' succession of ideas which he expounded like this:

The elements of a new revolutionary upsurge are accumulating in the capitalist countries.

Hence the task of intensifying the fight against Social Democracy, and, above all, against its 'left' wing, as being the social buttress of capitalism.

Hence the task of intensifying the fight in the Communist parties against the right-wing elements, as being the agents of Social Democratic influence.

Hence the task of intensifying the fight against conciliation towards the right-wing deviation, as being the refuge of opportunism in the Communist parties.[58]

Stalin set forth this rosary of 'tasks' in April 1929. In July, the Tenth Plenum of the ECCI began to carry them out, with assiduity, Bukharin having already been removed from his post as representative of the Russian party in the Comintern leadership. The main report to the plenum, presented jointly by Manuilsky and Kuusinen, did indeed seek to 'intensify' the Comintern line in all the directions mentioned. The identification of Social Democracy with Fascism was completed, and Social Democracy became Social Fascism. 'The aims of the Fascists and the social Fascists,' it was said, 'are the same; the difference consists in the slogans, and partly also in the methods. There is also a certain difference in that "pure" Fascism does not employ any left wing, while to social Fascism such a wing is absolutely necessary . . . It is the special task of the left wing of social Fascism to operate with pacifist, democratic and "socialist" slogans.' Nevertheless, even these slight differences were tending to disappear: 'It is clear that the farther advanced the progress of social Fascism, the closer it gets to "pure" Fascism.' This was 'a lengthy process'. And Stalin's spokesmen proceeded, with the precision of zoologists, to classify the parties of the Second International in accordance with the stage they had reached in this 'lengthy process' and biological development: 'British Labourism can perhaps be described as social Fascism in the caterpillar stage, whereas the Social Democratic Party of Germany is already in the butterfly stage.' But this alleged evolution towards Fascism of the parties enjoying the allegiance of the majority of the European working class did not trouble Manuilsky and Kuusinen overmuch. They even presented it as a positive phenomenon that would facilitate the revolution: 'Since social Fascism openly shows itself up as Fascism, it will no longer be difficult to win the majority of the working class in Germany for the proletarian revolution.'[59]

Thälmann and the other representatives of the KPD at this plenum of the ECCI declared that they fully agreed with the theses of Manuilsky and Kuusinen. For several months already the KPD's propaganda had been claiming that 'reformism is socialism in words and Fascism in deeds'. Nevertheless, Thälmann made a self-criticism before the ECCI, for only a month previously the party leadership, at the Twelfth Congress of the KPD (June 1929) had recorded their own failure to 'interpret immediately the big political change which is taking place within the Social Democracy as a decisive step towards the present social Fascism'.[60] This was an indirect acknowledgement of the resistance put up by some sections of the party to the ultra-sectarian 'new line

At the same time as it 'intensified' the struggle against Social Democracy, and above all against its left wing, the Tenth Plenum 'intensified' the struggle against the 'right-wing deviation' within the Comintern. Where this task was concerned, Stalin's official spokesmen left the responsibility for the onslaught to their semi-official colleagues. The German party leaders deserved this honour for, since the end of 1928, they had been carrying out a great purge of 'Bukharinist rights' from the ranks of the KPD, expelling Brandler, Thalheimer and other heretics. On this question too, however, Thälmann criticized himself, declaring that the purge had not gone far enough. He announced that numerous cadres would be replaced, at all levels of the party, by elements capable of fulfilling the tasks to be accomplished in the 'third period' – that is, elements who understood the Fascist character of Social Democracy and the need for an implacable struggle against the right-wing deviation in the party. Strong in the prestige that this achievement conferred on them, the German delegates at the plenum launched a formal attack upon Togliatti, who was suspected of Bukharinist inclinations and specifically accused of two sins: having, at the Sixth Congress of the Comintern, opposed the purge in the German party, and having shown excessive liberalism towards the 'rights' in the Italian party.

Thälmann brought forward as evidence these statements made by Togliatti at the Sixth Congress: 'As to the diverse currents which exist in the Political Bureau of the [German] party, we think that the differences which exist there are differences which can exist normally in the Central Committee of a party without necessarily causing factional and group struggles. If, on the strength of these divergences in the German party, it came to a group struggle or else to the adoption of organizational measures on the part of the majority of the Political Bureau against the minority, this would be a very dangerous state of affairs because it would be tantamount to a shrinking of the basis of the Central Committee: moreover it might also narrow down the political line of the party and its internal democracy.'[61]

'This' did indeed prove to be *molto pericoloso* for many sections of the Comintern. But the most harmful consequences were suffered by the German party, which was at the decisive stage in the struggle against Fascism, the moment when it was urgent and necessary to make the maximum effort to secure unity of action by the working class and raise the ideological, political and organizational level of the party. It must be emphasized that those who were accused of 'rightism' were, in general, the most resolute advocates of the policy of workers' united front against the Fascist menace that hung over Europe. In the specific case of Germany it was the Tenth Plenum of the ECCI that intitiated the grave errors committed by the KPD. Subsequently, after the catastrophe, the ECCI was to condemn these errors, but to keep silent about its own responsibility for them, and the responsibility borne by Stalin.

The Road to Catastrophe

The period improperly described as 'relative stabilization' of capitalism – in fact it was a period of rapid growth of the productive forces – the prosperity of which, hailed by the cheer-leaders of the bourgeoisie and by the Social Democrats, was only a façade behind which the great world economic crisis of 1929–33 was being prepared, was a period that should have been devoted to theoretical, political and organizational preparation of the Communist parties for new revolutionary situations in the future. But the process, already analysed, of theoretical paralysis and stifling of internal political life in the parties; the ever-heavier imposition of a sterilizing bureaucratic centralism; the successive purges of the 'right' and the 'left'; the increasing adaptation to the zigzags of the internal and external policies of the Soviet state; the liquidation of the fruitful element contained in the policy of the workers' united front worked out in Lenin's time – all this was inevitably bound to lead the parties to dissociate themselves further and further from national realities, to isolate themselves from the masses, and in practice to play into the hands of the reformist policy of the Social Democrats. The parties stagnated instead of becoming transformed into genuine vanguards of the proletariat. This situation did not, of course, prevail to an equal extent in all the parties. Depending on the objective conditions peculiar to each of them, the characteristics of the leading group, and so on, some parties put up better resistance than others to the steamroller that had been set moving. Some of them, such as the Spanish party, became insignificant groups. Others, such as the Italian party, managed to preserve to a certain extent the connection between their policy and national realities.

In the case of the German party, this period was marked by stagnation on both the political and organizational planes. The theoretical level was on the downgrade. Between 1925 and 1930 the party's membership remained practically stationary: 1925 – 122,755; 1926 – 134,248; 1927 – 124,729; 1930 – 124,000. At elections the percentage of votes won by the party followed an almost horizontal line: 1924 – 12·7 per cent, 1928 – 10·2 per cent, 1930 – 13·1 per cent.[62]

The month of October 1929 saw the beginning of the world economic crisis. Germany, where the effects of the crisis were experienced sooner and more seriously than in any other country, did not undergo the revolutionary upsurge that Stalin had been forecasting since 1927, but saw, on the contrary, a spectacular advance by Fascism. At the elections of 1930 Hitler's party received 6,400,000 votes, that is, five-and-a-half million more than in 1928, whereas the KPD gained only 1,300,009 votes (4,590,000, as against 3,262,584 in 1928), its percentage of the total votes rising from 10.2 per cent to 13.1 per cent. The Social Democratic Party lost half-a-million votes. The progress made by the KPD was certainly substantial, but it was also extremely relative when compared with the dizzy rise of the Fascists. A far from negligible share of the votes received by the Fascists came from working-class elements especially the unemployed. The KPD's position in the factories was even more disquieting than the election results. In January 1931 the percentage of factory committees led by the Communists was only 4 per cent, while the Social Democrats controlled 84 per cent. Towards the end of 1932 only 10 per cent of the party members belonged to trade unions. One of the main reasons for this situation was the slogan of breaking with the reformist trade unions and setting up parallel trade-union organizations which had been put forward by Stalin during the meeting of the Presidium of the ECCI held in December 1928. Stalin mentioned Germany specifically as one of the countries where such a line should be followed. The Fifth Congress of the Profintern, held in September 1930, decided that the trade-union opposition in a certain number of countries must leave the trade unions and form independent organizations. In practice, these were to become mere duplicates of the party organizations.

This trade-union tactic was bound up with the thesis about the beginning of the 'third period', that of the revolutionary upsurge. According to this thesis, it was better to have organizations which, though small were well under the party's control than to work perseveringly to convince the masses within the big traditional trade-union organizations. For the KPD the consequences of this line were translated into the figures given above. Its electoral gains among the workers were due mainly to the votes cast by the unemployed (as already mentioned, this was true also of the Fascists' electoral successes among the workers). The great majority of the workers in the factories and in the trade unions remained under the control of the Social Democrats. This accounts for the failure of all the KPD's attempts to organize political strikes, since it was not applying a tactic of workers' unity that would have enabled it to establish real contacts with the Social Democratic masses of the employed workers.[63] Moreover, the election results revealed the going-over *en masse* to the Fascists of the middle strata of the population in town and country.

In this context, to call for the dictatorship of the proletariat, as an immediate issue, meant blocking the road to unity of action by the working class and hurling the middle classes into the arms of Fascism. Yet this was the programme of the KPD. Many years after the catastrophe, Wilhelm Pieck was to admit that one of the worst mistakes of the German party had been to 'struggle for the establishment of a German Soviet Republic', to refrain from 'putting in the forefront the fight to defend democracy and the political rights of the masses', to 'attack the Nazis and Social Democracy at one and the same time', and 'not to have understood the seriousness of the Fascist danger'.[64] As an aggravating circumstance one might add the fact that Soviet Russia was always put forward as the model for the creation of a German socialist republic. It was in Germany that criticism of the anti-democratic aspects of the Soviet model had met with the widest echo among the workers, thanks to the efforts of the powerful propaganda apparatus of the Social Democratic Party. The aims of this propaganda were certainly far from pure – but what was said was factually true, nevertheless. If the KPD had undertaken such a criticism, on a revolutionary Marxist basis, while defending the Soviet revolution, and had put forward a new model of socialism for Germany, the course of events might have been very different. It must be acknowledged, of course, that, for this to have happened, a different type of Communist party would have been needed.

Pieck said essentially the same as Trotsky, with this difference, that Trotsky was already saying it in 1930, when there were still some chances of changing the situation. Opposing the theory of 'social Fascism', Trotsky showed the fundamental contradiction that existed between Fascism and Social Democracy. 'No matter how true it is that the Social Democracy prepared the blossoming of Fascism by its whole policy, it is no less true that Fascism comes forward as a deadly threat primarily to that same Social Democracy, all of whose magnificence is inextricably bound up with parliamentary-democratic-pacifist forms and methods of government.' 'One must be in a state of complete bureaucratic idiocy to refuse to utilize correctly and systematically the great, sharp contradictions between Fascism and the Social Democracy in the interests of the proletarian revolution.' On the basis of this assumption, Trotsky called for a consistent united-front policy as the only way to bar the path against Fascism: 'The policy of a united front of the workers against Fascism flows from this whole situation. It opens up tremendous possibilities for the Communist Party. A condition for success, however, is the rejection of the theory and practice of "social Fascism", the harm of which becomes a positive menace under the present circumstances ... We will inevitably have to make agreements against Fascism with the various Social Democratic organizations and factions.' In the war against Fascism we were ready to conclude practical military alliances with the devil and his grandmother, even with Noske and Zoergiebel.'[65]

In opposition to Thälmann's theses, Trotsky declared that the united front must not be put forward in conjunction with the slogan of immediate overthrow of capitalism, for 'the Social Democratic workers remain Social Democrats precisely because they still believe in the gradual, reformist road to the transformation of capitalism into socialism'. The Communists should address them in these terms: 'You put your stakes on democracy; we believe that the only way out lies in the revolution. Yet we cannot and we do not want to make the revolution without you. Hitler is now the common foe. After the victory over him we shall draw the balance together with you and see where the road actually leads.' In another of Trotsky's writings of this period we find the shrewd observation that 'the guilt of the Stalinist bureaucracy is not in that it is "irreconcilable" but in that it is politically impotent' in this attitude of 'irreconcilability'. For Trotsky, the attitude taken up by the middle classes, who were for the moment in sympathy with Fascism, was of great importance. 'For the social crisis to bring about the proletarian revolution, it is necessary that, besides other conditions, a decisive shift of the petty-bourgeois classes occur in the direction of the proletariat.'[66] However, he did not indicate *how* these middle strata were to be won to the side of the working class in the phase of anti-Fascist struggle.

The 'social Fascism' thesis even led the KPD to participate, alongside the Nazis and the Stahlhelm, in the referendum of 9 August 1931, against the Social Democratic government of Prussia. Many years later, the German Communist leaders were to see this as one of the most serious mistakes committed by their party. It made it possible to present the Communists as being 'allies of the Fascists in the eyes of a large part of the working class'. It set up a new barrier between Communists and Social Democrats at a moment when the Fascist danger was already grave and could not be dealt with otherwise than by united action of the working class.[67] But *Pravda* of 12 August 1931 wrote: 'The results of the voting signified . . . the greatest blow of all that the working class has yet dealt to Social Democracy.' For its part, the Comintern offered the event as an 'example of the application of the united front'! Trotsky's comment was: 'In what way the intervention in the plebiscite alongside the Fascists, against Social Democracy and the party of the centre, is an application of the policy of the united front towards the Social Democratic and Christian workers, will not be understood by any proletarian mind.' And he went on to say: 'To come out into the streets with the slogan "Down with the Bruening–Braun government!" at a time when, according to the relationship of forces, it can only be replaced by a government of Hitler–Hugenberg, is the sheerest adventurism.'[68]

In May 1932 Trotsky prophesied 'that if the most important organizations of the German working class continue their present policy, the victory of Fascism will be assured almost automatically, and in a relatively short space of time at that.' He urged that the KPD at once take the political initiative and 'propose an agreement for struggle [against Fascism] to the Social Democratic Party and the leadership of the Free Trade Unions, from below up to the very top ... There is no other path for the German working class. The question of the fate of Germany is the question of the fate of Europe, of the Soviet Union, and in a considerable measure, the fate of all humanity for a long historical period. No revolutionary can avoid subordinating his forces and his fate to this question.'[69]

Events were soon to show how clearsighted were Trotsky's analyses and suggestions in his writings of 1930–32 on Germany. But neither the Comintern leaders nor those of the KPD were willing to take account of them. The ferocious persecution of 'Trotskyism' in all sections of the Comintern, which proceeded side by side in these years with the no less relentless struggle against the 'rights' and 'conciliators', led to any proposal for a united front with the Social Democratic parties and bourgeois-democratic forces, to hold up the Fascist advance, being seen as an opportunist heresy. At the end of 1932, faced with the extreme aggravation of the Fascist danger, the KPD began to modify its policy towards Social Democracy, but it was then too late.

The whole political evolution of Germany from 1930, when the Fascist threat was first revealed in its full magnitude, gives grounds for assuming that the course of events could have been entirely altered if, from that time onwards, the Comintern and the German Communists, correcting their previous policy, had applied a flexible tactic of anti-Fascist unity. In fact, despite the ultra-sectarian policy of the Communist Party, a growing number of Social Democratic workers did become more and more aware of the danger, and took up left-wing positions in favour of unity. The ebbing of Nazi influence was shown by the elections of November 1932, when Hitler's party lost two million votes. The two workers' parties then had, between them, 13 million votes, as against 11·7 million votes for the Nazis. The Communist Party's vote came to 6 million, which was 1·3 million more than in 1930. An intelligent policy of anti-Fascist unity, undertaken in time, could clearly have expanded to a considerable degree the Communist Party's influence among the Social Democratic masses, the Catholic workers of the Centre Party, and the middle classes. It would have given support to the pressure from below in favour of unity that existed inside the Social Democratic Party, and helped the advance of its left wing. The historical value of Trotsky's pronouncements during this period does not lie merely in the fact that events proved him right, but also in the fact that they demonstrate that it was possible to put such proposals forward. They show that the lag by the Comintern in grasping the nature and gravity of the Fascist danger in Germany and in developing a policy to combat it is not to be accounted for by unclarity in the objective situation or by the communist movement's lack of experience in this matter. After the elections of 1930 the menace of Fascism in Germany was glaringly obvious. In Italy for several years the working-class movement had known what Fascism meant. The policy of workers' united front, including agreements with the Social Democratic leaders, had been worked out and put into practice in Lenin's time. And in that same period the Comintern had combated the ultra-leftism of Bordiga and other Italian Communists, which was hindering the united struggle against Mussolini's Fascism. Then and in subsequent years Gramsci clearly analysed the phenomenon of Fascism. So also did Togliatti, until, in 1929, he bowed to Stalin's thesis of 'social Fascism'. And yet, when the menace of Fascism began plainly to take shape in Germany, the Comintern, far from going forward with understanding of the Fascist phenomenon, adopted the line we have examined above, thereby wiping out all earlier experiences and analyses.

This political blindness on the part of the Comintern, in face of the advance of Hitler, cannot be explained merely by an accumulation of mistakes, as Dimitrov was to claim at the Seventh World Congress – throwing, moreover, all the blame for these upon the KPD. The mistakes were in this case the reflection of a deep-going sickness: atrophy of the theoretical faculties, bureaucratization of the organizational structures, sterilizing monolithicity, unconditional subordination to the manoeuvres of Stalin's camarilla, and – as a result of all these factors – widening divorce between the Comintern's policy and the actual situation, internationally and within each country. Hence the helplessness of the Comintern to intervene as a decisive revolutionary force in the terrible duel fought between proletariat and bourgeoisie against the background of the world economic crisis. Hence its impotence before Hitlerism. The historical bankruptcy of the Third International was consummated, like that of the Second, on the German scene. The Comintern collapsed in the very country where its own first congress had situated the new focus of the world revolution. The turn effected at the Seventh Congress would not revive it: that would be only its swansong.

THE PEOPLE'S FRONT EXPERIENCE

Capitalist Recovery and Working-Class Counter-Offensive

A wave of pessimism and alarm swept over the bourgeois world during the three years that passed between the outbreak of the economic crisis and Hitler's accession to power. The events that took place certainly boded no good for the capitalist system. The fall in production, and the confusion in trade and finance, went further than ever before in the history of capitalism's cyclical crises. At the lowest point of the curve of the depression the number of wholly unemployed varied between 25 and 30 million. Europe and the USA were shaken by waves of strikes, mass demonstrations, 'hunger marches' and clashes between the workers and the armed forces of the state. Social and political agitation reached a level unprecedented since 1919–20. Some European countries underwent political changes which the ruling classes feared might develop similarly to the Kerensky episode in Russia in 1917: the fall of the monarchy in Spain in April 1931; the formation in Bulgaria, in June of the same year, of a government of the 'National Bloc'; the defeat of the right wing in the French elections in May 1932. Liberation movements pressed forward in Asia and Latin America. But there was another side to the medal. Fascism and the traditional reactionary forces multiplied their activities, with unrestrained violence and demagogy, and found response among the millions of desperate members of the middle classes who had been severely affected by the crisis, and even among the proletariat. The reformist socialists and bourgeois liberals manoeuvred on two fronts: against the Fascist threat and against the threat of revolution. Indefatigably, the Communists called for 'Soviet power'. Hitler's triumph led to the beginning of a clarification process, eliminating the threat of revolution in the country where this represented the greatest danger to European capitalism. Later, the explosion of June 1936 was to occur in France, but it was in Spain that the spectre of revolution found embodiment. And just as, centuries earlier, the Europe of rising capitalism had united against Imperial Spain, so now mature capitalism united to crush revolutionary Spain.

Yet the fact that in Europe, as in the USA, capitalism succeeded in overcoming the crisis of the thirties cannot be explained solely by the victory of the ruling classes in the political sphere, whether won by resorting to Fascism or by more or less traditional methods. Victory on this political plane enabled the recovery mechanisms inherent in the crisis itself to operate fully on the plane of economic structures. The thesis in vogue in the Comintern during those years, describing capitalism as in the grip of its 'final crisis', resulted precisely from a denial of this capacity for recovery.[70] The production-structures of capitalism underwent 'self-rationalization' after 1929, just as in previous cyclical crises, by way of the ruin of millions of small producers in town and country, the bankruptcy of hundreds of thousands of medium-sized capitalists and of a certain number of big sharks, and the dismissal on the spot of millions of 'redundant' workers – in short, in accordance with the logic of its 'natural laws'. This time, however, practical capitalist economists, and certain theoreticians (the first edition of Keynes's *General Theory* appeared in 1936), became aware of the possibility and necessity of bringing these 'natural laws' under some form of control. This was the first challenge offered to the Marxist thesis that claimed it was not possible to correct the anarchy inherent in capitalist production. The very dynamic of this anarchy in the industrially advanced countries had brought about a high degree of monopolistic concentration, creating thereby the objective conditions for curbing this anarchy, since the mass of private capitalists were closely dependent on a few hundreds or dozens of big monopoly units. The linking of the state with these 'trusts' provided an incomparable instrument of coercive power at all levels – economic, political, ideological, scientific, cultural, etc.

Thenceforth the role of the state was no longer to be confined to keeping the exploited in a condition of obedience: it had, in addition, to subject the private interest of each individual capitalist to the general interest of capitalism. By one of those ironies that history knows how to produce, the first successful proletarian revolution contributed substantially to making the capitalist classes aware of the need to discipline its 'natural laws', and of the means that must be used in order to achieve this end. The Russian revolution helped them to appreciate better the risks involved in *laisser faire, laisser passer,* and the gigantic 'state trust' created by the revolution, together with its first five-year plan, helped them to perceive the services that the state might render in the economic sphere. Following the trail blazed by its enemy, the bourgeois state thus made its historic irruption into the holy-of-holies of capitalist economy. It had been obliged to do this more than once on previous occasions, during wars, but when this happened it was always an exception to the rule: now the exception became the rule. Fascism in Germany and the New Deal in the USA (symbolically, Hitler and Roosevelt came to power almost at the same time) represented the two poles of the set of political and economic solutions that monopoly capitalism was to make use of in order to restructure industrial society. But this polarity was mainly political. The barbaric nationalist, racial and anti-working-class violence of the former and the paternalistic idealism of the latter covered an economic process that was similar in their two countries. Contrary to what many believed at that time (in all political tendencies, even among Marxists), the Fascist variant was ultimately nothing but an emergency solution forced on monopoly capital in the great industrial power that Germany was, by virtue of its weakness in relation, internally, to the labour movement, and, externally, to the 'encirclement' by its rivals, with their colonial monopoly; whereas the American variant was to be revealed as the first try-out of the 'neo-capitalism' of the future.

To sum up, the most serious economic crisis in the history of capitalism, instead of being the 'final crisis' that was to result in the proletarian revolution, as the Comintern expected, turned out to be the birth-pangs of a new phase of capitalist development: state monopoly capitalism. Preparations for the Second World War, and the war itself, made it possible to pass quickly through the stages of this mutation, not only by hastening in every country the transformation of the state into the principal economic power, but also by obliging technical and scientific progress to develop at feverish speed and intensifying the dynamic of economic and political concentration. Once more the monstrous 'logic' of the capitalist mechanism showed itself stronger than the conscience of mankind and the class-consciousness of the proletariat, and more cunning than the strategic and tactical contrivances of the 'world party' of revolution.

Nevertheless, fresh opportunities to oppose this 'logic' and change the course of events arose in Europe between Hitler's coming to power and the start of the world-wide slaughter. In the countries where the labour movement had not been crushed by Fascist or near-Fascist dictatorships, the terrible lesson of Germany produced a salutary reaction among the masses, in the workers' parties and trade unions, and even in some political parties of the bourgeoisie and petty-bourgeoisie whose existence was traditionally bound up with the parliamentary regime and the freedoms bequeathed by the bourgeois revolutions. The increased danger of war also contributed to stimulating the masses to engage in political activity – though in some cases the fear of war inclined them to the most abject surrenders.

In the working class the anti-Fascist reflex was accompanied by a growing hostility to capitalism, stimulated by the harsh effects of the crisis. The reformist method was discredited among extensive sections of the workers, and left-wing tendencies gained ground rapidly in the Social Democratic parties and trade unions. The year 1934 showed several symptoms of this radicalization. In February, in Vienna, the Socialist workers' militia fought bravely against Dollfuss's dictatorship. In Paris, Communist and Socialist workers demonstrated in the streets against the Fascist-tending 'Leagues'. The same month saw the great 'Hunger March' on London, in organizing which Communists worked side by side with members of the Labour Party and the ILP, and trade-unionists. In October came the revolt in the Asturias. Although the movement against the entry into the Madrid government of the pro-Fascist Popular Action Party did not, in most of Spain, go beyond the stage of a revolutionary general strike, in the Asturias the miners seized power and defended it heroically for fifteen days against the greatly superior armed forces sent by the government to crush their revolt. During the Asturian Commune, Communists, Socialists and Anarchists fought shoulder to shoulder.

This counter-offensive of the working-class movement against the Fascist advance and intensified capitalist exploitation reached its climax in 1936. After the election victory of the People's Front in Spain and France, the working class did not wait passively for the election promises to be honoured. This was due not only to the fact that the programmes of the two People's Fronts were extremely moderate and offered no solution to the fundamental problems of the two countries, but also to the workers' lack of confidence in the new governments. They knew that the political situation their struggle had created was favourable to them, and they must profit from this situation without losing any time. Between February and July, strikes, demonstrations, attacks on prisons in order to release political prisoners, seizures of land, settlements of accounts with Fascists and reactionaries, and the formation of armed workers' groups spread ever more widely over Spain. And when the Generals rebelled, the workers replied with armed struggle and revolution. In France, without waiting for Blum to form a government, the working-class masses went on strike and occupied the factories during the month of June. The closeness of the two movements, Spanish and French, both in space and time, created a unique opportunity to begin a process that might have altered the European scene in a radical way. Undoubtedly, deep revolutionary feeling and fighting spirit were at that time stronger in Spain than in France. But the French movement did have a revolutionary potential that was deliberately held back by those who should have encouraged it. The Spanish revolution was thus isolated by the frustration of the revolutionary possibilities of the movement in France, and this was one of the essential reasons for its military defeat. The road was opened for Hitler's aggression and the Second World War.

The responsibility borne by international Social Democracy, and especially by the French Socialist Party, for the course that events were to take was no less great than that borne by the German Social Democratic Party for the triumph of Hitler. It is, however, highly unlikely that history will absolve the Communist International from all blame.

The Turn of 1934

A change in the attitude of the Socialist leaders towards the question of a united front with the Communists began to become apparent immediately after Hitler's accession to power. In a call addressed to the workers of all countries, the leadership of the Labour and Socialist International declared in February 1933 its readiness to open conversations with the Comintern for the purpose of organizing joint action against Fascism, giving as its only condition the ending of mutual attacks.[71] During the conference held by the LSI during August of the same year its 'left' wing, represented at that time by Nenni, Grimm, Zyromski, Spaak and others, took up a position similar to the one advocated by the Comintern: the only course open to the working class in face of the advance of Fascism was the direct struggle for power. Adler and Blum, representing the 'centre', kept to the traditional reformist positions, while accepting the principle of joint action with the Communists, provided the latter honoured the condition mentioned above.[72] In the early months of 1934 the Spanish Socialist Party declared itself in favour of the Workers' Alliances and proposed to the Communist Party that it join them.[73] In 1933 the French Socialist Party stated it was ready for concerted action with the Communist Party on condition that the latter put an end to 'insulting polemics between the two parties'. After the events of 6 February 1934 the leaders of the Socialist Party in the Seine (Paris) *département* proposed to the leaders of the Communist Party a joint meeting to 'decide the basis for an honest agreement and bring about united action by the working people'.[74] Similar moves by other Socialist parties could be mentioned.

The reasons for this evolution of an important section of Social Democracy towards a political alliance with the Communist parties were complex. One of the most widespread was, undoubtedly, a defensive reaction to the fact, then being made obvious, that Fascism did not confine its blows exclusively to the extreme left. The dramatic experience in Germany had shown that Fascism, as Trotsky pointed out in 1930, was 'a deadly threat to Social Democracy'. At the same time, the collapse of the great Social Democratic Party of Germany gave hegemony within the LSI to the Socialist parties of the Versailles powers threatened by the revenge-seeking spirit of Hitlerism. And these states, in which the Socialist parties played an important role, were beginning to contemplate the possibility of an alliance with the Soviet Union. Improved relations between the Socialist parties and the Comintern and its national sections might facilitate such an alliance. In some cases this evolution by Social Democracy was dictated by narrow party considerations: it was a matter of not clashing directly with the tendencies in favour of unity and a more radical line that were spreading among the masses.

However, it was not just opportunism. The experience of Fascism led some of the Social Democratic leaders – though not many, to be sure – to carry out a fundamental revision of their reformist doctrines. Otto Bauer, one of the outstanding figures of the 'Austro–Marxist' School, provides a typical instance. After the elections in Austria in April 1927, Bauer forecast in almost mathematical fashion the route that the Socialists would have to traverse in order, by means of electoral support, to come to power and introduce socialism. 'In 1920,' he said, 'we won 36 per cent of the votes. At the elections before last, we got nearly 40 per cent. In six and half years we have gained approximately 7 per cent of the votes. How many do we still have to obtain? The road that we still have to cover in order to reach power will require a period of time roughly the same as has elapsed since 1920 ... One or two elections more, and we shall have finished with government by the bourgeoisie.'[75] At the end of the journey, however, it was the bourgeois government that had finished with the Austrian Socialist Party. In 1936 Otto Bauer wrote that the experience of Fascism 'destroys the illusion of reformist socialism that the working class can fill the forms of democracy with socialist content and develop the capitalist into a socialist order without a revolutionary jump'.[76] This conclusion was widespread at the time among left-wing Socialists. An interest in the theoretical problems of the revolution was often to be observed among them, which contrasted with the pragmatism then prevailing in the Comintern. While condemning reformism, many of these Socialists advocated the creation of a new Marxist party that would unite revolutionary Socialists and Communists, without excluding the Trotskyists. (The left-wing Socialists of the 1930s had no prejudice against Trotsky; quite the contrary.) These attitudes were maintained in the left wing of the Socialist Party and its youth organization in Spain, in the Zyromski and Marceau Pivert tendencies in the French Socialist Party, in a section of the Independent Labour Party, in a group of German 'revolutionary socialists' who in September 1934 published a political platform entitled *Towards a Socialist German*y, etc.[77]

There were thus, for the first time since the split in 1919, real possibilities not only of united action by Social Democrats and Communists, but also of the unification in a single party of all the different revolutionary tendencies inspired by Marxism. Yet the year 1933, and half of 1934, went by without the Comintern modifying in any way the ultra-sectarian attitudes that had already caused the destruction of the KPD. It did not agree to the meeting proposed by the LSI in February 1933. It did not grasp the significance of the left-wing tendency that showed itself at the LSI conference in August 1933. Four months later, at its Thirteenth Plenum, the ECCI continued to counterpose the united front 'from below' to the united front 'from above', still regarding Social Democracy as a whole as the main social basis of the bourgeoisie, with its left wing as its most crafty and dangerous section.[78] Faithful to this principle, the Communist parties rejected all the offers of unity that were put to them. The Communist Party of Spain refused to join the Workers' Alliances. For its part, the leadership of the French Communist Party replied in these terms to the proposals, already mentioned, made by the Socialist leaders of the Paris area: 'More than ever do we fraternize with the Socialist workers, more than ever do we appeal to them for joint action with their Communist comrades. And more than ever do we denounce the Socialist leaders, the Socialist Party, lackeys of the bourgeoisie and last bastion of capitalist society.'[79] A few days later, demonstrations summoned separately by the Communist Party and the Socialist Party converged upon the same point, and a hundred thousand Paris workers hailed united action. For the French Communist Party leadership, however, this was merely an example of the united front 'from below'. During the months that followed, the campaign against the Socialist Party was strengthened still further.[80]

Moscow suddenly gave the signal for a 'turn'. *L'Humanité* of 31 May 1934 reproduced an article from *Pravda* of 23 May which said that it was perfectly admissible to propose united action to the Socialist leaders. The same issue of *L'Humanité* published an appeal 'to the workers and to the branches of the Socialist Party' which was also addressed *to the National Administrative Committee* of the Socialist Party.[81] From that moment onwards, pacts for united action between Socialists and Communists followed quickly one after another. The French one was signed in July and the Italian in August. In September the Spanish Communist Party joined the Workers' Alliances, despite the presence within them of the Trotskyist organization; and the Spanish Communist and Socialist youth organizations began talks with a view to merging. It became plain, in fact, that the initiatives for unity that had been coming forward for more than a year from the ranks of the Socialist organizations were no mere manoeuvres, and that the Comintern's persistence in its ultra-sectarian line had done grave harm to working-class unity during all that period. This was all the more serious because, in the situation created in Europe by Hitler's accession to power, 'gaining time' was a matter of life and death in preparing the revolutionary forces for the battles to come.

What were the factors that prevented the Comintern from making this 'turn' sooner? And why did it make the turn in May 1934? The situation, analysed above, in which the Comintern found itself in 1933 is adequate to explain the delay. The mentality and political habits created by ten years of sectarian rigidity, purges and steady increase in bureaucratic centralism were exactly the opposite of what the new situation called for. These characteristics were especially pronounced in the group of functionaries from the Soviet party who, after the elimination of Bukharin and the Bukharinists, formed, under Stalin's direction, the actual leadership of the Comintern (Manuilsky, Kuusinen, Pyatnitsky, Lozovsky, etc.). It is probable that some of the European Communist leaders had, in their hearts, already for some time been aware of the need for a change of tactics; they could not but be affected by the pressures of events, the urge for unity that was growing among the masses and in the Social Democratic parties, and also by the increasing threat from Fascism. In order, however, to revise the Comintern's policy in the way the situation required, it would have been necessary to abandon conceptions (such as that of 'social Fascism') and norms for action (such as the 'fundamental strategic rule') which had been laid down by Stalin. And after the elimination of the Trotskyist, Bukharinist and other oppositions it had become practically impossible to go against Stalin's views in the Comintern. One might break away, but one might not discuss. For the turn to be made, Stalin's 'green light' was indispensable.

We have not sufficient information to determine exactly how and why the decision was taken in May 1934, precisely. According to the Soviet historians Leibzon and Shirinya it was the Comintern leaders, and particularly Dimitrov, who took the initiative in making the turn during 1934–5. Given the danger that threatened the USSR Stalin did not oppose their moves, but he insisted that the tactical turn be effected without any criticism of the previously prevailing conceptions – which were his own. The change in policy must be based exclusively on the 'change in the situation'. There must be no questioning of the correctness of the general line followed during the previous ten years. The leaders of the parties, including those of the KPD, were alone to be held responsible for the 'mistakes made in applying' this line. In this way the infallibility of Stalin would be preserved.[82] Nevertheless, Leibzon and Shirinya, despite the obvious interest they have in providing support for their thesis and although it may be that they have consulted the minutes of meetings of the ECCI held in this period, do not adduce a single document to prove that the question of the turn was ever discussed by the leading group in the Comintern *before* the appearance of the article in *Pravda* which I have mentioned (and, indeed, no reference is made to this article in their book). This article, which, by recommending agreements 'from above' between Communist and Socialist parties, radically altered the rules that had been followed by the Communists for the preceding ten years, would never have been published by *Pravda* without Stalin's explicit approval. Moreover, the information given by the two Soviet historians proves that the discussion in the ECCI and in the preparatory commissions of the Seventh Congress began *immediately after Pravda* had given the go-ahead. The turn did not result from discussion in the leadership of the Comintern; on the contrary, the leaders were able to discuss it only because Stalin had decided that there should be a turn. This is not to say that the version given by Leibzon and Shirinya may not contain a part of the truth. I shall say something later about this aspect of the problem.

Why did Stalin give the signal for the turn at this time? To judge by the information available, the explanation lies – as with other turns made by the Comintern – in Soviet policy, and, more specifically, in Soviet foreign policy. I have already mentioned, in Chapter 2, that after Hitler came to power the Soviet government began actively to seek alliances with the 'democratic' capitalist states. For a certain period, however, between Hitler's triumph and the beginning of 1934, this endeavour was combined with an effort to preserve the 'spirit of Rapallo'. The protocol renewing the Soviet–German pact of 1926, which was a prolongation and amplification of the Treaty of Rapallo, was ratified three months after Hitler became Chancellor. After Japan and Germany left the League of Nations, the Central Committee of the Soviet Party declared (in December 1933) in favour of the USSR joining it, but at the same time Molotov said that the Soviet government had no reason to modify its policy towards Germany.[83] In his published writings Stalin maintained a prudent silence on the international situation during an entire year, between January 1933 and January 1934. He broke this silence at last on 26 January 1934, when he delivered his report to the Seventeenth Congress of the CPSU. He began by observing that, 'quite clearly, things are heading for a new war'. He considered all the forms that this war might assume, and warned the capitalist states that, in any event, the adventure could end very badly for them. They ran the risk of finding themselves face to face with revolution. However, of all the possible variants, Stalin emphasized: 'There can hardly be any doubt that [a war against the USSR] would be the most dangerous war for the bourgeoisie.' And he added:

The bourgeoisie need have no doubt that the numerous friends of the working class of the USSR in Europe and Asia will endeavour to strike a blow in the rear at their oppressors who have launched a criminal war against the fatherland of the working class of all countries . . . It can hardly be doubted that a second war against the USSR [he had referred earlier to the intervention of 1918–20] will lead to the complete defeat of the aggressors, to revolution in a number of countries in Europe and in Asia, and to the destruction of the bourgeois-landlord governments in those countries.

He then referred to the new rulers of Germany. Provided they did not depart from 'the old policy, which was reflected in the treaties between the USSR and Germany', there was no reason why Soviet–German relations should worsen. 'Of course, we are far from being enthusiastic about the Fascist regime in Germany. But it is not a question of Fascism here, if only for the reason that Fascism in Italy, for example, has not prevented the USSR from establishing the best relations with that country.' It would be a quite different matter if Germany sought to go over to 'a "new" policy, which in the main recalls the policy of the former German Kaiser, who at one time occupied the Ukraine and marched against Leningrad'. Stalin noted that 'this "new" policy is obviously gaining the upper hand over the old policy'. And, so that the Nazi leaders should have no more room for doubt regarding the alternative that was open to the USSR if they were to persist in this 'new policy', he went on to mention 'the very great significance for the whole system of international relations' of the then recent restoration of normal relations between the USSR and the USA (November 1933), not only, Stalin continued, because it contributed to the maintenance of peace, but also because it 'forms a landmark between the old position, when in various countries the USA was regarded as the bulwark for all sorts of anti-Soviet trends, and the new position, when that bulwark has been voluntarily removed, to the advantage of both countries'. And Stalin ended by saying: 'The USSR does not think of threatening anybody – let alone of attacking anybody. We stand for peace and uphold the cause of peace. But we are not afraid of threats and are prepared to answer the instigators of war blow for blow. Those who want peace and seek business relations with us will always have our support.'[84] Nowhere in this report was anything said to the effect that, in the event of a conflict between the capitalist states provoked by German aggression, the Soviet Union would come to the rescue of the countries attacked. Up to that time the Soviet state had concluded no pacts of mutual assistance with other countries, only pacts of non-aggression.

Everything in this report was carefully measured out and proportioned. The bogey of revolution if war should come was brandished as an argument to keep the capitalist states back from the slippery slope of armed conflict; but references to the class struggle in the capitalist countries were much less numerous than at previous congresses – and, for the first time in a report to a party congress, no mention whatever was made of the Communist International. An exemplary balance was kept in defining the relations between the Soviet Union and the capitalist states. The Fascist regime prevailing in Germany, it was made clear, constituted no obstacle to the preservation of good relations with that country. Everything depended on its attitude *towards the Soviet Union.*

In the light of this speech it is easy to understand why the moment for political alliances between Communist and Socialist parties had not yet come: Berlin might have interpreted such moves as signifying a one-sided orientation of the Comintern, and so of Stalin, towards the states that were Germany's rivals. But on that same day, 26 January 1934, when Stalin was making his so carefully constructed speech, Poland and Germany were signing a pact which – as Leibzon and Shirinya point out – constituted 'an obvious step towards aggression by Hitler against the USSR'. And it was indeed in that sense that the pact was interpreted in Moscow. Paris saw the pact as a serious crack in the system of anti-German alliances that had been patiently built up by French diplomacy. The Quai d'Orsay and the military leaders of France drew the conclusion that the time had come to give serious thought to a return to the traditional strategy of the French governments of the period before the First World War: neither under the Tsar nor under Stalin had Russia shifted its location – it still lay to the east of Germany. Nor had France shifted, they reflected in Moscow. Geography dictates. At the beginning of May, Barthou defined the French position, proposing to the government of the USSR a Franco–Soviet pact of mutual assistance which should be expanded into an 'Eastern Pact' and included in the frame-work of the League of Nations. Since this plan implied the assent of Great Britain, Barthou warned London that, if it were to offer oppo-sition, then France would conclude a direct military alliance with the USSR. On 25 May Barthou told the Chamber of Deputies that Russia's entry into the League of Nations 'would be a considerable event and, since I am concerned for peace, I say it would be a considerable event from the standpoint of the peace of Europe'.[85] Six days later came the article in *l'Humanité*, reproduced from *Pravda*, urging the Communist Party of France to reach an understanding with the French Socialist Party.

But agreement with the French Socialists was not the only aim; it was, indeed merely a stage. On 24 October, at Nantes, on the eve of the first day of the Radical Party Congress, Thorez put forward the idea of a 'broad people's front' in which the party of Édouard Herriot would have a place. This was the party which Trotsky said was the one 'with whose aid the big bourgeoisie preserves the hope of the petty bour-geoisie in a progressive and peaceful improvement of the situation'.[86] In his autobiography, *Fils du peuple* (1960 edition), Thorez wrote that this initiative of his was taken in despite of the Comintern's counsels, as transmitted to him by Togliatti, and he offers this as proof that, even at that time, the French Communist Party did not submit unconditionally to the Comintern's directives. In view, however, of what relations were like in the upper hierarchy of the Comintern, and considering the sub-sequent behaviour of Thorez in the face of directives sent from Moscow, it is hard to believe that he would have ignored the opinion of the Comintern representative unless a 'higher' authority had backed, or even suggested, his 'initiative'.[87] In any case, the appeal to the Radicals coincided perfectly with the tasks that Soviet diplomacy had on its agenda at that time. French reactionary circles, favourable to Germany, were trying by every means to torpedo the plan for a Franco–Soviet pact, and they profited by the assassination of Barthou (on 9 October) to intensify their manoeuvres. The support of the Radicals was indis-pensable if the plan was to succeed.

The Franco–Soviet Pact was signed in Paris on 2 May 1935, and, in the days immediately following, conversations were held in Moscow between Laval and Stalin. The communique published at the end of these talks included this passage: 'Comrade Stalin expressed complete understanding and approval of the national defence policy pursued by France with the object of maintaining its armed forces at a level consistent with its security requirements.' The Communist Party had until then kept up an unwavering opposition to any 'national defence policy', regardless of which particular bourgeois parties were in the government. The party's deputies voted regularly against the military budget. Six weeks before the signing of the pact Thorez declared in the Chamber: 'We shall not allow the working class to be dragged into a so-called war for the defence of democracy against Fascism.'[88] According to some historians Laval believed he had killed two birds with one stone: besides getting the pact he had put the Communists in an awkward situation and hindered their *rapprochement* with the Radicals. But the Communists' reply was a striking one. Throughout France party posters appeared proclaiming 'Stalin is right'. *L'Humanité* did its utmost to explain that there was national defence and national defence, army and army, so-called war for defence of democracy and genuine war for defence of democracy. In short what the party was saying was that from the moment when the defence of the Soviet Union was at stake, everything became different. That was plain enough. What, however, presented a problem to a revolutionary party was how to proceed from that general observation to the definition of a policy that would enable *this* contradiction to be resolved – namely, how to contribute to the defence of the USSR while at the same time fighting against a bourgeoisie which, by virtue of the pact, had become an important factor in the Soviet defence system.

There could be no doubt for a revolutionary that Stalin was right to sign a pact of mutual assistance with bourgeois-democratic France against the threat from Fascist Germany. But it was much more difficult to agree that he was right to give 'complete approval' to the national defence policy practised by Paris, even if the problem were to be looked at exclusively from the standpoint of the pact's military effectiveness. And it became highly questionable if one looked at the problem from the angle of the anti-Fascist and revolutionary struggle in France. Stalin's words, besides furnishing the bourgeois parties with a splendid argu-

⌐nent to justify *their* national defence policy, represented a transparent invitation to the French Communists not to restrict the 'breadth' of the People's Front to the Radicals alone. In the last resort, if the interests of the defence of the USSR should require it, ought one not to go so far as the *union sacrée*, as in 1914? On 17 May, two days after the publication of Stalin's statement, Thorez gave the party the 'theoretical' justification for it. If, he said, a war against the Soviet Union 'is not being conducted by all the imperialist countries, if some, owing to the contradictions of interest between them and the rest, are acting in concert with the land of socialism, then their action *objectively* serves the cause of peace, which *is identical with* the cause of the power of the working people, it *objectively* serves the cause of the proletariat, which cannot be separated from the safeguarding of the country where the working people have become masters of their fatherland.'[89] Consequently, if the French imperialist bourgeoisie organizes joint action with the Soviet Union against Germany, this action is identical with the cause of the French proletariat.

Not long after, Thorez was to put forward the slogan of the 'French Front'. For the moment, however, what mattered was to ensure the agreement of the Radicals. The General Secretary of the French Communist Party did not hesitate to offer the support of the party to a Radical government that would carry out the Radical Party's programme. On 31 May Thorez said in the Chamber of Deputies: 'We Communists, renewing the Jacobin tradition, would be ready to give you our support, *Monsieur le Président* Herriot, if you or any other leader of your party would take the leadership of a Radical government – since the Radical group is the largest of the left-wing groups in this Chamber – of a Radical government, I say, that would really implement the policy of the Radical Party.' And already at this stage Thorez put forward the idea that it would be appropriate to broaden this 'Front' in the rightward direction. 'It is even possible that the Radical Party may be joined by other Republicans, more or less moderate in tendency, but who simply have sufficient perspicacity, sufficient common sense and sufficient heart to appreciate the danger that the Fascists represent for the country and for peace.'[90] But '*Monsieur le Président*' could make nothing of this extraordinary piece of political intrigue. He exclaimed: 'I am not a man of the right, but I am tired of seeing my party taken in tow by the extremists. The Radical Party is in no sense a revolutionary organization.'[91] Daladier, however, and the 'Young Turks' of the Radical Party understood very well that it was not a matter of the Radical Party being taken in tow by the extremists, but rather of the extremists being taken in tow by the Radical Party. The latter would not have to give up its glorious historical role and become a revolutionary organization – the Communist Party would have to give up *its* historical role and cease to be a revolutionary party. Since the Communists had accepted the policy of the Radical Party, not excluding national defence, why not include them in the new *Cartel des Gauches*, styled 'People's Front'? When, on 25 July 1935, the Seventh Congress of the Comintern opened in Moscow, the French version of the People's Front was going strong. It had not yet taken, and indeed would never take, any of the 'new Bastilles', but it had already had its 14 July. Thorez, Blum, Daladier and the ten thousand representatives of the People's Front organizations who had come from all parts of France to the Buffalo Stadium that day swore a solemn oath to 'remain united to disarm and dissolve the factious Leagues, to defend and develop democratic freedoms, and to ensure peace for mankind'. Eternal France presided over this now historic day: Joan of Arc and 1789, the *Marseillaise* and the *Internationale*.[92] In a short time little of all that would remain, apart from holidays with pay.

The Seventh Congress of the Communist International

The policy of the united front of the working class was a *reprise*, under the conditions of the struggle against Fascism, of the policy followed by the Comintern in the years 1921–3. The People's Front policy, however, had no precedents in the history of the Comintern. Dimitrov tried to find some in the resolutions on tactics passed by the Fourth Congress, but in no way did these conceive of collaboration with bourgeois parties. Neither policy, however, originated in a critical analysis of the problems of the class struggle under the capitalist system, in the light of the experience of the revolutionary movement in the previous period. They were both adopted as a pragmatic response to the urgent requirements of

Soviet foreign policy, after Berlin, ignoring Stalin's warning, had given its policy a direction that clearly implied preparing war against the Soviet Union. If Hitler had remained faithful to the 'Rapallo line' and had concentrated his *revanchard* moves exclusively against the West, would *Pravda* have urgently called upon the French Communists to reach an understanding with Blum? It is enough to put this question – a far from arbitrary one, since German imperialism did in fact revert to the 'Rapallo line' in 1939–41 – to appreciate how decisive the 'Soviet foreign policy' factor was in the tactical turn made by the Comintern.

On this occasion, however, the urgent needs of the defence of the USSR coincided with the no less urgent need for working-class and anti-Fascist unity – whereas, during the previous ten years, the orientation of Soviet foreign policy, concerned to exploit German nationalism against the imperialist 'Versailles powers', had had a far from negligible influence, as we have seen, in giving a sectarian twist to the policy of the Comintern. It is nevertheless not possible to say that there was *complete* coincidence between these two needs. A section of the bourgeoisie in the 'democratic' capitalist states, and the right wing of the Social Democratic leadership, might agree with the Soviet government on preventive measures to be taken against the German danger, and might even support a form of People's Front which, in the new circumstances, could play a role similar to that played by the Social Democrats in the Entente countries during the First World War. Obviously, though, they could not support a policy of workers' unity and People's Front that had a revolutionary content. Any policy that could lead to a revolutionary solution of national and international problems would inevitably clash with their interests and foster tendencies in these social and political forces that would favour a compromise with the external foe. This was contrary to the interest of Soviet policy, which sought to build an alliance between the USSR and the 'democratic' capitalist states against Hitlerite Germany. The way the European situation developed between 1934 and 1938 showed that within this contradiction there lay fundamentally three possibilities, which were taken up more or less consciously by the different tendencies participating in the leadership of the workers' united front and the People's Front. Things might lead to a radical, revolutionary change, and then the defence of the USSR could be organized on new foundations – an alliance between the Soviet state and the new revolutionary states (without ruling out alliances of a different kind with capitalist states that were rivals or victims of Germany, and in which the working-class movement did not yet constitute a real danger to the bourgeoisie). Or workers' unity and the People's Front might be integrated in a national union under the hegemony of the bourgeoisie, and then the defence of the USSR would be based essentially on alliance with the capitalist state in question. Or, thirdly, the working-class and anti-Fascist movement, though not sufficiently strong to dictate the first of the three possibilities, might prove strong enough to terrify all sections of the bourgeoisie and make them compromise with Germany, thus isolating the USSR.

Logically, the bourgeois political groups and the right-wing Social Democrats participating in the People's Front worked in a conscious way to bring about the second of the three possibilities. In the political theses of the Seventh Congress of the Comintern both the first and second possibilities were indicated, though never explicitly defined. The policy followed by the Comintern, under the inspiration of these contradictory theses, contributed greatly, however, to bring about realization of the third possibility. At the time of Munich, workers' unity and the People's Front had been shipwrecked without having been able to develop their initial revolutionary potential. The USSR thus found itself isolated. Fortunately, the contradictions between the imperialists were strong enough to ensure that – the danger of revolution having been eliminated in *both* imperialist camps – these contradictions took precedence over the common class interest that might otherwise have led from Munich to a combined anti-Soviet intervention by all the capitalist states, Fascist and 'democratic' alike.

It is usually assumed, in studies of the Seventh Congress of the Comintern, that the basic purpose of its work was the formulation of tactics for the struggle against Fascism and against capitalism. The Congress certainly gave its greatest attention to this theme, and the main report, presented by Dimitrov, was devoted to it. In order to grasp the underlying significance of the political line adopted and appreciate how it was applied, it is necessary to start from what the Congress itself defined as the *central slogan* for the Communist parties: 'The fight for peace and for the defence of the USSR'. This meant that all the activity of the Communist parties, their policy and their actions, had to be considered and decided in relation to this supreme objective. The underlying reason for the contradictions that showed themselves in the tactical theses of the Congress, and in their subsequent application, lay precisely in this general line, which was made specific in the following directive from the Congress: 'The struggle for peace opens up before the Communist parties the greatest opportunities for creating the broadest united front. All those interested in the preservation of peace should be drawn into this united front ... The concentration of forces against the chief instigators of war at any given moment (at the present time – against Fascist Germany, and against Poland and Japan which are in league with it) constitutes the *most important* tactical task of the Communist parties.'

What *were* these forces interested in the preservation of peace that the Communist parties must draw into a united front? In the first place, obviously, the mass of the people, but also every group in the ruling classes that was interested in peace, including those states, large or small, which, at the given moment, had a similar interest. The resolution passed by the Congress stated that 'the mutual relations between the Soviet Union and the capitalist countries have *entered a new phase* ... The peace policy of the USSR has not only upset the plans of the imperialists to isolate the Soviet Union, but has laid the basis for its cooperation in the cause of the preservation of peace with the small states to whom war represents a special danger, as well as with *those governments which at the present moment are interested in the preservation of peace.*'[93] Dimitrov explained which states were meant by this cryptic allusion: 'Even some of the big capitalist states, afraid of losing in a new redivision of the world, are *at the present stage* interested in avoiding war.' These were, in short, the big European colonial powers and the USA, which were afraid of losing their monopoly of world exploitation in a war with Germany and Japan.[94] And Dimitrov went on to say that 'this gives rise to the possibility of forming a very wide united front of the working class, of all working people and whole nations against the threat of imperialist war'. Here the already equivocal notion of 'whole nations' attains the height of ambiguity – it would appear to mean 'whole states'. The 'world front', as Dimitrov was to call it on other occasions, was, in fact, nothing other than the Grand Anti-Hitler Coalition, which was not able to come into being until the Nazis had begun aggression against the Soviet Union.

Togliatti, whose role at the Congress was to give the report on the struggle against the war danger, declared that utilization, in order to preserve peace, of the contradictions between imperialist states was not a matter for the Soviet Union alone: 'It is obligatory for the proletariat and for the Communist parties of the capitalist countries, in so far as these parties can and must elaborate a positive stand in deciding problems of international policy, to interfere actively in the course of events and aid tendencies that retard the unleashing of war and hinder everything that constitutes a direct immediate menace to peace.'[95] At the time of the Seventh Congress this was not at all an academic question, but a highly topical one, presenting itself in a most concrete way. It confronted in practice the two principal Communist parties of Europe, the French and the Czechoslovakian. They were the only mass Communist parties left in Europe after the crushing of the KPD, and were political factors of some weight in their respective countries. (At the time of the Seventh Congress the Spanish party had not yet 'taken off' and was still suffering the effects of the October defeat.) On the other hand, France and Czechoslovakia were the countries with which, two months earlier, the Soviet Union had signed pacts of mutual assistance. They represented to perfection the two types of state 'interested in the preservation of peace' to which the Seventh Congress alluded: the 'big state' which was afraid of losing its dominant position in the world, and the 'small state' which was in danger of losing its national independence. What, then, must the respective Communist parties, and the Comintern in general, do to 'aid' this fundamental aspect of Soviet policy? It was the first time that the Comintern had been faced with such a problem.

Togliatti acknowledged in his report that the question gave rise to some misgivings among the Communists:

There have been some waverings, individual comrades even getting the idea that the conclusion of mutual-aid pacts meant losing sight of the prospect of revolution in Europe ... Certain comrades even compared the conclusion of mutual-aid pacts to a compulsory retreat under the pressure of the enemy. But these few comrades have demonstrated only that they are unable to distinguish between a retreat and an advance. Could one conceive a more remarkable success than the fact that a big capitalist country is compelled to sign an agreement of mutual aid with the Soviet Union, an agreement which stipulates defence against an aggressor, defence of peace and of the frontiers of the country of proletarian dictatorship? ... Practical experience has rapidly convinced these comrades that they were grossly mistaken ... The new pact by which the Soviet Union confirmed its peace policy could only enhance the prestige of the proletarian state in the eyes of the working people of all countries, in the eyes of the wide world, and consequently also the prestige of socialism and the proletarian revolution.

Reminding the Congress of the criteria that ought to guide the Communist parties in deciding their policy in this respect, Togliatti began by propounding an axiom that had already been implicit in the Programme of the Comintern approved by the Sixth Congress (which, as was shown in Chapter 2, formulated the 'principle' of the hegemony of the Soviet Union in the world revolutionary movement), but which was here set out with incomparable clarity: 'For us it is *absolutely indisputable* that there is *complete identity of aim* between the peace policy of the Soviet Union and the policy of the working class and the Communist parties of the capitalist countries. There is not, and cannot be, any doubt in our ranks on this score. We not only defend the Soviet Union in general. We defend *concretely its whole policy and each of its acts.*' This did not mean, Togliatti went on, that the 'tactics' of the Communist parties must always show 'complete coincidence in all acts and on all questions'. He adds: 'Numerous examples could be cited of the lack of coincidence in the positions of the proletarian parties in various countries in regard to some concrete question.' *Nevertheless, the examples quoted by Togliatti were all of earlier date than the appearance of the Soviet state and the Comintern. He did not quote a single case of a Communist party adopting a tactical position differing from that of the Soviet party.* There is perhaps no plainer confirmation to be found in all Comintern literature of the way the national sections of the Comintern were totally subordinated to the policy of the Soviet state.[96]

The criteria having been formulated 'in principle', Togliatti went on to apply them to the cases of France and Czechoslovakia. The respective parties had to act in a way that took into account 'the concrete circumstances'. They must 'staunchly defend the pact, because it is an instrument in the struggle for peace and for the defence of the Soviet Union'. They must 'vote for the pact in parliament' and 'expose any attempt to pursue a policy different from or in contradiction to the obligations ensuing from the pact'. They must at the same time say to the bourgeoisie that 'we have no guarantee' that the army would not be used against the working class, that it would not be the poor, as usual, rather than the rich, who would have to find the money for it, that, when the time came, the pact would actually be honoured, and so on. Consequently, they must say that, so long as no such 'guarantee' was available, they would not vote for the military budget or give up their fight against the governments in power. Togliatti concluded: 'Those who do not understand the profound inner consistency of this position adopted by our comrades in France and Czechoslovakia will never understand anything of the real dialects of events and of revolutionary dialectics, even though they fancy themselves to be highly intelligent and logical persons, as Léon Blum, for instance, fancies himself.'[97]

In a very short space of time the 'dialectics of events' in France, Spain, Czechoslovakia and elsewhere were to subject the 'profound inner consistency' of the Comintern's new tactic to a harsh test. But the delegates at the Seventh Congress found nothing to object to in the remarkable virtuosity with which Togliatti had solved the problem of the relation between possible revolutionary developments in some countries of Europe and the Soviet Union's alliance with the bourgeois states of these countries. At the time of the Seventh Congress this possibility of revolutionary developments was located in Spain and in France, and the problem of the 'relation' therefore arose concretely in the case of the latter country. If the French situation should come to the point of a revolutionary crisis, what ought the attitude of the Communist Party to be? Ought it to strive to intensify the crisis, urging it towards proletarian revolution, even if this situation risked endangering the Franco-Soviet Pact? It was no less justified, given the way the situation in France had evolved since 1934, to bring up this eventuality than it was for the

Dutch delegates to ask whether, in the event of German aggression against their country, the resulting war would not bear the character of a war of national defence, despite Holland's status as an imperialist colony-owning country. Togliatti, with the approval of the Congress, answered the Dutch Communists' question in the affirmative – though he added the usual qualifications, namely, that the line taken 'must never lead to renouncing the class struggle', and that in such cases 'our policy of defence of national freedom must never be detached from the real struggle for the liberation of the oppressed and exploited peoples of the colonies'. He mentioned that his reply was relevant not only to Holland but also to Belgium and other similar cases. This categorical answer was in line with the complete conformity which existed at that time between the prospect of national defence of Belgium and Holland and the system of alliances which the Soviet government was engaged in building in order to safeguard itself against possible German aggression. If the Congress did not examine specifically the problem presented by the situation in France, and if Togliatti skilfully avoided speaking about it, was this not because no such conformity existed in that particular case, and that, on the contrary, it was the problem of lack of conformity that arose?

In any case, the Congress gave an indirect answer to the question in so far as all the reports, all the speeches and all the theses were dominated by the idea that the supreme task was to ensure the defence of the USSR: 'Assistance to the USSR, its defence, and cooperation in bringing about its victory over all its enemies must therefore determine the actions of every revolutionary organization of the proletariat, of every genuine revolutionary, of every Socialist, Communist, or non-party worker, of every labouring peasant, of every honest intellectual and democrat ...'[98] Knorin, one of the Soviet members of the Comintern leadership, indicated very plainly that, from the point of view of the prospects of the revolution, what was essential was not to wage the revolutionary struggle in the capitalist countries but to ensure the development of the USSR. This it was that, in the long run, would cause the balance to tip in favour of the socialist revolution. The Communists, said Knorin in his speech to the Congress, were the party of peace, striving to do everything in their power 'to bar the way to war, so as to be able to convince the peoples, *through peaceful emulation and peaceful labour*, of the necessity of socialist revolution'. And he added that if the Communists were for peace, it was because peace would guarantee the further progress of socialism in the USSR and the growth of its economic and political might. 'If peace is maintained, then the international relation of forces in the class struggle will shift daily in favour of the proletariat and to the disadvantage of capitalism.'[99]

As we have seen in Chapter 2, the Seventh Congress of the Comintern, unlike any of the previous congress, did not tackle the specific theme of world revolution and its prospects. Dimitrov said: 'We intentionally excluded from the reports as well as from the decisions of the Congress *high-sounding phrases* on the revolutionary perspective.'[1] After what has already been shown it is hardly necessary to explain that, in my opinion, this 'exclusion' was due to more imperative reasons than the praiseworthy desire to avoid revolutionary verbiage (and, be it said in passing, it would indeed have been a question of verbiage). At the time of the Fifth Congress, or of the Sixth, when an objective coincidence of interests existed, on the plane of international relations, between defeated Germany and the encircled Soviet Republic, in face of the 'big states' of the capitalist world, and when Moscow considered that it was Britain, France and the USA that were heading the world-wide anti-Soviet drive (along with the Social Democrats and the 'demo-bourgeois' or 'demo-pacifist' parties, as Stalin called them), the Comintern could still *explicitly* formulate one or other strategy for world revolution – whether right or wrong is another matter – without the risk of coming into conflict with the 'peace policy' of the USSR.

But how, in the setting of the Seventh Congress, could any *explicit* strategy of world revolution be reconciled with the need for the USSR to conclude alliances with the imperialist colonial powers and the USA? This was why, after a period of seven years without a congress being held, despite what was laid down by the Comintern's statutes, at a time when the world system of imperialism had just been experiencing the worst economic crisis in its history, and the question of a Second World War was on the agenda, the Seventh Congress of the Comintern refrained from undertaking any theoretical analysis of the problems of imperialism, capitalism, the socialist revolution in the West and the anti-imperialist revolutions in the colonial and dependent countries. This also explains why, of the seventy pages of Dimitrov's report on the Congress (in the edition quoted here), only one-and-a-half were devoted to the anti-imperialist struggle in the colonies. It could be said that the Seventh Congress was the most 'Eurocentrist' of all the Comintern congresses – but for the fact that, behind the European themes, behind the prestigious figure of Dimitrov and the other Western Communist leaders who occupied the foreground, what was taking place in fact was the most 'Russocentrist' congress of them all.

It would nevertheless be a mistaken and over-simplified view to conclude that the Comintern and Stalin had renounced any and every *overall* conception of the world revolution. Actually, the Seventh Congress implicitly retained the conception set forth at the Sixth, adapting it 'tactically' to the situation created by the appearance of two serious threats on the Soviet frontiers – Hitler's Germany and militarist Japan. These countries constituted at the same time a grave danger not only to the working-class movement in Europe and the Chinese revolution, but also to bourgeois democracy and the independence of some European countries, as likewise to the independence of China. On the other hand, the ambitious moves of German and Japanese imperialism also threatened the interests of the great imperialist powers which had been victorious in the First World War. If we consider that the Sixth Congress had introduced, as the principal element in its conception of the world revolution, the idea that the Soviet Union was the international driving-force of the proletarian revolution, the base of the world-wide movement of the oppressed classes, the focus of the international revolution, the most important factor in world history, the essential factor in the international liberation of the proletariat, and so on (see Chapter 2), it is clear that, in the new world situation, the Comintern's strategy must consist in organizing around the 'central slogan' of 'struggle for peace and the defence of the USSR' (two ways of saying the same thing) all the interests, factors and contradictions that lay across the path of German and Japanese expansionism.

This strategic conception fitted into the general view of the condition of capitalism which the Comintern, under Stalin's direct influence, had begun to define at the time of the Sixth Congress, and to which the great economic crisis had seemed to give striking confirmation. According to this view, capitalism had entered – really entered, this time – the last stage of its already protracted 'death-agony'. It was from this angle that the rise of Fascism was interpreted by the Comintern. One of the dominant ideas of the Seventh Congress (taken from Stalin's report of 1934, already mentioned) was that the spectacular advance of Fascism showed that 'the bourgeoisie is already unable to rule by the old methods of parliamentarism and bourgeois democracy',[2] and this not only in Italy and Germany but on the world scale. Foster, delegate of the CPUSA and member of the ECCI, told the Congress that there were elements of Fascism in Roosevelt's policy. Other delegates said that it 'opened the way' to Fascism. And Dimitrov spoke of a danger of Fascism in the USA, because, as he said, 'the programme for the recovery of capitalism has collapsed'.[3] If this was the view taken by the Congress where American capitalism was concerned, it is easy to imagine how it saw the situation of capitalism in Europe. The logic of this conception led to Fascism being seen as the final politico-social form of imperialist capitalism, after which the latter was doomed to disappear. This was, in fact, the idea set forth by Dimitrov in his report, when he defined Fascism as 'the open terrorist dictatorship of the most reactionary, most chauvinistic and most imperialist elements of finance capital'. This formula, devised by Stalin, wrongly claimed to describe the class content of Fascism in Germany and Italy by reducing it to a mere section of finance capital. Starting from this idea, which implied that Fascism was intrinsically very weak, Dimitrov dangled before his hearers an optimistic prospect according to which the very dialectics of the development of Fascism must inexorably create conditions favourable to its destruction, and lead ineluctably to the downfall of capitalism.

His argument can be summed up like this. Contrary to its own aim, Fascism worsens instead of curing the contradictions of the bourgeois camp. It sharpens the economic conflict between the capitalist states and stirs up the hatred and anger of the masses, thereby helping to awaken their revolutionary spirit. It weakens illusions about bourgeois democracy, giving a decisive stimulus to the workers' united front, for the Social Democratic workers see in Fascism the consequence of the policy of class-collaboration with the bourgeoisie. 'The initiative shown by the

Communist Party in the organization of the united front and the supreme self-sacrifice displayed by the Communists, by the revolutionary workers in the struggle against Fascism, have resulted in an unprecedented increase in the prestige of the Communist International,' whose mission is to guide the revolution to its final triumph. 'Thus Fascism, which has undertaken to bury Marxism, the revolutionary movement of the working class, is, as a result of the dialectics of life and the class struggle, itself leading to the further *development of the forces* that are bound to serve as its gravediggers, the gravediggers of capitalism.'[4] Marx had forecast that the dialectics of motion of capital was digging capital's grave; Dimitrov explained that the last phase of this already long-drawn-out process had begun now that capitalism had assumed its final form, as Fascism.

Deducible from this schema was the idea that barring the way to Fascism where it had not yet come to power, and destroying it as a state form where it was in power, meant taking the decisive step towards the victory of the world revolution. The whole tactic of the workers' united front, the People's Front, and the world front for peace (and defence of the USSR) formed part of this view of how things would develop. Dimitrov ended his report with the words: 'And we want all this because only in this way will the working class at the head of all the working people, welded into a million-strong revolutionary army, led by the Communist International and possessed of so great and wise a pilot as our leader Comrade Stalin, be able to fulfil its historical mission with certainty – to sweep Fascism off the face of the earth and, together with it, capitalism.'[5]

The tactical turn made by the Comintern did not alter in any way the assumption that the revolution could be victorious only under the leadership of the Comintern and its national sections. The essential aim of the workers' united front was to regroup the working class of each country under the leadership of the corresponding Communist party. Agreements could be made with the Socialist parties during the transition period, which might involve the forming of governments of the anti-Fascist united front, but it was the Communist Party alone that would lead the movement when the time came to take up the direct struggle for the dictatorship of the proletariat (which could only take the

Soviet form, this being another of the unchanging assumptions of the Seventh Congress). After coming to power, the Communist Party intended to rule alone. True, the Congress contemplated the possibility of forming a single revolutionary party by uniting the Communist and Socialist parties. But the conditions laid down for this unification were such as to mean the retention pure and simple of a party of the Stalinist type, with its theoretical dogmas, tactical schemas, bureaucratic centralism, acceptance of Soviet hegemony, and so on. As a Spanish humorist of those days remarked, it was not a matter of unifying but of 'USSRifying'.

The People's Front policy called for by the Comintern had as its main purpose the regrouping around the workers' united front of the middle classes of town and country, who would thus be placed, albeit indirectly, under the leadership of the Communist Party. The immediate aim was to smash Fascism; but, in the course of the struggle, conditions would be created that would ensure that these middle classes stood by the side of the proletariat when the hour sounded for the socialist revolution. This was the standpoint of the Comintern. But just as forming the workers' united front presumed that agreements would be made with the Socialist parties during the anti-Fascist phase of the struggle, so the regrouping of the middle classes around the working class required – according to the theses of the Seventh Congress – understandings between the Communist parties and the political parties or other organizations representing these social strata.

The Comintern's governing idea was that the political platforms that must serve as the basis of the workers' united front and the People's Front must be adapted to the level of consciousness of the great majority, and must not include excessively radical aims that might 'frighten off' politically undeveloped sections. Given that the workers' united front and the People's Front were not two distinct movements, but that in fact the former was conceived as merely the tougher and more advanced nucleus of the latter, and that the essential aim of the latter was to draw the middle strata towards the proletariat, one had to ensure that the platform of the workers' united front did not 'go too far', that it must take into account the state of mind of the middle strata. Eventually, in its concern to attract the middle classes, the Seventh Congress adopted a

general policy that tended to align the entire movement with their outlook – this concern being fully understandable in the light of the fundamental role played by the middle classes in the victory, first of Italian,
and then of German Fascism. As a rule, the platforms were made up of
three sections: economic demands, perfectly compatible, in principle,
with the outlook of the reformist parties and trade unions; political
demands that did not go further than the defence or restoration of bourgeois-democratic freedoms and institutions and the suppression of Fascist activities and organizations; and a section on the 'fight for peace'.
Faithful to the line proclaimed by the Comintern, the Communist
parties systematically opposed the formulation of objectives of a socialist type, or what could be regarded as such, in the programmes of the
workers' united front and the People's Front. The French Communist
Party, for example, declared itself against the 'structural reforms' (a
certain number of nationalizations) proposed by the Socialist Party.
Two kinds of argument were put forward to justify this attitude. One
kind was 'leftist' in character: 'We Communists,' said Thorez, 'are for
socialization; we are for expropriation pure and simple of the capitalist
expropriators, but we consider that one condition must be fulfilled in
order to socialize, just one little condition: the possession of power, the
seizure of power. Now, there is only one method of seizing power that has
proved its worth up to now: that is, the method of the Bolsheviks, the
victorious insurrection of the proletariat, the exercise of the dictatorship
of the proletariat and Soviet power.' (Thorez could, of course, have said:
Good. Since you, who have up to now kept to a reformist line, are
advocating socialization of the banks and large-scale industry, this
means that we can unite the working class in a struggle to achieve these
aims – but to do that we must take power. In Russia, a backward
country, they proceeded in a certain way, and established a ruling
authority in which power was exercised by a single party. France is a
quite different sort of country, industrialized, and with other traditions
and other forms of the working-class movement: it may be, therefore,
that another road is open to us, which we must seek together; perhaps it
will be necessary to form a new type of revolutionary party – and so on.
Obviously, Thorez, being General Secretary of the French section of
the Comintern, could not talk like that. To do so he would have had to be a

revolutionary Marxist who, like Lenin, was seeking the particular path to be followed by the revolution in *his* country.) The other argument brought against the socialization proposals was a very simple one indeed: the Radical Party was against them. For Thorez this meant that 'socialization' would frighten away the middle classes.[6]

How, on the basis of this tactical schema, did the Comintern think it could bring the movement to the level of consciousness and revolutionary inclination necessary if the question of socialist revolution was to be raised concretely? The answer lay in the following thesis: capitalism was already incapable of 'absorbing' or 'integrating' the great wave of popular demands that was being prepared. Though the economic demands of the workers, peasants, civil servants, etc., were only 'minimum' demands, capitalism, being no longer in a condition to develop the productive forces (had not the 'recovery' plan of the most powerful capitalism, that of the U S A, already failed?), would be unable to meet them. It would find itself, in fact, in a situation with no way out: the masses drawn into the movement would become radicalized and would reach the conclusion that, as Dimitrov put it, salvation could be expected only from the establishment of Soviet power. The defence of bourgeois-democratic freedoms and institutions would lead to the same extreme situation. In fact, the defence against Fascism of political forms that capitalism was thenceforth unable to use in order to maintain its domination must inevitably force the ruling classes into a situation with no way out. Bourgeois democracy thus became a mechanism that was turning upon the bourgeoisie who had created it.

However, there was still the problem of peace and war. As the Comintern saw it, this was where the main danger lay: the dynamic just described might be jammed, for a whole phase of history at any rate. The Comintern feared lest Fascism, by means of a terrorist dictatorship established on the world scale, might succeed in prolonging the existence of capitalism, despite the irremediable impotence of the latter to develop new productive forces. Such an eventuality might occur if the capitalist states were to unite to destroy by force of arms the 'international driving-force of the proletarian revolution'. Here too, though, the dialectics of the phase of moribund capitalism came into play. Fascism was playing the sorcerer's apprentice by intensifying to the utmost the contradictions between imperialisms and raising the question of a new partition of the world. In order to protect their sacrosanct colonial profits, the great powers that had won the First World War found themselves forced into alliance with the Soviet state, which was threatened by the same foe – an alliance either to maintain the *status quo* or to fight alongside the Soviet state if it should come to war. (As for believing that these powers were 'peace-loving', as the Comintern's resolutions declared, that was a euphemism that deceived only the peoples and the Communist Party members themselves.)

In short, the Comintern considered that the irresistible dialectics of history, having brought capitalism to the brink of the abyss, would go on working in such a way that the Socialists would be compelled to line up with the Communists, so helping to create the right conditions for the establishment of Soviet power, which, once set up, would eliminate these same Socialists from the political scene. As for the parties representing the middle strata, these would follow a similar itinerary: they, too, would play the role of the man who was 'cuckolded, beaten and happy'. Finally, the big capitalist states that were in possession of colonies would be obliged to cooperate with the Soviet Union in order to destroy their rivals and, in doing so, to destroy Fascism, which was alone capable of keeping capitalism alive. In other words, these states would actually hasten the coming of the world revolution.

Looked at in this light, the essential task of the Comintern's tactics worked out at the Seventh Congress was above all to 'give a push' to this irresistible dynamic of history. This would be done, first, by acting so that the broad masses, whose political consciousness had not yet matured to the point of understanding that Soviet power offered the only salvation, would follow the vanguard even if they did not appreciate very clearly where they were being led; and, secondly, by doing what was needed to ensure that those social groups, political parties and state institutions that were destined subsequently to vanish from the scene would go to meet their fate offering a minimum of resistance. Once the world had entered the phase in which the extremely decrepit condition of the economic and political structures of capitalism was bringing society rapidly to the great moment of *Hic Rhodus, hic salta!* the most important thing was that nobody should take fright before that Great

Leap of which only the party of the world revolution knew the secret. The workers in the vanguard must avoid putting forward aims that might alarm the less advanced workers; the working class as a whole must refrain from proclaiming purposes – above all, that of proletarian revolution – which might upset the middle classes of the towns and the small and medium peasant proprietors; finally, the mass of the workers, civil servants, technicians, intellectuals, peasants, etc., must act so as not to scare those bourgeoisies that might be willing to ally themselves with the Soviet Union to combat the German revenge-seekers and the Japanese expansionists. Since this last consideration concerned the 'chief link' in Comintern strategy, it had to, and did, take priority over all other tactical preoccupations.

The entire tactical complex that has been outlined was conceived – both on the level of the alleged objective basis on which it was grounded and on that of the party's conscious activity – as a defensive–offensive tactic. *Defensive* in that the objective dynamic of the process created its own defences against the advance of the Fascist menace and in that the party's activity in order to unite the different social forces menaced by Fascism operated on the basis of the lowest common denominator. *Offensive* because this objective–subjective dynamic intensified the contradictions and polarized the social and political forces, and because, in proportion as this new situation took shape and the correlation of forces became favourable, it enabled the party to put forward more radical aims and forms of struggle. The Seventh Congress, taking account of the situation prevailing in Europe at the time, definitely stressed the defensive aspect. Nevertheless, in Dimitrov's report as well as in other contributions, reference was made to the offensive phase.

We want unity of action by the working class so that the proletariat may grow strong in its struggle against the bourgeoisie, in order that while defending today its current interests against attacking capital, against Fascism, the proletariat may reach a position tomorrow to create the preliminary conditions for its final emancipation . . . We must tirelessly prepare the working class for a rapid change in forms and methods of struggle when there is a change in the situation. As the movement grows and the unity of the working class strengthens, we must go further, and prepare the transition from the defensive to the offensive against capital, steering toward the organization of a mass political strike.[7]

Soon after the Seventh Congress the transition to the 'offensive against capital' was to arise as a real possibility in Spain and France.

'It is necessary to know how to end a strike': 1936 in France

The reasons for the upsurge of the working-class and anti-Fascist movement in France between 1934 and 1936 have been studied in a number of political and historical works.[8] They can be summarized very schematically as the combination of three main factors. First, the effects of the economic crisis, which hit France only after a certain delay, when recovery had already begun in the USA and other countries. This delay meant that the social discontent caused by the crisis coincided, and combined, with the second factor, namely, the anti-Fascist reaction aroused in the working-class movement and in other sections of society by Hitler's coming to power. The social struggle in France became interwoven with the political struggle against the reactionary forces (in particular against the notorious 'Leagues') which incarnated the 'Fascist danger'. Thirdly, the Comintern's tactical turn provided the will to unity that existed in the most conscious sections of the working-class movement with a framework in which they could come together and organize, the German experience having shown the tragic consequences of division. The pact between the Communists and Socialists, and the trade-union unity that followed from this, stimulated the workers' confidence in their own strength and increased the role played by the working class in the country's political evolution. The workers' parties became a pole of attraction for a substantial section of the urban middle strata, hard hit by the crisis. Discontent reached its climax with the deflationary decrees of Laval. As Thorez put it: 'The 800,000 civil servants – this bulwark of the state that Marx talked about in his *Eighteenth Brumaire* – are rising; the petty bourgeoisie is losing confidence in the leadership of the parties of the big bourgeoisie.'[9] Discontent grew among the peasants too.

Confronted with this rising popular tide, the Fascist forces organized themselves and intensified their activity. One of the principal historians of this period writes: 'Gradually a polarization took place: on the right, around the "Croix de Feu"; on the left, around what, since October 1934, the Communists called the "People's Front" . . . An atmosphere of latent civil war spread through the whole country.'[10] In mid-1935, in his speech at the Seventh Congress, Thorez spoke of the prospect of a revolutionary crisis: 'The drive of the mass movement can impose a People's Front government which our party would support and in which, if necessary, it might even participate. The anti-Fascist battle would become fiercer, since the reactionary and Fascist assault would be brutal and immediate. But the People's Front and the Communist Party would have occupied new positions, which we would have to utilize to prepare for the establishment of Soviet power, the dictatorship of the proletariat.'[11] For the moment, at any rate, the French Communist Party showed no less concern than the Socialists and Radicals that the 'anti-Fascist struggle' should proceed 'in a civic spirit'. In December 1935 Thorez, Blum and Ybarnegaray (the latter speaking for the 'Croix de Feu') promised in parliament that they would dissolve their respective paramilitary organizations.[12] Let the ballot decide. And on 3 May 1936 the ballot gave victory to the People's Front.

Nevertheless, the expression 'victory of the People's Front' does not truly express the real meaning of that event. The 'bourgeois party' belonging to the 'Front' suffered a heavy defeat, losing 43 seats and being left with 116 deputies instead of 159; a considerable section of those who had previously voted for it now voted for the Communists and Socialists, while others transferred their support to the bourgeois right. The victory was a victory for the two working-class parties; and, although the Socialists became the largest group in the Chamber (increasing the number of their deputies from 97 to 146, and beating the Radicals for the first time in the history of the French parliament), the major victor was the Communist Party (72 deputies instead of 10). It was also significant that the right-wing Socialist group which had broken off from the Socialist Party lost almost half of its parliamentary representation (26 instead of 45). All this testifies to the political polarization that was occurring in the country and the radicalization not only of the working class but also of an important part of the middle strata.

While, from the standpoint of revolutionary prospects, this political polarization revealed by the elections was highly encouraging, looked at from the angle of the Franco-Soviet Pact it could seem a cause for disquiet. What would become of France's military strength if the country slid into civil war? The Moscow correspondent of *Le Temps* wrote: 'Ruling circles here show no enthusiasm ... The relative failure of the Radicals is deplored.' Litvinov, accepting with a resigned air the 'popular will', told the correspondent of the *Petit Parisien*: 'What is essential is that France should not allow her military strength to be weakened. We hope no internal troubles will favour Germany's designs.'[13] If the wish voiced by the People's Commissar for Foreign Affairs was significant, the moment at which he voiced it was no less so. It was in the first fortnight of June. The French proletariat had committed itself to 'troubles' since the end of May, without waiting for the Blum government to be formed. The strike movement, accompanied by the occupation of factories, had spread wider and wider. The history of working-class struggle in France had never known a strike movement on such a scale. And the characteristics it displayed, taken together with the political foundation that the elections had revealed, justified the recalling by some contemporaries of that famous exchange: 'So this is a revolt?' – 'No, Sire, it is a revolution.' From the very first day, indeed, the movement bore the mark that is to be found at the beginning of every genuine revolution: spontaneous initiative by the broad masses, qualitative change in its state of mind, the joining together of millions of people in one single will to put an end to a certain order of things, the overflowing of habitual frameworks ... Nearly everyone who has studied the event, or who lived through it, agrees in their diagnosis. 'From the start,' says Jacques Fauvet, 'the movement assumed a twofold revolutionary aspect, attacking both authority and property.' Annie Kriegel writes: 'The big crowds, the uncontrolled masses, the reservists of revolutionary occasions, moved into action.' And Jouhaux, who used to the full the prestige that his long patriarchate in the trade-union movement had given him, in order to put out the fire, explained while the events were in progress: 'The movement began without anyone knowing exactly how or where. We were faced with an explosion of discontent by masses who, humiliated and repressed for years and years, had been chewing on their discontent and who now, in the free atmosphere resulting from the affirmation of the people's will on 3 May, found it possible to give expression to this discontent.'[14]

In fact, nobody had decreed the general strike, and still less the occupation of the factories. Everyone was taken by surprise: the trade-union and political leaderships, the government and the employers, the right and the left alike. The working class had taken advantage of the election victory of the People's Front. It was fully aware that this had been its *own* doing, above all, and the expression of its own new strength. However, the action taken also showed how few illusions the workers entertained regarding the fulfilment of election promises. What 'exploded' on this occasion was not merely economic discontent but also the distrust of parliamentary solutions which had accumulated over many years of elections. As the historian G. Lefranc rightly points out, some of the basic attitudes of French revolutionary syndicalism reasserted themselves: lack of confidence in the state and the political parties, confidence in the effectiveness of direct action by the proletarian masses.[15] The workers had no illusions regarding the cohesion and will to reform of the coalition they had themselves elected to power. They knew where their real strength lay, and occupied the factories.

General confusion prevailed. Blum, already installed as head of a Socialist–Radical government supported by the Communist Party, admitted to the employers' representatives that the most serious aspect of the situation was that the government did not know where the movement had sprung from or where it was heading. The leaders of the CGT were no less worried. They realized that the mass of the workers had partly escaped from their control and were tending to go farther than they considered reasonable. They sought to prevent the movement from spreading to the public services. Their sole aim was to arrive as soon as possible at a negotiated settlement.[16] The Communist Party leaders took the same line. Duclos said: 'We are concerned about two things – first, to avoid any disorder, and second, to get talks going as soon as may be, with a view to a quick settlement of the conflict.' But the first agreements made between the CGT, the employers' organization and the Blum government did not succeed in putting an end to the movement, even though *l'Humanité* proclaimed, over a whole page: 'IT'S VICTORY!'[17] By 11 June the number of strikers reached the two million mark. In the metal-working industry, the pilot sector of the great movement, the delegates from seven hundred factories issued an ultimatum on 10 June: if the employers would not agree to their demands, they would call for the nationalization of the enterprises, which would be operated by the technicians and workers engaged in them. On 11 June the rumour spread that the metal-workers were going to leave the factories and march in converging columns towards the centre of Paris. That same day, Thorez assembled the Communists of the Paris region and ordered them to use all their influence to bring the strike to an end: 'While it is important to lead well a movement for economic demands,' he said, 'it is also necessary to know how to end it. There is at present no question of taking power. Everyone knows that our aim remains unchangeably the establishment of a French republic of councils of workers, peasants and soldiers. But that is not something for this evening, or even for tomorrow morning.'

Marceau Pivert, leader of the revolutionary tendency in the Socialist Party, had just written in *Le Populaire*: 'Now everything is possible for those who are bold enough.' The slogan of the 'new Jacobins', however, was not boldness but caution. In his address to the Communists of Paris, Thorez replied to Pivert: 'No, everything is not possible at present.' And he called on the Communist militants to 'react against the leftist tendencies in the movement.' Next day, a meeting of the metal-workers, among whom the Communist Party had a lot of influence, agreed to sign a pact with the employers and go back to work. The party put forward the slogan: 'The People's Front is not the revolution.'[18] And indeed it was something different: in the France of June 1936 it proved to be a brake on the revolution, *after* having helped to open the sluice-gates.

In order to get the waters back into their bed what was most important was to propagate confidence among the masses in the policy that the leaders of the People's Front were going to pursue. The workers were well aware of what to expect from the Radicals, and their mere presence in the new coalition was in itself an obvious reason for mistrust. Blum's programme, as his chief political secretary has recently recalled, consisted in 'injecting into a democratic capitalist society like that of France the maximum dose of reform'.[19] Many workers appreciated more or less clearly that this 'maximum' would remain a 'minimum', and this was why, after voting for Blum because it was necessary to defeat reaction at the ballot-box, they 'repudiated' him by going on strike and occupying the factories without obtaining his permission. The third element in the coalition was the Communist Party. Despite the general lack of confidence on the part of the proletariat towards the new electoral-parliamentary grouping, a substantial section of the working class, which was looking for a revolutionary way out of the situation, was ready to trust the Communist Party – the only party not yet compromised by parliamentary combinations, the party which for fifteen years had untiringly accused the reformists of neglecting or betraying opportunities for revolution, and which appeared the authorized representative of the only proletarian revolution that had so far succeeded. This was why a new generation of revolutionaries came forward at this time to swell the party's ranks. Similarly, the influence of the Communist trade-union leaders grew rapidly within the CGT, now reunited. A considerable section of the working class voted for Communist candidates.[20]

But the fact of greatest importance was this: at the same time as the old revolutionary–syndicalist tendency revived to some extent, as I have mentioned, and that a comparatively important revolutionary tendency showed itself in the party of reformist socialism, the 'Marxist–Leninist' party became the leading party of the French proletariat. The way the situation would evolve now depended upon this party. It could – and in fact did – put in the scale the full weight of its 'revolutionary' prestige so as to canalize the spontaneous movement towards a governmental and reformist outcome; or it could work to develop the revolutionary potentialities that the situation held within it. The second of these solutions did not necessarily imply attempting an *immediate* seizure of power. Approaching the problem in this way, as Thorez did in his 11 June speech, was merely a trick to avoid facing the real question. This related to the two ways in which the People's Front tactic could be conceived.

The first of these was set out in the passage already quoted from Dimitrov's report to the Seventh Congress: 'As the movement grows and the unity of the working class strengthens, we must go further, and prepare the transition from the defensive to the offensive against capital, steering towards the organization of a mass political strike.' In the actual conditions that had arisen in France in June 1936 this meant raising the political and organizational level of the mass movement, linking the economic and trade-union demands put forward by it with other, more advanced political and economic aims, transforming the passive occupation of the factories into an 'active' one, taking advantage of the opportunities offered by this occupation to create forms of mass organization – workers' committees, workers' councils – which, in combination with the traditional trade-union and political forms of the French working class, would constitute the embryo of a new ruling authority.[21] Only in so far as a political process like this was begun would it be possible to answer the question whether the crisis of French society was such as to make possible a revolutionary outcome, or if it could go no further than more or less radical reforms within the framework of capitalism.

The other way of 'understanding' the People's Front tactic consisted in holding the mass movement back so that it did not go beyond the limits tolerable to the bourgeois or reformist wing of the 'Front'. As we have already shown, *this* line 'coexisted' with the first-mentioned in the theses of the Seventh Congress, and was in reality the predominant one of the two. Thorez carried it to caricatural extremes when he tried to show that the necessary conditions were not present for orienting the movement of May–June 1936 towards more revolutionary aims: 'We have not yet behind us, with us, as determined as we are to go through to the end, the whole population of the countryside. We should even run the risk, in certain cases, of losing some of the sympathy we enjoy at present among the strata of the petty-bourgeoisie and peasantry.'[22]

It hardly needs saying that if Lenin had waited until the *whole* of Russia's peasantry had been as determined as the Bolsheviks to carry out the socialist revolution, if he had waited until the openly announced prospect of a proletarian revolution would not deprive the Bolsheviks of the sympathy of certain groups of the petty-bourgeoisie and peasantry, there would have been no October revolution. The Bolsheviks were supported by a part of the peasantry, who were not fighting consciously for a *socialist* revolution, but for peace and land. And it is well known that the 'middle strata' put the Bolsheviks in the minority in the Constituent Assembly. In the France of 1936 there was no question of the important discontented and radicalized section of the 'middle strata' of town and country (whose existence Thorez did not deny in his speech of 11 June) being ready to follow the workers into an abstract 'socialist revolution', and still less of transplanting to France the Soviet one-party system. But this section could have gone along with the workers in fighting for a series of radical political and economic measures such as the timid programme of the People's Front did not include. (The attitude of a revolutionary party towards this programme could not be the same after as it had been before the 'social explosion' of May–June.)[23] For this to happen, of course, it was essential that the proletariat should not stop half-way. As the experience of all proletarian revolutions has shown, the masses of the petty-bourgeoisie of town and country, hesitant by nature, cannot be 'more royalist than the King' – they cannot bring themselves to march along the road of revolution unless they see the proletariat doing this in a way that demonstrates convincingly its strength and resolution.

The extreme weakness of Thorez's argument was due to the fact that the essential reason for the line taken by the party was not frankly set forth and analysed. It was only hinted at, like one of those shameful diseases that can only be spoken about in allusions: 'The present situation, due to the egoism and obstinacy of the employers,' wrote Vaillant-Couturier in *L'Humanité* of 6 June, 'cannot be protracted without danger to the security of the people of France.' And about the same time, Marcel Gitton, who was then one of the party's principal leaders, declared: 'We regard as unacceptable a policy which, in face of the Hitlerite menace, would risk putting the security of France at stake.'[24] 'What is essential is that France should not allow her military strength to be weakened. We hope no internal troubles will favour Germany's designs,' Litvinov had told a French journalist, as I have already mentioned.

This was where the heart of the problem lay. It would have been possible to argue indefinitely about what percentage of peasants or civil servants were ready to march alongside the working class in a revolutionary development of the movement of May–June, and this question could only have been settled in action; but there could be no doubt at all that, in the France of 1936, such a development must mean a bitter struggle in which the use of armed force, and even civil war, were not out of the question. What would become, if that should happen, of the 'military strength' of France, and the Franco-Soviet pact? There was, of course, a revolutionary answer to this question. Proletarian France would be a more reliable and more powerful ally for the USSR than bourgeois France. But suppose the revolutionary movement suffered defeat? Nobody could guarantee that it would win. The Jacobins of 1789 first stormed the Bastille and then made their stand at Valmy. Those of 1936 thought first of Sedan, and then decided that 'it is necessary to know how to end a strike'.

The basis of the French Communist Party's attitude became perfectly clear when, following the 'social explosion' in France, came the 'explosion' in Spain. The history, *War and Revolution in Spain*, written by an official commission of the Spanish Communist Party under the chairmanship of Dolores Ibarruri, quotes from Colette Audry's book on Blum a passage from a letter sent by the French Socialist leader to friends in the USA, dated 9 July 1942, in which Blum explains that giving aid to the Spanish Republic would have worsened the internal situation in France, and adds: 'As soon as the situation had become at all dangerously strained, we should have had in France something similar to Franco's *coup*. Before any foreign war had begun, France would have experienced a civil war, and one in which there was little chance of success for the Republic.' Directly after reproducing this statement by Blum, the Spanish Communist Party's historians write: 'Even though her book is an apologia for Blum, Colette Audry admits that he distorts reality here, since the French generals were incapable of establishing a reactionary regime, presided over by Pétain, until after the invasion of the German armoured divisions and the entry of the Hitlerites into Paris ... Under the conditions of 1936 a Fascist *coup* in France was doomed to failure. And yet this explanation that Blum gives of his policy of "nonintervention", as being due to fear of deepening the social and political conflict in France, does in a way bear some relation to reality.' Later on, the book reproduces the following commentary by Colette Audry: 'The Socialist leader of the government of the French People's Front *held in his hands the fate of two proletariats,* and it would have been enough for him to allow a bourgeois commercial treaty signed by his predecessors to be honoured, and advantage taken of a common frontier, *in order to save the one proletariat and strengthen the other.* Such an opportunity does not come twice in a lifetime.' The emphasis is provided by the Spanish Communists, who add: 'Here we touch the heart of the matter. What Blum wanted to avoid, what he feared, was that the revolutionary movement of the proletariat might be strengthened and that the People's Front might triumph completely not only in Spain but also in France.'[25]

It is worth noting once more the important role played by Blum in the betrayal of the Spanish Republic. It is also interesting to show that the chief reason for his policy was not the danger of war, as he alleged in his public statements in 1936 and 1937. By agreeing with Colette Audry in her view that a Fascist *coup* in France in 1936 was doomed to defeat, the leadership of the Spanish Communist Party makes a judgement of very great significance, for it amounts to admitting that there were in France conditions that were very favourable to a 'deepening of the social and political struggle' and a victorious outcome to the onward sweep of the 'revolutionary movement of the proletariat'. But the history written by the commission of the Spanish Communist Party is incomplete. Blum was not alone in fearing a 'deepening of the social and political struggle in France', and the possibility of civil war. Nor was he alone in invoking the bogey of Hitler in order to preach class peace in France. While Blum voiced his fears in a private letter of 1942, Maurice Thorez voiced his publicly on 25 July 1936: 'We must think what would become of our country,' he said on that day, 'if the Fascist gangs in the service of capital were to succeed in provoking, here as well, disorder and civil war, especially at a moment when besides the internal reasons that dictate calm and tranquillity [*sic*] there are also imperative necessities of an external order. Everyone realizes that a France weakened by civil war would soon fall a prey to Hitler.'[26] In these significant lines we see the underlying motivation of the policy followed by the French Communist leadership when faced, first, with the pre-revolutionary situation that was created in France in May–June, and then with the revolutionary retort made by the Spanish workers to the military *coup* in July. This policy was not, of course, decided by the French Communist leaders alone: it was the policy of the Comintern, the policy of Stalin.

The French Communist Party was to organize big campaigns, meetings, demonstrations and collections for 'Aid to Republican Spain', to denounce a thousand times the policy of 'non-intervention'. Its deputies were to make speeches and put down motions in parliament, and the party leaders were to express themselves with strong feeling, as when Thorez said:

Oh, I can no longer think of Spain, of the heroic battles being fought there, which are increasingly unequal as regards the material at the disposal of the Spanish Republicans, without a flush of shame reddening my brow! It is the anguish and shame of a proletarian loyal to working-class internationalism. The anguish and shame of a republican loyal to the traditions of the French people. The anguish and shame of a Frenchman who is concerned about the future of his country, threatened from within and from without by the bloody wave of Fascism.[27]

The French Communist Party was to help in the clandestine despatch of arms to the Spanish Republicans, and, above all, thousands of French Communists were to fight bravely in the ranks of the International Brigades. In short, the French Communist Party was to do everything to help the struggle of the Spanish proletariat *except* what would have tipped the balance decisively in favour of the revolution in Spain – to pursue a revolutionary policy in France.

It is not possible here to go into all the details of the 'other' policy, which, under the mask of opposition, connived at Blum's 'non-intervention' – the policy which, instead of promoting the revolutionary struggle in France, aimed at *union sacrée* under the banner of 'the Front of all Frenchmen', going so far as to agree to Blum's (abortive) suggestion in January 1938 that it should enter a government alongside Paul Reynaud.[28] I shall limit myself to mentioning that the decisive step towards this policy was taken when the leadership of the French Communist Party adopted the attitude I have described towards the explosion of May–June 1936. Not only did this line already contain all the factors that were to determine the subsequent course of the party's policy – it also helped to set in motion a politico-social process in which the objective possibilities that existed in 1936 for finding a democratic and proletarian way out of the French situation shrank ever smaller and smaller. Once the 'social explosion' had been damped down, the capitalists set about recovering with one hand what they had been obliged to yield with the other. A rise in prices followed the increase in wages. The shameful devaluation of the franc carried out by the Blum government (which had pledged itself not to devalue) helped to unload the burden of the economic crisis on to the shoulders of the workers and the middle strata. A growing proportion of the proletariat sank into passivity and scepticism once more. The petty-bourgeoisie and the peasants turned back towards the bourgeois parties. At the end of 1938 the Communist Party was again completely isolated. Its policy, ever 'broader', was producing ever narrower results. It ended by producing results exactly opposite to those desired by its highest mentors. Instead of reinforcing in France the foundations of the Franco-Soviet alliance in face of the Hitlerite danger, it culminated in . . . Munich.

On 8 September 1936 Thorez wrote in *L'Humanité:* 'In another period, without allowing itself to be affected by the demagogy of certain elements, the Communist Party had the courage to proclaim: it is necessary to know how to end a strike . . . Today we say, with resolution: it is necessary to end the blockade!' But the blockade of the Spanish Republic could not be broken, nor Munich avoided, nor the national catastrophe of 1940 prevented, otherwise than by revolutionary action of the French proletariat. And the impetus that could have led to such action was broken off short the day that the leader of the Communist Party declared it was necessary to end not a 'strike' but the mightiest movement of the French working class since the Commune.

The Untimely Revolution: Spain, 1936–9

The beginning of the Spanish revolution – the only revolution to occur in Europe during the Comintern's existence, apart from the ephemeral Soviet Republic in Hungary in 1919 – took the leaders of the 'world party' by surprise. In February 1930, Manuilsky, in a report to the ECCI, spoke of the 'enormous perspectives' that were opening up for 'the growth of the present revolutionary advance' which he saw taking place both in the developed capitalist countries and the colonial countries, into a 'revolutionary situation'. This revolutionary progress in the advanced capitalist countries had no existence outside the imagination of Stalin's representative in the Comintern: but shortly before this meeting of the ECCI the dictatorship of Primo de Rivera had fallen, and some of the delegates present at the meeting asked about the significance to be attributed to this event. Manuilsky replied: 'It is not Spain which decides the fate of the world proletarian revolution ... An individual partial strike may have more meaning for the international working class than this kind of "revolution" of the Spanish type, which takes place without the leading part being played by the Communist Party and the proletariat.'[29] But this revolution 'of the Spanish type' stubbornly persisted in advancing, even though it found no place in Manuilsky's forecasts and despite the almost complete absence from it of the party whose 'leading' role had been consecrated by history. At the time of the fall of the monarchy, in April 1931, the Spanish section of the Comintern had hardly 800 members.

Even more serious than its small size was its lack of real influence among the proletariat and its theoretical weakness.[30] This last feature was common to the whole labour movement in Spain. Neither the Socialists nor the Anarcho–Syndicalists – the two great tendencies that had divided the labour movement between them since the nineteenth century – had any clear notions about the revolutionary process begun in 1930–31. The former thought it was a purely bourgeois revolution, and clung to their 'minimum programme'. For them, the leadership of the Republic must be assumed by the bourgeois republican parties. All that the Socialist Party could do was to collaborate loyally with them in carrying out a programme of reforms that would also be of benefit to the working class. They were ready, in short, to follow in the footprints of European Social Democracy. The Anarcho–Syndicalists started from the same standpoint, namely that the revolution was purely bourgeois, but drew a quite different practical conclusion: they would in no way collaborate with the Republic born on 14 April 1931. It was necessary to press forward to the social revolution and the establishment of 'libertarian Communism'. The Communists, being for the first few months without clear guidance from Moscow, improvised in the light of the ultra-left general line being followed by the Comintern at this period. This position can be summed up in these slogans: 'Down with the bourgeois republic of the capitalists, generals and clergy! For a republic of Soviets of workers, soldiers and peasants!' The first slogan, very Spanish, had Anarcho–Syndicalist resonances. The second, in the given conditions, was utterly exotic and abstract.[31]

Actually, nobody in Moscow or in Madrid knew what was going to happen. Soon after its proclamation the 'republic of the clergy' was to resemble a crematorium of churches, and the generals were to conspire against the 'republic of the generals'. In an effort to clarify the situation, the Constitution proclaimed that the republic was a state of 'workers of all classes'. But the first-class 'workers' hastened to send their capital abroad, while those of the third class went on strike and occupied the estates of the landlords, with the avowed aim of reducing the republic to one class. The republican Constitution defined Spain as an 'integral state', but allowed for 'autonomy', and the peripheral nationalities, subjected since the sixteenth century to Castilian centralism, strove to break up this 'integral state' into three or four separate pieces. Azaña announced the surprising news that Spain had 'ceased to be Catholic', while parliament, which had appointed Azaña prime minister, elected the most Catholic Alcala Zamora to the post of President of the Republic. Araquistain declared firmly that 'no people is so radically [*sic*] socialistic as the Spanish people', while Unamuno exalted Spanish 'individualism'. Thus, when hardly born, the Republic presented many different images, but Ortega y Gasset, always profound, declared: 'It is necessary to alter the Republic's image.' All the cultivated ladies admired the philosopher's profundity, while the Civil Guard started 'altering' the image by machine-gunning the peasants. In short, the revolution 'of the Spanish type' offered a rather confused picture, but the Comintern hastened to classify it as belonging to the type of 'bourgeois-democratic' revolutions that fully conformed to the theory which Lenin had worked out for . . . Russia at the beginning of the century.

According to this theory – or, more precisely, to the dogmatic form of it produced by the Comintern – the Spanish revolution required a strategy of two stages, the schema of which should here be recalled. The first of these stages would see dealt with the problems left 'pending' by the unfinished bourgeois revolution; but, as the bourgeoisie was no longer revolutionary, it was the proletariat that must play the leading role in carrying out the liquidation of 'feudal survivals' (latifundia, domination by the Church, military castes, aristocracy, oppression of national minorities, etc.). Only when these problems had been disposed of could the proletariat go over to the attack on capitalist private ownership of the means of production – that is, pass from the 'bourgeois-democratic stage' to the 'socialist' stage, establishing the dictatorship of the proletariat. Down to the middle of 1934 this strategy was applied by the Comintern in Spain in the ultra-sectarian tactical form corresponding to the period of 'social Fascism'. During the elections to the legislature in November 1933, for instance, the platform of the PCE called for struggle for 'soviet Spain' and declared that 'the parties of bourgeois democracy, together with the Socialists . . . were and still are the centre of counter-revolution . . . Therefore' the document went on, 'in order to overcome fascism it is necessary to fight relentlessly against so-called bourgeois democracy, which foments and stimulates it.'[32] Fortunately, the turn made by the Comintern in the summer of 1934 enabled the PCE to begin following a policy that was closer to Spanish reality. The party joined the Workers' Alliances and entered into relations with the Socialist Party. Its substantial participation in the Asturias rising of October 1934 increased its revolutionary prestige. In April 1935, following the French example, the PCE proposed the creation of a 'people's anti-Fascist bloc'. The idea proved successful despite the resistance of the Socialist left wing, led by Largo Caballero, and of the Anarcho-Syndicalists, for, after the revolt in the Asturias, severe repression was imposed on the whole country, and the reactionary forces were preparing to introduce a dictatorship, the victims of which would not have been the workers' organizations alone, but also the 'left' republican parties. Anti-Fascist unity was timely, in order to erect an effective defensive front against the menace of dictatorship and to create more favourable conditions for a popular counter-offensive. It is not very likely, however, that it would have taken shape without the election situation of February 1936. The possibility of securing, in the event of a victory at the polls for the labour-republican bloc, an amnesty for political prisoners and the annulment of other repressive measures helped the 'Caballerists' to make up their minds and rendered possible the participation of the PSOE and the UGT in the People's Front. It was this, too, that decided a large proportion of the Anarcho–Syndicalist masses to vote for the People's Front candidates.[33]

For the Comintern, however, the People's Front policy had quite a different scope. 'A broad anti-Fascist People's Front,' Togliatti was to say later on, 'represents the peculiar form of the development of the Spanish revolution at the present stage,' that is, the 'bourgeois-democratic' stage.[34] The fundamental conception of the character and itinerary of the Spanish revolution to which I referred earlier remained the same; but the 'original form' taken by its development affected this conception in what could be called a 'moderating' way, if events had not revealed the illusory character of this 'moderation'. It tended, first, to accord greater importance to the role that the social and political forces of the petty-bourgeoisie, and even of some groups of the bourgeoisie (especially in the peripheral nationalities) could play in the unavoidable bourgeois-democratic stage of the revolution. The first concrete expression of this 'moderating' tendency was the election programme of the People's Front (which became the government's programme after the victory at the polls): this went no further than the traditional programmes of petty-bourgeois Republicanism. It contained no effective solution for the problems of the current 'stage'. The land question, the most important of all, remained in the air. The PCE undertook to respect absolutely the compromise arrived at, which meant sub-dividing the famous 'stage' into two parts – the first, confined to carrying out the programme mentioned, in which the party would support the government (formed exclusively by the petty-bourgeois and bourgeois Republican parties) which had been entrusted with the application of the said programme; and the second, in which the party would go forward along with all the forces that were ready to carry through the bourgeois-democratic revolution 'to the end'. Only after this 'end' was reached could the hour strike for the proletarian revolution.[35]

In contrast to the simplistic 'direct action' approach of the Anarcho–Syndicalists and the vagueness of the Caballerists' tactics, the strategic and tactical plan of the 'Spanish experts' of the Comintern seemed a model of method: clear distinction between phases and stages, concentration of forces against the main enemy in each of these, listing of the corresponding objectives in an order of increasing radicalism, etc. The PCE kept reaffirming that it did not renounce any of its revolutionary aims and that the end of the journey was still the dictatorship of the proletariat, on the Soviet model. At first glance, the plan seemed perfect. Actually, however, it had a major weakness, namely that it ran counter to the profound dynamic of the Spanish revolution. The latter had, indeed, travelled a long way since 1930–31. An extreme polarization of social and political forces had taken place. The main groups of the bourgeoisie, including most of the middle bourgeoisie and large sections of the petty-bourgeoisie of town and country – basically, those who exploited wage-labour – formed a *de facto* bloc with the landowning aristocracy, the ecclesiastical and military castes and the Fascist groups. It was certainly a heterogeneous bloc, not only in social composition but also in political tendencies, but it had a common denominator – fear of the advancing revolution. It was united by the idea that, in the face of this danger, the only way to save property, order, the family, religion, the fatherland and the other 'eternal values' was to return to a strong, dictatorial regime. And class instinct, even where there was no lucid grasp of the objective situation, did not deceive these social groups, for the proletariat had indeed gone over to extreme revolutionary positions. Deeply disappointed by the parliamentary republic of 14 April 1931 and by the liberal politicians, the proletariat no longer had confidence in anything but its own class organizations, and believed neither in 'minimum programmes' nor in half-measures. It could be said, without exaggeration, that the Spanish workers' 'minimum programme' was the social revolution. There might be all sorts of confusion among them – ideological, political and tactical – but one fixed idea dominated their minds: the capitalists and landowners must be expropriated, without further delay, and not only the big ones but also the medium and even the 'little' ones. (It must not be forgotten that, owing to the economic structure of the Spain of that time, a large part of the industrial and agricultural proletariat were exploited by medium and 'little' employers.)

This was the state of mind in 1936 not only of the Anarcho–Syndicalist masses but also of those Socialists who hailed Largo Caballero as the 'Spanish Lenin'. Stimulated by the revolutionary atmosphere that prevailed in the country, and attracted by the resolution that the proletariat displayed, other social strata also took up radical attitudes: the great mass of the poor peasants, semi-day-labourers, and some of the small peasants who cultivated their wretched bit of land without hired labour; important sections of the office-workers, civil servants, members of the liberal professions, etc., in other words the non-exploiting middle strata; and a substantial element of the student youth and the intellectuals. These groups had also been disappointed by the liberal–Republican politicians.

Though the metaphor of the volcano, so much used to describe socio-political situations, is often employed in a very loose way, in the Spain of 1936 it was rigorously appropriate. The election victory of the People's Front had hardly become known when the volcano began to erupt. And then, very soon, there became apparent the groundlessness of the 'sub-stage' foreseen by the Comintern's strategic-tactical plan and applied by the PCE. The petty-bourgeois and bourgeois-Republican parties which made up the government demonstrated immediately that they had remained themselves. Their policy was exactly the same as that of the period 1931–3, which had filled the people with disappointment and opened the way to the reactionary counter-offensive. The masses, however, *had* changed, and, as the Soviet historian Maidanik writes,

having confidence henceforth only in their own strength, they took control of the streets and, without waiting for the government's decisions, began to implement the People's Front programme from below, using revolutionary methods ... They released political prisoners, they compelled employers to re-engage workers they had dismissed for political reasons, and they began, in March 1936, to take over the land. In the middle of the same month began a wave of strikes caused by hunger, unemployment and Fascist provocation. The strike movement grew from month to month. Factories and workshops, mines and building-sites were paralysed, businesses closed down. In June and July an average of between ten and twenty strikes every day was recorded. There were days when the number of strikers amounted to 400,000 or 450,000. And 95 per cent of the strikes that took place between February and July 1936 were won by the workers. Great workers' demonstrations marched through the streets, demanding bread, work, the suppression of Fascism and total victory for the revolution. The first collective enterprises were set up. Meetings of tens of thousands took place, at which workers applauded with enthusiasm speakers who announced that the end of capitalism was at hand and called on them to do as they did in Russia. From strikes the workers escalated to occupation of enterprises that their owners had closed down. Their occupation of the streets, of enterprises and estates, and their ceaseless strikes urged the proletariat of towns and country on towards the highest forms of political struggle.

Maidanik's eloquent and truthful account is confirmed by all historians of the period. But what had this revolutionary explosion to do with implementing the People's Front programme? That did not provide for the occupation of estates or factories, or for the abolition of capitalism, but, on the contrary, sought to preserve private property at every level. Maidanik felt obliged, no doubt, to reconcile the actual course of events with 'proof' that the Comintern's policy was sound.[36]

Between February and July 1936 a *de facto* state of 'triple power' was established in Spain: the power of the legal government, which was actually very weak; the power of the workers, their parties and unions, which was manifested openly in the way I have described; and, finally, the power of the counter-revolutionaries, which, while outwardly expressed in aggressive speeches by their representatives in Parliament, in economic sabotage and in the activities of the Fascist storm-troops, operated above all in secret, in the barracks, preparing the military putsch. It was an open secret, though, for everyone knew that the Generals were conspiring, and their plans were publicly denounced in parliament and at meetings. Whoever studies those crucial months in the Spain of 1936 cannot but ask himself: why did the workers' parties and organizations not act in a concerted and determined way to nip the military rebellion in the bud and go forward resolutely along the road of revolution? The reply given by the proletariat to the rebellion when it came, crushing it over the greater part of the country, despite the advantage of surprise and initiative held by the rebels, showed how much in favour of the people was the balance of forces. Why did the workers' parties and unions not take the initiative? A quick look at their fundamental political positions will enable us, if not entirely to clear up this problem, at least to see what their vital motives were.

In the period that concerns us, the reformists were definitely in the minority in the Socialist Party and the UGT, although they retained the leadership of the party owing to the clever manoeuvres of the official machine. Under Indalecio Prieto, they stood for participation in the government in order to collaborate with the Republican parties in a new edition of the policy of the years 1931–3: a fight on two fronts, against reaction and against revolution. But the firm opposition put up by the majority of the local organizations of the party prevented them from practising this sort of role.[37]

The bulk of the workers belonging to the UGT, like the majority of the Socialist militants, supported the left-wing tendency led by Largo Caballero. The Caballerists were, in fact, an independent party which stood for the socialist revolution as an immediate objective, criticizing the idea of an intermediate (bourgeois-democratic, anti-Fascist) stage which was maintained by the Communists. We must go forward, they said, to direct establishment of the dictatorship of the proletariat. They did not define very clearly what the structure of this 'dictatorship of the proletariat' would be, but they were definite that it should be led by the Socialist Party, as the chief party of the Spanish working class. However, they favoured union with the Communists in order to form a single Marxist party. They also advocated merging the two great trade-union groupings, the UGT and the CNT. 'Caballerism' expressed the revolutionary radicalization of the bulk of the industrial and agricultural proletariat, grouped under the old flag of Spanish socialism – their will to finish once for all with the rule of the capitalists and landlords. Its main weakness lay in the lack of an effective tactic for the struggle for power. The Caballerists hoped that sheer attrition and the failure of the Republican government would cause the state power to fall into their hands like a ripe fruit. Furthermore, they underestimated the danger of counter-revolution.[38]

The other great traditional current in the Spanish labour movement, organized in the trade unions of the CNT, was equally radical in its revolutionary attitude. But its doctrinal basis made it very difficult to reach an agreement with the Marxist parties, and even with the trade unions of the Marxist tendency, those of the UGT. The continual repression to which the Spanish Anarcho–Syndicalists had been subjected by Republican governments with Socialist members had intensified their distrust not merely towards political parties in general but also towards the workers' parties. The idea of a state of the dictatorship of the proletariat filled the Anarcho–Syndicalists with almost as much hostility as that of the bourgeois state. In relation to the latter, moreover, they made in practice no distinction between parliamentary democracy and Fascism. They also underestimated the Fascist danger no less than the Caballerists did, though for other reasons. The way the Soviet state had evolved, the fate suffered by the Anarchists over there, and the reduction of the Soviet trade unions to the role of a bureaucratic instrument of the state all contributed to no small extent to reinforcing the apolitical and anti-state ideas of the Spanish Anarcho–Syndicalists, and especially of their leaders. Nevertheless, their experience of the failure of their previous attempts at revolution, and their recognition that the UGT was ceasing to be reformist and becoming revolutionary, brought about an important change within the CNT. Their Congress held in May 1936 offered to sign a 'revolutionary pact' with the UGT, so as to 'destroy completely the political and social order that at present rules the life of Spain' – leaving the problem of how to organize the new order 'to the free choice of the freely united workers'. The Congress drew up, all the same, a very detailed plan of the structure and working of the 'libertarian Communist' society that was to emerge from the revolution. And the CNT continued to be against any alliance with the workers' political parties.[39]

Within the setting of the strategic and tactical plan already described, the PCE advocated trade-union unity between the UGT and CNT, but on grounds quite different from those of the CNT. In the first place, for them there was no question of making a revolution, but rather of defending and consolidating the Republican regime, exercising pressure on the Republican government so as to make it apply the People's Front programme. In the second place, leadership of the united activity of the proletariat was to be undertaken by the workers' parties and not by the trade unions. The party emphasized especially the need to develop the unity in action already established with the Socialist Party, and urged that the two parties be united into a single Marxist–Leninist party. The PCE's proposals for unity, at all levels and in all fields, constituted this party's strong point, since they obviously corresponded to the pressing needs of the objective situation, especially to the threat of a counter-revolutionary *coup*, the seriousness of which was appreciated by the PCE more clearly than by the other organizations. At the same time, however, the content of these unity proposals contradicted some essential aspects of the objective situation. The real choice, in fact, lay not between the establishment of a counter-revolutionary dictatorship and the consolidation of the bourgeois parliamentary republic, but between a counter-revolutionary dictatorship and a proletarian revolution – if only because the sole force capable of preventing the counter-revolutionary dictatorship had not the slightest intention of going on to give its support to a bourgeois republic. (This was the fundamental difference between the situation in Spain and that in pre-Fascist Germany, where the majority of the proletariat had been ideologically and organically integrated into bourgeois democracy.) By stressing the urgency of united action *on the basis of the first alternative* the PCE produced a sympathetic response in the minority, reformist wing of the Socialist Party, but one of reticence, and even open disagreement, among the Caballerist Socialists, as well, of course, as open hostility on the part of the Anarcho-Syndicalists. The Caballerists and Anarcho-Syndicalists committed a serious mistake in underestimating the Fascist danger and not taking the initiative regardless of any doctrinal and tactical disagreements, for resolute and concerted action against it. What was of vital significance in their mistake, however, was not that they underestimated this danger as a threat to the parliamentary Republic, but that they did not grasp its seriousness as a threat to the proletarian revolution itself. By not putting *this* aspect of the problem in the forefront the PCE certainly failed to help the Caballerists and Anarcho–Syndicalists to perceive their error. Unintentionally, indeed, the party helped rather to strengthen them in this mistaken attitude. The possibility of nipping the military plot in the bud was so closely linked in those months with the proletarian revolution that the only way of achieving this end would have been to remove the petty-bourgeois Republican government (whose passivity, and even complicity, enabled the revolt to be prepared), so as to instal a government that would allow the revolutionary workers to take the bull by the horns.

Between February and July the Spanish revolution entered a situation that closely resembled that in Russia on the eve of the October days. Either the revolutionary proletariat would take the initiative or else the counter-revolution would. Casares Quiroga was a perfect Kerensky, but Spain had no Lenin. Instructors from the Comintern, however, were there in substantial numbers. Genuine revolutionaries like José Diaz and Pedro Checa, and people's tribunes like Dolores Ibarruri lacked the theoretical grounding needed to oppose the People's Front schemas which the Comintern imported into Spain from France. (It was the same with us Communists as with the Liberals of the Iberian Peninsula in the nineteenth century: we had no ideas of our own, based on analysis of Spanish society. Instead of adapting Marxism to the distinctive features of the Spanish revolution, we tried to adapt the Spanish revolution to the particular form of Marxism that had served for the Russian revolution. In 1936 we welcomed the People's Front, as presented by Thorez or by Togliatti, as the 'peculiar form' of the Spanish revolution, until the time should arrive for it to assume the 'Soviet form'.)

Throughout the existence of the Comintern, no Communist Party ever had a better opportunity than was now offered to the PCE to unite with the left wing of Social Democracy in a single Marxist party. Such a unification had in fact been possible since the end of 1934. The left-wing Socialists went over to clearly revolutionary Marxist positions and favoured unification. Their line was, of course, open to question on a number of points, and not all of their leaders always acted from the purest of motives. With some, including, no doubt, Largo Caballero himself, calculations of party advantage and strivings for hegemony obviously played a part. But the way in which the Comintern looked on this matter was not exempt from the same faults. It seemed paradoxical enough, given the role played by the Communist Party in the dictatorship of the Soviet proletariat, that one of the principal reproaches addressed to the Caballerists by the PCE was their claim to be the leading force in the dictatorship of the proletariat in Spain. The really insurmountable obstacle, however, was that the Comintern was quite sure that it possessed the absolute truth of Marxism and was alone obligatory, in its essential features, for all countries; that the 'Marxist–Leninist', party must be organized and must operate in conformity with the model created by the Comintern; that the theory of the Spanish revolution worked out by the Comintern was the only correct one; that the People's Front policy was no less suitable for Spain than for Italy or France; that a Marxist–Leninist party must look upon Trotskyism as the most disgusting of heresies and treat as above criticism the type of socialism being built in the USSR; etc. Even if the leaders of the Socialist left had all been little angels of revolution (and they were not), they clearly could not have accepted unification on those foundations. It was definitely possible, between 1934 and 1936, to form a big revolutionary party of the Spanish proletariat – but only on the basis of an open form of Marxism. Of course the Comintern could not contemplate such an approach without ceasing to be the Comintern. This is one of the heaviest historical responsibilities it bears, for the formation of such a party in good time would have considerably increased the chances of victory for the Spanish revolution, and might thereby have altered the course of events throughout Europe.[40]

The July days revealed the point to which the proletarian revolution had 'matured' in Spain, and how favourable to it was the balance of forces. Although the counter-revolutionary putsch enjoyed the advantages of having the choice of moment, of conforming to a general plan and being directed by a centralized general staff, and of being able to rely on the principal armed forces of the state, it was nevertheless defeated over most of Spain, in the regions that were decisive economically and in terms of population, by the resolute counter-attack of the proletarian forces, despite their dispersed order and lack of any plan or co-ordinated leadership on the national level (or even, in most cases, on the local level). No doubt the workers' organizations played a fundamental role, but the spontaneous *élan* that arose from the depths of the proletarian masses in town and country was no less decisive. The republican state collapsed like a sandcastle, and the passive, vacillating, and even openly capitulating behaviour of the petty-bourgeois parties contributed to the few successes that the counter-revolutionary forces did manage to achieve. After the first few days of fighting, though the revolution had not finally conquered, the balance of forces in the country as a whole was clearly favourable to it. Had the civil war that followed been restricted to Spaniards, the ultimate outcome could hardly have been in doubt. As was bound to happen, however, the armed combat between revolution and counter-revolution in Spain became automatically transformed into an international problem.[41]

Until this moment the contradiction between the idea held by the Comintern about the nature of the Spanish revolution and its actual content had not been linked in any direct way with the requirements of Soviet foreign policy. There was doubtless an indirect connection, in so far as the general line adopted by the Seventh Congress of the Comintern, and, in particular, the French version of the People's Front policy, were strongly conditioned, as we have seen, by the European strategy of the Soviet leaders. Spain as such, however, had not yet entered Stalin's field of vision. This problem was put before him suddenly and in far from easy terms. The USSR could not dodge its duty to show active solidarity with the Spanish people in arms without risk of losing all prestige in the eyes of the world proletariat. This duty coincided, in one way, with the anti-Hitlerite line of Soviet diplomacy in this period. In another way, however, it was in contradiction with the tactical forms, so to speak, assumed by this line. For the primary object of Soviet policy was to consolidate the military alliance with France and achieve an understanding with Britain. But neither the bourgeois France of Blum nor the Conservative Britain of Baldwin and Chamberlain could tolerate a victory of the proletarian revolution in Spain. Contributing to such a victory therefore meant, for the Soviet government, breaking with those powers. The only way in which, it seemed, 'aid for Spain' could be reconciled with the objective of Soviet diplomacy was to ensure that the Spanish proletariat went no further than was acceptable to the French and British bourgeoisies. And the most that they could accept in Spain was a parliamentary republic – democratic, anti-Fascist, 'People's Front' even, as far 'to the Left' as you like, but . . . bourgeois, above all, bourgeois! It was not even certain that a solution on those lines would be acceptable to the British Conservatives; but it was the only way open to Stalin whereby he could attempt to reconcile, so far as possible, the contradictory demands with which fate, once again, had burdened him in his dual capacity of 'tried and recognized, great and wise leader' of the Communist International, as Dimitrov called him at the Seventh Congress, and no less great and wise leader of the Soviet state.[42]

Unfortunately, the Spanish proletariat had already left this 'reasonable' limit far behind. In the weeks that followed 19 July, the capitalist regime virtually ceased to exist in the Republican zone: the means of production and political power alike passed, *de facto*, into the hands of the workers' organizations. All historians of the Spanish civil war agree on this point, apart from those whose concern is not to serve historical truth but to justify the policy of Stalin and the Comintern. The latter category of 'historians' still claim that the content of the Spanish revolution never went beyond the 'bourgeois-democratic stage', for to admit the contrary would mean admitting that Stalin's policy in Spain consisted precisely in obliging the revolution to retreat. The Soviet historian I have quoted was subjected to severe criticism because he dared to contradict the official theses on this question and others equally thorny. 'It seems to me,' he wrote in his book *The Spanish Proletariat and the National Revolutionary War, 1936–1937,*

that the events of 19 July marked the beginning of a qualitatively new stage in the Spanish revolution. The activity of the proletarian masses and their subjective outlook both support this conclusion. July–August 1936 saw settled, in fact, the basic problems of the revolution, those of political power and ownership of the instruments and means of production. Local authority passed, in practice, into the hands of the armed proletariat. Also into their hands, and to a lesser extent into those of the peasants, passed all the instruments and means of production belonging to the capitalists and landowners. A large part of the bourgeoisie and of its state machine was liquidated on the territory held by the Republic. All this went beyond the limits of a bourgeois-democratic revolution.[43]

Indeed it did. But it had to be got back into those 'limits' if Soviet aid to the Spanish republic was to fit into the 'limits' of Soviet diplomacy. And the substantial team of Comintern representatives installed in Spain with the mission of supervising the work of the PCE, together with the no less substantial team of Soviet military and political advisers, set themselves with all the zeal at their command to carry through this difficult operation. It was extremely difficult, for it involved nothing less than pushing the proletarian revolution back within the bourgeois-democratic bounds from which it 'should' never have escaped. And doing that was a lot more complicated than Thorez's 'knowing how to end a strike'. One had to begin by denying the anti-bourgeois reality of the revolution, so that activity aimed at restoring bourgeois institutions might seem different from what it actually was. The Comintern, the world party of the socialist revolution, could not allow itself to advocate a rectification of the socialist image of the Spanish revolution with the same freedom that Ortega y Gasset had shown in advocating a rectification of the plebeian image of Azaña's republic. The proper forms must be respected. And, for that, it was necessary to proclaim that the Spanish revolution was 'in essence a popular, democratic, anti-Fascist movement, the principal aim of which was to defend the Republic, freedom and national sovereignty against the Fascist rebellion and the brutal intervention by the armed forces of Hitler and Mussolini'.[44] Whatever went beyond those bounds was nothing but excesses by the Caballerists, the Anarcho-Syndicalists and the masses who were insufficiently educated in Marxism–Leninism.[45]

The safeguarding of the 'essence' was accompanied by reaffirmation of principles and symbols. The Constitution of 1931, embodying the principles of bourgeois democracy, was still in force. Parliament – half the deputies of which were on the side of the rebels, and, as regards the half of the remaining half that was made up of Republican deputies, it was hard to see what they could possibly represent in the Republican zone – retained its functions. Azaña, now President of the Republic, continued at his post. The Republican state continued to be the legal authority, even if real authority was in other hands. Juridically, capitalist ownership of the means of production was not abolished, even though in practice it had been smashed. 'Never put too much trust in the stupidity of your opponents,' Talleyrand advised, and the politicians of European bourgeoisie were clearly no imbeciles. The legal façade of the Spanish Republic did not deceive them. They required real restoration of the bourgeois regime. But the facade was useful to Stalin and the Comintern for other reasons. In the first place, it enabled them to present 'aid for Spain' as aid to the legal, Republican regime, as defined by the Constitution of 1931. In the second place, it helped to justify the theoretical fiction of the 'bourgeois-democratic' character of the Spanish revolution. In the third place, it furnished an ideological, political and juridical structure that could serve to welcome and promote the methodical transformation of this fiction into reality. Clearly, this last operation, the essential one, could not be carried through without the support and collaboration of the Spanish revolutionary forces themselves, and that this would be forthcoming was extremely doubtful. However, Stalin and the Comintern had at their disposal a decisive weapon – more precisely, they had *weapons*, 'arms for Spain'.

Regardless of whether the revolution asserted its proletarian content, or retreated in order to assume a bourgeois-democratic content, as the Comintern wished, or went back to the liberal-bourgeois content dreamed of by the Azañas and Prietos, one thing was quite plain: unless the military forces of the rebel Generals and their Italian and German allies were beaten, every possible 'content' of the revolution was doomed in advance. And, to win in the military field, the revolution needed *arms*, *urgently*, together with technicians to give instruction in how to use them. It became clear very soon that these could come from nowhere but the Soviet Union. And it was equally clear that the USSR would send them only if the Spanish leaders carried out the policy considered necessary by the Soviet government in order to harmonize their aid to the Spanish Republic with Stalin's general strategy. From the first months of the civil war, all the Spanish leaders, from Azaña to Nin, understood this condition and sought to adapt themselves to it, but they did not all do this in the same way.[46]

For the PCE, of course, there was no problem, since the Soviet Union's policy, that of the Comintern, and its own all formed an indivisible whole. What was required was to apply the general line of the Seventh Congress of the Comintern. In order to overcome Fascism, the main enemy, the essential task was to ensure united action on the widest scale by all its adversaries. There was no contradiction between the international policy of the Soviet Union (alliance with the bourgeois states threatened by Nazi Germany) and the national policy of the Communist parties (alliance with the liberal groups of the bourgeoisie). Once Fascism had been beaten, the road to the socialist revolution would be open – in the case of Spain a great deal more certainly than in any other country, since the proletariat occupied a position of hegemony within the alliance. Once the war had been won, it would be possible to go over to the next stage and proceed to establish the dictatorship of the proletariat. In order to win the war, however, it was essential to retain the anti-Fascist alliance, on the national plane no less than the international, and this required that socialist aims must not be proclaimed in Spain at this stage, and 'excesses' of the revolution must be corrected. Concessions should even be made to the Republicans and reformist Socialists, so as to test whether thereby Blum could be persuaded to help the Spanish Republic. The schema seemed at first sight to be highly coherent – provided that all the interested parties agreed to play the role assigned to them. This, however, was not at all the case.

The liberals of Azaña's type and the reformist Socialists like Prieto were readiest to do what was asked of them, for this line corresponded to their own chief preoccupations of the moment: to restore the Republican state, liquidate 'extremisms', get closer to the Western democracies, etc. It was not accidental that, during the month and a half of the existence of the Giral Government (20 July–4 September), a government composed exclusively of representatives of bourgeois Republican parties, 'the constructive, unity-seeking policy of the Communist Party, which subordinated everything to the needs of the war, found an increasingly favourable response in governmental circles'. Nor was it accidental that Azaña said to foreign journalists: 'If you want to know what the situation really is, and to meet men who really know what they want, read *Mundo Obrero*.'[47] But Azaña himself knew very well what he wanted; and that was certainly not to win the war in conditions that would give hegemony to the PCE and open its road towards the dictatorship of the proletariat. As his *Memoirs* clearly show, what he aimed at was restoration of 'the Republic of 14 April', and his tactics were to make use of the Communists, in a first phase, against the Socialist left and the Anarcho-Syndicalists, so as, in a second phase, to reduce the Communists to impotence, profiting by the fact that in the first phase they would have come into conflict with the majority of the revolutionary proletariat. The lines of Prieto and of Negrin were similar, and in Azaña's *Memoirs* we see revealed the close collaboration between these three – Azaña, Prieto, Negrin – in the second stage of the war, that which opened with the fall of the government of Largo Caballero in May 1937.[48]

The Caballerists also adapted themselves to the Stalinist strategy, without, however, giving up their own ideas and aims, the chief weakness of which, as I have said, was lack of precision – ultimately, the absence of a coherent policy. Reflecting the will of the proletarian masses, they proposed to preserve the socialist content of the revolution, but in pursuit of this end they relied neither on a programme that gave precise form to this content nor on tactics that could enable them to fight effectively in favour of it in the very complex situation of the civil war. They wanted to play the leading role in the bloc of the labour movement and the Republicans, although in reality they tailed behind the PCE on some questions and behind the Anarcho-Syndicalists on others. But it was just these characteristics that made the Caballerist Socialists the ideal formation to occupy the front of the stage in the drama that was now beginning. Their revolutionary reputation, and in particular the myth of Caballero himself ('the Spanish Lenin'), together with the vagueness of their assumptions, enabled them to represent the revolution in its most general expression: not the Bolshevik revolution, and not the *libertarian* revolution, but the Revolution of the Proletariat – with capital letters and no adjective. Their largely trade-union composition made it easier for them to reach understanding with the CNT. And the fact that they had neither a coherent policy nor a well-structured organization constituted an advantage in the eyes of those who had both. For the proletariat, Largo Caballero at the head of the government meant a guarantee of revolution. For Azaña and Prieto, as for Stalin and his representatives in Spain, it could mean a guarantee that the revolution would collaborate in 'rectifying' itself and restoring the bourgeois Republican state. For the Anarcho–Syndicalists it meant the possibility of retaining the enclaves of 'libertarian Communism' created in the areas where they were preponderant. For Largo Caballero and his supporters, alliance with the Republicans signified a sort of *ruse de guerre* in order to adapt to the international conditions in which the Spanish revolution had to take place, while preserving its proletarian purity.[49]

The adaptation of the CNT and the POUM to international conditions, and in particular to the Soviet line, was hindered by reservations which were similar to those made by the Caballerists, but much more radical, since they were expressed in political positions that were better defined and much harder to reconcile with restoration of the Republican state than those of the Caballerists. The 'libertarian revolution' that the Anarcho–Syndicalists had begun to carry out in Catalonia and Aragon, and which they wanted to extend to other regions, was not only quite incompatible with restoration of the bourgeois state, it was also quite incompatible with the most elementary necessities, military and economic, of the war.[50] For the POUM the socialist character of the Spanish revolution was perfectly clear, and they called for the establishment of proletarian power. But the POUM's strength was very limited. Practically confined to Catalonia, it there came up against the hegemony of the Anarcho-Syndicalists in the chief proletarian centres, while at the same time it was the object of implacable hostility on the part of the PCE The first months of the civil war coincided with the physical extermination of the opposition in the USSR, and the POUM, like the Trotskyists, became for Stalin and the Comintern a 'fascist agency' that had to be destroyed at any cost.[51]

The whole evolution of the internal situation in the 'Republican zone' during the civil war was governed by these initial facts and the contradictions and conflicts resulting from them. It developed in two well-defined phases: first, before the fall of Largo Caballero, in May 1937, and second after that event, down to the defeat (the 'Negrin phase'). In the first phase the front formed by the Republicans, the reformist Socialists and the Communists was successful, in the main, in forcing the revolution back within bourgeois-democratic bounds and restoring the Republican state, with the regular people's army as its principal instrument. In the second phase, the front formed by the reformist Socialists and Azaña's Republicans busied itself with systematically reducing the positions held by the Communists in the state machine, especially in the army, the forces of order and the special services, as well as in the economic sectors, reducing still further the advanced content of the Republic, and . . . preparing the eventual surrender. The line or the Comintern in the Spanish revolution ended by turning against the very objective in the name of which it had been imposed, that of winning the war. And yet it was this line that had made possible the protracted and tenacious resistance put up by the Republic.

This positive effect of the Communist line resulted above all from the fact that the Comintern and the PCE grasped from the start the decisive significance of the military aspect. With the help of Soviet technicians and Communist cadres from other countries, the PCE concentrated all its energy on solving this problem. Its structures, its way of working, the training of its cadres, all this made it particularly well qualified to accomplish the task in hand. Pierre Broué admits that the Communist Party proved to be a remarkable organizing force, 'a tremendously effective weapon'.[52] The semi-military features of the Bolshevik model upon which it had been formed enabled the PCE quickly to become the *military party* of the Republic, the organizing nucleus of the army that had to be built as speedily as possible, and without which *everything* was doomed: libertarian experiments, Republican state-forum, political parties and trade unions. The most elementary common sense told the masses, whatever their political or trade-union preferences might be, that without an army, without a unified command, without discipline, without a war economy, without 'iron' unity, as the PCE put it, between front and rear, without subordinating everything to the urgent necessity of beating the enemy forces that were advancing, then all would be lost. If the membership of the PCE and of its great ally, the United Socialist Youth (JSU), increased rapidly in the first months of the war, together with its political influence and authority, this was because the proletariat saw the Communists not as 'more revolutionary' than the Caballerists or the Anarcho–Syndicalists but as more clear-sighted and better able to deal with the crucial problem of the moment.

The prestige that the USSR acquired by the help it rendered to the Republic certainly contributed to the rise of the PCE, but the essential factor was the one I have just mentioned. It was symptomatic that the party made relatively little advance, as regards recruitment of members and increased influence, in the UGT, not to mention the CNT, that is, among the organized working class. Many petty-bourgeois elements hastened to join the PCE, attracted by its renown as the party of order and legality, the defender of small-scale property. But it was above all young persons, not yet shaped by the unions or the traditional workers' organizations, who joined the PCE (or put themselves under its leadership in the JSU) because they were attracted by the party's military virtues and by a simplified ideology in which the idea of revolution was identified with anti-Fascism mingled with patriotism.[53]

The PCE made a contribution of prime importance, therefore, to the organizing of the Republican army. The Comintern formed the International Brigades, and the Soviet Union was the chief supplier of arms to the Republic, not to mention the significant contribution made by Soviet military experts. Had the war been nothing but a technico-military enterprise there would be nothing for reproach in the contribution made by the PCE, Comintern and USSR to the Spanish people's struggle against Fascism (leaving aside for the moment the question of the quantity of arms supplied to the Republic by the Soviet government). As everyone knows, however, since Clausewitz pointed it out, 'war is not merely a political act, but also a real political instrument, a continuation of political commerce, a carrying out of the same by other means'.[54] And this is especially true, it may be added, where the war is a civil war. The thesis of the PCE, 'Unless we win the war, no revolution is possible', was obviously sound, but the other thesis that came to be associated with this one, 'By winning the war we achieve the revolution', was absolutely ambiguous.[55] For, as we have previously seen, each organization in the Republican camp had its own conception of 'the revolution' and was fighting to ensure the victory of this conception by *continuing to follow* its previous policy, from the first day of the civil war onward. 'The war' was not a distinct aspect of the total struggle, making it possible to put between parentheses the three principal 'variants' of the revolution that confronted each other: the proletarian, the bourgeois-democratic and the liberal-bourgeois. The fighting at the fronts and the directly military instruments were closely bound up with one or other type of social or political organization. And the entire future of the Republic depended ultimately upon the type of socio-political regime that would be established *during the war*. The military force created by the PCE, the Comintern and Soviet help was placed at the service of two main political aims: offering military resistance to the rebels and ensuring the triumph of bourgeois democracy, of a democracy acceptable to the Republicans, and in principle also to the 'Western democracies'. As the instrument of the second of these aims, however, the military force of the PCE-Comintern-USSR came into contradiction with the reality of the revolution and with the majority of the proletariat who regarded this reality as their greatest conquest. Such a contradiction could not but weaken the military power of the Republic. The two political aims that the military efforts of the PCE–Comintern–USSR endeavoured to serve were not complementary but contradictory. The second was prejudicial to the first, as events soon showed.

In the first months of 1937 the Caballerists, the Anarcho–Syndicalists and the militants of the POUM realized that their adaptation to the line laid down by Moscow, which had produced no positive effect on the attitude of the 'Western democracies', was, however, resulting in a steady reduction in the 'proletarian content' that the revolution had possessed at the start, and in a strengthening of the position of the PCE, the reformist Socialists and the bourgeois Republicans in the political and military structures. It was especially the powerful position held by the PCE in the army that worried them. And the terror launched by Stalin against the opposition elements in the USSR, added to purely Spanish concerns, brought this anxiety of theirs to a climax. The Stalin terror looked to the Caballerists, Anarcho-Syndicalists and POUM-ists as a prefiguring of what would happen to them in the event of the Communists being in a position of power when the war should come to a victorious end. The attitude immediately taken up by the PCE was not calculated to reassure them. In perfect synchronization with the 'Moscow trials' the party demanded, in effect, the extermination of the POUM, and it treated as enemies of the USSR and Fascist agents the Caballerists and Anarcho–Syndicalists who denounced Stalin's crimes.[56] Given their blind faith in the Soviet leaders, the Spanish Communists could not doubt that in the USSR they were exterminating 'enemies of the people', 'Fascist spies'. And when a fight to the death against Fascism was taking place in Spain, and the USSR was the only country to help the Spanish Republic, only other 'enemies of the people', other 'disguised agents' of Fascism could be capable of daring to defend those whom Stalin was putting down – so it seemed to the Communists. The introduction of this virus of mistrust and hatred brought to paroxysm the political and doctrinal divergences between the organizations and groups that represented the revolutionary proletariat.

During this period the reformist Socialists and bourgeois Republicans maintained a prudent discretion regarding the dramas that were taking place in Moscow. The gulf that opened between the PCE and the other sections of the revolutionary proletariat made Azaña and Prieto masters of the situation.

The 'May crisis' of 1937 resulted from this process. The Caballerists and Anarcho-Syndicalists were expelled from the government, and power remained in the hands of the right-wing Socialists, the bourgeois Republicans and the PCE.[57] Police action against the POUM began at once, followed by a political offensive against Largo Caballero and his supporters. While the PCE denounced them as accomplices of the POUM, Prieto's group manoeuvred to dislodge the Caballerists from the leadership of the UGT and from the positions they held in the PSOE. At the same time, the more moderate and reformist elements in the CNT strengthened their positions.[58]

A decisive step had thus been taken in the difficult task entrusted by Stalin to the Comintern – to make the Spanish revolution get back within the 'democratic' fence from which it 'ought' never to have escaped. But the chief beneficiary of this operation was not its chief executant, the PCE, but the bloc of bourgeois Republicans and reformist Socialists who occupied the key posts in the government – the premiership, and control of the army, foreign policy and the economy. It is true, that the PCE held a substantial part of the army in its own hands, but, given that the supreme purpose of its policy, Stalin's policy, was to retain the alliance with the bourgeois-reformist bloc, the PCE was quite unable to use this force against its 'sacred' allies. Prieto, at the head of the Defence Ministry, could therefore proceed methodically to reduce, little by little, the specific weight of the Communists among the cadres of the armed forces and the supply services.

At the same time, the government's general policy evolved rapidly rightward on internal matters, and moved in the direction of a negotiated settlement of the war. Eventually, it was Azaña's political line that began to predominate (see note 48, p. 704). For great social revolutions like the Spanish revolution either advance resolutely to their ultimate consequences, or else retreat and end in counter-revolution. Long before the Fascist troops entered Barcelona and Madrid, counter-revolution had quietly installed itself in the Republican zone. As the civil war went on and on, with its train of privations and sacrifices, and as the balance of military power changed in favour of the enemy (who was receiving from Germany and Italy much more substantial aid than the Republic was receiving from the USSR), discouragement and defeatism spread among the petty-bourgeois strata in town and country, not without contaminating the proletariat as well. The capitulation policy of Azaña and Prieto found a social basis that grew wider every day, whereas the resistance to the bitter end advocated by the Communists encountered growing scepticism.

The PCE strove desperately to check the deterioration in the situation, but neither its propaganda nor the steps taken with a view to strengthening the army and increasing the production of arms could make up for the vacuum left by the loss of what had been the mainspring of the people's fighting spirit in the first months: revolutionary enthusiasm. The most radical masses of the proletariat felt they had been cheated, and within the PCE itself, from behind the façade of official optimism, doubt and hesitation began to show through. The policy of alliance with the bourgeois Republicans and right-wing Socialists came under criticism, and the view was expressed that the party ought to take over exclusive control of the conduct of the war.[59] These tendencies were connected with the opinion held by many Communists that hopes of aid from the 'Western democracies' were quite illusory. Why, then, was such respect shown to those who in Spain itself were the political representatives of the Anglo-French 'democratic bourgeoisie' and Social Democrats who were betraying the Spanish people? Why sacrifice to an alliance with those who were moving towards capitulation the possibilities that still remained for a policy of revolutionary war that might revive the fighting vigour of the proletariat, impose iron discipline and make the fullest use of existing resources?

Ideas such as these managed to find expression in one of the central organs of the PCE, *Mundo Obrero*, which, being published in Madrid, escaped to some extent from direct control by the party leadership, whose headquarters was in Barcelona, with *Frente Rojo* as their official organ. In the issue of 23 March 1938 the editors of *Mundo Obrero* presented the problem in these terms: 'It is impossible to say, as one paper does, that the only solution is for Spain to be neither Fascist nor Communist, because this is what France wants ... The Spanish people will win despite opposition from capitalism.' The PCE leadership reacted immediately. In a letter signed by José Diaz and published in *Frente Rojo* of 30 March, the editorial board of *Mundo Obrero* was severely criticized:

The statement that 'the only solution to our conflict is for Spain to be neither Fascist nor Communist' is perfectly correct and corresponds precisely to the position of our party. As for the statement that 'the Spanish people will win despite opposition from capitalism', it corresponds neither to the situation nor to the policy of our party and the Communist International ... In my report to the November plenum we said: 'There is a terrain on which all democratic states can meet together and act jointly. This is the terrain of defence of their own existence against the common aggressor, Fascism, the terrain of defence against the war that threatens us all.' When we speak here of 'all democratic states' we are not thinking only of the Soviet Union, where socialist democracy prevails, but also of France, Britain, Czechoslovakia, the USA, etc., countries which are democratic but also capitalist. We want these states to come to our aid. We consider that by aiding us they are defending their own interests. We strive to make them see that this is so, and we appeal to them for aid. The attitude that you take up in your article is very different from this, and is not correct ... It would inevitably lead us once again to narrow the front of our struggle at a moment when we need to broaden it.[60]

Thus, on 30 March 1938, when it was more than obvious (actually, this had been so since Blum, a few days after the outbreak of the civil war in Spain, had lined up with the attitude of the British Conservative government) that 'democratic' capitalism was not going to stir a finger to come to the aid of the Spanish Republic, despite all the latter's efforts to 'broaden' its political appeal, the Comintern, over the signature of José Diaz, continued to comfort itself with the illusion (and to spread this illusion among the Spanish fighters) that France, Britain and the USA were going to help the Spanish people. Soviet historians today acknowledge that 'from the end of 1937, connivance [against the Spanish Republic] between the Fascist states and the USA, France and Britain was increasingly obvious'.[61] And only fifteen days after the reprimand to *Mundo Obrero* Britain made an agreement with Mussolini for the withdrawal of the Italian 'volunteers' after Franco had won the war, in mid-June the French government closed the frontier with Spain; and September brought the Munich agreement.

Meanwhile, the 'broadening' advocated in Diaz's letter was expressed in official abandonment (which merely recognized the actual situation) of the revolutionary content that the struggle had had when it began. Gabriel Jackson says quite rightly that Negrin's 'thirteen points', backed by the PCE, 'presented to world opinion the image of a regime whose aims and methods were similar to those of the Western democracies. It was a supreme effort to convince the Western governments of their own stake in the survival of the Republic.'[62] But the 'Western governments', unlike the Comintern, saw the problem from a class angle, and the most solvent representative of Spanish capitalism was not Negrin but Franco. 'Democratic' capitalism would not act as required except in return for the complete crushing of the Spanish proletariat, which would mean the crushing of a Republic that, over a period of almost a decade, had shown its historical inviability as a 'bourgeois-democratic republic'. The 'Western governments' might be sympathetic to the chimerical image of Spanish Republican reality that the PCE and Negrin endeavoured to present, but they were organically incapable of accepting the reality that was hidden behind this image, that of a revolutionary proletariat ready to raise its head again at the first opportunity. The drama drew near to its final outcome in the very terms in which classes and the class struggle (and not the theoretical dogma of the Comintern about the inevitability of a 'bourgeois-democratic stage') had presented the issue in the Spain of 1936: Fascism or Communism – understanding by 'Communism' here what everyone meant at that time where Spain was concerned, namely, the proletarian revolution with distinctive and non-transferable features (*Spanish* features, in short), that had swept like a tempest across the Peninsula in the second half of 1936.

The ideological and political concessions made by the PCE and Negrin in the last months of the war, in order to facilitate 'national unity', of 'all patriotic Spaniards' in either camp, the reduction of Negrin's thirteen points to three, served merely to convince the most optimistic that the Republic was on the brink of disaster. The 'party of capitulation' grew until it became the largest in the Republican zone. There followed the catastrophic collapse of Catalonia, and Casado's successful conspiracy, leading to the final crushing of resistance. At the last moment the PCE tried to react, disregarding all concern for its bourgeois and reformist allies or for 'democratic' capitalism, but it was too late.[63] All the sacrifice and heroism of three years went down with a policy that, from the first day of the civil war, had turned its back on the essential demands of Spanish revolutionary reality in order to adapt itself to the international strategy of Stalin.

The subjection of the PCE to this strategy constituted, indeed, a serious obstacle in the way of *full* development of the fighting reserves and creative initiatives of those forces, capable of performing miracles, that every great social revolution contains. *Within the limits* imposed by this subjection, the party set an example, as has been said, in organizing the army, and effectively exalted the fighting spirit of the masses, the anti-Fascist and national-liberation aspects of the struggle, etc. This was absolutely necessary, and even vital. But *full* realization of the potentialities mentioned above required, first of all and above all, that the proletariat, the decisive revolutionary force, should have no doubt at any stage that the fight to the death which had been begun would result in its liberation from capitalist slavery. And this not as a promise relating to a later stage but as an affirmation and development of the socialist content that the revolution in progress had possessed since the July days, as the translation of this content into a new legality and new institutions – in short, as the establishment of *workers' power*. All the other contents of the revolutionary war were important and none should have been underestimated, but only provided that they were subordinated to the socialist content. On this basis it appeared necessary – and it could have been understood in this way by the proletariat – to respect small-scale property which did not exploit the labour of others, to ally with the non-exploiting strata of the petty-bourgeoisie, to collaborate with the non-proletarian political groups which, because of the other aspects of the war (anti-Fascist, national, etc.), were ready to take part in the struggle. On this basis, the aspect of defence of national independence which the Italo–German intervention conferred upon the civil war could have meant for the proletariat something more than traditional patriotism, namely, defence of its own liberation.

Recognition of the absolute priority of the proletarian and socialist essence of the revolution, reaffirmation of this at all levels, taking it as starting-point for the solution of all problems posed by the war – this was all the more necessary, it must be emphasized, because this essence had *already* been put into practice by the masses themselves, and any retreat must inevitably provoke mistrust on their part, weaken their morale, and in the end cause them to conclude that it was not worth agreeing to such sacrifices just to re-establish the Republic of Azaña. The spirit that made possible the defence of Madrid was that of the proletarian revolution, and if there was any possibility of victory it could be found only in the spreading and deepening of this spirit. But that necessitated the setting-up of a revolutionary proletarian government that would leave no room for doubt as to the aims of the struggle and would undertake with inflexible firmness the solution of the tasks imposed by the war – the organization of the army and the production of armaments, the supplies needed, and so on, together with something that the government, concerned to restore the Republican state order, increasingly dominated by Azaña, Prieto and Co., who were exclusively preoccupied with resembling the 'Western democracies', did not contemplate and could never have contemplated, namely, the organizing of large-scale revolutionary guerrilla activity in the areas dominated by the rebel generals.

The political characteristics assumed by the 'restoration' policy were expressed in the 'conventional' way in which the war was waged. But, while the organization of a regular army, with positional and mobile warfare on the basis of large units, was essential under the specific conditions of the Spanish civil war, a guerrilla struggle was no less essential. All that it required was a different kind of government. This shortcoming needs to be emphasized, for it had considerable influence on the ultimate outcome of the struggle. Guerrilla activity on a wide scale, for which favourable conditions existed in a number of regions of Spain, would not merely have considerably reinforced the military power of the Republic and the likelihood of victory but would also have made possible, in the event of defeat in 'conventional warfare', the cre-

ation of bases for continuing the armed struggle over a long period, so as
to merge, when the world war came, with the anti-Hitlerite resistance.[64]

The failure of the Anarcho-Syndicalists to understand the problem of
the state, and the tactical and organizational inconsistency of the Caballerists, were undoubtedly a big obstacle in the way of organizing the
kind of revolutionary authority that the conditions of the civil war inexorably demanded. If, however, the PCE, which had a better appreciation of the needs of the situation, had criticized Anarcho-Syndicalism
and 'Caballerism' from the standpoint of the proletarian revolution and
revolutionary war, rather than in the name of the defence of bourgeois
democracy, it would have met with a big response among the Anarcho-
Syndicalist and Socialist masses, including the best of their cadres. Dur-
ruti was no exception, for the war and the revolution taught people very
quickly. In fact, substantial groups of the Anarcho-Syndicalists and left-
wing Socialists grasped very soon that a state power was needed, with
an army, discipline and so on. And they would have grasped this sooner
if the PCE had not presented these problems *in contradiction to* the
socialist content of the revolution. In the first months of the war there
were great possibilities for bringing about unification of Communists,
left-wing Socialists, POUMists and Anarcho-Syndicalists of the Dur-
ruti kind in one great revolutionary party, or at least for close collaboration between them in building a proletarian state. For that to happen,
however, it would have been necessary for the PCE to place itself unre-
servedly on the terrain of the revolution, casting aside all dogmatic
schemas. Such a party and such a state would have had to be completely
independent of the Comintern and of Moscow. Only thus could they
have been accepted by the other revolutionary sections of the Spanish
proletariat.

None of this was possible, of course, given what the Comintern and
Stalin's policy actually were. Even if we assume, for the sake of speculation, that the PCE had taken this line, the international situation of
such a hypothetical socialist republic would doubtless have been desperate, in view of the opposition to be expected from the Comintern and
from Stalin. To be sure, it would have been able to play cards that were
not available to the People's Front Republic, enslaved to Stalin's policy

and prisoner of its own petty-bourgeois essence: it would have been able, by its example and by direct appeal, to encourage the revolutionary struggle of the French proletariat (in the second half of 1936 the spirit of May and June was still alive in France). The same card could have been played in relation to Stalin. Refusal to help the Spanish proletariat, given the tremendous sympathy its fight would arouse, even in the Social Democratic labour movement, would have dealt a heavy blow to the standing of the USSR among the workers throughout the world. And although Stalin's international strategy was based fundamentally on using the contradictions between the imperialist powers, and not on developing the world revolutionary movement, he could not do without the support of the international labour movement. He needed that, even if only for exploiting inter-imperialist contradictions – to ensure for example, the alliance with France, and to bring about an understanding with Britain, the 'pressure' in this direction exercised by the respective working classes of those countries was needed. A Spanish socialist republic of the type described – that is, one independent of the Comintern and the USSR, and it was only conceivable as such – would command the weapon of open criticism, the possibility of denouncing frankly before the proletariat of the world the conduct of the Moscow government, should the latter refuse to help the Spanish revolution. It is not absurd to suppose that, faced with this danger, 'Moscow would have been forced to supply arms, and, possibly, at more reasonable prices', as Trotsky said.[65] If, however, we look at this problem in the light of subsequent events, and in particular of the German–Soviet pact and of the abandonment of the Yugoslav revolution in 1948, it is not absurd, either, to think that Stalin would have reacted by denouncing our hypothetical heterodox Spanish Communists for their alliance with the Anarcho-Syndicalists, Cabellerists and POUMists as a sinister provocation (organized by the Gestapo under the guidance of Trotsky) against the USSR and the Western democracies, in order to prevent them from coming to the help of the Spanish Republic – that legal, constitutional, parliamentary, etc., institution.

I will not pursue this speculation, the only point of which is to bring out the essential facets of what some Soviet historians themselves have begun to describe as Stalin's betrayal of the Spanish Republic.[66] Like

Western historians, the Soviet writers note especially the inadequacy of the military aid that Stalin gave to the Republic. The hypothesis I put up just now sought to show the possibilities that this 'betrayal' cut off by preventing the creation in the Republican zone of a revolutionary authority that would have considerably enhanced the fighting capacity of the Spanish people. Stalin's policy followed by the Comintern and the PCE, gave hegemony in the Republic to the bourgeois and reformist forces that sought to compromise with the enemy – with the aggravating circumstance that it did not even respect the legality and sovereignty that were the basis of the Republican state's respectability in the eyes of the Western democracies. Stalin's secret service operated in Spain just as they would have done in the Mongolian People's Republic. The most scandalous case, though by no means the only one, was the murder of Nin, after the plan to use him in a Spanish edition of the 'Moscow trials' had fallen through. As G. Jackson notes: 'The Nin case was a terrible moral blow to the credit of the Negrin government. Two months after taking office with strong pledges for the restoration of personal security and justice, the Prime Minister had been forced to tolerate the Communist outrage or to fight back, at the risk of being destroyed as Largo Caballero had been destroyed.'[67] This is a thoroughly correct judgement, except that the 'Communist outrage' was in reality, even more than an outrage against Negrin's prestige, an outrage against Communism.

The aspect of Stalin's 'betrayal' which is emphasized by the historians mentioned is also in accordance with the facts: the stifling of the revolution and the dependence to which the Republic was forced to submit were not even compensated by military aid at least equivalent to that which Franco's generals received from Germany and Italy, although the Soviet arms had been paid for in advance, as everyone knows, by the gold of the Bank of Spain. The problem of this inadequacy will not be finally cleared up until the relevant Soviet archives are opened. Then only will it be possible to determine how far it was due to technical difficulties (distance, the blockade, etc.) and how far it was a 'planned' inadequacy, corresponding to considerations of foreign policy. What seems beyond question is that this second factor was present. Stalin could not, without altering his international strategy, help the Spanish Republic to a greater degree than was compatible with his policy of alliances with the 'Western democracies'. And the latter did not accept at all that Soviet help should give a military advantage to the Republic. Azaña and the Republic's ambassador in Moscow (Marcelino Pascua, a member of the Socialist Party) understood this perfectly. In the President's notebook we find this record of a conversation with Pascua on 13 August 1937: 'I think [said Azaña] that, contrary to what is often supposed, there is a limit to Russia's cooperation, which is not set by the possible blockade but by Britain's official friendship. In my view, the USSR will do nothing to help us that might do serious harm to their relations with Britain or compromise their position in the policy of seeking friends in the West.' 'There can be no doubt about that [Pascua replied]. For the USSR the Spanish affair is *a matter of minor importance.*'[68] Stalin helped the Spanish Republic in order that it might prolong its existence and arrive at a compromise solution acceptable to the 'Western democracies', within the framework of a system of anti-Hitlerite alliances, and not in order that it might *win.*

This conclusion is forced on one by an analysis of the facts and of Stalin's foreign policy. At the time, however, it seemed to the Communists and to many Spanish anti-Fascists who were not Communists, to be the most monstrous calumny ever imagined. Subsequent events showed, nevertheless, clearly enough, that Stalin was not one to hesitate in sacrificing to *raison d' état* not merely a possibility of revolution but an actual revolution, even when this occurred close to the Soviet frontiers and there were no 'technical' difficulties in the way of supplying the aid needed to oppose imperialist intervention. The example of the Greek resistance at the end of the Second World War is sufficiently conclusive.[69] Between the two world wars, it is Stalin's Spanish policy, applied by the Comintern and the PCE, that provides the most obvious example of the sacrifice of a revolution to the interests of Soviet *raison d'état.*

THE COLONIAL EXPERIENCE

National Liberation Movements and the Policy of the Comintern

During the gloomy spring of 1939, after Franco's entry into Madrid and Hitler's into Prague, the only substantial section of the Comintern that remained on its feet in Europe was the French party. Apart from this, only the small Communist parties of Scandinavia, Britain, Belgium, Holland and Switzerland, whose political impact was almost nil, remained legal. All the other European sections had been reduced to clandestine existence after suffering heavy defeats. Soon after this the French party was to undergo the same fate: and the Second World War would begin.

Capitalism was able to hurl the world into the second great massacre of the century because, during the twenty years since the first one, the majority of the proletariat in the 'advanced' countries had steadily turned its back on the revolutionary mission which, according to Marxism, it should have assumed. Thus, the Comintern had failed in the main aim it set itself at the outset of its existence – to wrest the working class from reformism and organize it politically and trade-union-wise on revolutionary principles. The Comintern did not succeed in taking a single important step in this direction in the USA, which was already the metropolis of capitalism, or in Britain, the country that stood next in importance, despite its stagnation, on account of its colonial empire. It must be admitted that in both cases the task was no easy one, given the political and ideological state of the proletariat of the Anglo-Saxon countries at the time when the Comintern came on the scene. But the International failed in Germany too, where the objective conditions were at first very favourable and where a positive achievement would have altered the world situation to a serious degree. France was the only capitalist country of importance where the Comintern, seventeen years after its formation, held positions of strength in the working class.

When, however, we look at events with the advantage of hindsight, we may wonder whether the rise of Communism in France in the second half of the 1930s was not, rather than a victory for revolutionary Marxism, the first step in the Social Democratic retrogression of the Communist movement in the advanced capitalist countries. One conclusion is forced on us, in any case: the Comintern did not manage (far from that) to accomplish the principal task it had set itself, namely, to become the leading party of the Western proletariat. It is in this major fact that the key to the historical failure of the Comintern lies. This is why I have focused my critical analysis of its activity upon the cases where conditions were most favourable to the accomplishment of this task. I must, however, also refer, even though briefly, to the results obtained by the Comintern in another field of activity, which it regarded as being also of great importance from its very foundation: leadership of the fight of the colonial and dependent peoples against imperialism. The record here is not very impressive, either.

On the eve of the Second World War, membership of the Comintern in the colonies and dependent countries was still very small, except in China, where, as we shall see later, the strength acquired by the Communist Party from the last years of the 1930s onward was not exactly due to the policy of the Comintern. In all the other Asian Countries taken together there were, in 1939, no more than 22,000 Communists. In Africa there were 5,000, most of these being Frenchmen in Algeria and Morocco and white workers in the Union of South Africa. Throughout Latin America the total membership was 90,000,[70] a considerable percentage of these having been recruited after the Seventh Congress of the Comintern, when the Latin-American parties, following the directives of the International, were applying an opportunist policy of temporizing with Yankee imperialism. This numerical weakness well reflects the very light political weight represented by the Communist parties of the colonies and dependent countries in the national liberation movement. The latter experienced a great upsurge between the two world wars, but it was led – with the exception, already mentioned, of China after the Japanese invasion of 1937 – by bourgeois (and even feudal) nationalists. (The concepts of 'bourgeois' and 'feudal' are here used in the conventional way, although they do not correspond to socio-political categories that are wholly identifiable with the corresponding European ones.)

The first big difficulty that the Comintern came up against in dealing with the problems of the revolutionary struggle in the colonies and dependent countries arose from the fact that Marxist theory had not given much attention to this question down to that time. The heritage left by Marx and Engels in this domain was very slight, especially where questions of strategy and tactics were concerned. True, the idea of a connection between revolutions in backward countries, exploited by European capitalism, and the socialist revolution had been indicated by Marx as early as 1853. The 'formidable revolution' of the Taipings, he wrote in that year, may contribute to bringing about the revolution in Europe 'more . . . than . . . any other political cause that now exists'.[71] His views and analyses on the role of the 'national factor' and the 'peasant factor' in European revolutions contained suggestions that could be used when studying the problems that the colonial liberation movement of the twentieth century was to throw up. Marx's investigation of the 'Asiatic mode of production' might have been very useful to the Comintern in deepening its knowledge of the societies that the revolutionary anti-imperialist movement set out to liberate and transform. But Marx's principal writings on this subject remained unpublished down to 1939, and those writings that were known previously were regarded, by Plekhanov and other Marxist theoreticians, as hypotheses that Marx himself had abandoned. After the defeat of the Chinese Communist Party in 1927 a discussion took place on this subject in the Soviet Union, and the concept of the 'Asiatic mode of production' was condemned.[72] The contribution of Marx and Engels to the problematic of the revolution in the pre-capitalist world colonized by Europe thus turned out to be very slight and indirect – which was natural enough, since the question had hardly arisen in practice in the lifetime of the founders of Marxism. But the inner logic of Marx's theory of the world socialist revolution included two essentially 'Eurocentrist' ideas that were to weigh heavily upon the Comintern. The first, a strategic one, was that the liberation of the world exploited by capitalism must be a *result* of the socialist revolution in the West. The second, a cultural one in the widest sense, was that the socialist transformation of the world meant its *Europeanization.*

Lenin based himself upon this theoretical heritage. As was noted in Chapter 2, during the years following the Russian revolution of 1905 he became acutely aware of the new revolutionary force that was beginning to appear in the East. In contrast to the colonialist attitude of the right in the Second International and the anti-colonialism in words only of the 'orthodox' centre, Lenin declared with emphasis that the revolutionary proletariat of the West must make the cause of the oppressed peoples its own, render this cause resolute support, and see it as an important factor in the world socialist revolution, a factor contributing to the destruction of the very foundations of imperialism. Until the October revolution, however, Lenin had done no more than touch upon the problems of the revolution in the East.[73] The First Congress of the Comintern gave them little attention, and expressed very clearly the traditional ideas that were strongly rooted in the minds of Western Marxists: 'The emancipation of the colonies is possible only in conjunction with the emancipation of the metropolitan working class. The workers and peasants not only of Annam, Algiers and Bengal, but also of Persia and Armenia, will gain the opportunity of independent existence only when the workers of England and France have overthrown Lloyd George and Clemenceau and taken state power into their own hands.'[74]

Between the First and Second Congresses, however, three things were to happen that would cause the 'national and colonial question' eventually to acquire an important place in the discussions of the Comintern. First, the prospect of a proletarian revolution became more remote (even though, at the time of the Second Congress, there was a brief resurgence of hope – dashed by the halting of the Red Army before Warsaw). Second, the anti-imperialist national liberation movement experienced, in contrast with the ebbing of the revolutionary tide in the West, a considerable upsurge. Third, the national and colonial question had arisen sharply within Soviet Russia. Moreover, the Second Congress was attended for the first time by delegates from the Communist organizations that had begun to be formed in the colonies and dependent countries. As a result of all these circumstances, the first big discussion on the strategic and tactical problems of the revolutionary movement in the backward countries, oppressed by European capitalism, was to take place in the Communist International. The discussion revolved fundamentally around two points: (*a*) how the national liberation movement should be evaluated as an integral part of the world socialist revolution, and (*b*) what policy the Comintern ought to follow on this front (problems of strategy, tactics, organization, etc.).

Discussion of these questions was continued shortly afterward at the Congress of the Peoples of the East convened by the Comintern and held at Baku in September 1920. This congress was attended by representatives of the Communist parties of the colonies and dependent countries, as well as by representatives of the Communist organizations of the peoples who had been oppressed by Tsarism and liberated by the October revolution. At the Third Congress of the Comintern (1921) the colonial problem was hardly considered at all, for reasons that will appear later. It was discussed again at the Fourth (1922) and Fifth (1924) Congresses. In the analysis that follows I shall try to make a synthesis of the positions taken up at these first five congresses of the Comintern and at the Baku Congress, before going on to look at the Comintern's chief experience in the colonial field, its policy in the Chinese revolution. I shall concentrate my analysis on the points (*a*) and (*b*) mentioned above.

(a) Evaluation of the national liberation movement as an integral part of the world socialist revolution

The extreme 'European' viewpoint maintained by the First Congress was partly corrected by the Second. In face of the retreat of the revolution in the West, Lenin and the other Bolshevik leaders were readier to appreciate the significance for the defence of the Russian revolution that was represented by the anti-imperialist liberation movement now on the march in Asia. And the Communists of the Asian countries, filled with revolutionary enthusiasm and aware of the intolerable situation in which colonialism had placed their countries, could not accept that their liberation must wait upon the taking of power by the workers of London or Paris. Furthermore, some of these Asian Communists openly voiced their lack of confidence in the prospect of a proletarian revolution in the West. The one among them most qualified in theoretical knowledge, the Indian Communist M. N. Roy, defended an 'Asian' standpoint that was to some extent an anticipation of Maoism: Comrade Roy,

[says the report of the congress commission on the national and colonial question] defends the idea that the fate of the revolutionary movement in Europe depends entirely on the course of the revolution in the East. Without the victory of the revolution in the Eastern countries, the Communist movement in the West would come to nothing ... This being so, it is essential that we divert our energies into developing and elevating the revolutionary movement in the East and accept as our fundamental thesis that the fate of world Communism depends on the victory of Communism in the East.

Roy based this view on the hypothesis that, thanks to the resources drawn from the colonies, European capitalism was in a position to go as far as would be politically necessary in making economic concessions to the proletariat of Europe. 'The European working class,' he declared in the theses he put before the Congress, 'will not succeed in overthrowing the capitalist order until this source has been definitely cut off.' Lenin opposed Roy's ideas:

> Comrade Roy goes too far when he asserts that the fate of the West depends exclusively on the degree of development and the strength of the revolutionary movement in the Eastern countries. In spite of the fact that the proletariat in India numbers five million and there are 37 million landless peasants, the Indian Communists have not yet succeeded in creating a Communist Party in their country. This fact alone shows that Comrade Roy's views are to a large extent unfounded.

Nevertheless, Lenin and the Second Congress, despite the resistance of some representatives of Western parties, such as the Italian Serrati, did seriously modify the line of the First Congress. A re-formulation of Roy's thesis quoted above was adopted: 'Extra profit gained in the colonies is the mainstay of modern capitalism, and so long as the latter is not deprived of this source of extra profit it will not be easy for the European working class to overthrow the capitalist order.'[75]

Without giving up the traditional Marxist conception in which the proletariat of advanced capitalism and its socialist revolution constituted the key, the socio-economic and political basis, and the decisive agent of world revolution, the Second Congress assigned to the liberation struggle of the colonial peoples a role of front-rank importance in the world revolutionary process, and no longer subordinated the triumph of the colonial revolution in any particular country to the victory of the proletariat in the metropolis. This new line was to be further strengthened in the following years; and I have already mentioned that in one of his last writings Lenin expressed the view that the fate of the world revolution was in the last analysis guaranteed because peoples like those of China, India and other oppressed peoples, together with the Soviet peoples, made up the great majority of mankind.

However, this positive evaluation of the role of the colonial revolution in the process of the socialist world revolution was not to be reflected in any sustained effort by the Comintern either on the plane of theoretical and political thinking or on that of practical activity. The 'Eurocentrist' viewpoint continued to predominate in the leadership of the Comintern and in the Communist parties of the metropolitan countries, sometimes assuming a colonialist colouring. At the Third Congress Roy said:

I have been allowed five minutes for my report [on India]. As this theme cannot be dealt with adequately even in an hour, I wish to employ these five minutes for an energetic protest. The way in which the Eastern question has been dealt with at this Congress is purely opportunist, and is worthy rather of a Congress of the Second International. It is absolutely impossible to draw any practical conclusions whatever from the few sentences which the Eastern delegations have been allowed to speak.[76]

At the Fourth Congress Safarov, who collaborated with Lenin on problems of the East, said: 'In spite of the decisions of the Second Congress of the Communist International, the Communist parties of the imperialist countries have done extraordinarily little to deal with the national and colonial questions ... Worse still, the flag of Communism is used to hide chauvinist ideas foreign and hostile to proletarian internationalism.'[77] At the Fifth Congress, Katayama, representing the Japanese Communist Party, expressed regret that Zinoviev 'made scarcely any mention of the Eastern question. Comrade Varga's report and thesis is also incomplete, it takes account of no other countries except Europe and America ...' (Zinoviev, who was then President of the Comintern, had given the general report to the Congress, and E. Varga the report on the world economic situation.) Semaun, the delegate of the Communist Party of Indonesia, complained of the Dutch Communist Party's inactivity on colonial questions and advised the ECCI to 'pay more attention to the colonies'. Wolfe, for the Mexican Communist Party said: 'The attention of the European proletariat should be drawn to the fact that in the Latin American peoples it and the Comintern have a potentially powerful ally. It appeared that the Communist International did not sufficiently realize this.' The most severe criticism came from Nguyen Ai Quoc (Ho Chi Minh), who accused the European Communist parties of underestimating the significance of the colonies for the world revolution: 'In discussing the possibility of and the means for accomplishing the revolution, and in drawing up your plan for the coming war, you British and French Comrades, and also you comrades from other parties, have completely lost sight of this extraordinarily important strategic point. This is why I say to you with all the strength I can muster, "Take care!" '[78]

But translation into reality of the high evaluation that the Second Congress had made of the national liberation movement did not conflict only with the 'European' outlook of the Western Communist leaders. Even more, if possible, than in the case of the activity of the Comintern in Europe, its 'colonial' policy was affected by considerations of Soviet foreign policy.

The Third Congress provided an eloquent example of this. Discussion of the colonial problem was practically suppressed, as can be seen from the passage quoted from Roy's intervention. Zinoviev's main report devoted only a few general phrases to questions of the East and was concentrated on European matters. And yet there were weighty reasons why the discussion that had been begun in the previous year should have been pursued and carried deeper. Significant events had occurred during the Turkish and Persian revolutions. Sun Yat-sen had succeeded in establishing his base in Canton and had made contact with the Soviet government. In India the struggle against British rule was in 1921 assuming formidable proportions. As a Soviet historian writes: 'A wave of meetings, demonstrations and large-scale strikes shook the entire country. The Indians stopped work in government institutions, boycotted the courts and educational institutions, burnt British goods. Millions of workers took part in this activity, and in many places the colonial administration was practically paralysed.'[79] (This was the 'theme' which, as Roy said, could not 'be dealt with adequately even in an hour', and for which the Congress had 'allowed five minutes'.)

In short, between the Second and Third Congresses a rich experience of anti-imperialist struggle had been accumulated, and new problems had arisen which called for examination by the Comintern. The Turkish experience was especially significant. In 1920 Mustafa Kemal had appealed to Lenin for military and diplomatic aid on the part of the Soviet state, and had immediately been given a positive reply. In March

1921 a treaty of friendship and aid was signed with him. Despite the very great economic and military difficulties that the Russian revolution was then experiencing, Moscow gave Kemal ten million gold roubles and sent him substantial quantities of arms. This aid enabled the Turks to cope victoriously with the armed intervention of the Entente, carried through by means of the Greek army. All this was quite logical from the standpoint of the anti-imperialist struggle, but the question was greatly complicated by the internal policy of the Kemalists. While soliciting Soviet aid, the Turkish nationalists were inflicting pitiless repression upon the Turkish Communist Party, which had been formed in 1920, and upon the peasant movement fighting for agrarian reform. A month and a half before the signing of the Soviet–Turkish alliance in Moscow, the Kemalists arrested the best-known Communist militants, forty-two in all. Fifteen of them (including the party's leader, Mustafa Subhi, an intellectual of standing, who introduced Marxism into Turkey) were immediately strangled and their bodies thrown into the sea. The rest were put on trial for 'high treason'.

Ought the Soviet government to help a bourgeois nationalist movement which, on the one hand, resisted the imperialist powers, but, on the other, murdered Communists and repressed the peasant movement? What should the Communist International's policy be in this situation? The Turkish revolution brought up from the very outset, and in extremely sharp form, one of the crucial problems of the fight for national liberation: the definition and inter-relating of the policy of the Soviet state and the policy of the International – that of the Communists in the colonial countries – in relation to the bourgeois nationalist movements. The Third Congress of the Comintern constituted a good opportunity to deal thoroughly with this complex problem, especially as the development of events in Persia, India, China, Indonesia, etc., might give rise to comparable situations at any moment. True, the Second Congress had already examined some aspects of the problem (as we shall see later), but it had done this in very general terms, without having at its disposal any experience so rich as was provided by the events in Turkey. Why was the discussion not continued at the Third Congress? Why was all attention focused at this Congress on the ebbing of the revolutionary tide in Europe, without anything being said about the upsurge of the anti-imperialist movement in Asia? It could be explained – and this, apparently, was how the Asian delegates interpreted it – as a persistence of the 'Eurocentrist' spirit, despite the discussions at the Second Congress. Even if this element did play a part, however, two facts entitle us to assume that the 'Soviet foreign policy' factor was also involved.

The first is that the pact with the Kemalists was signed *after* the massacre of the Turkish Communists. This fact shows how deeply Soviet leaders were concerned to ensure an alliance that might guarantee their southern frontiers, the oil of the Caucasus and navigation on the Black Sea. If the problem were to be submitted to discussion by the Third Congress of the Comintern this would incur the risk of a breach with Kemal. Significantly, though the Congress adopted a resolution protesting against the measures taken to repress the German Communists after the 'March action', it said not a word about the murder of the Turkish Communists.

The second fact is even more revealing. At about the same time as the Soviet government signed its treaty with Kemal, it signed a trade agreement with Britain by virtue of which the two states undertook to refrain from any propaganda hostile to one another, and Russia, in particular, promised to abstain from any propaganda that might incite the peoples of Asia to act contrary to British interests.[80] If, three months later, the Third Congress of the Comintern, whose discussions were presided over by Lenin, had given serious consideration to means of encouraging the struggle against British imperialism, London might have regarded that as a violation of the compromise arrived at. For the British bourgeoisie, as for the Communists of the whole world, Lenin was not only the head of the Soviet state, he was also the head of the Comintern. And it must not be forgotten that 1921 was a critical year for the Russian revolution, the year that saw the beginning of NEP and great hopes were entertained of investments by foreign capital. Could the Soviet leaders put in jeopardy the first important step they had succeeded in making towards a *modus vivendi* with Western capitalism? In December 1922, when the Fourth Congress met, these hopes had largely evaporated. The Genoa Conference had not produced the expected results, but, on the other hand, the Rapallo treaty with Germany was now in being. The Soviet Union could look more serenely upon its 'Western front'. And Britain, which had not given up its rooted anti-Sovietism, had opposed Soviet participation in the Lausanne conference on the Turkish problem. The diplomatic motives that had existed a year and a half earlier for the Comintern to avoid tackling the colonial problem were no longer in existence, and this was, indeed, given considerable attention. But the Turkish question was still handled in such a way as not to cause difficulties with Kemal.

If already in Lenin's day considerations of Soviet foreign policy affected, to the extent we have just seen, the Comintern's activity in the colonial world, there is no need to stress that the importance of this factor grew steadily during the Stalin epoch. This is a point I shall come back to later on. First of all, though, mention must be made of the effects produced from the outset by another factor, namely, the policy of the Soviet leaders in relation to the national and colonial problem inherited from Tsarism.

Lenin's attitude of principle on this question is well known. It was vigorously reaffirmed during the period between February and October 1917, and immediately after the taking of power: the non-Russian nationalities and Russia's colonies must have the right to decide freely how they chose to exist as nations, the right of self-determination, up to and including the right to separate from Soviet Russia. This was one of the main points in the Bolshevik programme.[81] It attracted to the party a great deal of support from the peoples oppressed by Tsarism, who had been disappointed by the centralism and colonialism of Kerensky and such – support which substantially helped the Bolsheviks to establish their authority. Very soon, however, this point was to turn against them. In a number of nations the 'right of self-determination' was to become the banner of political groups of the liberal bourgeoisie, Mensheviks and socialist revolutionaries, and reactionary Muslim nationalists, who exploited it in order to win the sympathy of the masses against the central authority of Russia, now incarnate in the Bolsheviks. The White counter-revolution and the imperialist intervention also sought, during the civil war, to make play with the 'right of self-determination'. The problem was settled by force of arms. When this arbitrament went in favour of the Bolsheviks, it happened either because the Red Army enjoyed the support of the worker-and-peasant majority – as in the territories where the majority of the population were Great-Russian, and probably also in the Ukraine, Byelorussia and some other regions where the 'native' Bolshevik organizations were strong – or else because the Red Army established Soviet power even without enjoying the support of the majority of the population, as was the case in Georgia and some other regions. This latter practice, which departed farther and farther from the original doctrinal positions, led some Bolshevik leaders, including Stalin and Bukharin, to demand that the party delete from its programme recognition of the right to national self-determination, replacing this with 'the right of self-determination of the working masses'.

Lenin opposed this categorically. 'Self-determination' of the working people of an oppressed nation, said he, can result only from their self-differentiation from the national bourgeoisie and their struggle against the latter. If the proletariat of the nation which has been the oppressor – in this instance the Great-Russian proletariat – does not accord full recognition to the 'right of self-determination' of the oppressed nation, it hinders this process of differentiation instead of facilitating it. He took the example of Finland. The Soviet government had acted rightly in recognizing Finland's right of self-determination, even though that led to separation from Soviet Russia, for 'the [Finnish] bourgeoisie were deceiving the people, were deceiving the working people by alleging that the Muscovites, the chauvinists, the Great-Russians, wanted to crush the Finns.' And it was in this way that one had to proceed henceforth, said Lenin. He admitted that it was possible that the Ukraine and some other nations might form themselves into fully independent states. This discussion took place at the Eighth Party Congress, in March 1919.[82]

The 'right of self-determination' continued to figure in the party programme – but it was never to be applied again as it had been in the case of Finland. In 1921 Georgia was occupied by the Red Army although a Menshevik government, elected by universal suffrage, was in power there, and Moscow had signed a treaty with this government, recognizing Georgia's independence and undertaking not to interfere in her internal affairs. But there were the oilfields of the Caucasus to be considered: this was a vital area both economically and militarily for the Soviet state (see note 42, p. 680). At the same time, in the Muslim republics and regions, to which a certain degree of autonomy had been conceded within the framework of the Russian Federative Republic, the 'right of self-determination' enjoyed little better luck. From 1920 onward Stalin, as People's Commissar for the Affairs of the Nationalities, organized systematic repression not only of reactionary Muslim nationalism but also of the native Communists who, perceiving that the masses were becoming less and less enthusiastic for the Soviet regime, were trying to strengthen the positions of the latter on national foundations. During the summer of 1922 Stalin took the initiative in hastening the formation of the 'Union of Soviet Socialist Republics', which meant in practice doing away with the small degree of effective independence of autonomy that the non-Great-Russian nationalities still retained. The right to self-determination, including separation, still figured among the principles of the Union, but the state mechanism that had been set up negated any actual possibility of exercising this right.

How is Lenin's insistence on maintaining unchanged his traditional attitude of principle on the national question to be reconciled with a practice that systematically refuted it? It seems to me that what emerges from Lenin's writings and speeches of this period is that, for him, though such practice was inevitable owing to the exigencies of the revolutionary war against the Whites and their foreign allies, it should certainly not be institutionalized so as to become a permanent attitude of the party. In the second half of 1922, when illness prevented him from intervening directly in state affairs, the information that he received from the periphery, together with the plan to form the 'Union', increased his fears of seeing Great-Russian chauvinism permeate the structure and methods of party and state. The very day (30 December 1922) that the Congress of Soviets approved Stalin's schema, Lenin wrote a note to the party leadership which began with this significant piece of self-criticism: 'I suppose I have been very remiss with respect to the workers of Russia for not having intervened energetically and decisively enough in the notorious question of autonomization, which, it appears, is officially called the question of the union of Soviet socialist republics.' Though bowing to the accomplished fact, he expresses doubt whether the new state structure is opportune, and says: 'we cannot be sure in advance that as a result of this work we shall not take a step backwards at our next

Congress of Soviets, i.e., retain the union of Soviet socialist republics only for military and diplomatic affairs, and in all other respects restore full independence to the individual People's Commissariats.' The note amounts to a violent denunciation of Great-Russian chauvinism, with direct charges against Stalin. 'It is quite natural that in such circumstances the "freedom to secede from the union" by which we justify ourselves will be a mere scrap of paper, unable to defend the non-Russian from the onslaught of that really Russian man, the Great-Russian chauvinist, in substance a rascal and a tyrant, such as the typical Russian bureaucrat is.' Lenin was deeply anxious about the effect that this situation might have on the peoples fighting against imperialism and on the Comintern activity. 'The harm that can result to our state from a lack of unification between the national apparatuses and the Russian apparatus is infinitely less than that which will be done not only to us, but to the whole International, and to the hundreds of millions of the peoples of Asia, which is destined to follow us on to the stage in the near future.' The 'harm' referred to here is, of course, that represented by the unification of these 'apparatuses' under conditions of oppression for the non-Great-Russian nationalities. Lenin adds: 'It would be unpardonable opportunism if, on the eve of the *début* of the East, just as it is awakening, we undermined our prestige with its peoples, even if only by the slightest crudity or injustice towards our own non-Russian nationalities ... [or lapsing into] imperialist attitudes towards oppressed nationalities.'[83]

The problem of the Muslim peoples of Central Asia, the Caucasus, the Crimea, etc., was especially difficult. These peoples, made up overwhelmingly of peasants, constituted a far from negligible proportion of the total population inhabiting the territory under Soviet rule – nearly 25 millions out of 145 millions. They formed the principal colonies, in the strict sense of the word, of the Tsarist empire. From the 1905 revolution onward a national liberation movement developed among them, like that of the peoples of the Middle East who were subjected, directly or indirectly, to Western imperialism. Immediately after the capture of power, the Council of People's Commissars, in an 'Appeal to the Muslims of Russia and the East' (3 December 1917), informed the former subjects of Tsarism: 'Henceforward your beliefs and customs, your national and cultural institutions, are declared free and inviolable! Build your national life freely and without hindrance. It is your right.'[84] But 'hindrances' were to appear very soon. Tsarist colonization had taken in these regions, especially in Turkestan (with a Muslim population of four millions), an 'Algerian' form: settlement by Russian colonists (peasants, and also some workers), who inevitably acquired a colonialist mentality. When Bolshevik power was established in the heartland of Russia, this Russian minority in the Muslim regions at once became 'Soviet' and from its ranks were recruited many of the 'Bolsheviks' who were to take over the leading functions in the new institutions. The native Communists coming from the left wing of the national movement which had developed after 1905 began to find themselves in conflict with a new kind of colonialism. In 1920 Lenin sent one of his closest collaborators, Safarov, to study the problem on the ground.

It was inevitable [Safarov was to write some years later] that the Russian revolution should have a colonialist character [in Turkestan]. The Turkestani working class, numerically small, had neither leader, programme, party nor revolutionary tradition. It could therefore not protest against colonialist exploitation. Under Tsarist colonialism, it was the privilege of the Russians to belong to the industrial proletariat. For this reason, the dictatorship of the proletariat took on a typically colonialist aspect.[85]

The native Communists, who were mostly intellectuals, supported by the more revolutionary sections of the peasantry, tried to find a solution to this problem by setting up a truly independent Soviet republic, bringing together the Muslim peoples, and in which revolutionary ideology would allow for the national cultural tradition. They thought it would be possible to find support in the anti-imperialist wing of the Pan-Islamic movement, and that a Muslim Soviet republic could make a big contribution to stimulating and directing the struggle for national and social liberation among the 250 million Muslims of Asia and Africa. Against this tendency was unleashed what Lenin called, in the note quoted above, Stalin's 'spite' against 'social-nationalism'. The party organizations and Soviets in the regions in question were harshly purged, the native cadres replaced by reliable 'proletarians' (in other words, mainly by Russians), and national-cultural activity subjected to rigorous surveillance.[86]

It was inevitable that this policy, as Lenin feared would happen, should have harmful consequences for the Comintern's activity among the peoples of the Muslim East. An initial obstacle of major importance was the blanket condemnation of Pan-Islamism contained in the theses approved by the Second Congress of the International. This condemnation was probably not merely the result of the internal problem that this doctrine created for the Soviet state, but also expressed the 'Eurocentrist' cultural viewpoint dominant among Western Marxists (including Lenin, himself the author of these theses), which prevented them from grasping and taking advantage of the revolutionary potentialities contained in the anti-imperialist movements connected with traditional cultures. At the Fourth Congress of the Comintern, Tan Malaka, representing the Communist Party of the Dutch East Indies (Indonesia) strongly criticized the blanket condemnation of Pan-Islamism, explaining the revolutionary anti-imperialist significance of a considerable section of this movement, and how the attitude taken up by the Comintern had been skilfully used by the bourgeois nationalists of the Dutch East Indies in order to isolate the Communists from the peasant masses.[87] (This isolation, though not the only reason, was certainly one of the chief reasons why the Dutch authorities were able to crush the Communist Party of Indonesia at the end of 1926.).

It was no accident that the most resounding setback for the Comintern on the 'colonial front' occurred among the Muslim peoples of the Middle East, those most closely related to the Muslim minorities of the Soviet state. The bourgeois nationalists at the head of the national liberation movement in Turkey, Persia, Syria, Egypt and other countries of this region were able to exploit successfully the contradictions between the doctrinal positions of the Comintern and the inability of the Muslims liberated from Tsarist colonialism by the October revolution to set up their own national state. The Communists were presented by nationalist propaganda as agents of a state that oppressed part of the Islamic community. It is significant in this connection that until the end of the Second World War, and in some cases still to this day, the Communist parties of the Middle East and North Africa were never able to develop beyond the embryonic stage.

To sum up, we have seen that the Second Congress of the Comintern expressed high appreciation of the role that the colonial liberation movement was called upon to play in the world socialist revolution, and that this view was never formally changed throughout the history of the Comintern, but always figured, with slight variations, in its theses and resolutions. We have looked at three of the factors that contributed from the outset to weakening this evaluation and to diminishing or distorting its concrete expression in the Comintern's theoretical and political activity: the 'Eurocentrist' outlook of the Western Communists, including the Russians; the subordination of the Comintern, on the colonial front, to the interests of the foreign policy of the Soviet state; and the transformation into a dead letter of the right of self-determination, up to and including separation, where the peoples of the USSR were concerned.

In proportion as the Stalinist dictatorship became reinforced, it was the second factor that emerged as the most important: because of this, however, the consequences of the other two factors also weighed more heavily. It was in the epoch of the People's Front that the 'Eurocentrist' way of looking at the colonial problem was to develop to the full in the Comintern, precisely because it fitted in splendidly with the momentary needs of Soviet foreign policy. The third factor did not merely serve as a negative example reducing the influence of the October revolution, and so of the Comintern, among colonial liberation movements. For Stalin and his collaborators were also the real heads of the Comintern, and the 'Great-Russian chauvinist' mentality with which they approached the problem of the non-Great-Russian nationalities of the USSR, especially the more 'backward' of these, could not but affect the way in which they saw the colonial question beyond the Soviet frontier. This state of mind predisposed them to seeing in the colonial peoples, their liberation movements, and the small groups of Communists struggling to expand their influence, only subordinate factors in historical creativity.

The overall strategic conception by which the leading role in the world revolution belonged to the Western proletariat, with hegemony among them exercised by the Russian proletariat, and leadership of the latter held by the Bolshevik party, provided comfortable doctrinal pretexts for 'Great-Russian chauvinism'. In any case, it became daily more obvious that, as we shall see later, in the Stalinist hierarchy of 'subordination', the liberation movement in the colonies and dependent countries stood on the bottom rung of the ladder.

(b) The Comintern's policy on the colonial front

The main problem that faced the Comintern as soon as it prepared to intervene in the struggle of the subject people for liberation lay in the fact that this struggle already possessed, in the principal oppressed countries, a structure, line and leadership of its own. In all these countries, as the theses of the Fourth Congress noted, 'at first, the indigenous bourgeoisie and intelligentsia are the champions of the colonial revolutionary movements'. Moreover, 'as the bourgeois-nationalist intelligentsia draws the revolutionary working-class movement into the struggle against imperialism, its representatives at first also take the lead in the newly formed trade-union organizations and their activities'. By showing in practice that it was possible to overthrow the Western powers in a backward, semi-Asiatic country, the October revolution had had profound repercussions in all the liberation movements of the oppressed peoples. The bourgeois nationalists themselves saw in the new state a practical ally against imperialism. These same theses added, nevertheless, that 'the representatives of bourgeois nationalism, taking advantage of the political authority of Soviet Russia and adapting themselves to the class instincts of the workers, clothe their bourgeois-democratic aspirations in a "socialist" or "Communist" garb in order — although they themselves may not always be conscious of this – to divert the embryonic proletarian associations from the direct tasks of a class organization.'[88]

What attitude should be adopted towards these nationalist movements which were anti-imperialist and yet bourgeois, which saw in Soviet Russia a possible ally and at the same time assumed the clothes of the October revolution so as the better to establish their bourgeois influence among the peasant masses and in working-class circles? This was the problem that faced the Soviet state and the Comintern on the 'colonial front'. The different aspects of this problem were as follows: (1) the relations between Soviet Russia, as a *state*, and these liberation movements, as representatives of the oppressed *nations*; (2) the relations between the Comintern, as representative of *the revolutionary proletariat of the capitalist West*, and these same movements; (3) the relations that the Comintern should maintain, as the *Communist organization in the colonies*, with movements of which it was in fact the class enemy.

Two sets of draft theses, reflecting distinct points of view and divergent conclusions, were put forward during the Second Congress of the Comintern, in which an approach was made to this question of tactics – which could be considered as a question of strategy in so far as it was a question of defining a long-term political line. The first set was Lenin's, the second Roy's.[89] Lenin's way of looking at the problem gave priority to the first two of the aspects I have mentioned. Roy, however, based himself rather upon the third. Lenin considered that the main thing was to take advantage of the objective possibility for Soviet Russia to rally around her the oppressed peoples that were fighting as nations against imperialism. He therefore believed that the Comintern, representing the revolutionary proletariat of the West, 'must enter into a temporary alliance with bourgeois democracy in the colonial and backward countries'. Roy's view was this: 'There are to be found in the dependent countries two distinct movements which every day grow further apart from each other. One is the bourgeois-democratic nationalist movement, with a programme of political independence under the bourgeois order, and the other is the mass action of the poor and ignorant peasants and workers for their liberation from all forms of exploitation. The former endeavours to control the latter, and often succeeds to a certain extent, but the Communist International and the parties affected must struggle against such control and help to develop class-consciousness in the working masses of the colonies.' Roy did not allow for any collaboration with the bourgeois nationalist movement, and took the view that 'the first and most necessary task is the formation of Communist parties which will organize the peasants and workers and lead them to the revolution and to the establishment of Soviet republics'. He acknowledged, nevertheless, that the revolution in the colonies could not be Communist in its first stages, and that it would be necessary to realize progressively 'a programme which will include many petty-bourgeois reforms, such as division of land, etc.'. And he added, 'But from this it does not follow at all that the leadership of the revolution will have to be surrendered to the bourgeois democrats.' Lenin's theses implicitly admitted that for a long time to come the leadership of the colonial revolution would remain locally in the hands of the national bourgeoisie, even though on the world scale the leadership of the anti-imperialist struggle would be taken by the proletariat of the advanced capitalist countries and the Soviet state. Roy's thesis also recognized this leading role on the international plane as belonging to the Western proletariat, but considered that it was necessary to rely directly upon the exploited masses of the colonies, without having recourse to the mediation of the bourgeois nationalist movement. Lenin's theses stressed 'the need ... to give special support to the peasant movement against the landowners, against landed proprietorship, and against all manifestations or survivals of feudalism', while striving 'to lend the peasant movement the most revolutionary character by establishing the closest possible alliance between the West-European Communist proletariat and the revolutionary peasant movement in the East, in the colonies, and in the backward countries generally'. From Lenin's point of view, however, this constituted no obstacle to an alliance with the bourgeois nationalist movement, because for Lenin the peasants were the essential component of 'bourgeois democracy'. It was a question of giving this democracy a more revolutionary orientation.

Lenin's entire strategic conception was based on two assumptions. The first of these was that the contradiction between the basic aims of the bourgeois-democratic national movement – such as national independence and local capitalist economic development – and the interests of imperialism was sufficiently deep to ensure that, despite hesitations by the national bourgeoisie, the alliance between this movement, on the one hand, and Soviet Russia, together with the proletariat of the advanced capitalist countries, on the other, possessed an objective foundation that was comparatively firm. The second of his assumptions was that, given its extreme numerical, economic and ideological weakness, the working class of the colonies would be unable for a long time yet to play a leading role in the national liberation movement. The following passage, taken from his speech at the Second Congress of the Comintern, is highly significant in this connection:

It is beyond doubt that any national movement can only be a bourgeois-democratic movement, since the overwhelming mass of the population in the backward countries consists of peasants who represent bourgeois-capitalist relationships. It would be utopian to believe that proletarian parties in these backward countries, if indeed they can emerge in them, can pursue Communist tactics and a Communist policy without establishing definite relations with the peasant movement and without giving it effective support.[90]

The principal purpose of this statement is to stress the necessity for the proletarian parties in the colonies to 'establish relations' with and to 'support' – Lenin does not say 'lead', and this is evidently not just a slip of the tongue – the peasant movement which represents bourgeois-capitalist relationships or, what comes to the same thing, to 'support' the bourgeois-democratic national movement. At the same time, however, Lenin is doubtful whether such proletarian parties can be formed in the colonial countries. And this is logical enough if one thinks of the characteristics that were essential if a party was to be regarded as 'proletarian' from the Bolshevik standpoint.

In Roy's schema this difficulty was evaded. While, on the one hand, he regarded it as indispensable that the Communist vanguard take in hand the leadership of the colonial revolution from the outset, he also admitted, in these same theses, that the proletariat hardly existed in the colonies, and that the mass of agricultural workers and those employed in the few light or extractive industries were sunk in ignorance owing to the policy of the colonialists. In his theses Roy noted that, 'as a result of this policy, the spirit of revolt, latent in every subject people, found its expression only through the small, educated middle class'. Roy solved the problem by having recourse to the leadership given by the proletariat of the advanced capitalist countries. This made his schema of the revolution somewhat inconsistent in its 'Asiocentrism'. He entrusted to the proletariat of the West, which he regarded as incapable of making the revolution in their own home countries because the surplus value extracted from the colonies enabled the capitalists to inculcate a conformist outlook among them, the mission of educating, organizing and mobilizing the exploited masses of the colonies to carry on a revolutionary struggle.

Lenin took things as they presented themselves at the moment and would probably go on presenting themselves – seen from the angle of his theory of the revolution – so long as there was lacking in the colonies the social basis indispensable for creating a sufficiently solid proletarian party of the Bolshevik type. Roy's schema, centred on Asia, gave subjective expression to the revolutionary potential of the East, but without showing the paths and means by which it could rise up. Ten years after the Second Congress of the Comintern some Chinese Communists, enriched by harsh experience, were to discover these paths. It is interesting, though, to note that Lenin, while retaining in his theses the conception of the 'proletarian party' of the Western type, the creation of which in the colonies seemed to him problematical – which inevitably meant leaving the liberation movement under the leadership of the national bourgeoisie – was beginning to wonder about the validity of this conception of the party where the subject countries were concerned. In some brief notes written during the Second Congress, which remained unpublished until recently, we find the following reflection: it will be necessary, he thinks, to '*adjust* both soviet institutions and the Communist Party (its membership, special tasks) to the level of the *peasant* countries'.[91] This suggestion was not followed up by the Comintern. The Chinese Communist Party was to be the first to echo it, but without knowing that this was what in fact it was doing.

The discussion at the Second Congress of the draft theses of Lenin and Roy resulted in amendments being made to both documents which narrowed the differences between them. Lenin agreed that where he advocated support for the 'bourgeois-democratic movement' in the colonies this should read: support for the 'national-revolutionary movement'. Lenin had to explain to the Congress that every movement for colonial liberation is necessarily 'bourgeois-democratic' in character, given that the overwhelming majority of the population are peasants, but that it can, nevertheless, be either reformist or revolutionary. In order to show the significance of the amendments made to the draft theses, Lenin said: 'We, as Communists, should and will support bourgeois-liberation movements in the colonies only when they are genuinely revolutionary, and when their exponents do not hinder our work of educating and organizing in a revolutionary spirit the peasantry and the masses of the exploited. If these conditions do not exist, the Communists in these countries must combat the reformist bourgeoisie . . .'[92] Time and events were to show how hard it was to find this white blackbird, a bourgeois liberation movement that was willing not to prevent the Communists from educating and organizing the exploited masses in a revolutionary spirit. At the same time, however, the Turkish experience very soon showed that the Soviet leaders did not take this condition quite literally.

The theses laid down as another condition – not for the bourgeois liberation movements but for the Comintern itself and for each of its sections – that an alliance with national revolutionary movement must be realized, 'but it must not amalgamate with it; it must unconditionally maintain the independence of the proletarian movement, even if it is only in an embryonic stage'. It was also declared that 'a resolute struggle must be waged against the attempt to clothe the revolutionary liberation movements in the backward countries which are not genuinely Communist in Communist colours'.[93]

The Second Congress gave its approval to an important theoretical proposition which Roy brought up, and which Lenin adopted, presenting it in the following terms: 'The Communist International should advance the proposition, with the appropriate theoretical grounding, that with the aid of the proletariat of the advanced countries, backward countries can go over to the Soviet system and, through certain stages of development, to Communism, without having to pass through the capitalist stage.'[94] Marx had already in his day framed a similar hypothesis where Russia was concerned.[95] Basing himself on the first experiences provided by the Sovietization of the most backward regions of the former Tsarist empire, Lenin also came to the following conclusion: 'The idea of Soviet organization is a simple one, and is applicable not only to proletarian but also to peasant feudal and semi-feudal relations. Our experience in this respect is not as yet very considerable. However, the debate in the commission, in which several representatives from colonial countries participated, demonstrated convincingly that the Communist International's theses should point out that peasants' Soviets, Soviets of the exploited, are a weapon which can be employed not only in capitalist countries but also in countries with pre-capitalist relations.'[96]

These were the main points of the guidelines and directions adopted by the Second Congress of the Comintern on the subject of the colonial question. The Fourth Congress, the last in which Lenin took part, looked at the question afresh and, in the light of the experience acquired during the two and half years that had elapsed since the Second Congress, carried further its theoretical study of some aspects of the colonial revolution, especially those connected with the agrarian question. This more thorough study, together with the behaviour of the national bourgeoisie in certain countries of Asia, tending to seek conciliation with imperialism, led the Congress to sharpen its critical attitude toward the bourgeois nationalist movement. In most of the countries of the East, said the theses approved by this congress: 'the agrarian question is of primary importance in the struggle for emancipation from the yoke of the Great Powers' despotism ... Only the agrarian revolution, whose object is to expropriate the large estates, can set in motion the enormous peasant masses; it is destined to exercise a decisive influence on the struggle against imperialism ... The revolutionary movement in the backward countries of the East cannot be successful unless it relies on the action of the broad peasant masses.' And the theses emphasize a very important fact which makes comprehensible the attitude of the national bourgeoisie: 'The bourgeois nationalists' fear [in India, Persia, Egypt] of the agrarian watchwords, and their anxiety to prune them down as far as possible, bear witness to the close connection between the native bourgeoisie and the feudal and feudal-bourgeois landlords, and to the intellectual and political dependence of the former on the latter.' (The 'forgetting' of this circumstance was, as we shall see later, to be one of the reasons for the shipwreck of the Comintern's policy in the Chinese revolution.)

This internal characteristic of the colonial revolution, together with the fact that its accomplishment strikes at the very foundations of imperialism, that 'a decisive victory for this revolution is incompatible with the rule of world imperialism', carries the implication that 'the objective tasks of the colonial revolution go beyond the limits of bourgeois democracy'. This serves as the basis for a further conclusion, namely that 'the ruling classes among the colonial and semi-colonial peoples are unable and unwilling to lead the struggle against imperialism in so far as that struggle assumes the form of a revolutionary mass movement'. Proceeding from these premises, the Fourth Congress went on to declare with much more firmness and emphasis than the Second that it was necessary for the 'young proletariat of the colonies' to fight to win an independent position within the 'anti-imperialist united front' and become the leading force in it. (The formulation 'anti-imperialist united front' was only another way of describing the alliance with the national-revolutionary movement advocated by the Second Congress. Since, however, the Fourth Congress was taking place at the time when in the West there was talk of the 'workers' united front', the colonial vocabulary of the Comintern was obliged to pay its little tribute to Europe.)

The following passage in the theses summarizes the tactics that the Communist parties of the colonial and semi-colonial countries were to apply:

The refusal of the Communists in the colonies to take part in the struggle against imperialist tyranny on the ground of the ostensible 'defence' of their independent class interests is opportunism of the worst kind, which can only discredit the proletarian revolution in the East. Equally injurious is the attempt to remain aloof from the struggle for the most urgent and everyday interests of the working class in the name of 'national unity' or of 'civil peace' with the bourgeois democrats. The Communist workers' parties of the colonial and semi-colonial countries have a dual task: they fight for the most radical possible solution of the tasks of a bourgeois-democratic revolution, which aims at the conquest of political independence; and they organize the working and peasant masses for the struggle for their special class interests, and in doing so exploit all the contradictions in the nationalist bourgeois-democratic camp ... The working class of the colonies and semi-colonies must learn that only the extension and intensification of the struggle against the imperialist yoke of the great powers will ensure for them the role of revolutionary leadership, while on the other hand only the economic and political organization and the political education of the working-class and the semi-proletarian strata of the population can enlarge the revolutionary surge of the struggle against imperialism.

In another chapter, the theses stress the need for the proletariat to win the support of the peasant masses: only then will it become the real vanguard of the colonial revolution.[97]

The chief inconsistency in the theses of the Fourth Congress, as in those of the Second, lay in the fact that this proletariat which was to carry out such complex and gigantic tasks was an extremely weak group in colonial society – as, indeed, Roy's own theses acknowledged. Even in countries that had experienced a certain amount of industrial development, like China, India and the Dutch East Indies, the percentage of workers in the population as a whole was very slight. Moreover, it was a working class that had been formed very recently, lacking revolutionary traditions or political experience and with an extremely low cultural level. The great majority were illiterate. The proletariat of these countries soon manifested fighting spirit, but that quality would not suffice if it was to take on the role that the Comintern's resolutions allotted to it. It was not unusual, moreover, for some sections of the working class – those, at least, who belonged to the most up-to-date enterprises – to enjoy a material position that was privileged in comparison with the wretched majority of the population; this situation facilitated the penetration of reformist and corporatist tendencies into the trade-union organizations. The Communist parties of the colonial countries would have been hard put to it to carry out their mission as theoretical and political vanguard of the national revolutionary movement if their social composition had been, in accordance with the European model, fundamentally proletarian. In fact, the Communist parties of the colonies formed during the first years of the Comintern were made up entirely of students and intellectuals, who were then joined by a few small groups of workers. And the leading cadres were, with few exceptions, intellectuals. Yet the Comintern considered that this predominance of intellectuals constituted the chief *weakness* of the colonial Communist parties, and its chief concern was to 'proletarianize' them. The Comintern was obviously unable to conceive of a colonial revolution carried through under the leadership of a party that was essentially made up of peasants, as regards the mass of militants, and intellectuals, as regards its cadres. The only thing that comes over clearly in the successive colonial theses of the Comintern is the lack of clarity as to the means of solving the problem. Most of the time it was simply dodged.

Apart from this crucial problem, the theses of the Fourth Congress reflect a certain earnest endeavour to analyse, resulting from the experiences accumulated during the two and a half years that had passed since the Second Congress. They are not, however, free from the chief characteristics of the theses of the latter, being pitched on an excessively abstract plane, with general formulations that 'embrace' highly complex and diverse realities. Roy alluded to this in his speech:

We thought that, simply because they [the countries of the East] were all politically, economically and socially backward, we could lump them all together, and deal with this problem as though it were a general problem. But this was a mistake. We know today that the Eastern countries cannot be taken as a homogeneous whole, neither politically, economically nor socially. This Eastern question therefore represents for the Communist International a question of greater complexity than the struggle in the West – assuming that the International is prepared to take it seriously.[98]

In the theses of the Fourth Congress, however, this lack of differentiation persists. Despite such important recent experiences as the Turkish and Persian revolutions, and the movements in India and Egypt, the Congress failed to attempt any fundamental analysis of these experiences. Like all the other Comintern congresses it devoted itself above all to the problems of the West. While the system of an ultra-centralized world party clashed here with the fact of national diversity, this contradiction was to have even graver consequences for the theoretical and practical leadership of the revolutionary struggle in the colonies.

The Fifth Congress, held during the summer of 1924, not long after Lenin's death, was even more definitely slanted towards European problems, and this provoked, as at other congresses, criticism from delegates from the colonial countries. Manuilsky's report on the 'national and

colonial question' was basically devoted to the cases of national oppression created in Europe as a result of the settlement after the
1914–18 war, and to praise of the way the national and colonial question
had been solved in the USSR. 'A very interesting clause in our constitution ... states that every nation forming part of the Union of
Socialist Soviet Republics can leave it at any moment. This can be
carried out without any restricting formalities whatever, as a one-sided
act.'[99] Hidden from the delegates of the foreign Communist parties was
the critique formulated by Lenin in December 1922, when he feared
that this 'interesting clause' might prove to be a 'scrap of paper'. Nor
were they told that if the right to separation was not restricted by any
formality, this was because it was restricted by an absolute barrier that
had nothing formal about it, namely, the impossibility of exercising this
right in practice. Instead of undertaking a sincere analysis of the Soviet
experience of the colonial question, which would have been very instructive for the foreign Communists, Manuilsky engaged in a bamboozling
apologia.

The principal innovation of the Fifth Congress, as compared with the
line taken at the Fourth, was that the critical attitude of the colonial
Communist parties towards the national bourgeoisies was considerably
modified. The Fifth Congress laid stress on collaboration with these
bourgeoisies. Roy's positions were severely criticized. The period was
beginning in which the Soviet Union, whose axis in foreign policy was
the tacit alliance with Germany, was to see Anglo-French imperialism
as its chief enemy. In Stalin's view, there was serious danger of a war
against the USSR, and it was Britain that was pulling the strings of the
new anti-Soviet plot. In face of this danger Stalin looked for allies in the
enemy's 'rear'. He thought he had found them, in the West, in the shape
of those trade-union leaders who, because of the radicalization of the
British working-class movement in this period, were interested in
making a show of cordial relations with the Soviet trade-union
leaders. In the East, looking at things with Stalinist realism, the only
possible allies of any weight were the bourgeois nationalist movements
engaged in conflict with Anglo-French imperialism. If Stalin was scep-
tical about the revolutionary capacity of the Western Communist
parties (we have already seen what his views were in 1923 about the

KPD), he was even more so where the 'colonial' parties were concerned, for they played a very minor role at this period. At the time of the Fifth Congress, there were in the whole of Asia (including Egypt but excluding Outer Mongolia, which was *de facto* a Soviet protectorate) nine sections of the Comintern. These were in China, with 800 members; Java, 2,000; Persia, 600; Egypt, 700; Palestine, 100; Turkey, 600; and also Japan and Korea, where small illegal groups existed, and India, where the party was not yet structured on the national scale and there were only some scattered cells with very few members.[1]

It is therefore not surprising that Stalin staked all his hopes on the 'national bourgeoisies' of the colonial countries. This applied especially to the one which, starting in 1923–4, seemed disposed to carry out to the end its national and 'bourgeois-democratic' revolution in the Asian country of greatest importance for the strategic interests of the Soviet state – a revolution that was standing up against the two imperialisms that were most dangerous at that moment to the security of the USSR, namely, British imperialism, a threat in Europe and Asia alike, and Japanese imperialism, a permanent menace to the Soviet Far East. The idea of a China unified as a nation under Sun Yat-sen – a Sun Yat-sen who proclaimed himself a fervent friend of the Russian revolution and sought the help of the Soviet state for his liberating enterprise – and Sun's party, the Kuomintang, was sufficiently attractive for Stalin to accord absolute priority over every other doctrinal or political consideration to alliance with the 'national bourgeoisie' that Sun Yat-sen was supposed to represent: and, in any case, to cast into oblivion the theses of the Fourth Congress of the Comintern.

THE CHINESE REVOLUTION

In the first months of 1927 the Chinese revolution entered a critical phase. The army of the Kuomintang, commanded by Chiang Kai-shek, had undertaken in the summer of 1926 the 'Northern Expedition', the aim of which was the unification and independence of China, extending to the whole of China the republic of Sun Yat-sen. The latter had consolidated his position in the area around Canton from 1923–4 onwards, thanks to the Soviet aid that enabled him to create his own military forces.[2] The Republican army advanced rapidly, and at the end of 1926 the Kuomintang government was able to establish itself at Wuhan, on the Yangtse. Its authority already extended over about ten provinces in the southern and central regions of China. Nanking and Shanghai were liberated in March 1927. As the Republican forces advanced, however, the masses of workers and peasants went into action. Strikes and revolts followed, or even preceded and helped, the onward movement of the Kuomintang army. This happened in Shanghai, which fell into the hands of a workers' militia, organized by the Communist Party and the trade unions, before Chiang's men arrived. This movement of the worker and peasant masses assumed such proportions and manifested such features – in some districts the peasant leagues carried out *their own revolution*, an agrarian revolution – that it alarmed both the Chinese bourgeoisie and the imperialist powers. The latter at once sent military reinforcements to their bases on Chinese territory, the notorious 'concessions'; and with their aid the bankers and compradors of Shanghai organized a counter-revolution.

Up to that time the Communist Party had been the Kuomintang's ally, or, rather, it had formed an integral part of the Kuomintang. Its members were members of the party founded by Sun Yat-sen. They shared in the leadership, though as a minority element. The Comintern considered the Kuomintang an organization capable of carrying the Chinese revolution through to the end of its bourgeois-democratic 'stage'. It defined the Kuomintang as a 'bloc of four classes' – the workers, the peasants, the petty-bourgeoisie and the national bourgeoisie. In March 1926 the ECCI had admitted the Kuomintang to membership of the International as a 'sympathizing party' and Chiang Kai-shek had been made an 'honorary member' of the Presidium. A year later, between April and July 1927, Chiang Kai-shek turned on the Chinese Communist Party and did his utmost to destroy it.

On 12 April 1927 Chiang's troops, along with armed gangs formed by the Shanghai bourgeoisie, launched a surprise attack on the Communist and trade-union organizations in that city. Within a few days, thousands of Communists and revolutionary workers, including prominent leaders of the Communist Party and the unions, had been savagely murdered or flung into prison. The Comintern leadership saw

'Chiang Kai-shek's *coup d'état*' as the going-over of the 'national bourgeoisie', that is, the 'right wing' of the Kuomintang to the counter-revolution, while the 'left wing', representing the 'petty-bourgeoisie', remained in the camp of revolution. The government in Wuhan was in the hands of this left wing. According to the Comintern's analysis, the 'left' made up 90 per cent of the 'bloc of four classes' and was the *real* Kuomintang. At first the 'left' did indeed condemn Chiang's *coup d'état*, and the Kuomintang was split, politically and in terms of armed forces and territory occupied. The Wuhan government, with the forces that remained loyal to it, controlled the provinces in the interior of the country. Meanwhile, Chiang, who had formed his own government at Nanking, controlled the coast provinces, and extended to all the region in his power the terror he had launched against the Communists and the workers and peasants' organization of Shanghai. Wuhan became, according to the Comintern, the 'centre of the revolution', and two Communists entered the Kuomintang government there. However, the agrarian revolution grew more and more threatening in the territories subject to Wuhan, despite the efforts of the Communist Party to moderate it. On 15 July, three months after Chiang's betrayal, the 'left' Kuomintang took up the same attitude as the 'right', expelling Communists from the party and the army, and murdering and imprisoning revolutionary militants of the labour and peasant movements. A few months later, the 'right' and the 'left' came to terms, and Chiang was recognized as supreme leader of the Kuomintang. The Communist Party had been decimated, broken up and reduced to illegality, along with the trade unions and the peasant leagues. Following instructions from the Comintern the Chinese Communists tried to save the situation by organizing a series of desperate counter-attacks, one of these being the famous Canton Commune of December 1927. All were crushed, and by the beginning of 1928 the bloody destruction of the Communist Party of China was an accomplished fact.

Immediately after Chiang's *coup* the leading organs of the Comintern, the CPSU and the Chinese Communist Party began a discussion that went through several phases, as events contributed new items to the dossier, and lasted until the Sixth Congress of the Comintern, in the summer of 1928. The various lines taken up in this discussion all agreed, however, on one major point, which was reaffirmed later in the versions of its own history put out by the Chinese party, as well as those written by Soviet historians and by Western writers: namely, that the catastrophic defeat suffered by the Chinese Communists in 1927 was not the inevitable result of a certain relation of forces, but, first and foremost, the consequence of serious political errors committed by the Communist leadership. And, to some extent, the subsequent course of events was to supply practical confirmation to this view. The Communist groups that managed to escape from the repression, shifting the centre of their activity to the rural areas, succeeded very quickly in organizing revolutionary bases where leading organs were set up and armed forces created which became substantial in size in the years that followed. This revealed, *a posteriori*, that a different tactic would have been possible from that which had led to defeat. Even if the objective conditions for victory of the revolution on the all-China scale were not present, the Communist Party would have been able to avoid catastrophe if it had foreseen the 'betrayal' by the Kuomintang bourgeoisie (warning signs had been multiplying for a year previously) and had not let itself be taken by surprise by the counter-revolutionary *coup d'état*. The 'second revolutionary civil war' could have begun on the basis of positions much more to the advantage of the workers and peasants.[3] The analyses carried out in 1927–8 could not take this subsequent confirmation into account, but study of the forces present and of their dynamic did make it possible to conclude that the defeat suffered had not been the inevitable consequence of objective conditions, but rather that of political mistakes. On the basis of this conclusion, the problem was one of determining the nature of these mistakes and the responsibilities resulting therefrom.

After a year of discussion, Bukharin summed up in these terms, in his report to the Sixth World Congress, the point of view of the leadership of the International:

Here we can in retrospect deal once again with some of the major problems of the Chinese revolution. The Communist Party of China, as all of you know, has suffered a severe defeat. This is a fact. The question arises, was this defeat a result of the wrong tactics pursued by the Comintern in the Chinese revolution? Perhaps it was indeed inexpedient to have entered into a bloc with the bourgeoisie; perhaps that was the original sin, the basic error, which determined the other errors and gradually, step by step, brought about the defeat of the Chinese proletariat?

And Bukharin answered his own question thus:

On the whole, it is not the main line of tactics that was at fault, but the political actions and the practical application of the line pursued in China. Firstly, at the beginning of the Chinese revolution, in the period of collaboration with the Kuomintang, our mistake was that we *did not sufficiently criticize the Kuomintang.* Instead of being an ally, *our party was at times an accessory* of the Kuomintang. Secondly, the Communist Party of China failed to understand the change that took place in the objective situation, the transition from one stage to another. Thus, it was possible for a time to march together with the national bourgeoisie, but at a certain stage of development *it was necessary to foresee imminent changes* ... Thirdly, our party at times acted as *a brake on the mass movement, a brake on the agrarian revolution, and a brake on the labour movement.* These were fatal blunders and, naturally, they helped to bring about the defeat of the Communist Party and of the Chinese proletariat. After a whole series of defeats the party set to work resolutely to rectify its opportunist blunders. But this time, as frequently happens, some comrades fell into the other extreme. They did not prepare uprisings with sufficient care, they displayed glaring putschist tendencies and adventurism of the worst type.[4]

Here we have an excellent summary of the political mistakes that led to the defeat of the Chinese Communist Party in 1927 – provided we insert two fundamental corrections. These are: (*a*) the mistakes were not made merely at the level of the Chinese Communist Party's 'practical application of the line', they were rooted in the 'main line of tactics' adopted by the leadership of the Comintern and (*b*) when Bukharin speaks of the 'Chinese Communist Party' we should read 'leadership of the Comintern', or 'the Chinese Communist Party carrying out the line and the instructions received from Moscow'.

The justification for the second of these corrections follows more or less axiomatically from the type of relations that the Chinese Communist Party had with the supreme centre of the Comintern (like those between the latter and any other national section). This was especially obvious in the period between 1924 and 1927, when the Soviet government was intervening directly in the events in China, which attracted attention all over the world. It was inevitable that the ECCI, supervised by Stalin, should not merely determine the 'main line of tactics' but also that it should check closely on how this line was applied in practice. The facts made known during the last twenty years, through the extensive amount of historical and political writing that has been devoted to the Chinese revolution, allow us to assume that the 'tutelage' exercised by the Comintern and the Soviet government over the Chinese party in this period was very similar to that which they exercised over the Spanish Communist Party during the civil war.[5] By unloading all responsibility on to the shoulders of the Chinese party leadership, and in particular on its General Secretary, Chen Tu-hsiu, the ECCI merely followed practice that had already become a matter of routine. Trotsky showed brilliantly, in his writings of 1927 and 1928, that the mistakes listed by Bukharin were not simply mistakes of 'application' but followed from the 'main line of tactics'. On these two questions – the nature of the mistakes made, and the responsibility for them – it is here possible to do no more than mention very briefly the most outstanding facts.

The form and content of the alliance between the Kuomintang and the Chinese Communist Party were not discussed and decided on between the two parties. They resulted from direct negotiations between Sun Yat-sen and representatives of the Comintern, and more especially of the Soviet government. The document that laid down the line for the Chinese Communist Party was the declaration issued by Sun Yat-sen and the Soviet ambassador Joffe on 26 January 1923. This stated that 'neither the Communist system nor even the Soviet system can be introduced in China'. The common aim must be 'unification and national independence'.

The negotiations between the Soviet representatives and those of Sun Yat-sen also decided the form that collaboration between the Kuomintang and the Chinese Communist Party should take. Sun was against an alliance between the two parties as such, and would agree only to individual membership of the Kuomintang by the Communists, who must submit to the Kuomintang's discipline. At first the Central Committee of the Chinese Communist Party rejected this arrangement, arguing that it would mean mortgaging the party's political independence and sowing confusion among the masses. Eventually, however, the Chinese Communists accepted the Comintern's decision. Their Third Party Congress (June 1923) approved, though not without strong resistance, entry into the Kuomintang. Following the line laid down by the Comintern, the manifesto issued by the congress said that the Kuomintang 'should be the central force of the national revolution and should assume its leadership'.[6] There is no need to point out the extent to which an alliance contracted under such conditions ran counter to the theses of the Second and Fourth Congresses of the Comintern.

The Sun-Joffe declaration was obviously not the expression of a theoretical judgement on the immaturity of the Chinese economy for the 'Communist system', and the fact that it was stated that 'the Soviet system' was not suitable for China, either, was highly significant. Had not Lenin said at the Second Congress of the Comintern, and on other occasions, that the Soviet system was perfectly appropriate to the agrarian countries of the East? The declaration was a political compromise whereby the Soviet leaders, and therefore the Comintern and the Chinese Communists, reassured Sun Yat-sen that they would not seek to give the 'national revolution' a social-revolutionary content. This guarantee related especially to the agrarian revolution, the spectre of which haunted the Kuomintang bourgeoisie.[7] Moreover, the subjection of the Chinese Communists to the discipline of the Kuomintang proved still less reconcilable with the political and organizational independence of the Chinese Communist Party when the Kuomintang – aided by the Soviet advisers and Comintern delegates – transformed itself from 1924 onwards into a centralized party with structures similar to those of the Bolshevik party. In short, the essence of the 'main line of tactics' consisted, from 1923 onward, in accepting and supporting the leadership represented by the bourgeois nationalist movement of Sun Yat-sen. In the Comintern documents and in Stalin's statements of the 1924–7 period one can find a number of formulations which seem to contradict, formally at least, this essence of the 'main line'; however, contrary to the allegation made by Bukharin at the Sixth World Congress, the 'practical line' adopted in China was not in contradiction to the 'main line' but was an exact materialization of its essence.

At the start, the Chinese Communist Party, guided by the Comintern, acted in a plainly pragmatic way. It was necessary to harmonize the 'Chinese Communism' factor, which the party could not do without, with the alliance between the Soviet government and that of Sun Yat-sen. This alliance acquired extraordinary value in the eyes of the Soviet leaders in proportion as Sun's government saw opening before it the prospect of becoming the national government of China. Once, however, this harmonization had been accomplished on the practical and political planes, the Comintern and Stalin were obliged to provide it with a 'Marxist-Leninist' doctrinal justification. This was not at all easy if one started from the principle that the Kuomintang was the party of China's national bourgeoisie.

Accordingly, in May 1925 Stalin propounded the thesis that a differentiation had occurred in China between the conservative wing and the revolutionary wing of this bourgeoisie. The revolutionary wing formed part of the Kuomintang, representing essentially 'the revolutionary petty-bourgeoisie'. Consequently, the Kuomintang could be regarded as intrinsically a 'workers' and peasants' ' party, in which was realized 'a bloc of two forces – the Communist Party and the party of the revolutionary petty-bourgeoisie'. Such a bloc was acceptable and appropriate said Stalin, 'provided it does not bind the Communist Party hand and foot' and 'provided it facilitates the actual leadership of the revolutionary movement by the Communist party'. (When, some years later, Stalin's collected works were published, this passage was corrected so as to remove all reference to the Kuomintang. Events had shown very thoroughly that the 'national bourgeoisie', including its most reactionary wing, had not only been an element in the Kuomintang ever since the formation of the latter, but that it was in fact the real leader of the party, and that the expression 'bound hand and foot' described perfectly the situation of the Chinese Communist Party within the Kuomintang.[8])

The presence of the 'national bourgeoisie' was so flagrant that Stalin was obliged to alter his argument very soon, naturally without admitting that he was doing this. At the Sixth Plenum of the ECCI (March 1926) the Kuomintang was defined as 'a revolutionary bloc of workers, peasants, intellectuals and the urban democracy'. After Chiang's betrayal, in May 1927, Stalin explained that this formulation should be understood as meaning 'a bloc of the workers, the petty-bourgeoisie (urban and rural) and the national bourgeoisie'. And he also explained that he had not intended to say, in May 1925, that the Kuomintang was *already* a 'workers' and peasants' party' but that it *ought* to do everything to become such a party, that it was *tending* to become such a party.[9]

Unfortunately, the opportunist mistakes of the Chinese Communist Party prevented the actual Kuomintang from becoming the ideal Kuomintang that Stalin had outlined. However, if the Kuomintang included the 'national bourgeoisie', how was it to be explained that the Sixth Plenum of the ECCI had admitted this party into the International as a 'sympathizing party' and named its new leader (Sun Yat-sen having died a year previously) an 'honorary member of the Presidium'? In his explanation of 1927 Stalin preferred to 'overlook' this detail, which was never thereafter to be mentioned in Soviet historiography.

While Moscow was honouring him in this way, Chiang Kai-shek was launching his first attack on the Communists. During the night of 20–21 March 1926 he arrested the Communist cadres of the military school at Whampoa, put the Soviet advisers under house arrest, imprisoned a number of Canton Communists and trade-unionists, disarmed the strike pickets belonging to the Canton-Hongkong strike committee, and surrounded the headquarters of the trade unions with his troops. Chiang did not intend for the moment actually to crush the Communists, for the 'Northern Expedition' was being prepared and he needed Soviet military aid. His aim was to strengthen his position in the Kuomintang leadership by weakening the petty-bourgeois 'left' and 'binding the Communists hand and foot'. He succeeded completely in this. Wang Ching-wei, head of the Canton government and leader of the 'left', was obliged to go into temporary exile. At its meeting on 15 May the executive committee of the Kuomintang adopted, at Chiang's instigation, a series of anti-Communist measures. The Chinese Communist Party must undertake to observe strictly the 'Three People's Principles' of Sun Yat-sen, and hand over a complete list of Communist members of the Kuomintang; Communists would no longer be allowed to occupy leading positions in the Kuomintang, and their share of the membership of the party and state apparatuses must not exceed one-third of the total; the Communists were forbidden to form factions in the Kuomintang; the directives of the Chinese Communist Party and those it received from the Comintern, must be submitted for approval to a mixed Kuomintang–Communist Party committee.[10] Chen Tu-hsiu's immediate reaction was to propose to the ECCI that the Chinese party leave the Kuomintang and re-negotiate the alliance on a new basis.

This position of the Chinese party was severely criticized by *Pravda*, and, in Canton, Borodin, the representative of the Soviet government with the Kuomintang, adopted (and made the Chinese Communists adopt) a conciliatory attitude towards Chiang, bowing to the measures taken by the Kuomintang's executive committee. Chen Tu-hsiu was obliged to publish an article written in this spirit – an article that was to be used by the Comintern, after the catastrophe of 1927, in order to accuse Chen Tu-hsiu of opportunism. While submitting once again to the discipline of the Comintern, the leaders of the Chinese party suggested to Borodin that some of the arms being sent by the Soviet government for the Kuomintang army should be used to arm the military units controlled by the Communists, in order to prepare against a possible new attack by Chiang Kai-shek. The suggestion was rejected. Chen Tu-hsiu tells how the Comintern delegate explained the tactic that had to be followed in these words: 'The present period is a period in which the Communists should do the coolie service for the Kuomintang.'[11]

The 'Northern Expedition' began soon after this. The operational plans drawn up by the Soviet military advisers and their direct participation in the development of the expedition played a big part in ensuring its success. Chiang Kai-shek forbade all activity by the labour and peasant movements in the rear during military operations. The commander-in-chief's counter-revolutionary attitude and his dictatorial ambitions became increasingly obvious. The situation of the Chinese Communist leadership was more and more untenable, for it was caught between the pressure of the mass revolutionary movement, which was growing very rapidly – partly in a spontaneous way and partly through the initiative taken by the local Communist cadres – and the obligations imposed on it by the discipline of the Kuomintang. Day by day the numbers increased of those who wanted to cut this Gordian knot by leaving the Kuomintang and recovering complete freedom of action. But Stalin opposed this categorically when the problem was raised at the Seventh Plenum of the ECCI in November–December 1926. He expressed himself thus: 'It is said that the Chinese Communists should withdraw from the Kuomintang. That would be wrong, comrades. The withdrawal of the Chinese Communists from the Kuomintang at the present time would be a profound mistake. The whole course, character and prospects of the Chinese revolution undoubtedly testify in favour of the Chinese Communists remaining in the Kuomintang and intensifying their work in it.'[12] At the same time he criticized the Chinese Communists for not sufficiently intensifying the agrarian revolution and the labour movement. The ECCI passed a resolution which, in fact, required of the Chinese party (*a*) that it should remain within the Kuomintang at any cost and (*b*) that it should boldly develop the agrarian revolution. It was easy to write such a resolution in Moscow, but it seemed impossible to apply it in China, for the simple reason that almost all the leading personnel of the Kuomintang – 'right' and 'left' alike, army officers and state officials, members of the party apparatus – were connected in one way or another with landed property, and not by any means with the most modest variety.[13] In the concrete situation of China in 1926–7 priority had to be accorded to one or the other of these two demands. On the spot, the Comintern delegates and the Soviet advisers resolved the dilemma by giving priority to the alliance with the bourgeois leadership of the Kuomintang. Following their instructions, the Chinese party acted in the same way, and so became, as Bukharin was to put it later, a 'brake' on the peasant movement which was in full spate.

After Chiang's *coup* the Comintern intensified still further this 'practical line'. The Communist who headed the Ministry of Agriculture in the Wuhan government had to use his position in order to damp down the revolutionary peasant movement, for the 'excesses' of this movement jeopardized unity with the 'left' Kuomintang. On 30 June the Central Committee of the Chinese party passed a resolution that carried this appeasement policy to extremes. The resolution stated, among other things of a similar kind: 'Mass organizations – workers, peasants and others – must submit to the leadership and control of the Kuomintang authorities, the requests of the people's workers', peasants', etc., movements must conform with resolutions passed by the Kuomintang Congress or by its central executive committee, as well as with government laws and decrees.'[14] The party itself thus helped to paralyse and demoralize the forces which it still had at its disposal. Fifteen days later the 'left' Kuomintang was able with impunity to follow Chiang's example by unleashing terror against the Communists in the Wuhan government's zone.

The events in China coincided with the culminating phase of the duel between Stalin and the Trotsky–Zinoviev opposition. A few days before Chiang's betrayal the opposition had made a radical criticism of the policy being followed in China, forecasting that it would lead to the defeat of the proletariat. In the period following Chiang's *coup*, Trotsky carried this critique further, forecasting that the 'left' Kuomintang would go over to the counter-revolution. In this theoretical and political debate, Stalin's situation became more and more embarrassing: events in China were proving the opposition correct in far too obvious a way. Things began to take the same path in the Soviet Union's domestic situation as well. Stalin therefore went over from discussion to repression. In the press and in the Soviet organizations, oppositionists were prevented from expressing their views, especially on the subject of the Chinese revolution. Soon afterwards they were expelled from the party, and in January 1928 they were deported to Siberia.[15]

Yet the betrayal by Chiang Kai-shek and the Kuomintang (I use this term 'betrayal' for convenience only, since, as Trotsky said, 'they betrayed not their class but our illusions') could not be 'smothered' by such expeditious methods as those being used to gag the opposition. Until the last moment the press and the leading organs of the Soviet party had regarded the Kuomintang as the great party of the Chinese revolution, and Chiang Kai-shek had been glorified more than any leader of the Chinese party. It was the same in Comintern publications. Two methods were used in order to escape from this awkward situation – deception in words and adventurism in deeds. It was explained that Stalin's line had always been right, that betrayal by the 'national bourgeoisie' had always been foreseen, but unfortunately the Chinese Communists had proved incapable of applying the line and preparing themselves to deal with the betrayal when it came. Consequently, as a fitting punishment, the Comintern removed Chen Tu-hsiu from his post as Secretary General and replaced him by Chu Chiu-Pai. Thenceforth, all the woes of the Chinese Communist Party from its foundation down to 1927 were to be accounted for by means of this magic formula: Chen Tu-hsiu.[16]

The second method consisted in inciting the new leadership of the Chinese party, which was psychologically predisposed towards this by the twofold effect of betrayal by its allies and the criticism handed down by the Comintern, to launch a counter-offensive wherever it could still command some organized forces. A few 'revolutionary insurrections' in China, however ephemeral, could be useful for propaganda needs in Moscow and serve as 'dialectical weapons' against the opposition. In this way the party went over, without any transition period, from 'right' opportunism to 'left' adventurism, which cost it new defeats and new victims. The most tragic episode was the Canton rising, directly organized by the envoys of the Comintern. According to Trotsky the fact that it coincided with the Fifteenth Congress of the CPSU (December 1927) was not accidental.[17] When these efforts had failed and the Chinese party had been destroyed, the Comintern dismissed Chu Chiu-pai on a charge of 'putschism'. In order to 'proletarianize' the party, Chu was replaced by a worker, Hsiang Hsung-fa, who proved incapable of coping with the task. The real leader of the party came to be another intellectual, Li Li-san who was to suffer, like Chen and Chu, for his loyalty to the Comintern. In September 1930 he was dismissed, also on a charge of 'putschism'. The new general secretary, Wang Ming, sent directly from Moscow to take the party in hand, was to remain at his post until January 1935. Then, three months after the Red Army had begun its 'Long March', the leading group of the Chinese party elected, in the little village of Tsunyi, and for the first time without any intervention from Moscow, a new general secretary.

With the election of Mao Tse-tung there triumphed in the Communist Party of China a conception of the Chinese revolution which had been gradually worked out, since the defeat of 1927, in close relation to practice, by the group formed around Mao in the large 'Red base' in Kiangsi province. The line of the Comintern during those years was based on the same theoretical foundations as before, but on the tactical plane it was marked by the ultra-Leftism and adventurism characteristic of the 'Third Period'.[18] The successive official leaderships of the Chinese party which loyally tried to apply this line came up almost always against the resistance, sometimes subterranean and sometimes open, of the Mao group. The latter increasingly possessed real power – politico-moral authority and armed forces – in the rural bases where the party was developing, whereas in the towns it was growing weaker. In October 1932 the official leadership, hitherto clandestinely centred in Shanghai, had been obliged to seek refuge in the Kiangsi base, and apparently it there took over command of the armed forces, ousting Mao. This last attempt by the Comintern to re-establish its control and authority over the Chinese section almost resulted in a catastrophe even worse than that of 1927. The official leadership ordered a static strategy in face of Chiang Kai-shek's fifth campaign against the 'Red bases', and the Red Army of Kiangsi was left with no way out but to retreat to the northwest. This military setback doubtless facilitated the political victory of the Maoist faction.[19]

The 'co-existence' over such a long period of the Comintern line and the Maoist line was not due only to the 'position of power' that Mao held at the head of the Red Army and the Soviets of Kiangsi. It must have been facilitated by another factor. At first sight, the differences between these two lines were neither theoretical nor fundamental in character. They seemed to be of a tactical and limited kind, dependent on a state of affairs that was seen as only transient – for example, the fact that the workers' movement in the towns had been crushed for the time being, so that the party was obliged to rely mainly on the rural bases, a circumstance which accounted for the tendency of 'immature' Communists to exaggerate the role of the peasantry, etc. And, above all, Mao never explicitly challenged the theoretical conception of the Chinese revolution that was held by the Comintern. In his definition of the character of the Chinese revolution and the stages of its development, etc., Mao was formally on the side of Stalin and the Comintern and against Trotsky's line.

This theoretical conception amounted essentially to Stalin's dogmatization of Lenin's idea (in its 1905 version) of the bourgeois-democratic revolution: it was a transposition of this recipe to the Chinese scene (just as it was later to be transposed to the Spanish scene), with the addition of an element that was to mark the particularity of the Chinese bourgeois-democratic revolution as compared with the Russian, namely, anti-imperialism. This distinctive feature served Stalin as a justification for the alliance with the Kuomintang (and the form taken by this alliance) down to the defeat of 1927. According to Stalin, the anti-imperialist character of the Chinese revolution meant that the Chinese national bourgeoisie could play a progressive, and even revolutionary, role more thoroughly and over a longer period than the liberal bourgeoisie of Russia. Hence the theory of the 'bloc of four classes' and the division of the Chinese revolution into three stages (instead of two, like the Russian revolution), which had anti-imperialism in common but were differentiated by their social content, the role played by the different classes and so on. In the first stage, bourgeois-democratic in character, the proletariat had as its allies the peasants, the petty-bourgeoisie of the towns and the national bourgeoisie. The going-over by the national bourgeoisie to the counter-revolution, taking the urban petty-bourgeoisie with them for the time being, put an end to this stage. In the second stage, begun in 1927, the character of the revolution was still bourgeois-democratic, but the allies of the proletariat were confined to the peasants and, perhaps, the petty-bourgeoisie. Victory of the revolution in this stage would result in the establishment of a revolutionary-democratic dictatorship of the proletariat and the peasantry, under the hegemony of the proletariat. Once this regime had carried out its mission – abolition of feudal structures, continuation of the anti-imperialist struggle, etc. – it would be possible to go forward to the third stage, the socialist revolution.[20]

Trotsky criticizes this conception very severely. As regards the 'first stage' he calls it pure Menshevism, and sees in it the theoretical source of the policy which converted the Chinese Communist Party into a mere appendage of the bourgeois leadership of the Kuomintang, thus dooming it to defeat. Concerning the 'second stage', Trotsky accuses Stalin of forgetting the experience of 1917 (which showed that a 'revolutionary-democratic dictatorship of the proletariat and peasantry' was not possible as an intermediate regime between the bourgeois and proletarian dictatorships) and of repeating the mistakes he made after the February revolution, disregarding Lenin's 'April Theses'. For Trotsky, the Chinese revolution could not triumph otherwise than as a socialist revolution under the dictatorship of the proletariat. The fact that the main and immediate enemy of the Chinese revolution was imperialism, that it could not triumph otherwise than by overcoming imperialism, did not mean, as Trotsky saw it, that the Chinese bourgeoisie could play a more revolutionary role than the liberal bourgeoisie of Russia, but quite the contrary. On the one hand, the Chinese national bourgeoisie had interests in common with imperialism, even though it was oppressed by the latter. (Trotsky drew attention to this aspect of the matter, though without dwelling upon it; pointing out, for example, that there was no gulf between the *comprador* bourgeoisie and the 'national' bourgeoisie.) On the other hand – and this was his main argument – he emphasized the intrinsic *weakness* of the Chinese bourgeoisie. The latter was much weaker than the Russian bourgeoisie had been, if one considered the economic under-development of China and the umbilical cord that tied the Chinese bourgeoisie to the existing agrarian structures. The contrast between its weakness and the tremendous power of world imperialism ruled out any vigorous action against imperialism on the part of the Chinese bourgeoisie, drawing upon national forces. 'The Chinese bourgeoisie is sufficiently realistic and acquainted intimately enough with the nature of world imperialism to understand that a really serious struggle against the latter required such an upheaval of the revolutionary masses as would primarily become a menace to the bourgeoisie itself.'[21]

History was to prove Trotsky right in arguing that the Chinese revolution could be victorious only as a socialist revolution, but to prove him wrong (together with Stalin and the Comintern) regarding the road to victory and the role to be played by the various classes. For Trotsky the Chinese proletariat necessarily had to be the principal driving-force and leader of the revolution. Contradicting his own schema – since the organic weakness of the Chinese bourgeoisie could not but imply weakness of the working class as well – he applied to China the stereotype of Europe, and this caused him to underestimate the role of the peasant masses. After the defeat of 1927 he wrote: 'It will be possible to speak seriously about the perspective of an agrarian revolution only on the condition that there will be a new mounting wave of the proletarian movement on the offensive.'[22] In Europe's revolutions the proletarian 'mounting waves' had indeed usually preceded those of the peasants. After 1927, however, it was the opposite that happened in China: it can even be said that there were no more proletarian 'mounting waves' after that.[23] Trotsky's strategic conception of the revolution, which was even more 'European' than that held by Lenin towards the end of his life,[24] was to lead him to another conclusion that history has not validated, namely that the revolution could not triumph in Asia unless it had already triumphed in Europe. Undoubtedly it was his under-estimation of the revolutionary potentialities of the peasant masses in the colonies that induced him to make this assumption.

Needless to say, these ideas of Trotsky's were not likely to attract Mao. Under-estimation of the revolutionary role of the peasant movement and subordination of the revolution in Asia to the revolution in Europe ran directly contrary to his own conceptions. On the question of the national bourgeoisie he was closer to Stalin than Trotsky. The latter did not, of course, deny that it might be possible and opportune to make temporary compromises with the national bourgeoisie, but he had a much more negative conception of its role than Stalin had, as we have seen. Mao was never a 'leftist' on this point. He differentiated with care between the component parts of the bourgeoisie, not merely so far as the 'national' bourgeoisie was concerned but also among the *comprador* elements, and even among the latifundia-owners. He was always ready to enter into compromises and alliances, so long as these were beneficial to the revolutionary movement, and during the anti-Japanese war he showed his skill in this connection. What he never consented to was to subordinate the revolutionary forces to any ally whatsoever, bourgeois or petty-bourgeois, or to subordinate the Chinese revolution to either foreign models or foreign interests. In his 'Kiangsi writings' we see the clear awareness he already has of the distinctiveness of the Chinese revolution and of its great mission in history. It was on this basis that he came into conflict with Stalin's policy during the period of the 'Grand Alliance'.

Despite the differences mentioned, Trotsky shared with Stalin and the Comintern the same European way of looking at the Chinese revolution, which reflected the historical limitations of Marxist theory, produced in the laboratory of Europe. To transcend these limitations it was necessary to have been born in the province of Hunan; and even then the process was a laborious one, for the schemas of European Marxism had already conquered – even though considerably later than the commodities produced by Western industry – a substantial market among China's revolutionary intelligentsia.

The famous 'Report of an Investigation into the Peasant Movement in Hunan' (March 1927) certainly represents the first living and thorough 'fusion' of Marxism with Chinese reality, social and political. Without any stereotyped Marxist formulas, but using the Marxist method, here we have an analysis of the anatomy and the dynamic of the fundamental part of Chinese society, namely, the life of its countryside. The 'Report' shows us *this* world at every level – sociological and economic, political and cultural. It describes it under the impact of a sort of earthquake that leaves nothing standing – neither property, with political and economic power, nor family relations and ancestral customs. Here is the Chinese Revolution, in capital letters, the revolution born from the very womb of this society. In contrast with *this*, the heroic insurrection of the workers' vanguard in Shanghai shrinks to its proper, modest dimensions. The Hunan experience shows plainly who is the protagonist, the decisive force in the Chinese revolution. The Marxist Mao had written, one year earlier, another study, entitled 'Analysis of the Classes in Chinese Society', which, though of great interest, was obviously adjusted to fit an orthodox presupposition: 'The industrial proletariat,' he wrote, '. . . has become the leading force in the revolutionary movement.' In Hunan, however, he surrenders to. the evidence of reality. With peasant caution (which he was to continue to observe subsequently in his continuous conflict with the Comintern line) Mao does not explicitly question the role of the proletariat. He restricts himself to avoiding this thorny point and demonstrating with the eloquence of facts that the decisive force of the Chinese revolution lies in the masses of poor countryfolk. He says that the party must reconsider the views it has formulated up to now regarding the peasant movement, and calls upon the party to put itself resolutely at the head of this movement. This was the time, let us recall, when the Kuomintang was beginning its repression of peasant risings and when the leaders of the Chinese Communist Party, applying the Comintern line of unity at any price with the Kuomintang, were trying to damp down the agrarian revolution:

In a very short time, in China's central, southern and northern provinces, several hundred million peasants will rise like a mighty storm, like a hurricane, a force so swift and violent that no power, however great, will be able to hold it back. They will smash all the trammels that bind them and rush forward along the road to liberation. They will sweep all the imperialists, warlords, corrupt officials, local tyrants and evil gentry into their graves. Every revolutionary party and every revolutionary comrade will be put to the test, to be accepted or rejected as they decide. There are three alternatives. To march at their head and lead them? To trail behind them, gesticulating and criticizing? Or to stand in their way and oppose them? Every Chinese is free to choose, but events will force you to make the choice quickly[25]

Mao had already made his choice, from which he was never thereafter to swerve during his revolutionary activity. The Comintern continued imperturbably upholding the dogma of the 'bourgeois-democratic revolution led by the proletariat'. In his writings Mao bows, very briefly as a rule, to the ritual formula, but the content of these writings, the entire practical activity that they reflect, is faithful to the spirit of the 'Report' of 1927. Confronted with facts – the consolidation and expansion of the 'Red bases' in the countryside, the organization in them of an essentially peasant type of Soviet power, and the creation of a Red Army that showed itself able to repulse time and again the attacks of Chiang-Kai-shek's troops, whereas, during this same period the labour movement in the towns was unable to lift its head – the Comintern tried to force them into the framework of its theoretical schema. The Soviet power in the 'Red bases' had to be seen as an embryonic realization of the revolutionary-democratic dictatorship of the proletariat and peasantry under the leadership of the proletariat, and so on – whereas in reality the workers there were only a tiny minority, and played no role except in so far as they had ceased to be workers. At the same time, however, the Comintern strove to bring about a change in the situation so as to make reality adapt itself to its representation in theory. It constantly urged the Chinese party to concentrate their efforts in the towns and give priority to working-class forms of struggle: strikes, demonstrations, etc.[26] But the most serious aspect of the matter, something that was to have damaging consequences which jeopardized the very survival of the 'Red bases', was the Comintern's desire to make premature use of the armed forces organized in these bases in order to march to the conquest of the towns. The most striking example occurred during the summer of 1930, when the Red Army of the Kiangsi base and other bases in central China was thrown against the big towns of this region: Changsha, Wuhan and Nanchang. This operation was decided on by the leadership of the Chinese party in obedience to the Comintern's instructions, for two reasons.

The first of these was that the Presidium of the ECCI, at its meeting in February 1930, had come to the conclusion that there was 'an upsurge of the world labour movement' and that 'enormous perspectives [are opening] for the growth of the present revolutionary advance into a revolutionary situation in the leading capitalist countries and colonies'. China was especially aimed at, for 'we witness the decay of the Nanking reaction, the new outbreak of the generals' war in China, and the rise of favourable preconditions for a new upsurge of the revolutionary movement in China.'[27] In June, the ECCI passed a special resolution on China, in which it was said: 'Events are moving in such a way that the revolutionary situation will shortly encompass, if not the whole of Chinese territory, then at least the territory of a number of key provinces.' And a direct order was given to concentrate efforts on reinforcing the Red Army so as 'to be in a position to take over one or several of the industrial and administrative centres'.[28] On the basis of this resolution of the ECCI the Central Committee of the Chinese Communist Party passed one of its own, in this same month of June 1930, in which it declared: 'China is the weakest link in the chain of world imperialism; it is there that the volcano of world revolution is most likely to erupt. Consequently, thanks to the present aggravation of the world revolutionary crisis, the Chinese revolution may be the first to break out and spark off world revolution and decisive class war in the world.'[29] A month later, the plan worked out by the Chinese leadership – the brain involved seems to have been that of Li Li-san – was put into practice. But the volcano did not erupt. The operation resulted in heavy losses not only to the Red Army but also to the weak Communist and labour organizations in the towns attacked.[30]

I have already mentioned the other reason, which was always present in the Comintern's China policy: the urgent need for an urban, working-class base for the revolution, able to provide and secure the leadership of the proletariat over the whole of the revolutionary movement. It was necessary to establish workers' Soviet power, at least in a few towns, so that the peasants' Soviet power might be given the leadership without which the revolution 'could not' triumph. Since the workers' forces existing in these towns were unable for the moment to undertake this project on their own, the armed forces of the peasant bases must come to their aid. The thinking of the Comintern and the official leadership of the Chinese party was so clouded by the idea of proletarian hegemony that they failed even to consider the actual state of the Communist and labour organizations in the towns. And yet the plan accorded priority in the struggle to them. The resolution of the Chinese Central Committee says: 'The great struggle of the proletariat is the decisive force as far as preliminary successes in one or several provinces are concerned. Without a wave of strikes staged by the working class, without armed insurrection in the key cities, there can be no success in one or several provinces. It is a wholly mistaken idea not to pay attention to urban work and to count on the villages to surround the towns.'[31] Needless to say, this criticism was directed at Mao, who disagreed with the plan for an immediate attack on the towns and was already proposing the strategy that he was later to develop theoretically: spreading the revolutionary war in the rural areas, always avoiding battle with stronger forces, and maintaining as a long-term prospect the aim of gradually encircling and capturing the towns.

In conformity with the ideas of the June resolution, the plan of action worked out by the leaders of the Chinese Communist Party provided for a series of proletarian insurrectionary strikes, not only in the towns that were to be conquered by the Red Army – Wuhan, Nanchang, Changsha – but also in Shanghai, Nanking, Canton, Tientsin, etc. This 'proletarian' part of the plan proved to be a complete fiasco. At Changsha, the only urban centre that was actually occupied by the Red units – for a period of ten days – the majority of the workers maintained a reserved and passive attitude, even when the town was held by the Communists. And in nearly all the urban centres the plan of Li Li-san (and of his highly placed advisers) had as its main result the exposure of the weak Communist and trade-union nuclei, which were very severely crushed as a result. In the end the tactics of the Comintern in the period following the defeat of 1927 produced effects directly contrary to those aimed at: the political weight of the working class in the Chinese revolutionary movement was still further reduced, so that it became almost minimal.[32]

The events of 1927, 1930 and 1934 mark the decisive stages in the bankruptcy of the Comintern's China policy. Those of 1927 sealed the failure of the right-wing policy that made the Chinese Communist Party an appendage of the Kuomintang. Those of 1930 meant the failure of the adventuristic and 'ultra-proletarian' line that took the place of the previous policy, and which was a sort of Chinese version of the policy of 'class against class' (in the spirit of 'social Fascism') which was applied by the Comintern in Europe between 1928 and 1934. And the events of 1934 – the severe defeats suffered by the Red Army of Kiangsi in face of Chiang Kai-shek's fifth offensive, as a result of the military tactics laid down by the official party leadership – brought the collapse of the attempt to put the conduct of the revolutionary war under Comintern control.

This last episode determined the subsequent line of development of the Chinese party, for the two conceptions, which in the previous period had opposed each other in a 'subterranean' way, were now to clash openly. The deadly danger constituted by Chiang's fifth offensive against the great 'Red base' in Kiangsi subjected the two conceptions to the decisive test. Even though the dilemma presented itself mainly on the plane of military tactics, what was advocated by each of the two groups – the Maoist group and the pro-Comintern one – reflected their respective general conceptions of the Chinese revolution. The Tsunyi meeting consummated the victory of the Maoist conception in the Chinese party. When, at the end of 1935, the 'Chinese Soviet Republic', after a year's wanderings, installed itself in Yenan, a new chapter of the Chinese revolution was about to begin: the war with Japan. But the 'China chapter' of the Comintern's history was for all practical purposes at an end. As Mao said in 1943, in connection with the dissolution of the Comintern:

'Since the Seventh World Congress of the Communist International in 1935, the Communist International has not intervened in the internal affairs of the Chinese Communist Party. And yet, the Chinese Communist Party has done its work very well, throughout the whole Anti-Japanese War of National Liberation . . .'[33]

The Comintern's non-intervention in the Chinese party's policy after 1935 was certainly due to other reasons than merely the coming of the Mao group to the headship of the party. This latter aspect accounts for the attitude taken up by the new Chinese leadership; but if the Comintern did not try to oppose it, this was mainly because Mao's policy during the anti-Japanese war largely coincided with the Soviet Union's policy in the Far East. At first sight, indeed, the policy of the Chinese Communist Party was only a Chinese version of the European People's Front. In reality, however, there was a fundamental difference. Whereas in Europe this policy subordinated, *de facto*, the revolutionary forces to 'bourgeois democracy', in China the alliance between Mao and Chiang not merely did not hinder the independence of the revolutionary forces, but the latter succeeded in increasing their political potential and military strength. In contrast with the hesitations and weaknesses of the Kuomintang in the war with Japan, and its more and more obvious subjection to American imperialism, the Chinese party stood forward as the most uncompromising, radical and effective champion of national independence, after having in the previous period established itself as the party of the agrarian revolution. The fusion, in its programme and in its practice, of these two fundamental objectives of the Chinese revolution gave the Chinese Communist Party the social basis and political influence that enabled it to fight victoriously when, between 1946 and 1949, the struggle once again took the form of civil war – to fight victoriously not only against the Kuomintang and its American backers but also against Stalin's renewed attempt at interference.

The policy of the Comintern in the colonial and dependent countries, between the Seventh World Congress and the Soviet–German pact, was adapted perfectly, like its policy in Europe and America, to the central aim of Soviet foreign policy – the formation of an anti-Hitlerite alliance. Since the states whose alliance was sought were precisely the great colonial powers, this adaptation was expressed in a weakening, going

293

sometimes so far as actual abandonment, of anti-imperialist aims. In any case, revolutionary methods in pursuit of such aims were renounced. In practice, the anti-imperialist strategy was replaced by an anti-Fascist strategy – and this although the Seventh Congress resolutions spoke of 'anti-imperialist People's Fronts'. The Communist parties of Latin America, for example, declared that the main enemy of their peoples was no longer Yankee imperialism, but German imperialism. And, in 1937, Thorez pointed out that although the party's fundamental demand where the colonial peoples were concerned was 'the right to independence', it should be kept in mind that 'the right to divorce does not mean the obligation to divorce': 'If the decisive question of the moment is the victorious fight against Fascism, then the interest of the colonial peoples lies in their unity with the people of France, and not in an attitude that could favour the enterprises of Fascism – placing, for example, Algeria, Tunisia and Morocco under the yoke of Mussolini or Hitler, or making Indochina a base of operations for militaristic Japan.'[34] Suddenly interrupted during the period of the Soviet–German pact, this policy was to attain the zenith of its opportunism during the second phase of the Second World War and in the immediate post-war period, when the Comintern no longer existed. In the second part of this book I shall have occasion to examine that period. At this point I will merely point out that this policy did not contribute, of course, to strengthening the Comintern's role and its colonial sections in the anti-imperialist national liberation movement. As I said when beginning my analysis of this problem, the Comintern was to end its life without having succeeded in establishing solid and influential bases in the great majority of the countries under imperialist domination. Its base was still, as at the time of its birth, essentially European.

THE LAST ACT

Of all the 'turns' made by the Comintern, none was more contrary to the interests of the working-class movement or more prejudicial to the Comintern itself than the one that resulted from the Soviet–German pact of August 1939.

Since 1933, Fascism and, concretely, the Hitlerite state, had constituted a deadly threat to the proletariat and peoples of Europe. No Marxist doubted that. The Comintern's anti-Fascist strategy could be criticized from the left, with good reason – not, however, because it pointed to Fascism as the main enemy and sought to concentrate the maximum of forces against it, but because it did not measure up to this purpose. The opportunist spirit of its principal mentors, derived from subordination to the relations prevailing between the Kremlin and the Western powers, held back the revolutionary potential that anti-Fascism possessed, preventing it from developing fully. From the moment when, under this strategy, the revolutionary forces were subordinated to the 'anti-Fascist' bourgeoisie in the capitalist countries, and to Anglo-Franco-American colonialism in the rest of the world, not only was the revolutionary potential of the anti-Fascist front irremediably compromised, but its anti-Fascist edge was also blunted. The solution did not lie in giving up anti-Fascism and going back to the sectarian and ultra-left tactic practised by the Comintern down to 1934; it could come only from a consistent, that is, a radical, anti-capitalist anti-Fascism. Once it had seen its timorous anti-Fascism, dominated by *raison d'état*, result in the Munich agreement, the Kremlin leadership did not stop at signing a pact with its Enemy Number One; it also required, so as to accord greater weight and significance to this ignoble pact, that the Communists drop the banner of anti-Fascism at the very moment when the 'brown beast' was hurling its legions forth to reduce Europe to slavery.

The leaders of the USSR went very far indeed in the policy that was symbolized by the Soviet–German pact, and thereby facilitated, in practice, the German conquests in Europe, through contributing to demoralize the peoples oppressed or threatened by Fascism. I will limit myself to mentioning two of the most significant examples of such contributions.

Soon after the pact had been signed, Molotov, chairman of the Council of People's Commissars and Commissar for Foreign Affairs, in a speech to the Supreme Soviet, presented Germany as being 'in the position of a state which is striving for the earliest termination of war and for peace, while Britain and France, which but yesterday were declaiming against aggression, are in favour of continuing the war and are opposed to the conclusion of peace. The roles, as you see, are changing,' Molotov added, with perfect cynicism; and went on to say that 'Everybody realizes that there can be no question of restoring old Poland.' The 'peace' that Molotov spoke of meant recognizing the partition of Poland that Hitler and Stalin had just carried out between them. It was false, moreover, to suggest that such a 'peace' – ratifying as it did not only the enslavement of Poland but also that of Czechoslovakia and Austria, as well as the establishment of Fascism in Spain – formed any part whatsoever of the plans of Nazi Germany. The Soviet leaders knew better than anyone else what Hitler's real plans were. By ascribing 'peaceful' intentions to him they deceived those peoples of Europe who were marked down as the next victims of Hitlerite aggression, and put them off their guard. The roles were indeed changing. Now it was Stalin who had taken on the role played hitherto by the rulers of Britain and France. In the same speech, Molotov praised the new relations obtaining between Germany and the USSR: 'Our relations with Germany have radically improved. Here development has proceeded along the line of strengthening our friendly relations, extending our practical cooperation and rendering Germany political support in her efforts for peace . . . We have always held that a strong Germany is an indispensable condition for durable peace in Europe.'[35]

A little less than one year later, in August 1940, Molotov again addressed the Supreme Soviet. Hitler's armies had occupied Norway, Denmark, Belgium, the Netherlands and France. Molotov said: 'The people of France are now faced with the difficult task of healing wounds inflicted by the war, and, following this, the task of regeneration, which cannot, however, be realized by the old methods.' After reviewing the 'great successes' achieved by the German armies and noting that, of all Germany's enemies, 'only Great Britain . . . has decided to continue the war', Molotov stressed the positive role that had been played by the Soviet–German pact in the victory of the German armies: 'This agreement, strictly observed by our government, removed the possibility of friction in Soviet–German relations when Soviet measures were carried out along our Western frontier and at the same time it has assured [sic] Germany a calm feeling of assurance in the East.' Answering 'the foreign press, especially the Anglophil press, which often speculates about possible differences between the Soviet Union and Germany', Molotov affirmed: 'The good neighbourly and friendly relations that have been established between the Soviet Union and Germany are not based on fortuitous considerations of a transient nature, but on the fundamental interests of both the USSR and Germany.'[36]

I do not intend to discuss here the problem whether the Soviet–German pact resulted from a deliberate choice made by Stalin, when confronted by the alternatives of an alliance with Germany or an alliance with the 'democracies', or whether the second alternative was in fact non-existent, as Soviet historians still maintain. This question continues to provide material for polemics between specialists, and will not really be cleared up until the day when the Soviet archives are freely opened to historians.[37] I shall merely ask one question. Assuming that the main aim of Soviet diplomacy was to prevent the imperialist powers from forming a bloc directed against the USSR, and that in order to achieve this aim the Soviet government could do nothing in August 1939 but sign the pact with Germany, does this justify the *way* in which this pact was used and applied by Stalin? If the Soviet leaders were unable, owing to the pact, to encourage the struggle of the peoples of Europe against the occupying power, were they really obliged to deceive these peoples and lull them to sleep, as Molotov did in the first speech I have quoted, or to call on them to resign themselves to their fate, as he did in the second? Was it necessary for the Soviet government to encourage the Fascist aggressor by assuring him of the firmness of the pact that ensured him 'calm in the East'? Looking at matters from the present angle, however, it is legitimate to wonder whether behind this attitude there may not have lain something more than mere tactical manoeuvres, themselves already hard enough for a Marxist to accept. Was not the Soviet–German pact perhaps, in Stalin's mind, the beginning of a farther-reaching arrangement with Hitler's Germany? Some facts are known that seem to support this supposition. The Soviet historian Nekrich has reminded us that, on the eve of the German attack on the USSR, the Soviet government was ready to negotiate with Hitler 'a new, closer agreement'. And, according to the historian Melnikov, when, during the Hitler–Molotov talks of November 1940 the German leader put forward 'a very broad general plan for dividing up the world', Molotov replied with some concrete proposals, claiming for the Soviet sphere of influence 'the Straits, Bulgaria, Romania and Finland'.[38] If we consider these two pointers in the light of what has happened since, namely, the *de facto* partition of the world into 'spheres of influence' between the USSR and American imperialism which took place after the Second World War, and the pursuit of this policy by the USSR down to the present time, why should we not suppose that something like this was also the cornerstone of Stalin's policy towards that imperialism which seemed in 1939–41 to be the premier military power in the world? This hypothesis, if it should be confirmed, would furnish the key to the 'surprise' of which the Soviet army was victim when the Germans attacked. If this was indeed Stalin's plan, the idea that he held of the way history would go, then reality would for him, of course, have had to conform to this idea, and all the information supplied by the secret services of his future allies, together with all the glaring evidence of Germany's hostile preparations, would have had to be brushed aside, since they were in contradiction to Stalin's infallibility.[39]

As everyone knows, the main official argument used right down to the present time to justify the Soviet–German pact and the policy of 1939–41 was that the Soviet Union needed to gain time in order to prepare more effectively, and to avoid being involved on its own in a one-front war with Germany. As things turned out, however, the USSR had to cope, practically alone and for nearly two years, with the bulk of the German forces, strengthened by their European victories. Because of this situation, and of inadequate preparation, the USSR was brought to the brink of defeat, as Stalin himself acknowledged in 1945. This brings up another question: did the policy that followed the Soviet–German pact, if not the pact itself, constitute the best possible way of defending the national existence of the USSR?[40]

While the justification given *a posteriori* (that is, after 22 June 1941) was the one just recalled, the 'theoretical' justification for the pact offered between 1939 and 1941 was derived from the character which was attributed to the war, as being an exclusively imperialist one, equally unjust on both sides. In 1946, however, Stalin declared that 'the Second World War against the Axis states *from the very outset* assumed the nature of an anti-Fascist war, a war of liberation, one of the tasks of which was also to re-establish democratic liberties. The entry of the Soviet Union into the war against the Axis states *could only strengthen* – and actually did strengthen – the anti-Fascist and liberating character of the Second World War.'[41]

After the Twentieth Congress, this rectification made by Stalin was rectified in its turn, in Soviet accounts of the history of the war. It was now said that the war was imperialist on both sides from September 1939 until the fall of France in 1940 – meaning by 'both sides' the Axis powers and the governments of France and Britain – but was from the outset a just war – in defence of national independence and against Fascist enslavement – on the part of the peoples who were victims of Hitlerite aggression, and also on the part of the 'small states' (Poland, Norway, Netherlands, Belgium, etc.). And after the fall of France the war became a just war even as regards France and Britain considered as states. Until the start of the 'cold war' in 1948 the official Soviet version was that Britain, France and the USA had pursued purely liberating aims between 22 June 1941 and the end of the war in 1945. When the 'cold war' began, a rectification was introduced: the powers named, even though they were the USSR's allies, had never ceased to pursue imperialist, anti-popular, reactionary, colonialist, etc., aims.[42]

Needless to say, each of these successive rectifications corresponded to the state of relations between Moscow and the Western capitals at the relevant time. All of them, however, contained one element of truth, a truth that was hidden between September 1939 and June 1941, after having been vigorously brandished about in the period 1934–9, namely, that Hitler's Germany was the main enemy of the peoples of Europe, and the war against it, in reply to its aggression, was for these peoples an unquestionably just and necessary war, a war in defence of their national independence, and, at the very least, a war in defence of bourgeois democracy against Fascist tyranny.[43] But, if the war possessed this character from the outset, how can the Soviet–German pact be justified – and, above all, the policy of paralysing the anti-Fascist struggle in Europe, a policy denounced even by Soviet historians, such as Slezkin?

The Comintern leadership reproduced immediately, with an automatism unprecedented in previous 'turns', the Kremlin's *volte face* of

August 1939. At first sight, the Comintern documents of the pact years may seem highly orthodox, following the Leninist line of taking advantage of wars in order to bring about revolution. As mentioned in the first chapter, the Comintern now brandished once again the spectre of world revolution, which had been laid aside since the Seventh Congress. 'The working class,' wrote Dimitrov in October 1939, 'is called upon to put an end to the war after its own fashion, in its own interests, in the interests of the whole of labouring mankind, and thereby to destroy once and for all the fundamental causes giving rise to imperialist wars,' in other words, to do away with capitalism.[44] But the peoples were not called upon to organize a national-revolutionary war against Nazi Germany and against the traitors who betrayed their nations. In the form in which it was given out, and taking account of the fact that the German proletariat had been crushed since 1933 and was now largely under the influence of Nazi demagogy, the new line could have no other practical effect than to contribute to weakening the already feeble resistance of the states that Hitler attacked. In the Comintern manifesto, published at the same time as Dimitrov's statement, the main drive was against bourgeois democracy and the Social Democrats. Blum was blamed explicitly, but Hitler's name was not even mentioned. There was no direct attack on the Nazi dictatorship, but it was said of the bourgeois democracies: 'It is not for the freedom of nations that they are fighting, but for their enslavement. Not for the salvation of democracy from Fascism, but for the triumph of reaction.'[45] The Comintern's manifestos for 1 May 1940 and 1 May 1941 took a similar line.

All this meant, in brief, that Fascism was no longer the main enemy, *that* role having been taken over by bourgeois democracy and Social Democracy. The offensive was concentrated, moreover, against the latter, just as in the days of 'social fascism'. Less than a year before the invasion of the USSR, Koplenig, a member of the Presidium of the ECCI, wrote: 'It is therefore the most important duty of the revolutionary forces of the proletariat to wage a relentless struggle against Social Democratism in all its forms.'[46] As Deutscher writes:

When the balance of those strange twenty-two months is drawn, it is impossible to overlook the gratuitous service which the Comintern unwittingly rendered to Hitler. No sooner had Molotov and Ribbentrop put their signatures to the pact of August 1939 than the Comintern called off the anti-Hitler crusade to which its trumpeters had so long summoned governments and peoples. All the strategy and tactics of anti-Fascism, all its elaborate arguments were scrapped. The European shadows of the Russian General Secretary adopted an ambiguous pose of neutrality. Both belligerent camps, it was now said, pursued imperialist aims, and there was nothing to choose between them. The working classes were called upon to resist war and fight for peace . . . At times the opposition to war had an unmistakably pro-German twist as, for instance, in October 1939, when the Comintern echoed Molotov's and Ribbentrop's call for a negotiated peace and blamed France and Britain for the war. The effect of that policy, especially in France, was merely defeatist, not revolutionary. It supplemented the defeatism that corroded the top of French society with a quasi-popular brand of defeatism coming from below.[47]

And the French bourgeoisie did not miss this splendid opportunity to outlaw the Communist Party by accusing it of the national treason that the bourgeoisie was itself preparing.

This was a dark and tragic period for the Communists of Europe. Tens of thousands of them heard the news of the pact in the prisons and concentration camps of Hitler, Franco, Mussolini and the other dictators of the centre, south and south-east of the continent. Despite their blind faith in Stalin and the International, the moral and political blow they suffered was terribly hard. Many were unable to endure it. Overnight, the Communists, whether in prison or at large, found themselves isolated from the masses, deprived of any ally. In the countries of Fascist dictatorship, the Communists were the representatives of a party whose supreme head had made a pact with Hitler. In the countries threatened by Hitlerite aggression, the Communists were the representatives of a party whose supreme head had made a pact with the national enemy, objectively helping him in his aggression. As the countries of Europe were overrun one after another, the Communists found themselves, as a historian of the European resistance puts it, 'in an extremely difficult situation: when they were not being hunted down and imprisoned by their fellow-countrymen on charges of treason, they were suffering this fate at the hands of the German authorities.'[48] But the persecutions were not the worst of it. The most deadly aspect of the blow suffered by the Comintern was that it had given up the anti-Fascist struggle at the very moment when this was becoming most necessary, the very moment when the Hitlerite legions were marching out to enslave Europe. Renouncing the anti-Fascist platform in this situation meant not only throwing away the prestige and influence won since 1934, despite all the opportunist mistakes made: it meant committing suicide as a revolutionary force, however many manifestos might be issued against 'the imperialist war' – manifestos which, moreover, did not really call for revolutionary struggle but for a 'peace' which, in the circumstances of that time, could only be a 'Fascist peace'. If Hitler had kept a cool head despite his successes, if he had chosen to consolidate his conquest of Europe, taking advantage of the 'calm in the East' that the Soviet government guaranteed him, and had profited by Stalin's goodwill in order to expand the area over which they shared out 'spheres of influence' between them, it is hard to see how the Stalinist Communist parties could have survived. But Hitler invaded the Soviet Union, and the new phase of the war, which was to hasten the final collapse of the Comintern, made possible the spectacular revival of the Communist parties of Europe, and the consolidation of their Stalinist features.

After 22 June 1941, adapting itself once more with mathematical precision to the requirements of Soviet strategy and diplomacy, the Comintern made a 180-degree turn. Now, the distinction between bourgeois democracy and Fascist dictatorship, 'forgotten' for nearly two years was elevated into an idealization of the former. The responsibility of the 'democratic' capitalist states for the origin of the war was wiped out. The imperialist aims pursued by these states in their struggle against their German or Japanese rivals were glossed over, not only in the public propaganda of the Comintern and the Communist parties but also in the inner-party 'orientation' given to militants. And, as we saw in Chapter 1, the Comintern's last resolution announcing its own dissolution, and Stalin's declaration accompanying this, spread the illusion that the defeat of the Axis powers would by itself suffice for the construction of a world of peace and brotherly collaboration between nations, based on equality of rights. The illusion was spread that such an ideal world could be compatible with survival of the main forces of world imperialism. The capitalist allies of the U S S R were whitewashed. To judge by the documents issued by the Comintern in the last two years of its existence, the class struggle was no longer, on either the national or the international plane, the basic factor in world development. The anti-imperialist national liberation movement seemed to be doomed to the same fate. An era of universal brotherhood was proclaimed.

In the article quoted above (see note 46, p. 735) Koplenig waxed humorous at the expense of the Second International: 'The march of events, the whole course of the imperialist war and the rapidly growing influence of the Soviet Union are expediting the decay of the Second International. Its Executive Committee has virtually ceased to exist, although the fact has been scarcely noticed. It has been "lost on the way".' Less than a year later, the policy of the Third International was to be not essentially different from that of the Second. And less than three years later, it was the Third International that ceased to exist, whereas the Second would resume its activity. All this was perfectly logical: since the world had reached the threshold of universal fraternization between classes and states, the reformist International still had a mission to fulfil, whereas for Lenin's International there was nothing to do but dissolve itself.

Let us not pursue this irony any further. Neither Stalin nor the leaders of the Comintern had become choir-boys. But nor were the premeditated silences and the explicit intentions of the 1943 Resolution and Stalin's declaration, analysed in Chapter 1, merely *ruses de guerre*, either; they were the condensed expression of a general line that ran through all the activity of the Communist parties and determined, to a large extent, the balance of political forces in Western Europe at the end of the Second World War, so facilitating the conservation of capitalism in that part of the continent, as we shall see in the second part of this study.

The defeat of Fascism had to be the principal, immediate aim of every conscious revolutionary during the Second World War. The need for a policy of broad alliances between the proletariat and the bourgeois or petty-bourgeois forces that were interested in this same aim (though in a different way from the socialist forces) seems to me today, with the advantage of hindsight, to be hardly disputable. But there was not one way only of conceiving and applying this policy, either on the plane of relations between the powers or on that of the Comintern's general plane, or on that of the struggle inside each country. The way that Stalin chose – the logical continuation of his whole previous policy – meant sacrificing the possibilities created by the defeat of the Fascist powers and the bankruptcy of the other capitalist states of Continental Europe, in favour of a lasting partition of the world into 'spheres of influence of the USSR and the USA. The world of peace and brotherly collaboration between nations, of which the Comintern and Stalin spoke in 1943, was merely the false prospectus of a world divided between two super-powers.

NOTES

1. *The Dissolution*

1. See the resolution of the Executive Committee of the Comintern (ECCI), point 7, p. 42 below.

2. According to the statutes approved by the Sixth World Congress (1928) of the Comintern; in Jane Degras, ed., *The Communist International (1919–1943)*: *Documents*, OUP, London, 1956–65, II, pp. 465, 468.

3. Included in the introduction to the statutes of the Comintern approved at the Second World Congress (1920), in Degras, op. cit., I, pp. 162–3. The formula I have transcribed is not Marx's own but the summary of the latter which is given in the introduction to the statutes, after Marx has been quoted in full, as follows: 'The emancipation of labour is neither a local nor a national, but a social problem, embracing all countries in which modern society exists, and depending for its solution on the concurrence, practical and theoretical, of the most advanced countries.'

4. 'As I view European conditions, it is quite useful to let the formal organization of the International recede into the background *for the time being* ... Events and the inevitable development and complication of things will of themselves see to it that *the International shall rise again improved in form*' (letter from Marx to Sorge, 27 September 1873, in Marx and Engels, *Selected Correspondence*, Lawrence and Wishart, London, 1956, p. 348: my italics). In the resolution dissolving the Comintern (see below, p. 41, point 6) a parallel was drawn with the dissolution of the First International, but without anything being said on this essential point. In general, the account given in this document of the reasons why the First International was dissolved has only a remote connection with historical truth.

5. Letter of invitation from the Russian Communist Party (signed by Lenin and Trotsky) to other parties and revolutionary groups, calling on

them to attend the First Congress of the Comintern (Degras, op, cit., 1, p. 5).

6. Degras, op. cit., 11, pp. 472, 473. 'In order that revolutionary work and activities may be coordinated and given appropriate guidance, the international proletariat requires international class discipline, for which the most important prerequisite is the strictest discipline in the Communist parties. International Communist discipline must be expressed in the subordination of local and particular interests to the common and enduring interests of the movement, and in the execution without reservation of all decisions made by the leading bodies of the Communist International' (ibid., p. 525).

7. Employment of military terms was a typical feature of the language of the Comintern – carried over, as we shall see later, from the usage of the Bolshevik Party. The name 'Comintern' comes from the abbreviation used for *Kommunistichesky Internatsional* in Russian.

8. In the theses adopted by the Sixth Congress on the fight against imperialist war and the tasks of the Communist parties (theses 75 and 76); in *The Attitude of the Proletariat towards War*, Modern Books, London 1932, p. 21.

9. From the resolution of the Seventh Congress on 'the tasks of the Comintern in connection with the preparations of the imperialists for a new world war' (*Seventh World Congress of the Communist International, Abridged Stenographic Report of Proceedings*, Foreign Languages Publishing House, Moscow, 1939, pp. 591, 594).

10. In the theses against imperialist war and the tasks of the Communists which were approved by the Sixth Congress and ratified by the Seventh, 'three types' of war are held to be 'possible' in 'the present epoch': 'first, wars between imperialist states; second, wars of imperialist counter-revolution against the proletarian revolution, or against countries in which socialism is being built; third, national revolutionary wars, especially of colonial countries against imperialism, which are connected with wars of imperialist suppression' (*The Attitude of the Proletariat towards War*, op. cit., p. 21). How is one to classify the Second World War, in which all three types were mixed up together?

11. For the official version, besides the documents reproduced in full below, pp. 39 ff., which constitute our principal source, I have also taken account of the following works: B. N. Ponomarev (responsible, together with Suslov, to the Central Committee of the CPSU for questions of the international Communist movement), article 'Kommunistichesky Inter-

natsional', in *Bol'shaya Sovyetskaya Entsiklopediya*, 2nd edn, Vol, 22, 1953; 'L'Anniversaire de l'Internationale communiste', in *Nouvelle Revue Internationale*, February 1969; William Z. Foster, *A History of the Three Internationals*, International Publishers, New York, 1955; P. Togliatti, 'Alcuni problemi della storia dell'Internazionale comunista', in *Rinascita*, 7–8, 1959; G. Amendola, 'Venticinque anni dopo lo scioglimento dell'Internazionale comunista', in *Critica Marxista*, 4–5, 1968. In the summer of 1969 the Institute of Marxism–Leninism in Moscow published a new history of the Comintern (*Kommunistichesky Internatsional, kratky istorichesky ocherk*, Moscow, 1969) which I was not able to consult for the Spanish edition of this book. Having subsequently done this, however, I have no changes to make in what I have written, for this history simply repeats what was said in 1943.

From outside the Communist movement not many works have been devoted particularly to this subject. I will mention, from among these: Alfred Burmeister, *Dissolution and Aftermath of the Comintern: Experiences and Observations, 1937–1947*, Research Programme on the USSR, New York, 1955; Annie Kriegel, 'La Dissolution du Komintern', *in Revue d'Histoire de la Seconde Guerre Mondiale*, 68, 1967. The subject is dealt with marginally in Pierre Broué, *Le Parti bolchevique*, Éditions de Minuit, Paris, 1963, summing up the Trotskyist standpoint on this matter, and likewise in Isaac Deutscher, *Stalin*, OUP, London, 1949, and Milovan Djilas, *Conversations with Stalin*, Harcourt Brace and World, New York, 1962 (Penguin edition, 1963). Dominique Desanti also refers to the episode, in a mainly anecdotal way, in *L'Internationale Communiste*, Payot, Paris, 1970.

The only critical testimony available from a participant is that provided by the Yugoslav Communist leader Veljko Vlahović, who was present at the meeting of the ECCI where the decision was taken, as a representative of the Young Communist International. His account was published in the issue for 20 April 1959, of *Kommunist*, the journal of the League of Communists of Yugoslavia. However, this testimony throws little light on the question, merely confirming that all the leaders of the Comintern did was docilely to approve an order that could have come only from Stalin.

12. These documents will be found in the appendix to this chapter, on pp. 39 ff.

13. In the essay mentioned in note 11, in *Rinascita*, 7–8, 1959, p. 480 (my italics). More recently, the Italian Communist historian Alberto Caracciolo has mentioned the 'lamentable fact' constituted by 'the complete

absence down to the present time of Russian sources for this kind of research' (*Gramsci y el marxismo*, Proteo, Buenos Aires, 1965, p. 120: Spanish edition of *Studi gramsciani, atti del Convegno tenuto a Roma nei giorni 11–13 gennaio 1958*, Ed. Riuniti, 1958).

14. In 1967 the Feltrinelli publishing concern in Milan undertook republication of the principal public documents of the Comintern. But the most complete documentation is concentrated in the Institute of Marxism–Leninism in Moscow and other Soviet institutions, subject to the Central Committee of the CPSU. Since 1935 the *complete* texts of the theses, resolutions and reports of the six first congresses of the Comintern have not been reissued in the USSR, nor have the documents of the period of the Soviet-German Pact been re-issued since 1941. The only Comintern documents that are allowed to circulate in their entirety are those of the Seventh Congress.

As regards the internal conflicts within the Comintern, the only testimony available comes to us from a succession of 'heretics'. Of particular interest, besides the works of Trotsky and other Russian oppositionists, are the book by the German Communist Arthur Rosenberg, published in Germany at the end of 1932 (English trans., *A History of Bolshevism*, OUP, London, 1934); Jules Humbert-Droz, '*L'Œil de Moscou*' à Paris, Julliard, Paris, 1964; Vladimir Dedijer, *Tito Speaks*, Weidenfeld and Nicolson, London, 1953; and the archives of Tasca ('A. Rossi'), the representative of the Italian Communist Party at the Comintern, which Feltrinelli have begun publishing.

15. Ponomarev, op. cit., *Bol'shaya Sovyetskaya Entsiklopediya*.

16. Foster, op. cit., p. 439 (my italics). Foster's name does not appear among the signatories to the resolution of 1943 because the CPUSA had for legal reasons to leave the Comintern in 1940.

17. Wallace's speech was reported in the *New York Times* of 9 March 1943. A story that Roosevelt had asked Stalin to dissolve the Comintern circulated for a time in the West, without any evidence being given to support it. Branko Lazitch refutes the story in *Est-Ouest*, 135, 1955, pointing out that, if there had been any truth in it, mention of it would have occurred in Cordell Hull's memoirs, or in Elliott Roosevelt's book about his father, *As He Saw It*. Djilas, in his *Conversations with Stalin* (Penguin Books, 1963, p. 67), attributed to the Soviet dictator a statement that 'the Westerners' had never demanded the dissolution of the Comintern.

18. Even the leaders of the Yugoslav Communist Party, whose revo-

lutionary policy during the war of liberation had clashed with the advice to be 'moderate' which came to them from Moscow, expressed unconditional agreement with Stalin's declaration. See Dedijer, op. cit., p. 198.

19. In Chapter 5 I shall examine in detail Stalin's policy in the division of 'spheres of influence'.

20. Yugoslavia constitutes the exception that proves the rule. The Yugoslav Communist Party did not respect the 50–50 allotment of percentages agreed on between Stalin and Churchill (See Notes, Part 2, p. 17 note 45) and after 1945 carried through the revolution to the end.

21. Article I of the statutes of the Comintern, voted at the Second World Congress (1920) (Degras, op. cit., I, p. 164).

22. Togliatti, op. cit., p. 480.

23. See Chapter 3.

24. See the appendix to this chapter, the resolution, point 1 (p. 39). This definition has been repeated, word for word or with variations that do not affect the content, in all the documents or official histories of the Communist movement. It cannot, therefore, be regarded as a wartime 'improvisation'.

25. I say nothing about the content of this 'upholding' of Marxism, which became under Stalin a mere operation of confronting one kind of 'adulteration and falsification' with other varieties of the same crime. On that point, however, there was no 'dissembling' where the leaders of the Comintern were concerned. Like all the Communists of the time, they had been shaped by *this* variety of 'Marxism', and took it for the only authentic one. But that the majority of the working class were still under reformist influence constituted an obvious empirical fact. On this problem, as on others, dissembling is plain to be seen in the resolution of the Presidium.

26. See on this the article by Annie Kriegel, already mentioned (note 11): 'La Dissolution du Komintern'.

27. The sections have been numbered to facilitate reference.

2. The Crisis of Theory

1. Stalin distorted the views of Marx and Engels on this subject by ascribing to them the idea that the socialist revolution *in the sense of the capture of power by the working class* would occur simultaneously in all the advanced capitalist countries. On this basis he was able to demonstrate Lenin's 'originality' in maintaining the impossibility of such a simultaneous victory and the probability, on the contrary, of the revolution

proving victorious first of all in a single country. Subsequently a whole series of 'Marxologists' and 'Leninologists' have shared this opinion of Stalin's. Among the latter the most typical instance is that of Alfred G. Meyer, in his *Leninism* (Harvard University Press, Cambridge, Mass., 1957, and Praeger, New York, 1962). Nowadays, Soviet theoreticians are trying to get rid of Stalin's falsified version of the ideas of Marx and Engels and show that Lenin's innovations did not clash with his essential faithfulness to the Marxist theory of the revolution. (The most recent work dealing with this question is the philosopher Y. A. Krasin's, *Lenin, Revolution, and the World Today*, Progress Publishers, Moscow, 1971: see pp. 10–12.) But they continue to claim that Lenin assumed that it was possible for socialism to be victorious *in the sense of being completely constructed* in separate countries, a conception that is totally opposed to that of Marx, and which makes untenable the position they take up in their dispute with Meyer and others. The historical truth, as will be seen later, is that Lenin spoke of the possibility of a victory for socialism in a single country only in the sense of the capture of power by the working class, and *not* in that of the complete building of socialism. He regarded this first victory as the beginning of the advance of the world revolution, leading very soon to the capture of power by the working class in the advanced capitalist countries.

2. Marx, 'The Future Results of the British Rule in India' (1853), in *Marx and Engels on Colonialism*, Lawrence and Wishart, London, 1960, p. 82.

3. This view is upheld in the programme of the CPSU approved at the Twenty-Second Party Congress, in 1961. Stalin first propounded it in 1946.

4. See 'Nekotorye aspekti leninskoi teorii revolyutsii' ('Some Aspects of Lenin's Theory of the Revolution'), by N. G. Levintov, in *Voprosy filosofii*, 4, 1966, in which the working-out and application by Lenin of these two ideas is particularly examined. Lenin understands by a social revolution in the narrow sense (corresponding to what Marx embraced in the concept of 'political revolution') the period in which the essential form assumed by the social movement is the directly revolutionary struggle of the masses; by the revolution in the broad sense he means the process whereby all the fundamental historical tasks of the revolution are solved. Levintov shows that Lenin, referring to the French Revolution as a social revolution in the broad sense, sees it as going on from 1789 to 1871, and including in this long period the revolutions in the narrow sense of 1789,

1830, 1848 and 1871 (the Commune). The customary formulations 'social revolution' and 'political revolution' result in an undialectical differentiation between the 'social' and the 'political'. For this reason I have preferred to use the formulations introduced by Lenin.

5. Trotsky mentions a single exception among the Marxists of the late nineteenth century, that of the German Socialist Georg Vollmar, who in 1878 upheld the possibility of an 'isolated socialist state' (he had Germany in mind) – appealing for support to that 'law of uneven development' the discovery of which Stalin credited to Lenin (Trotsky, *The Revolution Betrayed*, Pioneer Publishers, New York, 1957, pp. 293–4).

6. 'Russia – and I have studied conditions there from the original Russian sources ... – has long been standing on the threshold of an upheaval; all the elements of it are prepared ... This time the revolution begins in the East, hitherto the unbroken bulwark and reserve army of counter-revolution' (Marx, letter to Sorge, 27 September 1877, in Marx and Engels, *Selected Correspondence*, Lawrence and Wishart, London, 1956, p. 374).

7. Kautsky, 'The Slavs and the Revolution' (1902), quoted by Lenin in *'Left-Wing' Commission, an Infantile Disorder, Collected Works*, 4th edn, Vol. 31, English version, pp. 22, 23. In 1848 Bakunin had prophesied that, one day, 'in Moscow the star of Revolution will rise high and beautiful, out of the ocean of blood and fire, and it will become the guidepost for the happiness of all liberated mankind' (in the final variant of Bakunin's 'Appeal to the Slavs', quoted in E. Pyziur, *The Doctrine of Anarchism of Michael A. Bakunin*, Milwaukee, 1955, p. 34).

8. Lenin, 'The Revolutionary-Democratic Dictatorship of the Proletariat and the Peasantry', op. cit., Vol. 8, p. 304.

9. Lenin, 'The Stages, the Trend and the Prospects of the Revolution', op. cit., Vol. 10, p. 92. The idea that the Russian revolution and the proletarian revolution in the West 'complement each other', with the former acting as 'prelude' to the latter, and the latter in turn enabling the Russian revolution to become a socialist revolution, had already been formulated by Engels in his preface of 1882 to the Russian edition of the *Communist Manifesto*. Lenin borrowed from Engels the expression about how the workers of Europe, by carrying through the socialist revolution would show the Russian proletariat 'how to do it' (Engels, 1894 postscript to his essay *On Social Conditions in Russia*, 1875). For an English translation of the passage referred to, see Karl Marx and Friedrich Engels (ed. P. W. Bienstock and B. F. Hoselitz), *The Russian Menace to Europe*,

Allen and Unwin, London, 1953, p. 234. In 1917, arguing directly with Preobrazhensky and indirectly with Lenin, Stalin was to express the idea that would later take more definite shape and govern his entire strategy: 'The possibility is not excluded that Russia will be the country that will lay the road to socialism ... We must discard the antiquated idea that only Europe can show us the way' (Stalin, *Works*, Vol. 5, English edn, pp. 199–200).

10. Lenin, 'Paul Singer' (1911), in op. cit., Vol. 17, p. 95.

11. Lenin, 'Meeting of the International Socialist Bureau' (1908), in ibid., Vol. 15, p. 237.

12. Lenin, 'The Successes of the American Workers' (1912), in ibid., Vol. 18, p. 335.

13. Lenin, 'The Awakening of Asia' (1913), in ibid., Vol. 19, pp. 85–6.

14. Lenin, 'Democracy and Narodism in China' (1912), in ibid., Vol. 18, 163–9.

15. Marx and Engels never gave any consideration to the question of what role the Russian revolution might play among the peoples subject to the yoke of colonialism.

16. Lenin, 'The Tasks of the Proletariat in Our Revolution', in ibid., Vol. 24, p. 67.

17 Lenin, 'Lessons of the Crisis', in ibid., Vol. 24, p. 215.

18. ibid., Vol. 26, p. 190.

19. Lenin, 'Imperialism', in ibid., Vol. 22, pp. 187, 302.

20. See Y. A. Krasin, op. cit., p. 23. According to Krasin, Lenin defined imperialism as 'transitional, or moribund, capitalism', whereas what Lenin actually wrote was that imperialism must be seen as 'transitional or, *more precisely*, moribund capitalism' (my italics). In other words, Lenin here corrected himself and gave a more precise definition. In my view, the point of this self-correction of his was that the term 'transitional' defines only one of the aspects revealed by Lenin in his analysis, namely, the high degree of socialization of production that is characteristic of the monopoly phase, and which prepares to the utmost the material conditions for socialism. By using the epithet 'moribund', it seems to me, Lenin indicates that this advanced socialization (together with a series of other political economic and social factors) has brought about an *extreme* intensification of the contradictions of imperialism (let it not be forgotten that Lenin's work was written in the midst of a world war) and made the socialist revolution *imminent* on the world scale – an idea that he formulates very clearly in all his writings of this period.

8

21. The Italian Communist writer Vittorio Strada, in his essay 'Brest-Litovsk: The Discussion about War, Peace and Revolution' (in Italian), in *Critica Marxista*, 4, 1963, makes, in my opinion, the mistake of supposing that Lenin's position in the discussion with the 'left-wing Communists' was based on an assumption that the Russian revolution could hold on even if the revolution should not prove victorious in Europe. Actually, in his report to the Seventh Party Congress, after the Brest-Litovsk peace had been signed, Lenin declared quite unequivocally that 'it is the absolute truth that without a German revolution we are doomed' (op. cit., Vol. 27, p. 98). His differences with Trotsky, on the one hand, and with the 'left-wing Communists' (Bukharin, etc.) on the other, were of a merely tactical order. Lenin did not at all base himself on the possibility of maintaining the socialist revolution in being in an isolated Russia. His entire argument related to the impossibility of successfully waging a revolutionary war at that time, given the extent to which the army had disintegrated. It was solely a question of securing a momentary respite while awaiting the revolution had begun.

22. Lenin, 'Letter to Sverdlov', 1 October 1918, in ibid., Vol. 35, pp. 364–5. All Lenin's articles and speeches during the last months of 1918 and throughout 1919 reflect his profound conviction that the world revolution had begun.

23. Lenin, 'The Proletarian Revolution and the Renegade Kautsky', in ibid., Vol. 28, p. 113. (This is not Lenin's well-known book, but a short article, bearing the same title, which gives the essence of the longer work.)

24. Marx and Engels, *Werke*, Vol. 27, Dietz, Berlin, 1965, p. 190. It is possible to speak of Lenin's 'Blanquism' only as regards his ideas on the organization of the revolutionary party, and then only to a certain extent. For Lenin the highly centralized and highly disciplined nucleus of professional revolutionaries, organized on strictly conspiratorial lines, is linked with a large body of 'non-professional' revolutionaries, and with mass organizations of various kinds. And where the role to be played by the party is concerned, Lenin is not 'Blanquist'. The party does not 're-place' the revolution: it organizes and leads the revolution when this is already on the march. But when reality proves that the revolution is *not* there – as was obviously the case with the world revolution in 1919–20 – the party's activity based on the assumption that it *is*, 'really', there becomes *objectively* Blanquist. As everybody knows since Hegel pointed it out, what men believe they are doing is one thing and what they are

actually doing is another. This is true even of Marxists of Lenin's stature.

25. Togliatti regarded it as of 'exceptional importance' to stress the fact that Lenin proclaimed the necessity of creating the Third International *before* the Russian revolution had been victorious, since this 'deals a blow at malicious allegations that the Comintern was never anything but a tool of the Soviet state' (art. cit., pp. 469–70). Lenin did indeed proclaim this necessity when the First World War had hardly begun. And the idea of transforming the Comintern into a tool of the Soviet state was wholly alien to his thinking, both before and after the October revolution. But this does not alter the fact that, after Lenin, the Comintern became transformed into a tool of the Soviet state – and that the premises for this transformation were created in Lenin's own time, as we shall see later.

Lenin's initiative was opposed by the majority of the little group of internationalists who had participated in the conference at Zimmerwald (September 1915) and Kienthal (April 1916), and even by a section of the Bolsheviks, who kept up their disagreement with him on this point even after the February revolution. The October victory, which gave Lenin world-wide prestige, enabled this idea of his to make progress among the revolutionary groups in various countries. Its practical realization, however, could not begin until the coming of the German revolution. On the objections raised by the Spartacists, see Chapter 3, below.

26. Lenin, 'Concluding Speech at Closing Session', in op. cit., Vol. 28, pp. 476–7, and 'Founding of the Communist International', in ibid., p. 485. In another speech delivered at the end of March 1919, Lenin said: 'All over the world the association of Communists is growing. In a number of countries Soviet power has already triumphed. Soon we shall see the victory of Communism throughout the world: we shall see the foundation of the World Federative Republic of Soviets' (ibid., Vol. 29, p. 241).

27. Referring to the circumstances in which the Second Congress met, Trotsky wrote in 1921: 'It will be remembered that the Red Army was marching on Warsaw. In view of the revolutionary condition of Germany, Italy and other countries, it was believed that in its function as a force additional to and strengthening the forces in operation in Europe, this military blow (which was of no importance by itself) might serve to dislodge the avalanche of revolution from the ledge on which it had come to rest. This did not happen. We were driven back' (quoted in Rosenberg, op. cit., p. 157).

At the time of the Second Congress, however, optimism was still the reigning mood. 'The decisive hour is approaching,' says one of the Congress resolutions. 'In practically every country where there is a substantial labour movement the working class, arms in hand, is faced by a series of bitter struggles' (Degras, op. cit., 1, p. 128).

28. In writings about this period by members of the Communist parties, Lenin's judgements and analyses on the actual progress of the world revolution, which were not confirmed by history, are usually passed over very quickly, if not completely ignored. Togliatti proves no exception to this rule in his article of 1959. For instance, when he quotes Lenin's warning to the Second Congress that 'there is no situation from which the bourgeoisie can find no way out', he says nothing about the point that it was Lenin's theses of 1917–20 that had largely contributed to implanting this notion in the then recently formed Communist parties. According to Togliatti, Lenin did not express the idea that 'the war would be followed by a settlement of accounts between governments and governed' (Togliatti, art. cit., p. 470). How, then, are we to understand the statements I have just quoted, and all the others to the same effect? Soviet writers go farthest of all in this treatment of the matter. In Krasin's book, previously mentioned, a work of 320 pages (in the English edition) devoted entirely to Lenin's theory of the revolution, the reader will seek in vain for the slightest critical note. Everything Lenin wrote or said was perfect, coherent and confirmed by practice. It need not be emphasized that this apologetical treatment of Lenin's work adds nothing to his historical merits, while considerably hindering Marxist appreciation of his teachings. In working out a theory of socialist revolution that answers the problems of the world of today one must of necessity proceed by way of a critique of Lenin, no less than of Marx.

29. In his report to the Fifth Congress of the Comintern, Zinoviev was obliged to recognize this fact, *a posteriori*: 'In 1921–2 the tactics of the united front meant the realization that we have not yet won a majority of the working-class; secondly, that the social-democracy is still very strong' (*Fifth Congress of the Communist International, Abridged Report,* CPGB, London, 1924, p. 27).

30. This assumption had a precedent in Lenin's optimism already before the war about the revolutionary predisposition of the proletariat of the advanced capitalist countries, as we have seen in previous pages. During the war, he wrote: 'We find that the socialist and labour organizations are now split into two big camps in all countries of the world. *The smaller section*, the leaders, functionaries and officials, have betrayed

11

socialism and have sided with their governments. The other section, to which *the mass of class-conscious workers* belong, continues to gather its forces and to fight against the war and for the proletarian revolution' (op. cit., Vol. 22, p. 124). There is no need to describe how greatly Lenin's confidence in the Western proletariat was enhanced when the German revolution began, followed soon afterwards by the Hungarian. On 22 October 1918 he declared: 'Bolshevism has become the world-wide theory and tactics of the international proletariat' (ibid., Vol. 28, p. 116). In March 1919 he said: '*The masses of workers turned their backs* on these traitors to socialism' (i.e. the reformist leaders) (ibid., Vol. 29, p. 240). And in July 1920: 'Now, a year or a little more after the First Congress of the Communist International, we have emerged victors over the Second International . . .' (ibid., Vol. 31, p. 233). (All italics mine.)

31. Lenin, 'Theses and Report on Bourgeois Democracy and the Dictatorship of the Proletariat,' in ibid., Vol. 28, p. 470.

32. Lenin, 'Letter to the Workers of Europe and America', in ibid., Vol. 28, p. 435.

33. Lenin, 'Meeting of Moscow Party Activists, 27 November 1918', in ibid., Vol. 28, p. 216.

34. Marx and Engels made the same mistake with regard to the capitalism of the nineteenth century. The idea that it had reached a terminal situation is found in the *Communist Manifesto* and reappears thereafter on numerous occasions. For instance, in a letter to Engels dated 8 October 1858, Marx, after mentioning the world-wide expansion of capitalism in this period – the colonization of California and Australia, the opening-up of Japan and China to the world market – concludes: 'We cannot deny that bourgeois society has experienced its sixteenth century for the second time – a sixteenth century which will, I hope, sound the death-knell of bourgeois society just as the first one thrust it into existence ... On the continent the revolution is imminent and will immediately assume a socialist character' (Marx and Engels, *Selected Correspondence*, Lawrence and Wishart, London, 1956, p. 134).

35. Stuart R. Schram and Hélène Carrère d'Encausse, *Marxism and Asia*, Allen Lane The Penguin Press, London, 1969, p. 22.

36. In Lenin's analysis of imperialism, the scientific rigour is greatly affected by his political concern with the fight against reformism, and doubtless also by the way that the 'orthodox' theoreticians of the Second International waged their struggle with Bernstein. The latter built up his revision of Marx on a basis of attributing to the latter a theory of the

'collapse' of capitalism as a result of its purely economic contradictions. In answering Bernstein, some Marxists made the mistake of accepting that this 'collapse' theory was indeed to be found in Marx, and this helped the revisionist offensive to progress on the plane of economic theory, the most important example being Tugan-Baranovsky's critique. Trying to refute him and uphold Marxist orthodoxy, Kautsky took up a defensive position with his theory of 'chronic depression' as the prospect inevitably facing capitalism. As for Rosa Luxemburg, her investigation of 'the accumulation of capital' led her, in fact, to a new 'theory of collapse', according to which capitalism was incapable of carrying out expanded reproduction on its own foundations, this being possible only so long as it could go on integrating additional pre-capitalist structures. When this ceased to be possible, capitalism would be left with no way out. After the war, Hilferding accused Lenin of having, in his turn, upheld the theory of *economic* collapse – which is not, in fact, to be found in Lenin's theoretical hypotheses. For Lenin, no economic crisis, no contradiction on the plane of economic structures, can by itself bring about the collapse of capitalism. Revolutionary Intervention by the proletariat is essential. Lenin's mistake, both on the general theoretical plane (analysis of the structures and dynamic of imperialism) and on that of analysis of the European and world situation in 1914–20, seems to me to have been committed on two levels: (a) although he does not share the ideas of the 'economic collapse theory', he nevertheless underestimates the factors that make it possible to offset the elements of crisis; (b) he overestimates the revolutionary inclinations of a proletariat formed in a period of 'peaceful' expansion of capitalism and of the flowering, on this basis, of the reformist ideology. Driven by his anger at the reformist evolution undergone by Kautsky and Hilferding, Lenin did not take sufficient account of the rational elements in the former's theory of ultra-imperialism and, especially, in the latter's theory of 'organized capitalism'.

37. Quoted by Branko Lazitch, *Lénine et la IIIe Internationale*, La Baconnière, Neuchâtel, 1951, p. 176. (This passage, which will be found in the Russian verbatim report of the Congress – *Tretiy vsemir'ny kongress Kommunisticheskogo Internatsionala, stenografichesky otchet*, Petrograd, 1922, pp. 45–6 – is omitted in the text of Trotsky's speech given in *The First Five Years of the Communist International*, I, New Park Publications, London, 1973.)

38. *Decisions of the Third Congress of the Communist International*, CPGB, London, p. 4.

39. Degras, op. cit., 1, pp. 242–3 (my italics).

40. ibid., p. 237 (my italics).

41. *The First Five Years of the Communist International*, 1, op. cit., p. 292.

42. Degras, op. cit., 1, pp. 233–4.

43. Lenin, 'Better Fewer, but Better', in op. cit., Vol. 33, pp. 499–501.

44. Alfred G. Meyer, *Leninism*, Praeger Paperback, New York, 1962, Chapter 12.

45. Lenin, op cit., Vol. 33, p. 206.

46. Lenin, 'Five Years of the Russian Revolution and the Prospects of the World Revolution', in ibid., Vol. 33, p. 430.

47. ibid., pp. 430–31 (my italics).

48. ibid., p. 420. It is significant of Lenin's state of mind in the last period of his life that, in this report on 'five years of the Russian revolution and the prospects of the world revolution', he says practically nothing about the prospects. He puts all the emphasis on the need to study and re-study the *problems* of the revolution. Moreover, after the Second Congress of the Comintern, Lenin never missed an opportunity for criticizing revolutionary verbiage. At the Third Congress, he wrote in February 1922, '... I was on the exreme right flank. I am convinced that it was the only correct stand to take, for a very large (and influential) group of delegates, headed by many German, Hungarian and Italian comrades, occupied an inordinately "left" and incorrectly "left" position, and far too often instead of soberly weighing up the situation that was not very favourable for immediate and directly revolutionary action, they vigorously indulged in the waving of little red flags' (ibid., Vol. 33, p. 208).

49. Degras, op. cit., 1, p. 444.

50. Stalin, op. cit., Vol. 8, p. 65.

51. ibid., Vol. 6, p. 388.

52. ibid., Vol. 6, p. 414.

53. These were some lines from Lenin's article 'On Co-operation', written at the beginning of 1923, in which, after mentioning that the means of production are in the hands of the state, the state is in the hands of the proletariat, and the proletariat is allied with millions of peasants, he says that this means they have 'all that is necessary for building a complete socialist society' (Stalin, op. cit., Vol. 8, p. 74). From the context of Lenin's article it is clear that for him 'a complete socialist society' means here the including of the peasantry, through co-operatives, in the orbit of collective production-relations. Of course this isolated phrase of Lenin's may seem

to justify Stalin's argument . . . if one forgets the whole of Leninism and, specifically, what Lenin had written only one year before his article on co-operation: 'We have always urged and reiterated the elementary truth of Marxism – that the joint efforts of the workers of several advanced countries are needed for the victory of socialism' (Lenin, op. cit., Vol. 33, p. 206). Had Lenin forgotten in one year that 'elementary truth'?

54. Stalin, op. cit., Vol. 8, p. 67.

55. Trotsky, *The Permanent Revolution* (introduction to German edition), New Park Publications, London, 1962, p. 27.

56. Degras, op. cit., II, p. 491. By 'victory of socialism' is meant the complete construction of socialism within a national setting. As Trotsky points out in his critique of the programme approved by the Sixth Congress: 'If we are to interpret the words "victory of socialism" merely as another expression for the dictatorship of the proletariat, then we will arrive at a general statement which is irrefutable for all and which should be formulated less equivocally. But this is not what the authors of the draft have in mind. By a victory of socialism they do not mean simply the capture of power and the nationalization of the means of production, but the building of a socialist society in one country. If we are to accept this interpretation then we would obtain not a world socialist economy based on an international division of labour but a federation of self-sufficing socialist communes in the spirit of blissful anarchism, the only difference being that these communes would be enlarged to the size of the present national states' (Trotsky, *The Third International after Lenin,* Pioneer Publishers, New York, 1957, p. 54).

A year and a half before the Sixth Congress the Executive Committee of the Communist International had already fully adopted Stalin's view. In the resolution approved by the Seventh Enlarged Plenum of the ECCI, held in November–December 1926, we read this: '. . . the CPSU is carrying through its policy of socialist construction quite correctly, in the firm conviction that the Soviet Union disposes within the country of everything that is "necessary and sufficient" for the construction of a completely socialist society' (Degras, op. cit., I, p. 330).

57. Degras, op. cit., II, pp. 491, 486.

58. ibid., II, pp. 488, 511–13.

59. Stalin, op. cit., Vol. 13, p. 41.

60. Degras, op. cit., II, p. 472.

61. Trotsky, *The Permanent Revolution,* op. cit.

62. ibid., p. 155.

63. Antonio Gramsci, *Selections from the Prison Notebooks*, Lawrence and Wishart, London, 1971, p. 241.

64. Trotsky, 'The Death Agony of Capitalism and the Tasks of the Fourth International' (commonly referred to as 'The Transitional Programme'), in Isaac Deutscher and George Novack, eds., *The Age of Permanent Revolution: A Trotsky Anthology*, Dell, New York, 1964, pp. 255–8. (My italics.)

65. Trotsky, *The Revolution Betrayed*, Pioneer, New York, 1957, p. 231. Trotsky here slips into what Lenin called 'the chief mistake made by revolutionaries', namely, 'that they look backwards at the old revolutions . . .' (Lenin, op. cit., Vol. 24, p. 141).

66. Trotsky, *The Revolution Betrayed*, op. cit., pp. 231–2.

67. ibid., p. 227.

68. ibid., p. 228. 'And, finally, if the "scraps of paper" should preserve their validity during the first period of military operations, there is not a doubt that groupings of forces in the decisive phase of the war would be determined by factors of incomparably more significance than the oaths of diplomats . . .'

69. 'The situation would be radically different, of course, if the bourgeois allies received material guarantees that the Moscow government stands on the same side with them, not only of the war trenches but of the class trenches too. Availing themselves of the difficulties of the Soviet Union, which will be placed between two fires, the capitalist "friends of peace" will, of course, take all measures to drive a breach into the monopoly of foreign trade and the Soviet laws on property . . . And if you assume that the world struggle will be played out only on a military level [i.e., without a revolution occurring in the West] the Allies have a good chance of achieving their goal' (ibid., pp. 228–9).

70. ibid., p. 229.

71. For Bukharin the building of socialism in one country – or, more precisely, in Russia – was possible on condition that this process be adapted to the slow pace of the peasantry. 'The peasantry is to be remodelled by the aid of the co-operatives, the peasant is to be induced to join us by means of the co-operatives. We have the banks and the credit. In the course of decades we shall transform the peasant, without concerning ourselves about the fact that he is a property owner. We are to remember that he has to be our ally, and that we have to remodel him' (Bukharin, 'Concerning the Theories of Permanent Revolution', in *Inprecorr*, English edn, Vol. 5, No. 13, 7 February 1925, p. 171). It was a matter of

building socialism 'at a snail's pace', as Bukharin himself put it. From his theorization of this Russian road to socialism Bukharin deduced that the course of the world revolution, too, would have to adapt itself, in the last analysis, to the circumstance that the huge majority of the world's population consists of peasants. The colonial problem, says Bukharin, is actually a peasant problem. On the world scale as on the scale of Russia, the proletariat has no choice: 'The proletariat, after its victory, must maintain friendly relations with the peasantry at any price ... Nothing but an entire lack of comprehension of international economic relations can cause anyone to ignore this task ... The proletariat has here no alternative. It is forced to carry the peasantry with it when building up the socialist structure. It must learn how to do this, or it cannot maintain its power' (ibid., p. 165).

But this highly interesting problematic outlined by Bukharin is situated within an assumption that the proletariat has already taken power in the metropolitan countries of capitalism.

72. Lucio Magri, 'Valeur et limites des expériences frontistes', in *Les Temps Modernes*, January 1966, p. 216. While agreeing with Magri when he says that the doctrine of 'socialism in one country' reflected objectively the relative and reciprocal autonomy between the Russian revolution and the world revolution, I cannot go along with him when he says that it 'provided the basis, objectively and subjectively, for a new strategy' (based on this autonomy). In my view, what Stalin created was a strategy which totally *denied* this autonomy.

73. Among these an outstanding place certainly belongs to the German Communist historian Arthur Rosenberg, whose *History of Bolshevism* constitutes, as George Haupt rightly observes in the thought-provoking preface he wrote for the French edition (Grasset, Paris, 1967), 'a profound and critical meditation, the lucidity, breadth and scope of which justify us in including this book among those important works of political thought that are indispensable for understanding the past and even the present of Communism'. In the course of this investigation of the Comintern I have more than once had occasion to acknowledge the 'stimulating' quality of Rosenberg's work – without, however, agreeing with his general ultra-left outlook or with many of his specific conclusions.

74. Trotsky, *The Revolution Betrayed*, op. cit., pp. 186–7. Rosenberg, who gives numerous facts and arguments regarding this utilization of the Comintern for the needs of Soviet foreign policy, considers nevertheless that the Comintern was more of an embarrassment than otherwise to the

USSR, both on the diplomatic plane and on that of its endeavours to win 'the friendship of the workers throughout the world'. 'Russian diplomacy would work better and be more fruitful of results if it was not compromised by the existence of the Third International ... The path leading to the friendship of the majority of European and American workmen is closed and not opened to Soviet Russia by the activities of the Communist International.' And Rosenberg goes on to remark that 'it appears all the more extraordinary that the Soviet government should not have long ago cast off the Third International' (p. 180). In his opinion, the Soviet government continued to concern itself with the Comintern so as to keep alive 'the proletarian and socialist fable which even Russian Bolshevism cannot dispense with and whose importance for Russian domestic policy has grown even greater since 1928. If a dictatorship of the proletariat really existed in Russia, the fact would be recognized by the international proletariat or at least by its revolutionary element. If all the international labour organizations were to certify that Soviet Russia is a middle-class state, their testimony would not overthrow the Soviet government but would certainly prejudice its relations with the Russian proletariat' (p. 181). As will be seen, this argument contradicts the one according to which the Comintern is an embarrassment to the Russian government in seeking 'the friendship of the workers throughout the world'. Quite apart, however, from this contradiction in Rosenberg's thinking, the problem is in reality a great deal more complex than he makes it out to be. In the first place, the Comintern was a reality the existence of which did not depend *exclusively* on the Soviet leadership, despite the decisive role they played in creating and, subsequently, in leading it. It was a response to an objective need, born of the reformist degeneration of Social Democracy, even if it did not respond to this need in the most satisfactory fashion. The fact that the world revolution followed a path different from the one the idea of which inspired the creation of the Comintern did not do away with the need for an international revolutionary organization – a problem, indeed, that is still with us today. Actually, Stalin and the other Soviet leaders had to reckon with the Comintern as with an objective reality which, even if manipulated, subordinated, emptied of its original purpose, could not be completely suppressed. (Its dissolution in 1943 was ultimately, as we shall see in more detail later on, only one of the ways whereby this reality was *adapted* to the interests of the Soviet state.) Considerations bound up with the internal conditions of Soviet society also affected, doubtless, the different forms taken by this adaptation. But this did not exclude other considerations, of an international character: moreover, the two aspects were closely linked. It is true – and this is, fundamentally, the reason why Rosenberg said that the Soviet state was not interested in the Comintern for reasons of foreign policy – that, while being an instrument susceptible to being used in accordance with the needs of Soviet foreign policy (as an instrument of 'pressure' on the bourgeoisie, to use Trotsky's expression, and also, let it be added, as a genuinely revolutionary instrument where this function did not conflict with Soviet interests), the Comintern represented, at the same time, an embarrassment in relations between the USSR and the imperialist states. But the importance of that aspect, like the importance of the other aspects mentioned, varied with circumstances. The relations between the Soviet state and party, on the one hand, and the Comintern, on the other, need to be analysed in a way that takes a number of variables into account. In the passages that follow, I am concerned to analyse the variable constituted by the 'embarrassment' factor.

75. Bukharin, 'The International Situation and the Tasks of the Communist International', report to the Fifteenth Congress of the CPSU, in *Inprecorr,* English edn, No. 73, 1927, p. 1676.

76. Down to 1926 Zinoviev had been president. At the Seventh Plenum of the ECCI, in October 1926, he was removed and the post of president abolished. Bukharin took over leadership of the Comintern until the Tenth Plenum, in April 1929, which unseated him. The main reports of the congresses preceding the Seventh had always been presented by Soviet Communists.

77. Dimitrov, closing speech at the Seventh Congress, in *Seventh Congress of the Communist International, Abridged Stenographic Report,* FLPH, Moscow, 1939, p. 557.

78. In *Rosa Luxemburg: Selected Political Writings,* ed. Robert Looker, Jonathan Cape, London, 1972, p. 250. In the context of this work, 'devilishly hard conditions' and 'fatal circumstances' means the general conditions of Russia (backwardness, predominance of agriculture, etc.) and the circumstances resulting from the imperialist armed intervention, the absence of revolution in the West, etc. The concept of 'tactics' is used in the broadest sense, embracing the strategical problems of the revolution. Rosa Luxemburg appreciated so early as 1904 – in connection with the conception of the party that was upheld by Lenin – the danger inherent in isolating the Bolshevik experience from its political and social setting. Referring to the connection established by Lenin between opportunism and decentralizing tendencies, she wrote in her essay 'Organizational

Problems of Russian Social Democracy': 'However, to separate these phenomena, which arose on a concrete historical base, from their context, making them into abstract models having universal and absolute value, is the greatest of sins against the "Holy Ghost" of Marxism – namely against its historical-dialectical mode of thought' (Rosa Luxemburg, *Selected Political Writings*, ed. Howard, Monthly Review Press, New York, 1971, p. 298).

79. Other facts could be added to these. The tremendous international repercussions of the October revolution helped to conceal how essentially Russian it was, in the type of objective contradictions involved, in the characteristics of its social agents, its strategic paths and tactical methods, etc. As regards the theoretical forces initially available to the Comintern, account must be taken not only of the fact that nearly all the theoretical cadres of the Second International remained in the reformist camp but, also that, in the preceding period, a divorce had occurred between the theory of the revolution in the strict sense, which remained congealed, so to speak, in the 'outline' form in which Marx and Engels had left it, and the development of the social sciences (economics, sociology, history, philosophy), which, although greatly influenced by Marxism, took an essentially positivist direction.

80. Lenin, op. cit., Vol. 31, pp. 21–2, 91.

81. Bukharin, *Historical Materialism*, English edn, Allen and Unwin, London, 1926, p. xii.

82. Nevertheless, one can mention, so far as philosophy is concerned, Karl Korsch's book entitled *Marxism and Philosophy*, which was published in 1923 (English translation, New Left Books, London, 1970), and was immediately condemned by the Comintern. In 1923 also there appeared *History and Class-Consciousness*, by George Lukács (English translation, Merlin Press, London, 1971). While defending Bolshevik orthodoxy on problems of party and state, this book, like Korsch's, constituted, on the philosophical plane, a re-examination of the problems of the Marxist dialectic, going back to investigate its origins, the relation between Marx and Hegel. This was why it was condemned by Zinoviev at the Fifth Congress of the Comintern (1924), along with Korsch's book.

83. *Bolshevik* (Moscow), No. 10, 5 September 1924, p. 53. This journal began to appear after Lenin's death, in the context of the struggle with the Trotskyist opposition.

84. The comparison made by Zinoviev between the relation of the Marxists to Marx and that of the Darwinists to Darwin does not take account

of an essential difference which has been pointed out by the Spanish Marxist philosopher Manuel Sacristan, in his preface to the Spanish edition of Engel's *Anti-Dühring* (Grijalbo, Mexico City, 1964). 'As a general rule,' he writes, 'a classical writer serves, for men who practise the same science as he, only a source of inspiration which defines, more or less clearly, the essential motivations of their thinking. The classical writers of the working-class movement, however, defined, in addition to certain essential intellectual motivations, also the bases for the practical activity of this movement, its general objectives. The classics of Marxism are classics of a whole conception of the world, not just of a particular positivist scientific theory. This results in an attitude of militant partisanship on the part of the working-class movement towards its classics. Given this inevitable attitude it is after all quite natural for the lazy tendency not to criticize, but to rest concerned only with one's own moral and practical security, to take over when these classics are read, thus *wrongly consecrating whatever historical state of the theory happens to be found in them*, conferring upon this the same untouchability as a politico-social movement gives to the programmatic objectives which define it' (pp. 22–4; my italics). After Lenin's death the Comintern not only did not combat this 'lazy tendency' but, on the contrary, encouraged it, justifying it with all manner of practical, political and even 'theoretical' arguments.

85. These quotations have been taken from Zinoviev's work *Le Léninisme* (Bureau d'Éditions, Paris, 1926), pp. 11, 13, 14. The emphasis in each case is Zinoviev's own.

86. *Report of the Fifteenth Congress of the CPSU*, CPGB, London, 1928, p. 264. In the Russian report of this Congress (*XV s'yezd . . .*, Moscow, 1935, 1, p. 593), Bukharin says that, generally speaking, the Communist parties had, in any case, very few intellectuals to start with.

87. ibid., pp. 217–18 and *Inprecorr*, English edn, No. 73 of 1927, pp. 1672–5.

88. *Inprecorr*, English edn, No. 73 of 1927, p. 1680.

89. It was in March 1926 that Mao's study of the classes in Chinese society appeared, and in March 1927 his report on the investigation he had himself carried out into the peasant movement in the province of Hunan. So far as I know, politico-sociological inquiries like these – comparable to the ones made by Lenin in relation to Russian society at the end of the nineteenth century and at the beginning of the twentieth – were never undertaken in any of the Western Communist parties during the period of the Comintern.

3. Monolithicity

1. Quoted in B. Lazitch and M. Drachkovitch, *Lenin and the Comintern, I*, Stanford, 1972, p. 61.

2. Degras, op. cit., I, p. 171.

3. The official title of the document is: 'Conditions of Admission to the Communist International'. See Degras, op. cit., I, pp. 168–72.

4. Lenin, 'Speech on the Italian Question' (Third Congress of the Communist International, 28 June 1921), in op. cit., Vol. 32, p. 467.

5. Directly after the First World War, the trade-union organization of the working-class made a real leap forward in quantitative terms. Between 1913 and 1919 the number of organized workers increased in Germany from four million to eleven million; in Britain from four to eight million; in France from one million to two-and-a-half; in Italy from nearly a million to nearly two million; in Austria from about 250,000 to 800,000. (These are round figures.) The reformist or non-political leaders retained decisive influence over the great majority of this mass of trade-unionists.

Between 1918 and 1924, in all the countries mentioned, elections were held which probably took place under conditions of greater bourgeois freedom than any subsequent ones between the two world wars. The results give a certain idea of the relationship of forces and influence within the working-class between the traditional Socialist parties and the new Communist parties:

Country	Date of Elections	Party	Votes (in round figures)
Britain	1918	Labour	2,200,000
Britain	1922	Labour	4,300,000
Germany	1919	Majority Socialists	11,500,000
		Independent Socialists (Centrists)	2,300,000
Germany	1920	Majority Socialists	6,100,000
		Independent Socialists (Centrists)	5,000,000
		Communists	400,000
France	1919	Socialists	1,700,000
France	1924	Socialists	1,700,000
		Communists	900,000

Country	Date of Election	Party	Votes (*in round figures*)
Italy	1919	Socialists	2,000,000
Italy	1921	Socialists (Serrati)	1,500,000
		Communists	300,000
Austria	1919	Socialists	1,200,000
Austria	1920	Socialists	1,000,000
		Communists	22,000

(Figures quoted by Branko Lazitch, *Lénine et la IIIe Internationale*, op. cit., pp. 249–50.)

According to Arthur Rosenberg (op. cit., pp. 166–7): 'The majority of European workmen supported the Third International during the years 1919 and 1920.' This estimate hardly squares with the figures given above or with the results of the revolutionary struggles, but it does contain an element of truth. Substantial sections of the workers sympathized with the new International, which they saw as representing the Russian revolution; but they accepted neither its view of the situation nor its methods – the '21 Conditions' in particular. It is to this circumstance, no doubt, that Rosenberg alludes when he says: 'As a result of dissensions, and their rejection of large sections of the working-class, the Communists found themselves once more in the minority. The SPD, strengthened by the addition of a part of the USPD which had not gone over to the Third International, had a far greater membership than the Communist Party in Germany. The Social Democrats in 1921 were once more supported by a clear majority of the workmen in England and Italy, Sweden and Denmark, Holland and Belgium, Austria and Switzerland. Only in France, Czechoslovakia and Norway were the Communists in 1921 supported by the majority of organized workmen. Communism was forcibly suppressed by the governments of the Baltic and Balkan states, Poland and Hungary The syndicalists, who were supported by the majority of the Spanish workmen, left the Third International ... Communism hardly existed in non-European countries.'

In his essay on the Comintern, already quoted, Togliatti says: 'It was easier to break with the Social Democratic leaders than to get rid of Social Democracy.' But he draws no critical conclusion regarding the methods employed to achieve this 'break'.

6. The 'turn' began at the Third Congress, in June–July 1921, but the

first theses on the 'workers' united front' were not drawn up by the ECCI until the end of that year, being approved at its plenary meeting held in December.

7. Annie Kriegel, *Les Internationales onvières*, PUF, Paris, 1970, pp. 112–13. The subsequent period, following Hitler's coming to power (the 'People's Front' period), showed a certain increase in the membership of the legal parties, especially in France and Spain. Nevertheless, the official figures given at the Seventh Congress (785,000) seem surprising in view of the collapse of the German Communist Party which had occurred in the meantime, and the grave losses suffered by the Communist Party of China in the course of the armed struggle in 1934 and the first half of 1935, as a result of which its numbers fell from 300,000 in October 1933 to 30,000 in the first half of 1935. The Soviet historians B. M. Leibzon and K. K. Shirinya cast doubt, for the first time, upon the official figures, in their book *Povorot v politike Kominterna* ('The Turn in the Policy of the Comintern'), published in Moscow in 1965. They consider that the losses suffered by the Chinese party need to be deducted from these figures. In that case, the membership of the Comintern (apart from the Soviet party) would have stood, at the time of the Seventh Congress, at about 500,000 (p. 103, note 3).

8. *Stenografichesky otchet VI Kongressa Kominterna,* Moscow and Leningrad, 1929, part V, p. 109. (For the documents of the Second and Fifth Congresses quoted above, see Degras, op. cit., I, p. 165, and II, pp. 119–20.)

9. Lenin, op. cit., Vol. II, pp. 412–13.

10. Quoted in G. Fiori, *Antonio Gramsci*, English trans., New Left Books, London, 1970, p. 124.

11. Rosa Luxemburg began criticizing Lenin's theory on the party as soon as this assumed systematic shape in *What Is To Be Done?* and *One Step Forward, Two Steps Back.* Her essay 'Organizational Questions in Russian Social Democracy', published in *Neue Zeit* in 1904, constituted a direct critique, on the theoretical plane, of Lenin's conceptions. In this she makes an observation which is very much to the point: 'To attribute to opportunism, as does Lenin, the tendency to prefer some specific form of organization – say decentralization – is to totally mistake its inner nature' (Rosa Luxemburg, *Selected Political Writings,* ed. Howard, Monthly Review Press, New York, 1971, p. 300). In the same essay she points out the negative effects that ultra-centralism has on the party's political activity: 'Granting, as Lenin wants, such absolute powers of a negative

character to the top organ of the party, we strengthen, to a dangerous extent, the conservatism inherent in such an organ. If the tactics of the socialist party are not to be the creation of a Central Committee but of the whole party, or, still better, of the whole labour movement, then it is clear that the party sections and federations need the liberty of action which alone will permit them to develop their revolutionary initiative and to utilize all the resources of a situation. The ultra-centralism asked for by Lenin is full of the sterile spirit of the overseer. It is not a positive and creative spirit. *Lenin's concern is not so much to make the activity of the party more fruitful as to control the party—to narrow the movement rather than to develop it, to bind rather than to unify it*' (in Rosa Luxemburg, *Selected Political Writings*, ed. Robert Looker, Jonathan Cape, London, 1972, pp. 103–4).

12. Ryazanov proposed to lay it down definitively, in the resolution 'on unity', that never again could delegates be elected to a party Congress on the basis of political platforms put forward by various groups or individual members of the party, as had happened in connection with the Tenth Congress. Lenin opposed this amendment with the following arguments: 'I think that, regrettable as it may be, Comrade Ryazanov's suggestion is impracticable. We cannot deprive the party and the members of the Central Committee of the right to appeal to the party in the event of disagreement on fundamental issues ... In the circumstances, the elections may have to be based on platforms ... If we are united by our resolution on unity, and, of course, the development of the revolution, there will be no repetition of elections according to platforms. The lesson we have learned at this Congress will not be forgotten. But if the circumstances should give rise to fundamental disagreements, can we prohibit them from being brought before the judgement of the whole party? No, we cannot! This is an excessive desire, which is impracticable, and I move that we reject it' (op. cit., Vol. 32, p. 261). Lenin saw the problem in a dialectical way: whether groups with differing programmes, in other words, factions, are going to appear or not is not something that can be decided by decree. It depends on the development of the real movement whether important divergences do or do not appear in it. If they should arise, then the only way to resolve them is to have an open discussion in the party.

Lenin's opinion on the way that discussion should proceed in the event of important divergences is also very instructive: '*All* members of the party must make a calm and painstaking *study* of (1) the essence of the disagreements and (2) the development of the party struggle. A study must be made of both, because the essence of the disagreements is revealed, clarified and specified (and very often transformed as well) in the *course of the struggle*, which, passing through its various stages, always shows, at every stage, a *different* line-up and number of combatants, *different* positions in the struggle, etc. A *study* must be made of both, and a demand made for the most exact, printed documents that can be thoroughly verified. Only a hopeless idiot will believe oral statements' (op. cit., Vol. 32, pp. 43–4). There can be no doubt about it, a great expert in the field of factional struggles is speaking here. After Lenin, however, persistent efforts were made to transform Communists into such 'hopeless idiots'.

13. Trotsky, *The Permanent Revolution*, op. cit., p. 113.

14. Engels to Kautsky, 23 February 1891, in Marx and Engels, *Selected Correspondence*, 1956 edn, p. 511.

15. The first of these passages forms part of the communication of the General Council to the International Alliance of Socialist Democracy, 9 March 1869 (in *The General Council of the First International, 1868–1870, Minutes*, Progress Publishers, Moscow, 1966, p. 310). The second is from 'Fictitious Splits in the International', dated 5 March 1872 (in Marx-Engels-Lenin, *On Anarchism and Anarcho-Syndicalism*, Progress Publishers, Moscow, 1972, p. 73).

16. Trotsky, 'Against National Communism!' (1931), in *The Struggle Against Fascism in Germany*, Pathfinder, New York, 1971, p. 110.

17. *Seventh World Congress of the Communist International* ..., op. cit., p. 558. (My italics.)

18. Dimitrov, 'The Soviet Union and the Working Class of the Capitalist Countries' (November 1937), in *Selected Articles and Speeches*, Lawrence and Wishart, London, 1951, p. 184. In the second half of the 1930s, when Stalin launched a campaign of terror against the Bolshevik 'Old Guard', and against millions of Soviet citizens, there were living as exiles in Moscow, carrying out tasks on behalf of their respective parties or for the Comintern, a number of leaders and officials of those European Communist parties that were working in illegal conditions under Fascist or reactionary regimes (Germany, Italy, Poland, Hungary, Yugoslavia, Bulgaria, etc.). Stalin's repression fell upon them as well, on the pretext of relations or complicity with Trotskyism, Bukharinism, etc. The victims were invariably accused of being in the service of the police of their own countries and of various capitalist secret agencies. At the Eighteenth Con-

gress of the CPSU, Manuilsky even asserted that the Communist Party of Poland had been penetrated by police agents, just as, he claimed, had previously happened with the Hungarian and Yugoslav parties (*World News and Views*, No. 19 of 1939, p. 382). Among the Yugoslav Communists murdered by Stalin's secret police were the first two secretaries of the party, Filip Filipović (Bosković) and Sima Marković, together with Josip Čizinski (Gorkić), who held the position in 1937. The entire leadership of the Communist Party of Yugoslavia was swept away in that year, apart from Josip Broz-Tito, who was entrusted by the Comintern with the task of forming a new leadership (see Branko Lazitch, *Les Partis communistes de l'Europe*, Les Îles d'Or, Paris, 1956, p. 145). The party most affected was that of Poland. K. S. Karol, in his book *Visa for Poland* (MacGibbon and Kee, London, 1959, pp. 49–50), gives the following account. In January 1938 'all the Polish Communists in the Soviet Union were arrested and summarily shot. Adolf Warski, 71-year-old veteran of the working-class movement, friend of Lenin and of Rosa Luxemburg, who had retired from political life for several years, was the first victim. Lenski, though considered the most loyal Polish Stalinist, Wera Kostrzewa, who had been a comrade of Stalin when the latter had been deported to Siberia, Henryk Walecki and all the others shared the same fate. And since the list was not complete, Stalin summoned all the other Polish Communist Party leaders from Spain, where they were fighting in the first International Brigade – it bore the name of the Polish hero of the Paris Commune, Jaroslaw Dombrowski. Prochniak, a former member of the Comintern executive committee, Brand, Bronkowski, Bronski and many others kept this rendezvous with death. Hundreds of minor leaders were deported to concentration camps in the Arctic Circle . . . In April 1938 the Comintern officially decreed the dissolution of the Polish Communist Party, "which had been infiltrated by *agents provocateurs*, Trotskyites and other enemies of the working-class". The activities received orders to disperse, and were solemnly warned that any attempt to re-form the party would be looked upon as provocation. What the Pilsudski regime had not managed to do after long years of merciless struggle, the Comintern achieved in a few hours; the extreme left in Poland, as an organized force, ceased to exist.' Also shot were German, Italian and other foreign Communists. (Regarding the Germans, see p. 40, note 67, below.)

19. Foster, op. cit., p. 439.
20. The Fourth International was established in 1938.

4. *The Crisis of Policy*

1. O. Piatnitsky, *World Communists in Action*, Modern Books, London, 1930, p. 5.

2. At the general elections of November 1932 the Nazi Party lost 2,000,000 votes. Nearly all historians agree that the Hitlerite tide had begun to ebb, and that the political operation by which power passed into Hitler's hands was not at all dictated by the balance of forces. Some writers have spoken of the 'suicide of the Weimar Republic'. It would perhaps be more precise to speak of the suicide of the German labour movement.

3. Trotsky, 'The Tragedy of the German Proletariat', in *The Struggle Against Fascism in Germany*, op. cit., p. 375.

4. *Seventh Congress of the Communist International* ..., op. cit., pp. 136–7, 370.

5. ibid., p. 134.

6. The proposal invariably put forward was for a general strike, in full awareness that the reformist leaders would reply in the negative. Trotsky called this method 'ultimatism'. The party kept on indefatigably presenting its 'ultimatum' not only to the leaders but to the masses as well, demanding that they submit to its leadership and acknowledge the alleged historic mission of the Comuunist Party. (See Trotsky, 'What Next?', section entitled 'Bureaucratic Ultimatism', in op. cit., pp. 162–70.)

7. Gilbert Badia, *La Fin de la République allemande (1919–1933)*, Éditions Sociales, Paris, 1958, p. 88. The author notes that 'even when the Fascist danger became more pressing, no determined attempt was made to secure unity at the top' (p. 63).

8. W. Ulbricht, *Zur Geschichte der deutschen Arbeiterbewegung*, Vol. I, Dietz, Berlin, 1953, p. 455.

9. Lenin, op. cit., Vol. 33, p. 334.

10. On 16 December, 1926, Scheidemann, a leader of the Social Democratic Party and a former Chancellor, made a speech in the Reichstag that caused a sensation throughout the world. The Social Democrats were in opposition at that time, and the Social Democratic leader denounced the fact that the Reichswehr was engaged in secret rearmament and constituted a state within the state. After adducing a great deal of information on this subject, Scheidemann revealed that the Reichswehr general staff was using the services of, *inter alia*, an industrial company called GEFU for the purpose of installing in Russia an armaments industry working for the German army. Here are some excerpts from his speech:

'The task of GEFU consists in setting up an armaments industry abroad, in Russia. The agreements were signed with false names. The go-between for the agreements made by the Junkers firm, on 14 March 1922, was General Hasse. (Uproar on the Right, shouts: "Traitor!" "Scoundrel!" "Throw him out!") We know from an absolutely reliable source,' Scheidemann went on, amid a growing din, 'that cargoes of Russian arms arrived from Leningrad in several ships at the end of September and during October 1926. These vessels belong to the Stettin Shipping Co., and are named *Gothenburg, Rastenburg,* and *Colberg*. The Communist cell in the port is fully aware of all this. (Embarrassed laughter on the Left.) It offers an unbecoming and dishonest spectacle for Soviet Russia to be preaching world revolution while arming the Reichswehr. (Interruptions from the Left, shouts.) We can no longer tolerate a state of affairs which is contrary to the establishment of a truly republican and democratic army. The Reichswehr is in need of thoroughgoing reform. (Applause in the centre and on the Left, uproar on the Right)' (quoted by J. Benoist-Méchin, *Historie de l'Armée allemande*, Albin Michel, Paris, 1938, Vol. 2, p. 371: new edn, 1964, Vol. 2, pp. 369–70).

Gilbert Badia, in his *Histoire de l'Allemagne contemporaine* (Vol. I, pp. 234–5, and the corresponding notes), fully confirms the collaboration between the Reichswehr and the Soviet government and gives a number of details about this matter. See also A. Fontaine, *History of the Cold War, 1917–1950*, Secker and Warburg, London, 1968, p. 61. According to Deutscher (*Stalin*, op. cit., p. 409, note 2) the collaboration between Red Army and Reichswehr continued until 1935.

The Soviet historian Nekrich, in his book *22 June 1941*, mentions one of the aspects of this collaboration. A number of leaders of the Red Army attended courses at the German military academy. The relations established at this time between the German and Soviet military chiefs led to correspondence between them, and this enabled the German secret service, towards the end of the 1930s, to fabricate false documents for the purpose of compromising the leaders of the Red Army and convincing Stalin of the existence of a generals' plot, headed by Tukhachevsky and Yakir. The purge that was to destroy many of the commanders of the Soviet armed forces began in this way. (See V. Petrov, ed., '*22 June 1941*': *Soviet Historians and the German Invasion*, Columbia (South Carolina), 1968, pp. 131–5.)

11. Badia, *Histoire de l'Allemagne contemporaine*, op. cit., p. 132.

12. The Independent Social Democratic Party (USPD) emerged from

the split that took place in the German Social Democratic Party in 1917. The 'Independents' included Kautsky and Bernstein as well as the Spartacists (who broke with it in November 1918, to found the Communist Party). The common denominator of this motley group was their opposition to the war policy of the SPD leadership. Klara Zetkin left the 'Independents' before the majority of them went over in a body to the KPD, which happened at the end of 1920.

13. Badia, *Histoire de l'Allemagne contemporaine* op. cit., pp. 176–7. There is, as Badia shows, some reason to think that the government deliberately provoked this premature insurrection by the Communists.

14. Degras, op. cit., I, p. 240.

15. Here are a few examples. At the conference of the Russian Social Democratic Labour Party, when it had been temporarily reunited after the split of 1905, eight of the nine delegates from the Bolshevik faction proposed a boycott of the Duma. Lenin joined with the Mensheviks, the Polish Socialists and the Bund in order to ensure the rejection of this proposal. Not long before the October insurrection, in view of the resistance that his proposals had encountered in the Central Committee of the Bolshevik party, Lenin sent a letter ('The Crisis has matured') tendering his resignation and 'reserving for myself freedom to campaign among the rank and file of the party'. Zinoviev and Kamenev set forth publicly, in a journal not belonging to the party, their differences with Lenin on the subject of the insurrection plan. In 1918 the Moscow regional bureau, headed by Bukharin, issued a document opposing the peace of Brest–Litovsk and declaring that a split in the party was inevitable. Many other examples of the same kind could be quoted.

16. Lenin, op. cit., Vol. 33, pp. 281, 302.

17. In the first days of 1923 a dollar was worth 18,000 marks, in August it was worth 4,600,000 and in November 8,000,000. In other words, the mark became quite valueless. This monstrous devaluation of the currency was reflected in a steady increase in prices. Protests and strikes broke out all over the country. At the same time, the forces of Fascism and militarism began to move. In Bavaria, where Hitler's party already had a certain amount of strength, a 'march on Berlin' was discussed. The KPD set up organizations of proletarian self defence, the 'revolutionary hundreds'. On 1 May, 25,000 members of these groups marched through Berlin. On 29 June, an 'Anti-Fascist Day' was held, organized by the party. On 11 August, the workers of Berlin came out on strike for three days. Cuno's government resigned and Stresemann formed a government, in

which the SPD participated – until then it had been in opposition, and this circumstance had encouraged the Social Democratic workers to join in the wave of protests. The new government decided to halt the 'passive resistance' to the occupation of the Ruhr, took a number of economic measures (with the help of Anglo-American capitalism) in order to stabilize the currency, and declared martial law, in other words, gave *de facto* ruling authority to the army. In October, coalition governments of Communists and left-wing Socialists were formed in Saxony and Thuringia: but in Germany as a whole the movement had begun to ebb. The Social Democratic workers of Saxony and Thuringia rejected the Communists' proposal to organize armed resistance to the troops sent by the Reichswehr to 'restore order' in these two provinces. 'Order' was indeed restored, and the Communist ministers were ejected from the two provincial governments.

18. Trotsky, interview given on 20 February and published in the *Manchester Guardian*, 1 March 1923. In Degras, ed., *Documents on Soviet Foreign Policy,* OUP, London, 1953, I, pp. 375–6.

19. Quoted by Trotsky in his *Stalin*, Hollis and Carter, London, 1947, pp. 368–9.

20. Lenin, op. cit., Vol. 33, p. 148. Lenin went on to say that they were ready to make such concessions and sacrifices, 'but not any kind and not for ever'. The general sense of his theses was that one must go as far as might be necessary in order to preserve peace, but without endangering the essential conquests of the Russian revolution.

21. At that time Radek was the Comintern's specialist on German questions. At the Fifth Comintern Congress (1924), where the 'German question' formed the central theme of discussion (to such an extent that at one moment Pepper, the representative of the Communist Party of the United States, intervened to say: 'I was afraid that the Congress had become onesidedly a German congress, or at best a central European congress. So far it has been too little of a world congress'), Radek refuted the excessively facile statements made by Zinoviev and other leaders of the Comintern about the situation in Germany and other European countries: 'Comrade Zinoviev has said in his report that in the important centres in France and Germany we are advancing towards winning the majority of the proletariat. That is the kernel of the question. If Comrade Zinoviev asserts that, he is mistaken. And this error, together with the idea of our left-wing comrades, who declare that they are ready every day to take up the struggle for complete power ... (Interruption: Ready, ready!) One is not

ready to do that which one cannot do' (*Inprecorr*, English edn, Vol. 4, No. 47, p. 483, and No. 42, p. 421 – 23 and 17 July 1924).

22. Brandler said at the Fifth Congress, 'The entry into the Saxon government was made in spite of my objections and the opposition of the Saxon comrades' (*Inprecorr*, English edn, Vol. 4, No. 42 (17 July 1924), p. 425, and *Fifth Congress of the Communist International, Abridged Report*, London, CPGB, 1924, p. 65).

23. Ruth Fischer, *Stalin and German Communism*, OUP, London, 1948, pp. 316–17.

24. While upholding the official view of the Zinoviev leadership of the Comintern, blaming Brandler's policy, G. Badia comes to the conclusion that the conditions for regarding the conquest of power as feasible did not actually exist. In a long note in his *Histoire de l'Allemagne contemporaine* (p. 201), he refutes the statements of Thälmann and Stalin. (Stalin, who had supported Brandler, made a sharp about-turn and defended the opposite view. The reason for this turn-round was that the Brandler–Thalheimer group were supporting the opposition inside the Russian party. Stalin's arguments were that, while it was not possible to contemplate the seizure of power in August, that had become possible two months later, for 'the revolutionary wave had risen and broken the Social Democratic Party, and the workers were beginning to go over *en masse* to the Communist Party'.) The concrete facts of the situation show the opposite to have been true. The workers' councils in Saxony supported the attitude of the left-wing Social Democrats, who were against the general strike. The Hamburg revolt, as is shown by the description of it that Thälmann himself gave, did not succeed in drawing in even the majority of the members of the Communist Party in that city. Moreover, as Badia points out: 'Neither Thälmann nor Stalin, who formulated their views long after the events, take sufficient account of the state of the forces of the bourgeoisie. Despite the conflict between Munich and Berlin, the German bourgeoisie was stronger in 1923 than it had been in 1918. The right-wing parties had more influence. Above all, there was now such a well-organized instrument of repression as the Reichswehr, which did not exist in December 1918.' He quotes the view of Walter Ulbricht, expressed at the Ninth Congress of the KPD, held at Frankfurt in April 1924: 'The October battles [meaning the Hamburg rising] have shown the party what happens when a little group of courageous Communists allow themselves to be decimated while the broad masses, including even the broad masses of workers on strike, stand passively by, watching the struggle.'

25. The theses on the 'workers' united front' adopted by the Fourth Congress of the Comintern (1922) explicitly endorsed the tactics followed by the German party (Degras, *The Communist International (1919–1943): Documents*, 1, pp. 311–12). At the plenum of the ECCI on 12 June 1923, Zinoviev held up the KPD as an example to all as a party that took account of advice received from the ECCI. (*Na plenume ispolkoma Kominterna 12.VI.23*, Moscow, 1923, pp. 29–30.)

26 *Inprecorr*, English edn, Vol. 4, No. 47 (23 July 1924), pp. 485–6.

27. The resolution of the Fifth Congress on the 'Russian question' included the following: 'The congress also observes that the opposition in the Russian Communist Party was supported by groups in other parties in the Polish, German and French parties, etc.; this, like the RCP opposition, is a manifestation of a right (opportunist) deviation in these parties ...' (Degras, op. cit., 11, p. 142).

28. *Bolshevising the Communist International*, CPGB, London, 1925, pp. 107–8.

29. *Inprecorr*, English edn, Vol. 5, No. 32 (16 April 1925), p. 423.

30. Ruth Fischer, op. cit., Chapter 20, and p. 538, note.

31. J. Humbert-Droz, who was then one of the secretaries of the Comintern, reveals the details of this affair in his book, '*L'Œil de Moscou' à Paris* (Julliard, Coll. Archives, Paris, 1964, pp. 256–9). Soon after the Sixth Congress of the Comintern a crisis occurred in the KPD. The party secretary in Hamburg, Wittorf, had stolen 2,000 marks from the party funds, and Thälmann had prevented the matter from becoming public, forbidding the militants involved in checking the details to say anything about it, on pain of expulsion. The Central Committee of the party unanimously dismissed Thälmann. The scandal had been discovered by Eberlein, the representative of the Spartacists at the foundation congress of the Comintern, who in 1928 was auditor of the Comintern's finances. Fearing lest the leadership of the KPD fall into the hands of Bukharin's supporters, Stalin summoned a meeting of the Presidium of the ECCI, that is, the few members who were present in Moscow at that time. He compelled the Presidium to annul the decision of the Central Committee of the KPD, to rehabilitate Thälmann, and to administer a public reprimand to the German Central Committee. Several members of the Presidium, including Manuilsky, Bela Kun and Humbert-Droz himself, who were then on holiday in the Caucasus, learnt of this decision from the pages of *Pravda*.

32. At the end of 1919 and in 1920, there was in Berlin a Comintern

secretariat for Western Europe, working closely with the leadership of the KPD. Its line differed from that of the Moscow centre, and reflected the influence of the German leadership, within which the Luxemburgist tendency was marked. In January 1920 this secretariat published in its journal some draft theses on the tactics of the Comintern in the struggle for the dictatorship of the proletariat, in which an attempt to determine policy independently of the Bolsheviks was observable. Ideas that had been expressed at the foundation congress of the KPD were reasserted, including the notion that the socialist revolution constitutes a complex historical process, differing in accordance with circumstances and countries. The German revolution, and the revolution in Europe generally, it was said, presented problems and followed rhythms that were different from those of the revolution in Russia. (See the essay by Giorgio Caforno, in *Critica Marxista*, July–August, 1965, pp. 122–3.)

33. Engels, Preface to *The Peasant War in Germany*, FLPH, Moscow, 1956, p. 32.

34. Stalin, op. cit., Vol. 8, pp. 116–17.

35. This tendency arose in parties and groups which, although they had broken with the Second International, were in disagreement with the Third mainly on questions of organization and tactics. The '21 Conditions' greatly contributed to the development of this tendency, driving large groups of the Social Democratic left into it. In February 1921 the representatives of these parties and groups assembled in Vienna – the Austrian Socialist Party was the largest complete party among them, though some of the groups enjoyed extensive influence in their respective parties. Eighty delegates were present, representing thirteen countries. They decided not to form a new International but, instead, a 'Union of Socialist Parties for International Action', with as its chief mission 'working to create an International uniting the revolutionary proletariat of the world' (see Amaro del Rosal, *Los congresos obreros internacionales del siglo XX*, Ed. Grijalbo, Mexico City, 1963, pp. 149–52).

36. Degras, op. cit., I, p. 314.

37. The Second International was represented at the Berlin conference by Vandervelde, MacDonald, Wels and Huysmans, among other frontrank personalities; the Two-and-a-half International by Adler, Otto Bauer, Crispien, Paul Faure, Longuet, etc.; and the Third International by Radek, Bukharin, Klara Zetkin, Frossard, Bordiga, Katayama, Rosmer, Šmeral, Warski and Stojanović. Serrati attended as an observer for the Italian Socialist Party, which did not belong to any of the three Inter-

nationals. The delegations of the Second and the Two-and-a-half Internationals included Russian Menshevik and socialist revolutionary leaders like the Georgian socialist revolutionary Tsereteli and the left-wing Menshevik Martov. The meeting was held in public, with journalists present, representing both the press of the working-class movement and the world's press generally. A verbatim report of the proceedings was published soon afterwards. Working-class militants of all tendencies were thus able to acquaint themselves fully with the discussion. (The quotations given below are taken from *The Second and the Third Internationals and the Vienna Union: Official Report of the Conference between the Executives* ..., Labour Publishing Company, London, 1922. See also J. Braunthal, *History of the International*, Vol. 2, Nelson, London, 1967, p. 246.)

38. Degras, op. cit., I, p. 427.

39. ibid., I, pp. 249–50 (my italics).

40. ibid., I, pp. 309, 310.

41. Paul Faure, speaking for the Two-and-a-half International, said that 'the formation of a really united labour front ... can only succeed if the conflicts between working-class parties are conducted exclusively with intellectual and moral weapons, and are not poisoned by terroristic methods of combat of one workers' party against the other. The Executive of the International Union of Socialist Parties states the facts that in Soviet Russia, under the dictatorship of the Communist Party, the masses of the working people are deprived of all political rights and trade-union freedom; the socialist parties are persecuted with terrorist means and deprived of all possibilities of existence; and that Socialist Georgia has been robbed of her right of self-determination by military occupation. The IUSP Executive considers it a necessary condition of a real united front of the whole proletariat that equality of political rights shall be restored to socialist parties of Russia, the freedom of political and economic activity to the workers and peasants of Russia, and the right to self-determination to the toiling people of Georgia.' He warned that execution of the socialist revolutionaries who had been sentenced to death in Moscow would make the conference impossible.

Otto Bauer, also speaking for the Two-and-a-half International, declared, 'We consider it entirely impossible, incompatible with the idea of the proletarian united front, that full rights of citizenship should not be given to all proletarian and socialist parties in Russia ... One of the most incomprehensible phenomena in the Soviet policy is this, that at the very moment that their party had proclaimed the watchword of the united front they began preparations for criminal trials for acts perpetrated four years ago, under totally different circumstances, in a time of open civil war, although they must have known what difficulties this would raise against the realization of the proletarian united front.'

Bauer expressed his concurrence with the 'moral conditions' put forward by the representatives of the Second International, though not with the method they had chosen, namely, to formulate these conditions and expect the Third International to accept them. 'Let the masses first fight together, whatever their different political convictions may be, then I am convinced that in this *common struggle*, on the common battlefield, the feeling of comradeship and solidarity will develop, until no proletarian party will allow itself to oppose the fulfilment of these moral conditions. (Applause from Vienna and Moscow) . . . Do not ask the Communists what they want. That may soon change. Every day in Moscow they take up a new position. It is no good speculating, however interesting it may be to do so, as to what our comrades want; ask them what they are going to *do*. That is the important thing . . . I am convinced that action will impose its own conditions and necessities. With regard to the Communist International, I am not such a child as to believe that they will heed my appeal, because it comes from me. I am a traitor, so I read today, and have been sent here to represent the interests of the bourgeoisie. That is their way of speaking: we have grown too well accustomed to it to take it amiss. They will not listen to what I say . . . but they know quite well that when I appeal to them to create the necessary conditions *I am only voicing the desires of millions of workers in every country.*'

42. The Soviet government had formally recognized the independence of the Georgian Republic by a treaty of peace signed on 7 February 1920, followed three months later by a pact of reciprocal non-interference. It was a case similar to that of Finland. But Caucasia meant oil. At the end of 1920 the Bolsheviks resolved to settle the problem by the brisk means of armed intervention. This began on 11 February 1921, in combination with an attack by Kemalist Turkey from the south-west, which began on 15 February. The Soviet government justified its invasion of Georgia by referring to a call for help received from the Georgian Bolsheviks. (There was thus a remote historical precedent for the 'call for help' that served as pretext for the invasion of Czechoslovakia in 1968.) However, in the report that Makharadze, leader of the Georgian Bolsheviks, sent to Moscow on 6 December 1921, he said very plainly that the intervention

had not in fact counted on support from the working people of Georgia: 'The arrival of the Red Army and the establishment of Soviet power in Georgia had the outward appearance of a foreign occupation because in the country itself there was nobody who was ready to take part in a rebellion or a revolution. And at the time of the proclamation of the Soviet regime there was, in the whole of Georgia, not even a single member of the party capable of organizing action or providing leadership and this task had been accomplished mainly by doubtful or sometimes even criminal elements ...' (quoted by David Marshall Lang, *A Modern History of Georgia*, Weidenfeld and Nicolson, London, 1962, p. 240). Makharadze and other Georgian Bolshevik leaders were later accused of nationalism by Stalin, and eventually liquidated.

43. Radek sent back the 'Georgian' ball by referring to Ireland, India, etc., and justified the intervention by the Soviet Republic's need for oil. Otto Bauer agreed with Radek as regards the responsibility of the parties of the Second International in a series of violations of the rights of the peoples since 1918, but he also said: 'We admit, however, that the case of Georgia stands apart ... because here there were proletarian and socialist parties on both sides, who were responsible for what happened; because it was an army flying the red flag which in this case supported the military occupation; because whenever the proletariat now raises a protest against the violent deeds of imperialism it is met with a scornful reference to Georgia.' It may well be that the attitude taken by the leaders of Social Democracy, even those most favourable to the Russian revolution, had a certain influence on the corrections made by Lenin to Bolshevik policy in Georgia, which brought him into sharp conflict with Stalin.

44. Lenin, op. cit., Vol. 33, pp. 330–34, and Vol. 36, p. 611.

45. ibid., Vol. 33, pp. 332–3.

46. Degras, op. cit., I, p. 422.

47. ibid., II, p. 139 (my italics).

48. *Fifth Congress of the Communist International, Abridged Report*, CPGB, London, 1924, p. 22.

49. Degras, op. cit., II, p. 139.

50. ibid., II, pp. 151–2.

51. The MacDonald government was formed in January 1924, as the first Labour government in Britain's history. It did not keep its election promises on social questions such as nationalization. In the trade unions a left wing grew strong, giving expression to the radicalization of the masses. Under pressure from the masses, and of a section of the bourgeoisie

interested in exports to the USSR, the MacDonald government partly fulfilled its promise at the election to normalize relations with the Soviet Republic, recognizing the latter *de jure* but without effecting an exchange of ambassadors. At the end of 1924 the Labour Party (and the Liberals to an even greater extent) suffered defeat at a general election. A Conservative government came in, and proceeded to carry out a sharply anti-working-class policy. The radicalization of the masses was intensified. It was under these conditions, with the aim of seeming more 'left' and also of opposing the Conservatives, that some of the principal leaders of the British trade unions decided to enter into negotiations with the Soviet trade-union leaders. The Anglo-Russian Trade-Union Committee was set up at the beginning of 1925.

Behind this opportunist manoeuvre by the ECCI must be seen the interests of Soviet foreign policy, one of the main purposes of which at this time was to counter the anti-Soviet policy of the new British government. When he spoke at the plenum of the Central Committee of the Russian Communist Party in July 1926, Stalin gave this definition of the significance of the Anglo-Russian Trade-Union Committee: its task was 'to organize a broad movement of the working class against new imperialist wars in general, and against intervention in our country by (especially) the most powerful of the European imperialist powers, by Britain in particular' (Stalin, op. cit., Vol. 8, p. 193).

In May 1926 there began the most important working-class struggle in the whole history of Britain. Under mass pressure, and in order to prevent radical *political* demands from being raised, the leaders of the trade unions proclaimed a general strike, which lasted for nine days. All over the country, strike committees, councils of action and similar organs arose spontaneously, sometimes becoming embryonic ruling authorities. Meanwhile the trade-union leaders negotiated with a view to ending the strike. The situation became increasingly tense. The government prepared to use the army, and tanks appeared in the streets of London. On 11 May a Chancery judge declared that the strike was illegal. On 12 May the General Council of the TUC ordered a return to work. The miners, in support of whom the general strike had been called, stayed out on their own until December 1926, being then obliged to accept a reduction in their wages.

The great strike of the British workers evoked a vast international solidarity movement, and the Soviet trade unions sent large sums of money through the channels of the Anglo-Russian Committee. But the British trade-union leaders refused to accept it. Nevertheless, the Soviet leaders decided to keep the Committee in being, though it now served only to screen the policy of surrender being followed by its British members. The Committee eventually came to an end in 1927, on the initiative of the British side, at the time of the breach of diplomatic relations between Britain and the USSR (May 1927). At the Fifteenth Congress of the Russian Communist Party, held at the end of 1927, Kamenev and other opposition spokesmen criticized the policy followed in relation to this Committee, declaring that the break should have been made at the moment when the British trade-union leaders betrayed the General Strike. Bukharin replied that the policy had been correct, because 'disruption came over the most acute question of the international movement, the question of war [i.e., the threat of intervention against the USSR], and because the odium for the disruption happened to rest with the British' (*Report of the 15th Congress of the CPSU, CPGB*, London, 1928, p. 236).

52. Stalin, op. cit., Vol. 6, pp. 295, 295–6, 297 (my italics).

53. Stalin, op. cit., Vol. 6, pp. 401–4. For Lenin's actual position, see op. cit., Vol. 9, p. 100 ('Two Tactics', 1905).

54. See Ruth Fischer, op. cit., pp. 416–26.

55. Stalin, op. cit., Vol. 7, p. 99.

56. ibid., Vol. 10, pp. 292, 293, and Vol. 12, p. 22.

57. Trotsky considered that the turn implied by the idea of the 'third period' was 'directly contrary to the actual turn of the historical road'. The 'abrupt and direct revolutionary rise (the "third period")' was contradicted by 'the objective situation existing after the great defeats in Britain and China, the weakening of the Communist parties throughout the world, and particularly under the conditions of a commercial and industrial boom which embraced a series of the most important capitalist countries.' According to Trotsky, this turn gave rise to adventuristic tendencies and a still greater separation between the Communist parties and the masses ('The Turn in the Communist International and the Situation in Germany' (1930), in *The Struggle Against Fascism in Germany*, Pathfinder, New York, 1971, p. 56).

58. Stalin, op. cit., Vol. 12, pp. 17–18.

59. *Inprecorr*, English edn, Vol. 9, No. 40 (20 August 1929), p. 848.

60. ibid., Vol. 9, No. 51 (17 September 1929), pp. 1104–9. (See also No. 59, pp. 1281 ff.)

61. ibid., Vol. 8, No. 53 (23 August 1928), p. 942. Togliatti succeeded in escaping the fate of the other 'conciliators' by effecting a skilful 'tactical' retreat, which necessitated his making important concessions, such as

accepting the doctrine of 'social Fascism' and purging the Italian party of its 'right-wingers'. Tasca ('Serra', 'Rossi') was the chief victim, but Gramsci himself, who was already in prison, also suffered certain consequences – a matter which has not yet been completely cleared up. (See G. Fiori, *Antonio Gramsci*, NLB, London, 1970, pp. 257–8.)

62. Branko Lazitch, op. cit., pp. 163–4.

63. The facts about the factory committees are given by Trotsky, in 'What Next?' (*The Struggle Against Fascism in Germany*, op. cit., p. 233). Those on the percentage of Communist party members in trade unions come from Dimitrov's report to the Seventh World Congress (Congress report, op. cit., p. 167). Stalin's remarks of December 1928 are in Vol. 11 of his *Works*, pp. 314–15.

Of great interest is the graph on p. 190 of *L'Époque contemporaine*, by Maurice Grouzet (Vol. 7, published 1957, of the *Histoire générale des civilisations*, edited by Grouzet, PUF, Paris). Three curves show the extraordinary parallel between the progress of National Socialism (in terms of party membership and of votes received) and the percentage of unemployed, from 1929 onwards. In accordance with the 'logic' of the capitalist system, the increase in unemployment was paradoxically accompanied by a lengthening of the working day, and this intensified the 'privileged' situation of the workers engaged in production, who formed the main basis of Social Democracy, in contrast to the unemployed.

64. Quoted by Gilbert Badia, *Histoire de l'Allemagne contemporaine*, op. cit., I, p. 277.

65. Trotsky, 'The Turn in the Communist International . . .' and 'What Next?', in *The Struggle Against Fascism in Germany*, op. cit., pp. 70 and 171, and 'Letter to the Barbusse Congress Against War', in *The Militant*, 16 July 1932. For the KPD, Noske, who had been responsible for the repression of the Spartacists in 1919, and Zörgiebel, the Social Democratic police chief of Berlin who directed the bloody suppression of the demonstration of 1 May 1929, organized by the Communists, were typical representatives of 'social Fascism'.

66. Trotsky, 'The Turn in the Communist International . . .', 'The Only Road', and 'Before the Decision', in *The Struggle Against Fascism in Germany*, op. cit., pp. 59, 292, 342.

67. The phrase in quotation-marks is from an article by the French Communist leader George Cogniot, *'Social-démocratisme et léninisme, les deux lignes du mouvement ouvrier an XXe siècle'* (*Cahiers du communisme*, 10, 1968, p. 59). Faithful to the legend forged by Stalinist histori-

ography, Cogniot explains the mistake made by the KPD as due to 'the influence of certain leaders, such as Heinz Neumann, who were opposed to the workers' united front policy defended by Thälmann'. And he adds (in 1968!) that it was 'a bad inspiration of the ECCI'. Something that resulted from a policy carried out for several years becomes a 'bad inspiration'. Neumann, Remmele and the rest of the 'certain leaders' alluded to by Cogniot had neither more nor less responsibility than Thälmann. After the catastrophe of 1933, however, they served as scapegoats for Stalin's policy (just as Thälmann himself would have done, had he not fallen into the hands of the Nazis). Along with other German Communist leaders who had taken refuge in the USSR, like Eberlein, one of the founders of the party, Kiepenberger, who was in charge of the party's military intelligence organization, etc., they were killed during the great purge implemented by Stalin at the end of the 1930s.

68. Trotsky, 'Against National-Communism', in *The Struggle Against Fascism in Germany*, pp. 95, 96, 113.

69. Trotsky, 'Interview with *Montag Morgen*', in *The Struggle Against Fascism in Germany*, op. cit., pp. 263, 264.

70. See B. M. Leibzon and K. K. Shirinya, *Povorot v politike Kominterna* ('The Turn in the Policy of the Comintern'), Mysl, Moscow, 1965. On pp. 42–3 they write: 'For a long time, as Dimitrov was subsequently to point out, the Communists persisted in the mistake of regarding the world economic crisis that opened in 1929 as the final crisis [of capitalism], from which the bourgeoisie could find no way out, and the necessary result of which must be the triumph of the proletarian revolution. This thesis often took the place of a rigorous analysis of the extent to which the revolution had matured, on the basis of the development of class contradictions in each country.' But these writers, whose book is probably the most important of those so far written by Soviet historians about this period of the Comintern, confine themselves to noting the fact. They do not see (or, more probably, it is not permitted to them to see) the organic connection between this mistake and the whole conception of the state of capitalism that prevailed in the Comintern from its very foundation.

71. 'The Labour and Socialist International has always recognized that civil war within the working class was the chief cause of its weakness and was thus the biggest asset of Fascism. The Labour and Socialist International has always been convinced that the power of the workers can only be exercised to the full if the ranks are closed and working-class unity established ... The Labour and Socialist International is striving for

united working-class action on the basis of an open and frank understanding. In view of the tragic dangers with which they are faced, we call upon the German workers, the workers of all countries, to cease their attacks upon each other and join together in the fight against Fascism. The Labour and Socialist International has always been ready to negotiate with the Communist International with a view to common action as soon as this body is also ready' (quoted in Julius Braunthal, *History of the International*, Vol. 2, Nelson, London, 1967, p. 391, and *Report of the 33rd Annual Conference (1933) of the Labour Party*, p. 16).

72. See Annie Kriegel, *Les Internationales ouvrières*, PUF, Paris, 1966, p. 104.

73. The Workers' Alliance was first formed in Catalonia at the end of 1933. The manifesto announcing its formation was signed by the Socialist Party and other Catalan Socialist groups, together with the trade unions which they led, a section of the Anarcho-Syndicalists, the Workers' and Peasants' Bloc (a Marxist organization formed after most of the members of the Communist Party in Catalonia had broken with that organization), and the Communist left (Trotskyists). In February 1934 the Spanish Socialist Party took the initiative in forming Workers' Alliances all over Spain, calling on all workers' organizations to join.

74. See Jacques Fauvet, *Histoire du Parti Communiste français*, Fayard, Paris, 1964–5, I, pp. 121, 134.

75. *Arbeiterzeitung*, Vienna, 28 April 1927.

76. Otto Bauer, *Zwischen Zwei Weltkriegen?*, p. 142, quoted by Paul Sweezy, *The Theory of Capitalist Development*, Dennis Dobson, London, 1946, p. 252.

77. The reference to the group of German 'revolutionary socialists' is taken from the book by Leibzon and Shirinya (see note 70, above), p. 195. The book also mentions Otto Bauer's going to revolutionary positions. Other examples could be cited: e.g., in Poland, the left-wing Socialists proposed a programme of struggle for power, and at the congress of the Polish Bund, in March 1935, three-quarters of the delegates voted to break with the Second International.

78. See Leibzon and Shirinya, op. cit., p. 55. Subsequently the Comintern leadership acknowledged that it had been a mistake not to accept the proposal for conversations made by the LSI in February 1933 (ibid., p. 50).

79. Fauvet, op. cit., I, p. 135.

80. ibid., p. 137. Some days after the demonstrations there took place

the funeral of the Communists killed in the fighting with the police on 9 and 12 February. The Socialists were officially represented at the funeral. The editor-in-chief of *L'Humanité* wrote next day that this must not be seen as a 'realization of the united front', and warned: 'We do not forget that our comrades were killed by bullets paid for out of the credits voted by the Socialist deputies' (ibid., p. 138). The same journalist wrote in *L'Humanité* of 19 February: ' "Defend the Republic", as Blum puts it? As though Fascism were not also the Republic, as though the Republic were not already Fascism.'

Another example, from among thousands, of how little the German experience had taught the Comintern and its national sections is provided by the commentary in *Inprecorr* (Spanish-language edition) of 23 March 1934, on the Madrid printers' strike which paralysed the press of Spain's capital for several days. The strike was organized and led by Socialists, and the trade union had responded vigorously to provocative action by the employers, who were mostly reactionary. *Inprecorr* wrote: 'The social-Fascist leaders cannot let themselves appear completely indifferent in face of a Fascist provocation. They have to try to keep up among the masses the illusion that they are "enemies" of Fascism, that "there is a real conflict between the Socialist Party and Fascism", as some petty-bourgeois counter-revolutionaries seek to make the workers believe.'

81. Fauvet, op. cit., I, p. 143. A few weeks before this, Thorez had been summoned to Moscow by the ECCI to settle the Doriot affair. Jacques Doriot had been maintaining for months that it was necessary to come to an agreement with the Socialist Party, and he had begun to put this policy of alliance into practice in his stronghold at Saint-Denis, despite directives to the contrary from the leadership of the Communist Party (one of whose most influential members he was) and from the Comintern. In Moscow the ECCI denounced Doriot's attitude and authorized the leaders of the French Communist Party to expel him if he did not submit; but, at the same time, it began to make the turn, doubtless in obedience to orders from the Kremlin. A few days after Doriot's expulsion, the Comintern and the French Communist Party started to apply the policy he had advocated.

82. Leibzon and Shirinya, op. cit., pp. 307–9. The spirit animating the authors of this work can be regarded as 'anti-Stalinist' to the extent that this is possible in legal publications in the USSR.

83. Fontaine, op. cit., pp. 79–80.

84. Stalin, *Works,* Vol. 13, English edn, pp. 298, 303, 304, 308, 309, 310, 312.

85. *Vsemirnaya Istoriya* ('World History'), Akademiya Nauk SSSR, Moscow, Vol. 9, 1962, pp. 301–2. Barthou's statement in the Chamber of Deputies is quoted by Fauvet, op. cit., I, p. 144.

86. Trotsky, *Whither France?,* Pioneer, New York, 1936, p. 12. Down to the end of May 1934 the French Communist Party had opposed any idea of an agreement with the Radical Party or with similar political groupings. The *Cahiers du bolchevisme* of 15 May had violently attacked Marceau Pivert, leader of the Socialist left, with the charge that he wished to draw the anti-Fascist movement into a bloc with the 'left' bourgeoisie (quoted by Daniel Guérin, *Front populaire, révolution manquée,* Julliard, Paris, 1963, p. 75).

87. Thorez, *Fils du peuple,* Éditions Sociales, Paris, 1960, p. 102. Thorez writes: 'On the very morning of the meeting at Nantes I received, transmitted by the leader of a brother-party, advice to abandon the formula and the idea of a People's Front. I replied that in a few minutes' time I was going to board the train for Nantes, and that I would there deliver a speech calling on the Radicals to join in forming a People's Front, as the Political Bureau had mandated me to do' (Jacques Duclos, in his *Mémoires,* names Togliatti as the 'leader of a brother-party' in question). 'Some time after this,' Thorez continues, 'I saw Stalin. He congratulated our party on its bold policy in pursuit of unity, which was in conformity, he stressed, with the spirit of Leninism. He said to me: "You have found a new key with which to open the gates of the future." ' If Stalin was thinking of the 'gates' of the socialist revolution, it would seem that this 'key' has not produced many results so far, some thirty-odd years since it was discovered. On the other hand, it did aid considerably in opening the 'gates' of the Franco-Soviet pact of mutual assistance, which was signed a few months later. And after all, it was perhaps at this that Stalin was ironically hinting.

88. *Débats parlementaires,* Paris, 1935, p. 1038.

89. Thorez, *Œuvres,* Vol. 9, p. 17. Thorez himself emphasized 'objectively': the emphasizing of 'is identical with' is mine.

90. ibid., p. 26.

91. *L'Œuvre,* 2 July 1935.

92. Fauvet, op. cit., I, pp. 165–6.

93. *Seventh Congress . . .,* pp. 591, 589–90; also in Degras, op. cit., III, pp. 375, 374 (my italics).

94. *Seventh Congress . . .*, p. 555. Togliatti ('Ercoli'), who presented the report on problems of peace and war, mentioned that this was the position of France and the USA. Great Britain, despite her colonial empire, was not for the moment following 'a policy of peace', for she was trying to urge German imperialism against the USSR. However, 'If we bear in mind that the war of 1914–18 was due largely to the conflict between British imperialism and German imperialism . . . it is clear that the problem will crop up again just as in 1914–18, but this time in a much sharper fashion' (*Seventh Congress . . .*, pp. 407–8).

95. ibid., p. 410.

96. ibid., pp. 426–7 (my italics). The 'examples' are given on pp. 428–30.

97. ibid., pp. 430–31.

98. ibid., pp. 492–4 and 603.

99. Quoted in Leibzon and Shirinya, op. cit., p. 144 (my italics).

1. *Seventh Congress . . .*, p. 559.

2. ibid., pp. 125–6. Cf. Stalin, op. cit., Vol. 13, p. 299.

3. Leibzon and Shirinya, op. cit., p. 119; *Seventh Congress . . .*, p. 151.

4. *Seventh Congress . . .*, pp. 125–6, 138–42. The analysis of Fascism made at the Congress was not based on a serious investigation of its historical development and its social, economic and political foundations, and this enabled the German and Italian cases to be wrongly transposed so as to apply to world capitalism as a whole. The definition quoted also helped to obscure the internal contradictions of Fascism, for it made no reference to the specific role played by the petty-bourgeoisie of town and country, which did not content itself with being a tool of finance-capital but also strove to acquire power for itself at various levels of the Fascist state. For Italy, see the excellent books by Robert Paris, *Histoire du fascisme en Italie* (Maspero, Paris, 1962), and Angelo Tasca, *Naissance du fascisme* (Gallimard, Paris, 1967). An earlier edition of Tasca's book was translated into English as *The Rise of Italian Fascism, 1918–1922*, by A. Rossi, Methuen, London, 1938. For Germany, see the full bibliography in Gilbert Badia, *Histoire de l'Allemagne contemporaine*, quoted earlier. Since the Spanish edition of my book came out there has appeared the important work by Nicos Poulantzas, *Fascisme et dictature* (Maspero, Paris, 1970).

5. *Seventh Congress . . .*, p. 193.

6. ibid., p. 223; Thorez, op. cit., Vol. 9, pp. 133, 143.

7. *Seventh Congress . . .*, pp. 144, 147. Dimitrov mentioned in the

context of the offensive phase the possibility of governments of the workers' united front, in which the Communist Party would participate alongside other parties and organizations of the working class and peasantry. But he pointed out that such governments could not be regarded as forms of the dictatorship of the proletariat. The latter could exist only under a one-party system, in accordance with the Soviet model. Governments of the workers' united front must serve to create the conditions making it possible to go over to the dictatorship of the proletariat – which implied, therefore, that the other parties and groups in it were helping to prepare for their own elimination.

This was one of the tactical and strategic dogmas of the Comintern that was to do most to hold back the unification of the different revolutionary tendencies in the working-class movement in the period of the People's Front. Its effect was especially harmful in Spain and France.

The distinction made at the Seventh Congress between workers' united front governments and People's Front governments was rather vague. In general, the latter were seen as having a broader composition, with a substantial participation by petty-bourgeois political forces, and as being capable of coming into existence even in the defensive phase of the anti-Fascist struggle. It is important to stress that the Congress did not study the possibility of People's Front governments in which parties or groups of the bourgeoisie would take part. But it did take as an example of the People's Front policy that of the French Communist Party, which had already offered its support to a Radical government.

8. Among the works devoted entirely to this period the ones by Georges Lefranc seem to me particularly useful: *Histoire du front populaire*, Payot, Paris, 1965; *Le Front populaire, 1934–1938*, PUF, Paris, 1965; and, especially, *Juin 1936*, Julliard, Paris, 1966, which brings together an excellent mass of material. The standpoint of the left-wing tendency in the French Socialist movement is represented by Daniel Guérin's book *Front populaire, révolution manquée*, and that of the French Communist Party in No. 3/4 of the *Cahiers de l'Institute Maurice-Thorez*, on 'Le Front populaire et l'action de Maurice Thorez', and *Le Front populaire*, by Jacques Chambaz (Éditions Sociales, Paris), among other writings.

9. *Seventh Congress* ..., p. 227. On discontent in the countryside see Lefranc, *Juin 1936*, pp. 37–41. To the factors mentioned must be added the reflex of national defence against the resurgent danger from Germany, a reflex which at that moment told in favour of anti-Fascism.

10. Lefranc, *Juin 1936*, p. 22.

11. *Seventh Congress* . . ., p. 218.

12. Lefranc, op. cit., p. 25.

13. Quoted, respectively, by Daniel Guérin on p. 104 of his book mentioned in note 8 and by G. Lefranc in *Le Front populaire*, p. 59.

14. Fauvet, op. cit., p. 197; A. Kriegel, *Le Socialisme français et le pouvoir*, EDI, Paris, 1966, p. 117; G. Lefranc, *Juin 1936*, p. 130. Trotsky wrote on 9 June an article entitled: 'The French Revolution Has Begun' (in *Whither France?*, Pioneer, New York, 1936, pp. 149–55). In this article and others written in this period Trotsky exaggerates, it seems to me, the revolutionary character of the situation that had been created. Thus, in the article mentioned, he writes: 'To be sure, Léon Jouhaux, trailing behind Léon Blum, keeps assuring the bourgeoisie that this is a purely economic movement within the rigid framework of the law. The strikers, indeed, are seizing factories for the duration of the strike, establishing control over the bosses and their staffs. But one may shut one's eyes to this deplorable "detail".' That the occupation of the factories went beyond 'the rigid framework of the law' is indisputable; but that this meant workers' control over their ownership and administration is extremely disputable. The weakness of the movement lay precisely in the circumstance that the occupation of the factories remained passive in character, and was not transformed into real control over production and management, that is, into the organizing of the foundations of a new ruling authority.

For a well-documented study of the actual development of the movement, the workers' demands, the attitudes of the trade unions, parties, employers, the government, etc., see, especially, Lefranc's book *Juin 1936*.

15. Lefranc, *Juin 1936*, p. 228.

16. ibid., pp. 125, 128.

17. Fauvet, op. cit., 1, p. 198.

18. Thorez's speech was published in *L'Humanité* of 13 June 1936. The reference to the slogan: 'The People's Front is not the revolution' comes from the *Histoire du Parti Communiste Français* in three volumes written by a group of well-known party members, some of whom were expelled in the 1950s for their anti-Stalinist line, while others managed to stay in the party to carry on oppositional activity (op. cit., Vol. 1, Édition Veridad, Paris, 1960, p. 191). The group published a bulletin entitled *Unir* (now renamed *Unir-Débat communiste*), and subsequently I shall refer to this work as *Histoire du PCF (Unir)*. Another watchword of the period, quoted in this work, was: 'We do not intend to attack private property.'

19. See the discussion of the People's Front in *Démocratie Nouvelle*, 5, 1966. The phrase quoted from André Baumel appears on p. 42.

20. Here are some figures showing the trend. At the elections of 1932 the party received 794,883 votes, and at the elections of 1936 it received 1,487,336. Its membership figures in the 1930s were as follows: 1933, 28,000; 1934, 40,000; 1935, 86,000; 1936, 280,000; 1937, 328,647; 1938, 320,000; 1939, 300,000. These figures are taken from Annie Kriegel's book *Les Communistes français*, Éditions du Seuil, Paris, 1968 – a substantial contribution to the study of the French Communist Party (pp. 31 and 294).

21. Trotsky made the (already classical) mistake of interpreting and forecasting the development of the French situation in accordance with the schemas of the Russian revolution of 1917. After the first wave of the revolutionary movement this would come to a halt and a reactionary counter-blow would be struck (as in July–August 1917), which would be followed by the decisive offensive of the revolutionary forces. As regards the new mass organization that needed to be formed, he wrote: 'The combat organization would not be identical with the party even if there were a mass revolutionary party in France, for the movement is incomparably broader than the party. The organization also cannot coincide with the trade unions, for the unions embrace only an insignificant section of the class and are headed by an arch-reactionary bureaucracy. The new organization must correspond to the nature of the movement itself. It must reflect the struggling masses. It must express their growing will. This is a question of the direct representation of the revolutionary class. Here it is not necessary to invent new forms. Historical precedents exist. The workshops and factories will elect their deputies who will meet to elaborate jointly plans of struggle and to provide the leadership. Nor is it necessary to invent the name for such an organization; it is the *Soviets of Workers' Deputies*.' Trotsky was optimistic, thinking that events would take this course because, during the first wave, new 'leaders have come forward in the industries and in the factories' and 'in the atmosphere of revolution the masses are swiftly re-educated, the cadres swiftly selected and tempered' ('The French Revolution Has Begun', in *Whither France?*, op. cit., pp. 154, 155). Trotsky considered the French situation to be as revolutionary as that in Russia in 1917, which was far from the truth. He further underestimated the degree to which the French working class was structured in trade unions and political parties – a degree incomparably greater than that of the Russian working class of 1917. He did not allow

for the fact that, though the policy of the French Communist Party and of the trade unions was not revolutionary, the main nucleus of revolutionary workers was in these organizations and had confidence in their leaders. Finally, contrary to his assertion, there was a great deal needing to be *invented* in the France of 1936, as regards tactics and the forms of revolutionary struggle.

22. *L'Humanité*, 13 June 1936.

23. I have already mentioned the Communist Party's opposition to including 'structural reforms' in the People's Front programme (see note 6, p. 45 above). However, as a concession to the Socialists, a passage was inserted in the preamble to the programme in which it was stated, in very vague terms, that the demands contained in the programme would be supplemented by more far-reaching measures in order finally to tear the state from the grip of 'industrial and financial feudalism'. The powerful workers' movement of May–June furnished an exceptionally favourable opportunity to the party to give concrete content to these abstract formulas. But the Communist Party leadership was determined to do nothing that might spoil their understanding with the Radicals and thereby endanger the Franco–Soviet pact.

24. Lefranc, *Juin 1936*, p. 140; Fauvet, op. cit., p. 198.

25. *Guerra y revolución en España*, Ed. Progreso, Moscow, 1966, Vol. I, p. 241. (Quotations from Colette Audry, *Léon Blum, ou la politique du juste*, Julliard, Paris, 1955, pp. 122, 126–7.)

26. Quoted in Fauvet, op. cit., I, p. 203.

27. From Thorez's speech at the Parc des Princes, 4 October 1936, in op. cit., Vol. 12, p. 233.

28. See Fauvet, op. cit., I, p. 221. The *Bol'shaya Sovyetskaya Entsiklopediya*, 2nd edn, later described Paul Reynaud thus: Bourgeois politician, Minister of Finance, then of the Colonies and of Justice, in the Tardieu and Laval governments (1930–32), opponent of the People's Front, Minister of Justice between April and November 1938, and between November 1938 and March 1940 Minister of Finance in the governments headed by Daladier. He supported the Munich agreement and was one of the authors of the special decrees directed against the social achievements of the workers, preparing the way for the suppression of the Communist Party in September 1939; in the post-war period connected with United States industrial and financial circles; etc. (Vol. 36, 1955, p. 302).

29. *Inprecorr* (English edn), Vol. 10, No. 21 (30 April 1930), p. 393, and

No. 23 (15 May 1930), p. 423. The development of the situation during 1930, and especially the fall of the monarchy in April 1931, caused the leaders of the Comintern to alter their opinion.

30. The history of the Spanish Communist Party constitutes one of the most telling examples of the harm done by the methods that were used in order to build, outside Russia, a revolutionary party 'of the Bolshevik type' (see Chapter 3).

When the Comintern was founded, the Spanish working class was organized in two main ideological camps: Marxist–Socialist and Anarcho-Syndicalist. In the Socialist Workers' Party of Spain (PSOE) and the unions it led, which were grouped in the General Workers' Union (UGT), as well as in the unions of Anarcho-Syndicalist orientation which were grouped in the National Confederation of Labour (CNT), the revolutionary wing was in the majority. The October revolution had a profound impact on both camps. The majority of the CNT and the majority of the PSOE–UGT alike declared for joining the new International. Clearly, adhesion by the CNT to the Comintern (which took place, but was soon rescinded) was lacking in basis, given the big divergences of principle between Marxism and Anarcho-Syndicalism; but it did show the possibilities that existed for collaboration and discussion. As regards the PSOE, it might have joined the Comintern but for the '21 Conditions'. In any case, very favourable conditions were present for creating a strong revolutionary-Marxist tendency within the party.

Instead of striving to foster a process of this kind (akin to that which had made possible the creation of the Bolshevik party), it was decided to set up forthwith the Communist Party of Spain (PCE), on the basis of splits in the PSOE and the CNT. The great majority of the revolutionary masses remained in their traditional organizations, and the new party was looked upon from the start as being responsible for a further division in the Spanish working-class movement, already so seriously divided. And this was a division that was no organic result of the movement itself, of a theoretical development and political struggle rooted in the distinctive conditions of the Spanish revolutionary process, but one imposed by the importation of doctrines and methods that had been employed in other latitudes. The PCE remained isolated, with this aggravating circumstance that it thought itself possessed of all the keys to the Spanish revolution. These did not have to be sought in the realities of Spain, they had been supplied ready-made from Moscow. The party was thus deprived of the stimulant that would have been given by an ideological and political struggle *within* the Spanish labour movement. It became a mere repeater of ready-made formulas.

The sectarian phase of the Comintern begun in 1924 (which coincided with the going underground of the PCE at the time of the dictatorship of Primo de Rivera), worsened still further the faults of the artificially created Spanish section. The internal struggle in the Soviet party also had serious repercussions in the PCE, some of whose best cadres supported Trotsky's line. By 1930 the party had lost more than nine-tenths of its original membership (about 10,000 in 1922).

In 1930 one of the principal organizations of the PCE, the regional federation covering Catalonia and the Balearic Islands, broke away, and soon afterward merged with the (independent) 'Catalan Communist Party' to form the Workers' and Peasants' Bloc. Later, in 1935, this united with the Communist left (Trotskyists), led by Andres Nin, giving rise to the POUM (Workers' Party of Marxist Unity). (The details of the process that led to the creation of the POUM will be found in the article by Pedro Bonet published in *La Batalla* in December 1965.) Before the civil war, the PCE was unable to set up an organization of its own of any importance in the principal industrial area of Spain, Catalonia.

31. The PCE leadership had adopted this line in agreement with the representatives of the Comintern (Humbert-Droz and Rabaté, as revealed by José Bullejos, the then General Secretary of the party, in his book *Europa entre dos guerras*, Ediciones Castilla, Mexico City, 1945, p. 135), but the Moscow centre laid the entire responsibility for it on the shoulders of the Spanish leaders. On 21 May 1931 the ECCI sent an open letter to the Central Committee of the PCE criticizing the party's mistakes. The chief of these was that it had not grasped the 'bourgeois-democratic' character of the revolution and the 'leading role' that the PCE ought to play in this revolution. The letter directed, among other things, that 'soviets of workers, peasants and soldiers' be formed; these soviets were to act as 'the driving force that will lead the democratic revolution to the end and ensure its development into a socialist revolution'. The PCE, said the letter, must utilize 'the furious resistance of the Anarcho-Syndicalist and reformist leaders to the forming of soviets in order to show the counter-revolutionary nature of Spanish Anarcho-Syndicalism and reformism'. One of the most clear-cut instructions in this document (which served as the PCE's guide through 1931–2) was that 'the Communist Party must in no circumstances conclude pacts or alliances, even temporary ones, with any other political force'.

As we see, the way in which the Comintern set about correcting the sectarian mistakes of the PCE was somewhat peculiar. After April 1931 a conflict broke out, which became more acute as the months went by, between the PCE leadership and the Comintern. Once the Spanish leaders had realized the absurdity of their original position, they took a line which in some ways came close to the first analysis of the Spanish revolution made by Trotsky, and which also showed an independent attitude in relation to the Comintern representatives in Spain. The most important of these, Codovilla, acted as though he were General Secretary of the party – which, *de facto*, he was, and continued to be down to the civil war, when Comintern functionaries from a higher level took charge. The conflict became a crisis at the time of the attempted *coup d'état* of General Sanjurjo (10 August 1932). The leaders of the PCE issued a call to 'defend the Republic', and the Comintern leaders described this as 'opportunist'. Soon afterwards Bullejos (the General Secretary), Adame, Vega and Trilla (the latter being the PCE's representative at the Comintern) were expelled from the leadership, and subsequently from the party, being accused of forming a 'sectarian-opportunist group'.

The essence of Trotsky's line was that, between the stage that the Spanish revolution was passing through, under the hegemony of the bourgeoisie and the petty-bourgeoisie, and the proletarian stage, under the hegemony of the working class (the dictatorship of the proletariat), there could be no 'bourgeois-democratic' stage under proletarian hegemony that confined itself to abolishing 'feudal survivals'. The history of the Spanish revolution down to 1939 showed that he was right. See on this, 'The Revolution in Spain' (January 1931) and 'The Spanish Revolution and the Dangers Threatening It' (May 1931). These and other essays are collected in *The Spanish Revolution (1931–1939)*, Pathfinder, New York, 1973. In the second of the articles mentioned Trotsky wrote: 'The immediate task of the Spanish Communists is not the struggle for power, but the struggle for the masses, and furthermore this struggle will develop in the next period on the basis of the bourgeois republic and to a great degree under the slogans of democracy' (op. cit., p. 128).

32. In the elections the PCE obtained, in the whole of Spain, 400,000 votes, as against 60,000 in the elections to the Constituent Assembly of July 1931. At the elections of November 1933 there were 8,711,136 votes cast altogether, and of these the Socialists received about 1,800,000.

33. From October 1934 the government was in the hands of a coalition formed by the Radical Republicans led by Lerroux (a right-wing bourgeois

party) and the CEDA (Spanish Confederation of Independent Right Groups, a bloc of parties and groups of the big bourgeoisie and large-scale landowners), led by Gil Robles. The workers' and republicans' protest movement against the repression carried out after the October rising (30,000 political prisoners, several of whom were shot), and the corruption of Lerroux's party, gave rise to a crisis in the CEDA–Radical coalition. The President of the Republic, Alcala Zamora, who entertained hopes of forming a big centre party, thought the situation was now ripe for this, and called on Portela Valladares, a politician in his confidence, to form the new government. As the latter could not find a majority in parliament, the Assembly was dissolved and new elections were held. Like Alcala Zamora and his circle, Gil Robles and his followers were by no means displeased to have these new elections, which they hoped to win (even though they would have preferred to organize them themselves). However, it was the union of the left, under the name of People's Front, that emerged victorious from the elections, reducing these plans to nullity and creating a new situation.

The People's Front was made up of the Republican parties of Azaña and Martinez Barrio, the Socialist Party, the Socialist Youth, the UGT, the Communist Party, the Syndicalist party and the POUM. Its programme was in reality that of Azaña's Republicans. Under the pressure of Caballero's followers, the PSOE had proposed nationalization of the land and of the banks, and workers' control in industry, but the Republicans were against this. They even refused to agree to another point proposed by the Socialists – unemployment insurance. All the basic problems were avoided, and the timid reforms that did get into the programme were formulated in an ambiguous way. As the Socialist historian Antonio Ramos-Oliveira observes: 'Everything here was equivocal, each section had a vague and evasive air about it' (*Historia de España*, Mexico City, Vol. 3, p. 240). The People's Front pact provided, moreover, that the Republican parties were to rule alone. This was all that was needed to open the way to civil war, which had already in fact partially begun.

34. Togliatti (Ercoli), 'Specific Features of the Spanish Revolution', in *Inprecorr* (English edn), Vol. 16, No. 48 (24 October 1936), p. 1294. Togliatti wrote this essay when the civil war had already begun, but the 'stage' to which he refers also includes the previous period. Togliatti played a role of prime importance in the political guidance and even the practical leadership of the PCE during the civil war. Along with him were the Bulgarian Stepanov, the Hungarian Gerő, the Argentinian

Codovilla and, of course, the eminent Soviet 'advisers', both military and political.

35. Both in its election propaganda and in its statements of policy the PCE differentiated clearly, in the February–July period, between these two 'sub-stages'. In his speech of 9 February 1936 José Diaz said: 'Let it be clearly understood that there is a minimum programme which must be carried out by the government the realization of which will create the conditions for the subsequent development of the democratic revolution in Spain' (José Diaz, *Tres años de lucha,* Ed. Nuestro Pueblo, Toulouse, 1947, p. 70). After the election victory the party kept strictly to the line of support for the government and respect for the compromises effected, while bringing pressure to bear on the Republican leaders for them to carry out rapidly the 'minimum programme'. This line left, in practice, the political initiative in the hands of the government, which could and did resist this pressure. In that respect the Azaña government gave proof of great 'firmness', such as it lacked when putting down the counter-revolutionary plot. Referring to this crucial problem, José Diaz said in his speech of 1 June: 'I must emphasize, comrades, that the government cannot do this on its own. Mass struggle provides the only effective guarantee that everything will implacably be done to sweep away reaction and Fascism. I hope that if the government sees that we have a resolute will to do this and insist upon it, then it will bring to their senses all these enemies of the Republic and of the workers' (ibid., p. 161). This was one way of sowing illusions among the masses, for there was no sign that the government had any intention of bringing the army plotters 'to their senses'.

The basic weakness of this policy was that it did not meet the peremptory demands of the situation. Even if the government had put the 'minimum programme' into practice, no essential problem would have been solved, and the decisive question of the *power* that could nip the counter-revolutionary plan in the bud remained unsettled. Only a new ruling authority headed by the revolutionary working class could fulfil that task. The party called on the masses to mobilize, but at the same time it held them back, so as to ensure that the 'mass struggle' remained compatible with total support for the government. In this same speech of 1 June, for example, José Diaz declares that it is right for the workers to use the strike weapon to defend their interests, but adds: 'Nevertheless, it is not to the advantage of the proletariat and the revolution that strikes be called for any reason at all, without careful consideration of the possibilities of solving disputes without having recourse to this method' (ibid., p. 165).

36. K. L. Maidanik, *Ispansky proletariat v natsionalnoye-revolyyt-sionni voiny, 1936–1937gg.* ('The Spanish Proletariat in the National-Revolutionary War, 1936–1937'), Izd. Akad, Nauk SSSR, Moscow, 1960, pp. 64–5.

Referring to this same period, the American historian Gabriel Jackson writes: 'All over central and southern Spain the atmosphere of class hatred was almost palpable' (*The Spanish Republic and the Civil War, 1931–1939*, Princeton, 1935, p. 218). It is hard to find a historian who does not concur in this view. The only exception, perhaps, is the *Histoire du Parti Communiste d'Espagne*, written by a commission presided over by Dolores Ibarruri, in which it is said: 'The main significance of 16 February [1936] from the political and historical standpoint is that it opened a possibility of peaceful, constitutional and parliamentary development of the democratic revolution in Spain' (Éditions Sociales, Paris, 1960, p. 113). In the book *Guerra y revolución en España*, brought out later by the same commission (Ed. Progreso, Moscow, 1966), this view is no longer to be found, but it is said that the civil war could have been avoided if the path advocated by the PCE had been followed: 'Effective and rapid implementation of the programme of the People's Front and the taking of vigorous measures to deprive reaction of its power to do harm, and cause miscarriage of the plot that it had already prepared for a military revolt' (p. 86). 'Unfortunately' neither the Republicans nor the reformist Socialists nor the Caballerist Socialists listened to the PCE. But was anything different to be expected of the first two groupings? And, as for the Caballerists, why did the PCE never propose to them a line of independent action? The authors of *Guerra y revolución en España* avoid the fundamental problem: owing to its inherent characteristics, the coalition that had won the election *could not* accomplish the eminently revolutionary task of crushing the armed counter-revolution. For that, a different type of coalition, a different strategy would have been needed – a coalition of the revolutionary organizations of the proletariat (PCE, left-wing Socialists, Anarcho-Syndicalists) and a strategy of taking power by taking advantage of the weakness of the Republican government. If the PCE had followed that road, and the plan had still failed owing to refusal on the part of the left-wing Socialists, and Anarcho-Syndicalists, it would at least have saved the party from historical responsibility for the defeat. Since, however, its policy was what it was, a far from negligible share of responsibility for the course taken by events must lie with the PCE.

37. The reformists had managed to get hold of the leadership of the PSOE at the end of 1935 by taking advantage of a clumsy move by Largo Caballero, who resigned from the party chairmanship over a matter of secondary importance. But the influence of the left kept on increasing in the months that followed. The congress of the PSOE should have been held during the summer of 1936. Election of delegates by the local organizations showed a majority for the left. The party leadership, headed by Prieto, resorted to shameless manipulations in order to put off the meeting of the congress.

38. Since April 1936 the Caballerists had their own daily paper, *Claridad*. In April the Socialist organization in Madrid adopted a resolution which expressed the basic position of the left wing: 'The proletariat must not confine itself to defending bourgeois democracy, but must ensure by every means the conquest of political power, so as thereby to realize its own social revolution. In the period of transition between capitalist and socialist society, the form of government will be the dictatorship of the proletariat.' On 1 May 1936 the Young Socialists paraded in uniform, with the slogans: 'A workers' government' and: 'A Red army'. The Caballerists were firmly in control of the UGT, membership of which reached a million and a half between February and July 1936. Within the UGT the powerful Landworkers' Federation included several hundred thousand agricultural labourers.

39. See José Peirats, *La CNT en la revolución española*, CNT, Toulouse, 1951, p. 116. Pages 111–36 of this book are devoted to the Saragossa Congress of May 1936, and give the text of the programme on the 'confederal conception of libertarian Communism', in which the organization of society to follow the 'libertarian revolution' was set out in detail. But no resolution of this Congress indicated what the working class ought to do to prevent the imminent and obvious danger of a counter-revolutionary rising.

40. José Diaz said in his speech of 11 April 1936: 'This single party must be formed on the basis of the points that were analysed at the Seventh Congress of the Comintern, and as these points have been accepted by the left-wing Socialist comrades, we shall soon be able to reach agreement.' Then, however, he added that the new party must join the Comintern, and mentioned that 'some comrades' among the left-wing Socialists had shown a certain mistrust towards that body. 'The mistrust that some comrades feel in relation to the Comintern must be liquidated, for it is obvious that

the single party of the proletariat can only be in the Third International, the International of Marx, Engels, Lenin and Stalin' (*Tres años de lucha,* p. 143). What was really obvious was that this condition constituted an insurmountable obstacle for men like Largo Caballero and other leaders of the Socialist left. If success was achieved in uniting the Communist and Socialist youth leagues, this was because most of the leaders of both of those organizations tacitly accepted this condition. Another important obstacle to the creation of the single party arose from differences regarding the character of the revolution, for, on the problem of collaboration with the bourgeois Republican parties, the PCE's line was closer to that of the reformist wing of the PSOE than to that of its left wing. The attitude of the PCE towards Trotskyism constituted a further obstacle, for the Caballerist leaders were closer to the ideas of Trotsky than to those of the Comintern where the character of the Spanish revolution was concerned. According to the PCE, however, 'in order to hasten and facilitate political unity of the working class, a merciless struggle must be waged against the degenerate sect of Trotskyism, whose basic mission is to disorganize the working-class movement, working systematically to hinder and sabotage unity of the working class, disarm the proletariat before the onslaught of Fascism, and drag it into the camp of the crusaders against the USSR, against victorious socialism, against the fortress of the world revolution' (speech by José Diaz, 1 June 1936, op. cit., p. 176). And at that time the POUM was the PCE's ally in the People's Front!

41. The PCE acknowledges, in the work already mentioned (*Guerra y revolución en España*), that at the decisive moment the bourgeois Republican government not only failed to do anything useful in face of the Fascist rising but also that, wherever the military registered a success, this was largely due to the Republican authorities. 'The working class were the sinews and soul of the people's struggle, which they filled with their fighting spirit and determination. The principal methods of action were: the political general strike, arming of the people through revolutionary initiatives that were subsequently legitimized by the Republican authorities, attacks on the barracks, and armed street fighting against the Fascist rebellion. These methods of struggle were of decisive importance, and it was thanks to them that the Republic was able to withstand the Fascist military insurrection. Wherever the masses were unable, or did not know how, to substitute themselves for the passivity, hidden behind legalistic pretexts, of the ruling authorities, they were beaten. Wherever this "legalism" was overcome in good time, wherever the masses secured arms by

one means or another and went over to the attack against the rebels, they were victorious' (pp. 175–6).

What would have happened if this 'legalism' had been 'overcome' already in the preceding months? If, instead of attacking the barracks *after* the military had taken the initiative, the working class had begun by seizing the state power that was practically in its grasp on 16 February, and using this power to organize an attack on the barracks?

42. *Seventh Congress* ..., p. 385. Gabriel Jackson, in the book from which I have already quoted (see note 36), analyses the Soviet point of view with great clarity, and what he says coincides more or less with what has been written by almost all the historians who have dealt with the question: 'If the Western nations, seeing themselves threatened by the spread of Fascist power, could be brought to cooperate with the Soviets in defence of a legitimately elected democratic government, such collective action might halt the uninterrupted series of Fascist triumphs since the rise of Hitler. With this in mind, all Soviet and World Communist litera‑ ture emphasized the entirely bourgeois composition of the Republican cabinet and the very small total representation of the Communists in the Cortes ... The Soviets also ostentatiously refrained from sending arms during the months of August and September, when it seemed even faintly possible that the Non-Intervention scheme would curb the aid of the Fascist powers to the Insurgents' (Jackson, op. cit., p. 258).

43. Maidanik, op. cit., p. 103.

44. This passage from *Guerra y revolución en España* (Vol. I, p. 256), written thirty years later, summarizes very well the analyses made and the propaganda line used by the PCE from July 1936 onwards. The Comintern directly inspired this line, which, in the hope of seeing the Spanish revolution 'accepted' by the Western democracies, went so far as to idealize the role of the bourgeois and petty-bourgeois political groups. Togliatti, for example, quotes these words of Azaña's: ' "What was left for us to do when the greater part of the army had broken its oath of loyalty to the Republic? Should we have abandoned defence of the Republic and submitted to a new tyranny? No! We had to *give the people the possibility of defending themselves.*" ' And Togliatti goes on: 'The Republican petty-bourgeoisie agreed to use plebeian methods in the struggle against Fascism, *consented* to give arms to the workers and peasants, *supported* the organization of people's tribunals, which are acting no less energetically than the Committee of Public Safety at the time of Robespierre and St Just' (Togliatti, op. cit., note 133, p. 1293. My italics).

45. 'The peculiarity of the Spanish People's Front,' wrote Togliatti, 'consists in the fact that the split in the ranks of the proletariat, the relatively slow pace at which the masses of the peasantry are being drawn into the armed struggle, the influence of petty-bourgeois anarchism and of social-democratic illusions which have not been outlived, and *expressed in the striving to leap over the stage of the bourgeois-democratic revolution,* are creating a series of additional difficulties in the struggle of the Spanish people for a democratic republic' (Togliatti, op. cit., note 133, p. 1295. My italics).

46. In the first weeks of the war, the Caballerists, the Anarcho-Syndicalists and the POUM were for the formation of a revolutionary workers' government. According to H. Rabasseire (*Espagne, creuset politique,* Paris, 1939, p. 98) and Clara Campoamor (*La Révolution espagnole vue par une républicaine,* Paris, 1937, pp. 143–5), this plan assumed concrete form at the end of August at a meeting between leaders of the CNT and the UGT. The idea was to set up a Junta presided over by Largo Caballero, with representatives of the Communist and Socialist Parties and the FAI (the Anarchist political organization), as well as of the CNT and UGT. The bourgeois Republicans would be excluded. When he heard of this plan, Azaña threatened to resign. But the decisive intervention was made by the Soviet ambassador, Rosenberg, who had just arrived in Madrid. He set out the serious international consequences that such a move would have, depriving friends of Spain of the argument about the 'legality' of the Republican government. And he proposed that, instead of a workers' Junta, a government should be formed, also under the leadership of Largo Caballero, in which all the workers' organizations would be represented, but also the bourgeois Republican ones. This solution to the crisis would make it possible for the USSR to send help. Pierre Broué and Emile Témime give this version of what happened in their book *The Revolution and the Civil War in Spain,* Faber and Faber, London, 1972, pp. 199–200.

In *Guerra y revolución en España* (Vol. 2, pp. 45–6) this plot by the CNT and UGT is denied. 'The story given by some historians, according to which Largo Caballero organized a conspiracy of UGT and the CNT to overthrow the Giral government, is not a serious one.' The authors add, however: 'But it is true that Largo Caballero hurled continual attacks and criticisms against the Giral government, especially at the end of August, when the Republic's military situation worsened. Some of his closest collaborators, like Araquistain and Baraibar, put around more or less publicly the idea that it was necessary to eliminate the Republican ministers, so as to give power to Largo Caballero, in order to establish a "workers' dictatorship" or a "government of the trade unions", a scheme that had something in common with the ideas of the Anarchists and Trotskyists.' This almost amounts to confirming what they began by denying.

The official history of the PCE says nothing about the intervention by Rosenberg and his team of advisers. But the interview between Largo Caballero and Mikhail Koltsov, described by the latter in his *Ispansky dnevnik* ('Spanish Diary': Moscow, 1957, pp. 77–80), leaves little doubt as to the reality of this intervention and its significance. It would be ingenuous, to say the least, to suppose that Soviet diplomacy did not exercise 'pressure' in the same direction as one of its chief political collaborators. What is doubtless incorrect in Clara Campoamor's version is that the UGT–CNT 'plot' went so far that Azaña threatened to resign. Azaña in any case, says nothing to this effect in his own *Memoirs* (see note 48).

47. *Guerra y revolución en España*, Vol. 1, p. 259.

48. The 'Cuaderno de La Pobleta' (1937) and the Pedralbes diary (1938–9), which form part of Azaña's *Memoirs*, unpublished (the author died in 1940) until they were brought out by Ediciones Oasis, of Mexico City, in 1968, provide extremely important materials for historical reconstruction of the Spanish civil war. They show that Azaña played a bigger role than historians have hitherto allowed him, especially after the Negrin government was formed. His basic line, with which both Negrin and Prieto were in agreement, was focused on two closely connected objectives: to bring about, as soon as possible, restoration of the bourgeois Republican state system, and to reach a compromise with the rebel generals, a compromise to be endorsed by the great powers. On 31 August 1937 he notes the conversation he had that day with Negrin and Giral, after an interview with Prieto, and writes, among other things: 'I went over once more the views that I had previously expressed: for peace, the Republic, and a pact guaranteeing that in Spain there would be neither dictatorship nor Bolshevism. While safeguarding Republican institutions so far as essentials are concerned, a number of concessions can be made. We must assume in these talks the role of *collaborators* for peace, in Spain as in Europe generally, and must whisper in the ear of the French government the words that the situation calls for, on the basis of the general desirability of making peace. I believe we reached agreement' (Manuel Azaña, *Obras*

completas, Vol. 4, *Memorias políticas y de guerra*, p. 761). Azaña is referring here to the talks that Negrín was about to have in Geneva with representatives of various countries, France and Britain in the first place, taking advantage of a meeting of the League of Nations. On 30 September he met the Cabinet. He records: 'I told them to go before the Assembly with the knowledge that this government, owing to the policy it incarnates, has the President of the Republic behind it. This government means for me that we have finished with anarchy, and that everyone is going to be obliged to see reason – first, with "reasons" and then, if that is not sufficient, by means of the force of law. The only thing I see wrong in the government's general policy is that it is not moving as fast as would be desirable. I emphasized the need to pursue relentlessly the recovery of functions, duties etc., that have been usurped from the state, and I repeated to the government my decision not to sign anything that aims at validating such usurpation' (ibid., pp. 807–8).

In a number of places in his *Memoirs*, Azaña mentions the favourable reactions of the P C E to his policy. On 31 May 1937, when Largo Caballero had only just been removed and replaced by Negrín as head of the government, he writes: 'I am told that the Communists are very pleased with me – especially Díaz, despite the way I criticized him on the afternoon of the crisis. He says that I ought to be in charge of everything. Hm! If I were to be in charge for twenty-four hours, one could imagine what could happen. In any case, if, despite all appearances, Díaz understood what was really happening behind that scene, he deserves promotion' (ibid., p. 606). The scene in question, described by Azaña a few pages earlier, was the meeting he had called with the leaders of the parties making up the People's Front, in order to find a solution to the crisis of the Largo Caballero government. And what was hidden behind the scene was the plan of the Republicans and the reformist Socialists to make the Communists appear responsible for the elimination of Largo Caballero. The latter had laid down as his condition for accepting headship of the new government that he must also be given the Ministry of War. The Socialists and Republicans did not want this but said that they would accept it 'on condition that the Communists accepted it too'. Azaña summed up the situation: 'If you all agree that the trade-unionists should enter the new government, some because they are in favour of this and the rest because they will submit or resign themselves to it, and Largo Caballero being the only Premier acceptable to the trade-unionists, – it is necessary to make it perfectly clear that, if the government is not formed, the reason is that the Communists refuse to yield on the question of Largo having the War Ministry, and that Largo will not renounce that portfolio' (ibid., pp. 601–2). The PCE did not 'yield', and so took upon itself responsibility for the formation of a government without the UGT or the CNT. It did not yield on the question of Largo Caballero at the Ministry of War, but it accepted Prieto in that post – Prieto, who, already at that time, as Azaña's *Memoirs* show, was in agreement with the President of the Republic on the need to seek a compromise peace, guaranteed by what Azaña called a 'five-power pact' (Britain, France, the USSR, Germany, Italy), on the basis (naturally) of a bourgeois regime which, while retaining Republican forms, would make 'a number of concessions' to the Fascists. Azaña and Prieto knew that this line coincided with that of the Soviet government, and for this reason they risked little in formally agreeing to Largo Caballero's demands: they knew that the Communists could not yield to them.

The 'Government of Victory', as the PCE entitled Negrín's government, had in reality the task of carrying through Azaña's plan. To do this it proved necessary to 'resist' rather than to 'win'. And the conflict that arose later between Azaña and Prieto, on the one hand, and Negrín, on the other, did not concern the basis of this policy, but was simply due to the fact that, by the middle of 1938, and especially after Munich, Azaña and Prieto considered that the war was lost, whereas Negrín thought that resistance could be kept up, with a view to 'linking up' the Spanish war with the world war which he saw was coming soon.

On 13 October 1937 a delegation from the PCE leadership, headed by Dolores Ibarruri, called on Azaña in order to tell him that the party did not agree with the moving of the government from Valencia to Barcelona. Azaña gives this account of the interview: 'La Pasionaria, speaking for all of them, talked of the demoralizing effect that this move would have on public opinion. In passing, she added that her party was not very keen on the policy the government was pursuing. She thought she detected a tendency towards dictatorship on the part of the Socialists. On this matter of the shifting of the seat of government, the Premier [Negrín] had acted alone, not consulting anyone, though everybody knew of his plans, and steps had actually been taken in Barcelona to find suitable offices before the Cabinet had even discussed the proposal. It was fifteen days since the Cabinet had met. They are not in favour of any dictatorship, even though that of the proletariat figures in their programme. "I assume," said I, laughing, "that you have postponed that little matter of the dictatorship of the proletariat for the time being?" "Yes, President, because we possess common sense" ' (ibid., p. 819).

As soon as the supporters of Largo Caballero and the Anarcho-Syndicalists had been put out of action for practical purposes, with the help of the PCE, the policy of the reformist leaders of the Socialist Party became one of restricting the positions held by the Communists in all fields: state machine, army, trade unions, etc. If the PCE had put off any idea of 'the dictatorship of the proletariat' for the 'time being', the reformists, closely allied with the Republicans, had not renounced the idea of restoring the 'dictatorship' of the bourgeoisie, which was their ultimate aim.

49. The resounding defeat suffered by Caballerism was due to the ambiguity of its policy, or rather to its lack of policy. Under the conditions of the Spanish civil war, in-between positions proved untenable. Either one waged the war in the name of bourgeois democracy, on the basis of reorganization and reinforcement of the Republican state, and in that case it was necessary to deal firmly with those sections of the proletariat who were trying to assert and develop 'their revolution' – or else one took a resolute line towards the establishment of a revolutionary authority capable of waging the war by its own methods. The Caballerists wanted to keep in with everybody – something that the personality of their leader made difficult, incidentally – and they ended by quarrelling with everybody. In proportion as restoration of the Republican state progressed, they became an increasingly serious obstacle in the path of carrying this restoration through to its ultimate consequences.

Pressures on Largo Caballero grew heavier, not only from the PCE, the delegates of the Comintern and the Soviet advisers, but also from Stalin himself, who did not shrink from intervening directly in problems of Spanish internal politics. In a letter signed by Stalin, Molotov and Voroshilov, dated 21 December 1936 and addressed to Largo Caballero, the latter was given some 'friendly advice': 'The urban petty and middle bourgeoisie must be attracted to the government side ... The leaders of the Republican Party should not be repulsed; on the contrary, they should be drawn in, brought close to the government, persuaded to get down to the job in harness with the government ... Above all, it is necessary to ensure the government the support of Azaña and his group, doing everything possible to help them to overcome their hesitations. This is necessary in order to prevent the enemies of Spain from presenting it as a Communist Republic, and thus to avert their open intervention, which represents the greatest danger to republican Spain.' And another 'suggestion' was offered, too: 'It is quite possible that the parliamentary path will turn out to be a more effective means of revolutionary development in Spain than in Russia' (Degras, ed., *Documents on Soviet Foreign Policy*, OUP, London, 1953, III, pp. 230, 231. The Spanish text is given in *Guerra y revolución en España*, Vol. 2, pp. 101–3, together with Caballero's reply).

There is no need to explain what was really meant by this 'friendly advice' from the leader of the state that controlled the supply of arms to the Spanish Republic and held its gold reserve. Caballero replied, in effect, that everything he was advised to do had already been done, which amounted to saying that the advice was unnecessary. And he allowed himself to put forward an objection: 'In reply to your suggestion, it must be said that, whatever fate the future may have in store for the institution of parliament, there are no enthusiastic defenders of it to be found here, even among the Republicans.' This remark, together with the claim that everything Stalin recommended had already been done, was not likely to reassure the addressee.

Stalin then intensified his pressure. At the end of February 1937 he sent Caballero another piece of 'advice', this time very urgently: it was necessary to proceed at once to unite the Communist and Socialist parties. Caballero declined. (Araquistain revealed this when the war was over, and it is his version that is given in the book by Peirats already mentioned (note 39), in Vol. 2, pp. 375–6. Maidanik confirms it in these words: 'Caballero again rejected the proposal for immediate unification of the two parties, put to him by the PCE and by the leaders of the international labour movement.' He does not mention Stalin, but gives as his source ... the book by Peirats. See Maidanik, op. cit., p. 293.)

Confronted with the stubborn refusal of Caballero to act like a good secretary of a national section of the Comintern, the only thing left for Stalin to do was to get rid of him, as was done with bad secretaries of national sections of the Comintern. This operation was accomplished at the end of May 1937, as we have already seen (note 48).

50. Quite apart from the question of the validity of the Anarcho-Syndicalist notions regarding the social system that is to take the place of capitalism, their absolute incompatibility with the demands of the war became plain. Practical experience furnished unquestionable proof of this, and it is significant that, on the plane of analysis, even writers most sympathetic to the social measures carried out by the CNT during the civil war are obliged to recognize their failure. In so far as the Anarcho-Syndicalists tried to face up to the war in a serious way, they were compelled

to give up their essential assumptions one after the other. And in so far as they did not give them up, the attempt to put them into practice raised an enormous obstacle in the way of solving the most immediate and agonizing problem that confronted the revolution – that of vanquishing the counter-revolution personified by the Spanish generals and their foreign allies. This task called for a dictatorial authority, the maximum unity, temporary sacrifice of all aspirations to material betterment, and so on. This task could be accomplished either by a revolutionary proletarian authority or by a bourgeois one. But it could not be accomplished at all *without any authority*. The tragedy of the Spanish revolution was that it proved unable to establish for itself either a revolutionary ruling authority like the Bolshevik dictatorship of the Russian civil war or a bourgeois Jacobin authority like that of the French revolutionaries of 1793.

51. Regarding the origin of POUM, see note 30, p. 51. The beginning of the Spanish civil war coincided with the opening of the 'Moscow trials'. Kamenev and Zinoviev were condemned to death in August. The POUM, by denouncing the crimes of Stalin against the Bolshevik Old Guard, became the dictator's *bête noire*, and, consequently, also that of the Comintern and of the Spanish Communists. In November the latter made the other parties of the People's Front agree to exclude the POUM from the Junta for the defence of Madrid. The Socialist Albar told the POUM leaders that Rosenberg had vetoed them (see Broué and Témime, op. cit., p. 239, note 30). On 28 November the Soviet consul in Barcelona sent a note to the newspapers describing *La Batalla*, the organ of the POUM, as a journal 'sold to international Fascism'. Soon afterwards, the POUM was excluded from the Council of the Generalitat. On 17 December *Pravda* was able to write: 'So far as Catalonia is concerned, the cleaning up of Trotskyists and Anarchists has begun and it will be carried out with the same energy as in the USSR' (quoted in Hugh Thomas, *The Spanish Civil War*, Eyre and Spottiswoode, London, 1961, p. 363). In other words, the Anarchists and POUMists were to be physically destroyed. The press of the PCE launched a violent campaign against the Trotskyists and 'uncontrollables' (in Spain itself it was impossible to refer openly to the Anarchists, as *Pravda* had done), accusing them of being 'enemies of the people' just like the Fascists. The Plenum of the Central Committee of the PCE held on 5–8 March 1937 resolved on putting an end to the POUM, as a concrete immediate task. In José Diaz's report he said: 'Who are the enemies of the people? The enemies of the people are the Fascists, Trotskyists and the "uncontrolled" elements ... Our chief

enemy is Fascism, against which we concentrate all our fire and all the hatred of the people. But our hatred is directed with equal force against the agents of Fascism, against those who, like the POUM, these Trotskyists in disguise, conceal themselves behind pseudo-revolutionary phraseology so as the better to fulfil their role as agents of our enemies in our own country.' Later in the same report he said: 'Fascism, Trotskyism and the "uncontrolled" elements are the three enemies of the people who must be removed from the political life not only of Spain but also of all civilized countries' (José Diaz, *Tres años de lucha*, pp. 322–4; abridged version in *Communist International* (English edn), Vol. 14, No. 4 (1937), pp. 1006–7). The campaign was intensified, culminating in the events of May in Barcelona: the armed clash between the forces of the government (mainly represented by the forces of the PCE) and the POUM, together with a section of the Anarcho-Syndicalists. On the basis of a German document the PCE alleged (and the allegation has never yet been withdrawn) that the persons mainly responsible for the events were the leaders of the POUM, manipulated by Fascist 'agents'. As Broué rightly observes, however, the document quoted by the PCE does not in fact specify at all that these 'agents' acted through the POUM rather than through some other organization. In any case, no 'agent' or group of 'agents' could have succeeded unless a situation lending itself to a clash had first been created (Broué-Témime, op. cit., pp. 286 and 294, note 40). And this situation had been created by the ideological and political campaign directed against the POUM by Moscow. It seems to me that the political theses of the POUM at this time played into the hands of the provocation that was being prepared against it and of which it was fully aware. On 14 March 1937 Nin said that, 'although less favourable than in the first months of the revolution, the relation of forces is such that the proletariat can *now* take power without having recourse to armed insurrection' (reproduced in *La Batalla*, July–August 1966). This was quite untrue. The sections of the proletariat which in this situation might in theory agree with Nin's attitude – some of the Caballerists and Anarcho-Syndicalists, as well as the POUM itself – *could not have tried to take power otherwise than through an armed struggle against the forces of the PCE* (and the Republicans and Socialists who shared the PCE's political ideas), which meant the greater part of the army. To look at the problem the way Nin did was to move towards civil war within the Republican camp. And civil war within the Republican camp could safeguard neither the proletarian revolution nor the bourgeois-democratic Republic: it could only hasten the victory of the Fascist counter-revolution. To see the 'relation of forces' in the Republican camp without taking the 'other camp' into account was a monumental mistake. Trotsky wrote, on 28 September of that year: 'The Stalin–Negrin government is a quasi-democratic obstacle on the road to socialism; but it is also an obstacle, not a very reliable or durable one, but an obstacle nonetheless, on the road to Fascism. Tomorrow, or the day after tomorrow, the Spanish proletariat may perhaps be able to break through this obstacle and seize power. But if it aided, even passively, in tearing it down today, it would only serve Fascism' ('Ultra-Lefts in General and Incurable Ultra-Lefts in Particular', in *The Spanish Revolution (1931–1939)*, op. cit., p. 296). This clear-sighted judgement – not long afterwards Trotsky was to formulate other, less clear-sighted judgements that contradicted this one – applied perfectly to the situation of March 1937. Nin's mistake was perhaps due, in part at least, to the dramatic situation of encirclement in which the POUM found itself. In any case, it facilitated Stalin's criminal plans. After the bloody May days there began the final, well-known phase of the smashing of the POUM (see, among other recent writings on this theme, the moderate article by Juan Andrade in *La Batalla*, June 1967). For my part I will only add that the repression of the POUM, and in particular the vile murder of Andres Nin, constitute the blackest page in the history of the PCE, which acted as accomplice in a crime committed by Stalin's secret service. We Spanish Communists were undoubtedly put out of our right minds, like all the world's Communists at this time and for a long time after, by the monstrous lies that were fabricated in Moscow. This, however, does not rid us of our historical responsibility. Fourteen years have passed since the Twentieth Congress of the CPSU in 1956, yet the PCE has still not made any self-criticism, or helped to clear up the facts. Even if we assume – and in my view this is probably the case – that the leaders of the PCE cannot themselves contribute much more to what is already known, they could at least call upon the CPSU to make public the information which it alone possesses. The Nin affair belongs to the history of Spain, and not only to that of the USSR.

52. Broué-Témime, op. cit., p. 232.

53. In his report of March 1937 to the plenum of the central committee of the PCE, José Diaz (*Tres años de lucha*, p. 326) gave the following data regarding the social composition of the 249,140 members of the party 'in the provinces ruled by the Republican government. This figure includes 50,000 members of the United Socialist Party of Catalonia. The

social composition of the party is as follows: 87,660 industrial workers; 62,250 agricultural labourers; 76,700 peasants; 15,485 from the middle classes and 7,045 representatives of the intellectuals and the liberal professions.' (An abridged version of this report appeared in *Communist International*, Vol. 14 (1937), from p. 1007 of which the above quotation is taken. A few lines on, in the original, Diaz says that his figure does *not* include the '45,000 or more' members of the United Socialist Party of Catalonia. By 'peasants' must here be understood small and medium landowners, and by 'middle classes' members of the urban petty-bourgeoisie, owners of small industrial or commercial businesses, etc.) Of these 249,140 members, 131,600 were said to be 'fighting at the front'. In the spring of 1937 nearly two-thirds of the army was under PCE control and at least a third of the soldiers were party members, according to Maidanik (op. cit., pp. 278–80). These last-mentioned percentages may be exaggerated, but there can be no doubt that the majority of the 150,000 industrial and agricultural proletarians in the party, who were mostly very young, were in the army. Maidanik himself writes: 'A Bulgarian Communist who arrived in Spain at the beginning of 1937 [probably "Stepanov", a delegate of the Comintern] wrote that "the Communist Party is essentially a military party" ' (ibid., p. 280). And he adds: 'It must be admitted at the same time that the conquest by the Communists of the working masses in the rear, except in Catalonia, was relatively slow, especially where the agricultural proletariat was concerned ... In the rear and in the trade unions the weight of tradition continued to work in favour of the Socialists and Anarchists' (ibid., pp. 280–81). It is questionable whether Catalonia should be excepted here: in the spring of 1937 the party had only 45,000-odd members there, and its chief growth had been among distributive workers, petty-bourgeois, etc.

54. Carl von Clausewitz, *On War*, English edn, Vol. I, Kegan Paul, London, 1908, p. 23.

55. José Diaz, *Tres años de lucha*, p. 350.

56. See note 51. In the report by José Diaz mentioned in that note (a report *delivered* by Diaz, but drawn up in its main lines by the Comintern team which was overseeing the PCE) we read: 'And now a plot has been discovered, a plot by the Trotskyists in the Soviet Union, and the accused, traitors to the socialist fatherland, having confessed their guilt, are going to be judged by the proletarian court. The German and Italian Fascist press is hurling insults at the Soviet power because it has discovered this plot by their agents. The Spanish Trotskyists cannot do otherwise than

run to the defence of their friends, using the same language as the Fascists. *La Batalla* of 24 January 1937 – to quote only one issue of this paper – contains the following statement: "A new crime is being prepared in Moscow. The most elementary forms of workers' democracy have been abolished in the Russia of today, which has fallen under a bureaucratic regime of personal dictatorship. The international proletariat cannot be called upon to defend Russia's cause if it is denied the right to know what is going on in Russia." What need is there to quote further? What I have read is enough to show the identity between Fascists and Trotskyists. As we see, these people have nothing in common with the proletariat or with any tendency that has regard to honesty. If we fight against the Trotskyists, it is because they are enemy agents who have made their way into the anti-Fascist ranks. It is a grave mistake to regard the Trotskyists as a tendency in the labour movement. They are an unprincipled group of counter-revolutionaries who are to be classified as agents of international Fascism. The recent Moscow trial has shown irrefutably that the leader of this gang, Trotsky, is an agent of the Gestapo' (op. cit., p. 323).

57. The two trade-union centres, the UGT and the CNT, refused to take part in the new government. In the succeeding months the reformist leadership of the PSOE, with the help of the state machine, succeeded in removing the Caballerists from the leadership of the UGT and getting the latter to agree to enter the government. A year later the moderate elements were similarly able to capture the leadership of the CNT, which was once again represented in the government (April 1938).

58. In José Diaz's report to the plenum of the Central Committee of the PCE in November 1937 he said: 'After the fall of the government of Largo Caballero a tendency appeared which aimed at the formation of a bloc in opposition to the People's Front government. The axis of this bloc was the defeated Largo Caballero group, which had fallen under Trotskyist influence, and which, linking up with counter-revolutionary Trotskyism, sought to draw the CNT into an anti-government policy ... Largo Caballero's group is also fighting against the People's Front. This complements its splitting and defeatist policy. It is no accident that this group has become the protector of General Asensio and the POUMists. Its links with Asensio and with the Trotskyist spies are integral to its policy' (*Tres años de lucha*, pp. 416–17).

Though the most important representatives of the defeatist and capitulatory policy, Azaña and Prieto, occupied the Presidency of the Republic and the Ministry of War, the PCE concentrated its fire on the Largo

Caballero tendency, using the same sort of 'arguments' as it had used in the attack on the POUM.

Meanwhile, the reformist leaders of the PSOE carried on the fight against the Caballerists in the PSOE and the UGT, to the applause of the PCE. An article in *Frente Rojo* of 16 August 1938 commented favourably on the 'firm and vigorous decision' of the national committee of the Socialist Party to direct 'all party organizations to take adequate steps to ensure unity of all the militants, not tolerating the formation and operation of any tendencies or factions' (*Tres años de lucha,* pp. 470-71).

Soon after the fall of Largo Caballero as head of the government, the PCE drew closer to the reformist leadership of the PSOE, and agreed on a common programme with it on 17 August 1937.

59. Already at the time of the November 1937 plenum of the PCE's Central Committee, mention was made of the serious symptom represented by the 'great weakness of party work at the front, although 60 per cent of our members are there' (*Tres años de lucha,* p. 433). At the same plenum it was said: 'We must fight energetically against hesitancy [in the party]. We must fight against those who hint, sometimes very indirectly, at their disagreement with this or with that, even after meetings and plenums have been held. This phenomenon has two causes. One is the lack of understanding that still exists regarding the imperatives governing our party and our policy, for there are many new members among us ... But there are other comrades too, long-standing party members, who hesitate. They say that they do not understand things very well, and make insinuations which naturally, in times like these, endanger more than ever the unity of the party' (ibid., p. 439).

60. Diaz, op. cit., pp. 461-3. In the November 1937 report to which he refers, Diaz does indeed speak of 'the terrain on which all democratic states can unite', namely, 'the terrain of defence against the war that threatens us all'. That, a year and a half after the Spanish war had begun, a PCE document should speak of a war 'that threatens us' reveals the non-Spanish hand that participated in the writing of this document.

61. *Vsemirnaya Istoriya,* Moscow, 1956-62, Vol. 19, pp. 349-50.

62. Jackson, op. cit., p. 453.

63. In the first days of March 1939 the leaders of the PCE tried to take over the principal commands in the central zone (all that was left to the Republic after the loss of Catalonia), where there were still substantial

military forces and resources for continuing resistance. But Casado's revolt in Madrid and the flight of the navy from Cartegena, and, above all, the general attitude of the population, caused the PCE's plan to miscarry.

64. It is enough to read the reports and articles by José Diaz published in *Tres años de lucha* to realize how thoroughly the question of guerrilla struggle in the enemy-occupied zone had been dropped. After the defeat it was recognized in the leading circles of the PCE that this had been one of their chief weaknesses. But it was obviously not an accidental shortcoming. On this question as on others, the party had come up against incomprehension and resistance on the part of the bourgeois Republicans and of Socialists like Prieto, and it had bowed to them, on this matter as on others, in order to preserve the alliance.

65. Trotsky, 'The Lessons of Spain', in *The Spanish Revolution (1931–1939)*, op. cit., p. 319.

66. On 16 February 1966 a meeting was held at the Institute of Marxism–Leninism attached to the Central Committee of the CPSU, at which Soviet historians, including specialists in military history, were present. The purpose of the meeting was to discuss the book by Alexander Nekrich called *22 June 1941*, published in Moscow in 1965 by the Nauka publishing house. We shall have occasion later to refer to this book in connection with the problems of the Comintern in the period of the German–Soviet pact (Nekrich shows Stalin's responsibility for the defeats suffered by the Red Army in the first phase of the Soviet–German war). This book, which was received with immense interest by Soviet readers, was soon after its appearance made the object of a violent campaign by the Stalinists, culminating in a ban upon it and measures taken against its author. At the discussion of 16 February, however, most of the participants supported Nekrich. And, during the discussion, other matters were brought up. One of those who spoke, Snegov, said in passing that Stalin had 'betrayed the Spanish Republic, Poland, and all Communists in all countries'. What was most significant, though, was that Deborin, who represented the official standpoint at this meeting, while replying vigorously to Snegov on the question of Poland, had nothing to say about Spain (see V. Petrov, ed., *'22 June 1941'*, op. cit., p. 260).

67. Jackson, op. cit., p. 404

68 Azaña, *Obras completas*, Vol. 4, p. 734. It is not possible here to undertake a detailed analysis of the Soviet attitude in relation to the non-intervention policy imposed by London. Clearly, however, the acceptance

of this policy by the Soviet government and its strict observation during the months of August and September and part of October 1936, while it was being openly violated by Germany and Italy, prevented the Spanish Republic from profiting by its initial advantage over the rebels. In general, moreover, entry into the game of non-intervention already meant placing on a basis unfavourable to the Republic the question of giving assistance to it.

69. At the end of 1944 the Greek resistance, largely led by the Communists, had made itself practically master of the whole country, and had a frankly revolutionary programme. Intervention by a British expeditionary force gave power back to Greek reaction, without any move on Stalin's part to prevent this from happening. In the second part of the present book I shall examine Stalin's policy on this question and, subsequently, on the civil war in Greece.

70. B. Ponomaryov et al., *World Revolutionary Movement of the Working Class*, Progress, Moscow, 1967, p. 338.

71. Marx, 'Revolution in China and in Europe', in *Marx on China, 1853–1860*, Lawrence and Wishart, London, 1951, p. 1. Marx's reflection was based on this schema: capitalism is a world system; British industry depends to a large extent on the great markets of Asia; in 1853, British industrial production, which had been expanding since 1850, was about to enter a crisis of over-production: 'If one of the great markets suddenly becomes contracted, the arrival of the crisis is necessarily accelerated thereby'; 'Now the Chinese rebellion must, for the time being, have precisely this effect upon England' (ibid., p. 4).

In an article of 1857 ('Persia–China', in ibid., pp. 50–51), Engels speaks of the war against foreigners which was developing in China as 'a popular war', and prophesies that 'the death-hour of the Old China is rapidly drawing nigh ... Before many years pass away we shall have to witness the death struggles of the oldest empire in the world, and the opening day of a new era for all Asia.'

But Marx and Engels did not deal with revolution in the colonial countries as a specific problem. The general idea that one can deduce from their writings is that these countries have to pass through the stage of capitalism. And just because it hastens the break-up of the petty agrarian communities which serve as basis for 'Oriental despotism', Marx sees positive, progressing aspects in colonization, at the same time as the cruel and inhuman ones. The founders of Marxism judged non-European civilizations through the prism of European civilization. The road to progress for the backward peoples they saw as the road of Euro-peanization, not only from the socio-economic standpoint but also culturally.

72. See Maurice Godelier, *La Notion de 'mode de production asiatique' et les schémas marxistes d'évolution des sociétés,* Centre d'Études et de Recherches Marxistes, Paris, n.d., pp. 5, 24.

73. See the reference in Chapter 2 to the way in which Lenin places the revolution of the East in his strategic schema of the world revolution. See, for the discussion of the colonial problem in the Second International, the extracts from the debates that took place at the Amsterdam (1904) and Stuttgart (1907) Congresses, published in Stuart R. Schram and Hélène Carrère d'Encausse, *Marxism and Asia (1853–1964),* pp. 125–33.

74. Degras, *The Communist International (1919–1943): Documents,* I, p. 43.

75. Schram and Carrère d'Encausse, op. cit., pp. 151–2, 160. The theses voted by the Congress on the national and colonial question are given in Degras, op. cit., I, pp. 139–44.

76. Schram and Carrère d'Encausse, op. cit., p. 187.

77. ibid., p. 193. Safarov is here referring to a letter addressed to the Comintern by the Sidi-bel-Abbès section of the French Communist Party. In May 1922 the ECCI had issued a call in connection with the national liberation movement in North Africa. The Communists of the Sidi-bel-Abbès section protested in their letter against this call, expressing a clearly colonialist outlook. 'There are peoples in tutelage,' said the letter, 'which are, as of now, capable of governing themselves alone, and others which as yet are not; and if Communist duty orders that liberty be given to the former, it even more imperiously orders that the latter be not abandoned to their miserable fate, it strongly orders that we serve them as humane and disinterested preceptors. If an Egyptian sovereignty is necessary, a sovereignty of cannibals is undesirable ...' The authors of the letter considered that 'the "revolt of the Algerian Muslim masses" which is spoken of in Paragraph Five [of the ECCI's appeal of May 1922 concerning the nationalist movement in French North Africa] would at the present time, that is to say before any victorious revolution in the mother country, be a dangerous folly of which the Algerian federations of the Communist Party, who have above all a Marxist sense of situations, do not wish to make themselves accomplices before the judgement of Communist history' (ibid., p. 196). This letter was used at the Fourth Congress, and again at the Fifth, as a typical example of the colonialist spirit of some Western

Communists (see *Fifth Congress of the Communist International, Abridged Report*, op. cit., p. 191).

78. *Inprecorr* (English edn), Vol. 4, No. 49 (24 July 1924), pp. 500–501, and Schram and Carrère d'Encausse, op. cit., p. 200.

Manuilsky, reporting to the Fifth Congress on the 'national and colonial question', also subjected the French and British Communists to severe criticism. In relation to the former, besides mentioning the celebrated letter from Sidi-bel-Abbès, he gave another example: 'The editors of the central organ of the party, *L'Humanité*, in publishing the appeal [of the Comintern to the French workers and to the colonial peoples], deliberately cut out from the text the words "to the colonial peoples".' To the British Communists he said: 'In none of the documents on the relations of the British Communist Party to the colonies which have been brought to us for perusal have we found a single declaration in which our British comrades have clearly and unmistakeably demanded the separation of the colonies from the British Empire' (*Fifth Congress of the Communist International, Abridged Report*, op. cit., pp. 191–3).

When, however, he spoke on Stalin's 'national policy' towards the non-Russian peoples of the USSR, Manuilsky passed from critique to dithyramb. And yet, as we shall see later, grounds for criticism were not lacking. The 'chauvinist ideas, foreign and hostile to proletarian internationalism', of which Safarov spoke, had representatives in the International that were far more dangerous than the Communists of Sidi-bel-Abbès.

79. *Vsemirnaya Istoriya*, op. cit., Vol. 8, p. 440.

80. Schram and Carrère d'Encausse, op. cit., p. 41.

81. In May 1917 the Bolshevik deputies to the soviets defended the following platform, drawn up by Lenin: 'The Russian people, the workers and the peasants, do not wish to oppress and will not oppress any nation; they do not wish to and will not hold by force within the boundaries of Russia a single non-Russian (non-Great-Russian) nation ... This means that the Great-Russians shall not forcibly retain either Poland or Kurland, or Ukraine, or Finland, or Armenia, or any other nation. The Great Russians offer a fraternal union to all the nations and propose the formation of a common state by voluntary consent of each individual people, and under no circumstances by means of violence, direct or indirect. The Great-Russians ... undertake ... to allow these nations and all other nations without exception freely to decide whether they wish to live as a separate state, or in union with whomsoever they please (Lenin, op. cit., Vol. 24, pp. 354–5). In the famous 'report on peace' which Lenin de-

livered to the Congress of Soviets the very day after the taking of power, Lenin said that the Soviet government 'conceives the annexation or seizure of foreign lands to mean every incorporation of a small or weak nation into a large or powerful state without the precisely, clearly and voluntarily expressed consent and wish of that nation, irrespective of the time when such forcible incorporation took place, irrespective also of the degree of development or backwardness of the nation forcibly annexed to the given state, or forcibly retained within its borders, and irrespective, finally, of whether this nation is in Europe or in distant, overseas countries.' And he made it clear that the question of 'the forms of its state existence' must be left open to decision 'by a free vote ... without the least pressure being brought to bear' upon the nation concerned (ibid., Vol. 26, p. 250).

82. ibid., Vol. 29, pp. 170 ff. Lenin was here arguing against Bukharin on the draft for a new party programme, but Stalin had taken up a similar position from January 1918 onward. In his report on the 'national question' to the Third Congress of Soviets, Stalin, after stating that 'the principle of self-determination was being exploited by the bourgeois chauvinist elements in the Ukraine in their imperialist class interests', went on to say: 'All this pointed to the necessity of interpreting the principle of self-determination as the right of self-determination not of the bourgeoisie but of the labouring masses of the given nation. The principle of self-determination should be a means in the struggle for socialism and should be subordinated to the principles of socialism' (Stalin, op. cit., Vol. 4, pp. 32–3).

83. This document of Lenin's, known under the title of 'The Question of Nationalities or of "Autonomization" ', remained for a long time hidden by the Stalinist leadership. It was not included in the original plan for the fourth edition of Lenin's collected works, being published for the first time in 1956, in the journal *Kommunist*. It is included in the fifth edition of the collected works, and in the extra Vol. 36, added to the fourth edition. (In the English version of this Vol. 36 it appears on pages 605–11.)

No details are known concerning the repercussions that this prophetic denunciation by Lenin of the danger of Great-Russian chauvinism had among the leading circles of the party. They must have been considerable, to judge by the proceedings of the Twelfth Party Congress (April 1923), in which Lenin did not take part. In his report 'on national factors in party and state affairs', Stalin sought to give the impression that he took up the same position as Lenin. He referred to 'Great-Russian chauvinism' in terms that seemed to confirm this impression; but a detailed analysis of this report of Stalin's reveals that his main attack was directed against 'local nationalism'. And some of the delegates were not deceived. Referring, as Stalin himself mentions, 'to notes and articles by Vladimir Ilyich' (Stalin, op. cit., Vol. 5, p. 271), these delegates tried to ensure that the fight against 'Great-Russian chauvinism' was not merely verbal. Bukharin even proposed that the point about 'local nationalism' be deleted from the draft resolution, so as to concentrate fire against the 'Goliath' of Great-Russian chauvinism. But Stalin had already secured control of the party machine, the majority of the delegates to the Congress were completely devoted to him, and the attempts made to translate into deeds the warnings uttered by Lenin remained ineffectual.

84. Degras, ed., *Documents on Soviet Foreign Policy*, I, OUP, London, 1951, p. 16.

85. Safarov, *Revolyutsiya i Kultura*, Tashkent, 1934, Vol. I, p. 10 (quoted in Schram and Carrère d'Encausse, op. cit., p. 32). At the Baku Congress, in the presence of foreign Communists from various Asian countries, the delegations of the Communist organizations of Turkestan and other Muslim nationalities included in the Soviet state put forward firm and outspoken criticism of the situation that had been created in their regions. Narbutabekov, for example, said in his speech: 'We people of the East ... have faith in our ideological guides and the leaders of the world proletariat – Comrades Lenin, Trotsky, Zinoviev and others, but all the same we must state at this congress what we want, and the voice of the Muslim workers and the peoples of the East must be heard. If it is heard, then the state power will find it easier to fulfil its tasks and aims in implementing the great principles of social revolution in the East. We demand genuine realization of the principles of freedom, equality and brotherhood in fact and not merely on paper ... Everyone knows that the East is utterly different from the West and its interests are different – thus, rigid application of the ideas of Communism will meet with resistance in the East. And so, if we want the four hundred millions in the Muslim world to adopt the Soviet system, some special criterion will have to be applied in their case ... We Turkestanis state that we have never before seen either Comrade Zinoviev or Comrade Radek or the other leaders of the revolution. They should come and see for themselves what is happening in our country, what exactly the local authorities, whose policies drive the working masses away from the Soviet power, are up to. I feel it my duty as a delegate to say this, precisely because I am staunchly behind the policy

of the Soviet power ... In shedding our blood on the Turkestan fronts against the enemies of the Soviet power, we bound up our lives closely with the working masses of the whole of Russia and the accusations of chauvinist tendencies made against Turkestani leaders must be dropped, for our workers have proved the contrary in shedding their blood ... I tell you, comrades, that our Turkestani masses have to fight on two fronts. On the one hand against the evil mullahs at home, and on the other against the narrow nationalist inclinations of local Europeans. Neither Comrade Zinoviev nor Comrade Lenin nor Comrade Trotsky knows the true situation in Turkestan, and what has been going on in Turkestan these past three years. We must speak out frankly and paint a true picture of the state of affairs in Turkestan, and then the eyes of the leaders will be opened ... We say: remove your counter-revolutionaries, remove your alien elements who spread national discord, and remove your colonizers working behind the mask of Communism!' (Schram and Carrère d'Encausse, op. cit., pp. 174–5).

86. One of the principal leaders of the Muslim peoples who was eliminated in this purge was Sultan-Galiyev, Stalin's assistant in the Commissariat for the Nationalities after the October revolution. For Sultan-Galiyev's theoretical and political views, see Schram and Carrère d'Encausse, op. cit., pp. 35–6, 178–80.

87. Here are some extracts from Tan Malaka's speech at the Fourth Congress: 'Pan-Islamism is a long story. First of all I will deal with our experiences in India [Indonesia], where we collaborate with the Islamists. We have in Java a very large union comprising many very poor peasants, viz., Sarekat Islam. Between 1912 and 1916 this union had one million members, perhaps it had three or even four million. It was a very large proletarian union which sprang up spontaneously and was very revolutionary. Until 1920 we collaborated with this union. Our party, consisting of 13,000 members, went to the National Assembly and carried on propaganda. In 1921 we succeeded in making Sarekat Islam adopt our programme and it went into the villages agitating for the control of production and for the watchword: "All power to the poor peasants and to the proletariat." Thus, we carried on the same propaganda as our Communist Party, only sometimes under another name. However, a split occurred in 1921, owing to the tactless criticism of the leaders of Sarekat Islam. The government, through its agents, made use of this split, and also of the decisions of the Second Congress of the Communist International, to fight against Pan-Islamism. The government agents said to the simple peasants

77

that the Communists did not only want to create a split among them, but also that they wanted to destroy their religion. This was too much for a simple Moslem peasant. The peasant thought to himself that he had already lost everything in this world and that he was not willing to lose heaven as well. Such was the mood of these simple-minded people, and the government propagandists and agents made use of it. Thus we have a split.' (Chair [Marchlewski]: 'Your time is up.') 'I have come from India, it took me forty days to come here.' (Applause.) 'The Sarekat Islamists believe in our propaganda. They are with us "with their stomachs" (to use a popular expression), but with their hearts they remain with the Sarekat Islam – with their heaven, which we cannot give them. Therefore, they boycotted our meetings and we could not carry on propaganda any longer.' Later, Tan Malaka explained that Pan-Islamism was acquiring a different significance from what it had previously possessed: 'At present Pan-Islamism now means the fraternity of all Mahomedan peoples and the liberation not only of the Arabian but also of the Indian, Javanese and all other oppressed Mahomedan peoples. This fraternity is called the liberation struggle against the British, French and Italian capitalists, consequently against world capitalism ... Just as we are willing to support the national war, we shall also support the liberation struggle of the very active and energetic 250 million Mahomedans who are subject to the imperialist powers' (*Bulletin of the Fourth Congress of the Communist International*, No. 7, pp. 6–8).

88. Degras, *The Communist International (1919–1943): Documents*, I, pp. 387, 388.

89. Lenin's 'preliminary draft theses' will be found in his *Collected Works*, Vol. 31, pp. 144–51. Roy's draft theses are given in Schram and Carrère d'Encausse, op. cit., together with the modifications made in the Congress theses after the discussion (pp. 150–63).

90. Lenin, op. cit., Vol. 31, pp. 241–2.

91. ibid., Vol. 42, p. 202.

92. ibid., Vol. 31, p. 242. Lenin's speech at the Second Congress reveals that the views expressed by Roy and other representatives of the colonial peoples had had a definite influence on him, as a result of which he considerably altered some of his original ideas. We see this, for example, when he says: 'There has been a certain *rapprochement* between the bourgeoisie of the exploiting countries and that of the colonies, so that very often – perhaps even in most cases – the bourgeoisie of the oppressed countries, while it does support the national movement, is in full accord

with the imperialist bourgeoisie, i.e., joins forces with it against all revolutionary movements and revolutionary classes. This was irrefutably proved in the commission, and we decided that the only correct attitude was to take this distinction into account and in nearly all cases, substitute the term "national-revolutionary" for the term "bourgeois-democratic" [2] (ibid.).

In Stalin's time, the theses of Lenin and Roy, as approved by the Congress, were simply pushed out of sight, while popularizing Lenin's original *draft* theses, on which Stalin could lean more confidently in order to justify his policy of tailing behind the 'national bourgeoisie' in China, for example.

93. Degras, op. cit., I, pp. 143, 144.

94. Lenin, op. cit., Vol. 31, p. 244

95. Marx and Engels put forward this hypothesis in relation to Russia in the 1870s and 1880s. It is found, for example, in the preface to the Russian edition of the *Communist Manifesto*. Even if related only to Russia, the theoretical importance that this hypothesis acquired around 1920, when revolution was concretely on the agenda in Asia, seems clear. However, for this original path, different from that of Europe, to be followed, it was indispensable, in the eyes of Marx and Engels, that the socialist revolution should first have triumphed in the capitalist countries of the West.

96. Lenin, op. cit., Vol. 31, p. 243.

97. Degras, op. cit., I, pp. 385–9

98. Schram and Carrère d'Encausse, op. cit., p. 190. In this speech, Roy undertakes an interesting analysis in which he tries to establish a differentiation that was not reflected in the theses eventually adopted by the Congress.

99. *Fifth Congress of the Communist International, Abridged Report*, p. 195, and *Inprecorr* (English edn), Vol. 4, No. 54 (4 August 1924), p. 573.

1. *Inprecorr* (English edn), Vol. 4, No. 57 (12 August 1924), p. 607.

2. On 7 April 1921 two hundred deputies of the parliament elected in 1913 met in Canton and resolved to form a national and republican government in opposition to the reactionary Peking government, which was in reality only one among the numerous reactionary militarist cliques which had divided up China among themselves after the revolution of 1911 – the so-called 'war-lords'. The Canton assembly elected Sun Yat-sen head of the new government, with the title of President of the Chinese

Republic. In June 1922, however, Sun's government was ousted by one of the 'war-lords', and had to flee to Shanghai. Sun re-established his power in 1923 and succeeded in consolidating it in the region around Canton as a result of an agreement with Soviet Russia which brought him arms and military specialists, so that he was able to form an army loyal to him. (See Jacques Guillermaz, *A History of the Chinese Communist Party, 1921–1949*, Methuen, London, 1972, pp. 5. 77–8.)

3. In the 'Resolution on some questions in the history of our party' adopted on 20 April 1945 by the Seventh Enlarged Plenary Session of the Central Committee of the Chinese Communist Party, elected at the Sixth Party Congress, the following explanation was given for the defeat of 1927 (not without a protracted discussion having previously taken place among the party's leading circles): 'The revolution ended in defeat because the reactionary clique in the Kuomintang, then our ally, betrayed it in 1927; because the combined force of that clique and the imperialists was very strong; and *particularly* because in the concluding period of the revolution (about six months) the right-wing viewpoint in our party, with Chen Tu-hsiu as its exponent, developed into a line of capitulation ...' (Mao Tse-tung, *Selected Works*, Vol. 4, Lawrence and Wishart, London, 1956, p. 172. My italics). The rigorous and detailed study by Jacques Guillermaz arrives at much the same conclusions, even though this author gives more emphasis to the general objective conditions that rendered victory impossible in the situation that then existed. There seems little doubt that this was so, but the impossibility of winning is one thing and quite another is the aspect assumed by defeat. This is in the main the conclusion reached also by Lucien Bianco (*The Origin of the Chinese Revolution*, OUP, London, 1972). This period of the Chinese revolution, and the overwhelming responsibility borne by Stalin and the Comintern for the defeat as it occurred, were first subjected to general analysis in *The Tragedy of the Chinese Revolution*, by Harold Isaacs (London, 1938).

4. *Inprecorr* (English edn), No. 41 of 1928, pp. 733–4 (my italics). Bukharin was the leader of the Comintern – though already subordinate to Stalin – during the critical period of the Chinese revolution (1926–7).

5. In the various versions of the history of their party that the Maoist leaders have put out up to now, they have carefully refrained from making any critical analysis of the role played by Stalin and the Comintern, concealing the information and documents that they must have in their possession (even if some of the relevant documentation is available only in the Soviet archives). Until the Sino-Soviet conflict began, not only

did they refrain from criticizing, but the role of Stalin and the Comintern was presented in an apologetical way, exactly as in the other Communist parties. Once the conflict had begun, the Chinese leaders decided that it would be 'profitable', in their struggle against the Soviet leadership, to take on themselves the defence of Stalin and the Stalinist heritage, while recognizing in a formal way 'some mistakes' made by Stalin – some related to non-Chinese problems, others specifically concerning the Chinese revolution. In the document published in *Renmin Ribao* and *Hongqi* on 13 September 1963 under the title 'On the Question of Stalin', it was said: 'While defending Stalin, we do not defend his mistakes. Long ago the Chinese Communists had first-hand experience of some of his mistakes. Of the erroneous "left" and right opportunist lines which emerged in the Chinese Communist Party at one time or another, some arose under the influence of certain mistakes of Stalin's, in so far as their international sources were concerned. In the later 1920s, the 1930s and the early and middle 1940s, the Chinese Marxists–Leninists represented by Comrades Mao Tse-tung and Liu Shao-chi resisted the influence of Stalin's mistakes; they gradually overcame the erroneous lines of "left" and right opportunism and finally led the Chinese revolution to victory. But since some of the wrong ideas put forward by Stalin were accepted and applied by certain Chinese comrades, we Chinese should bear the responsibility' (*On the Question of Stalin*, Foreign Languages Press, Peking, 1963, p. 8). There is undoubtedly something correct in this attitude. The Chinese Communists, like the Communists of Germany, France, Spain, etc., ought not to – and cannot, historically – evade their responsibility for the mistakes made by their respective parties even if these resulted from strict application of the lines received from Moscow. But it is an attitude that shows an extremely harmful side when it is used to evade the fundamental problem, which is not so much the personal responsibility of Stalin or of some particular leader of the Comintern, but the 'responsibility' of an ideological, political and organizational system – of a mechanism that subjected unconditionally the requirements of the revolutionary movement in each country and on the international scale to the interests of the Soviet state, without even the Soviet working people having power to exercise choice in the determining of these interests, this power being monopolized by the bureaucratic stratum, itself subject to a personal dictatorship. The historical merit of the Maoist leaders, and of Mao in particular, consists, in fact, in their having succeeded in gradually freeing the Chinese revolutionary movement, after the cruel defeat of 1927, from control by Stalin and the Stalinist Comintern. This merit will become greater, however, when they decide to enrich the experience of the international revolutionary movement by an objective and critical analysis of the role played by Stalin and the Comintern in the Chinese revolution. One of the obstacles at present standing in the way of such an analysis being made is doubtless the cult of Mao's personality, for such a step would necessarily mean critically revising a whole series of views expressed by Mao regarding Stalin and the Comintern. The moment does not seem to be nigh when the Chinese Communists will be able to demonstrate, as K. S. Karol puts it, that 'de-Maoization could be an enrichment and not a denial of the writings of the man who was together the promoter, the theoretician and the historian of the Chinese revolution' (K. S. Karol, *China: The Other Communism*, Heinemann, London, 1967, p. 142). Describing the contacts he made during his visit to China, Karol vividly presents in his book the history of the Chinese Communist Party 'as they see it today'. They 'see' it, we find, by refusing to look at some of its essential aspects.

6. See Guillermaz, op. cit., pp. 77–8. The passage quoted from the manifesto of the Third Congress of the Chinese Communist Party is taken from G. D. H. Cole, *History of Socialist Thought*, Vol. IV, Part 2, Macmillan, London, 1958, p. 783. Cole mentions that a note in Sun Yat-sen's handwriting exists in which he agrees to the Communists entering the Kuomintang on condition that they accept the discipline of the Kuomintang leadership (ibid., p. 782).

7. In January 1922 representatives of the Kuomintang attended a congress of Eastern peoples held in Petrograd, and there affirmed – disagreeing on this point with the Communist delegates – that agrarian reform could be accomplished in China only after the country had been reunified under a nationalist government (Guillermaz, op. cit., p. 71).

8. In Schram and Carrère d'Encausse, op. cit., on pp. 226–7, Stalin's original words are reproduced from *Pravda* of 22 May 1925. The 'corrected' version will be found in Vol. 7 of Stalin's works (English version, pp. 149–50).

9. Stalin, *Works*, Vol. 9, English version, pp. 250–51: Degras, op. cit., II, p. 277.

10. Guillermaz, op. cit., pp. 99–100.

11. From the letter which Chen Tu-hsiu addressed to the members of the Chinese Communist Party in December 1929 soon after he had been expelled from the party for insisting on the need to have a thorough

discussion of what had occurred. This letter is of great human interest as well as historical importance. It appeared in English in the New York *Militant*, in instalments between 15 November 1930 and 1 February 1931.

12. Stalin, op. cit., Vol. 8, p. 383. In June 1926 the plenum of the Central Committee of the Chinese Communist Party had decided 'to propose that the party resume its own existence and replace its current submission inside the Kuomintang with a formal two-party bloc', but the Comintern considered this decision mistaken, and it was not put into effect (Harold R. Isaacs, *The Tragedy of the Chinese Revolution*, 2nd revised edn, Stanford, 1961, p. 103).

13. Chen Tu-hsiu explains, in his letter mentioned in note 11, that the Comintern had instructed them to confiscate the land of the big land-owners and rich peasants but without touching the estates of the officers of the Kuomintang army. However, 'not a single one of the bourgeoisie, landlords, tuchuns and gentry of Hunan and Hupeh provinces but was the kinsman, relative or old friend of the officers of that time. All the landowners were directly or indirectly protected by the officers.' In the excellent study by Lucien Bianco (op. cit.) this aspect of the Chinese revolution, namely, the close connection of the bourgeoisie, at all levels, with the agrarian structures, is brought out very clearly.

14. Quoted in Guillermaz, op. cit., p. 137.

15. A detailed analysis of the part played by the Chinese question in the struggle between Stalin and the opposition will be found in Deutscher's biography of Trotsky. Deutscher points out, with objectivity, that the opposition took up this question only very late in the day. Even though from 1924 onward, Trotsky reaffirmed on a number of occasions his dis-approval of the subordination of the Chinese Communist Party to the Kuomintang, he did not really get to grips with the problem until shortly before Chiang's betrayal. Moreover, there were theoretical differences between Trotsky and the Zinoviev–Kamenev group about the strategy to be followed in the Chinese revolution. Zinoviev and Kamenev criticized the subordination of the Chinese Communist Party to the Kuomintang, but they were basically in agreement with Stalin that the Chinese revolution could triumph only as a bourgeois-democratic revolution.

16. Chen Tu-hsiu was, with Li Ta-chao, the man chiefly responsible for introducing Marxism into China. A personality enjoying prestige among the intelligentsia, he was one of the founders of the Chinese Communist Party. Chen possessed great intellectual honesty and always clearly ex-pressed his disagreements with the Comintern's directives, even though he

ended by submitting to them. When Stalin and the Comintern made him the scapegoat for the party's defeat, he did not accept this role, in the main out of intellectual honesty. His letter to party members (see note 11) begins thus: 'Since I followed our comrades to found the Chinese Communist Party, I sincerely executed the policy of opportunism of the international leaders, Stalin, Zinoviev, Bukharin and others, making the Chinese revolution suffer a shameful and sad failure. Though I have worked night and day, yet my demerits exceed my merits. Of course, I should not imitate the hypocritical confessions of some of the ancient Chinese emperors: "I, one person, am responsible for all the sins of the people," taking upon my shoulders all the mistakes that caused the failure. Nevertheless, I feel ashamed to adopt the attitude of some responsible comrades at times – only criticizing the past mistakes of opportunism and excluding oneself.' After his expulsion from the party, in 1929, Chen joined the Trotskyist opposition for a time, though maintaining the same critical attitude in relation to this: 'Even the banner of the opposition is not the incantation of the "Heavenly Teacher" Chang (the head of the Taoist religion, who has the "power" of driving out devils).' Arrested by Kuomintang police in 1932 and sentenced to thirteen years forced labour, Chen Tu-hsiu died in 1942. Jacques Guillermaz (op. cit., pp. 46–51) gives a biographical account of Chen's intellectual and political development down to the foundation of the party.

17. Guillermaz, op. cit., p. 161. The Canton rising was directly organized by two representatives of the Comintern, the German Heinz Neumann and the Georgian former Komsomol leader Besso Lominadze. They were both at that time among Stalin's trusted henchmen; which, however, did not save them from execution during the purges of 1936–8.

Soon after the 'left' Kuomintang began its persecution of the Communists, Stalin wrote an article in *Pravda* in which he compared this episode to the blow sustained by the Bolsheviks in July 1917 and considered it 'the more likely prospect' that 'in the near future – not necessarily in a couple of months, but in six months, or a year from now', there might be 'a new upsurge of the revolution'. In that event, said Stalin, 'the question of forming soviets of workers' and peasants' deputies may become a live issue, as a slogan of the day, and as a counterpoise to the bourgeois government' (Stalin, op. cit., Vol. 9, p. 366). The purpose of this article was to minimize the importance of the defeat suffered by the Chinese Communist party and justify the policy followed until then in relation to the 'left' Kuomintang. He wanted to compare the betrayal by the latter to that by

Kerensky and Co., and show the course followed by the Chinese revolution as leading to victory in the same way as had happened with the Bolsheviks in 1917. Once this prediction had been made, Stalin had to do everything possible to ensure that facts confirmed it. This provided the key to the adventuristic policy followed in the final months of 1927, leading to the Canton rising.

18. See note 57, p. 39, and the passage in the text to which it refers.

19. The official historians of the Chinese Communist Party explain this period like this: 'During this campaign [the fifth encirclement campaign waged by Chiang Kai-shek] the Red Army failed to smash the enemy's encirclement, owing to the completely wrong military line of remaining solely on the defensive and other wrong policies pursued by the central leading organs of the party ... During the Long March of the Central Red Army, the central leading organs of the party continued to commit military blunders which several times put the Red Army in dangerous predicaments and caused extremely heavy losses with the enemy blocking the route of advance and pursuing from the rear. In order to save the imperilled Red Army and China's revolutionary cause, comrade Mao Tsetung and other comrades conducted a resolute struggle and secured the calling of an enlarged conference of the Political Bureau of the Central Committee of the party in January 1935, at Tsunyi, Kweichow Province. With the majority of the comrades conscious of the issues and with their support, the Tsunyi Conference removed the "left" opportunists from the party leadership, and established Comrade Mao Tse-tung's leading position in the whole party' (Hu Chiao-mu, *Thirty Years of the Communist Party of China,* Lawrence and Wishart, London, 1951, p. 39).

20. I am here summarizing Stalin's views of the Chinese revolution, which he set out in a number of writings. See, in particular: 'Questions of the Chinese Revolution' and 'Notes on Contemporary Themes: 11, China' (Stalin, op. cit., Vol. 9, pp. 224–34 and 337–69).

21. Trotsky, *The Third International after Lenin,* New York, 1957, p. 174. It should be mentioned however, that Trotsky did not reject the possibility and appropriateness, in certain situations, of temporary compromises with the national bourgeoisie.

22. ibid., p. 195.

23. Even for the 1924–7 period it cannot be said that the development of the workers' movement preceded that of the peasant movement. In the eastern part of Kwangtung province, the organization and

mobilization of the peasant leagues reached a remarkably high level so early as 1922. (See Guillermaz, op. cit., 88–90.)

24. Not only because Lenin, in the last phase of his life, had glimpsed the possibility that the revolution in Asia might precede and open the way for the revolution in Europe, but also because of his greater appreciation of the revolutionary potential existing in the peasant masses of the East.

25. Mao Tse-tung, *Selected Works*, Vol. 1, Foreign Languages Press, Peking, 1965, pp. 18, 23–4.

26. In the resolution of the Tenth Plenum of the ECCI (February 1928) on the Chinese question, it was said that the spontaneous actions of the peasant partisans 'can become a starting point for a victorious national uprising only on condition that they are linked with the new upsurge of the tide of revolution in the proletarian centres'. In a letter from the ECCI dated November 1930 it is stressed that the Red Army 'is not sufficiently in the hands of the Chinese Communist Party. The social composition of the Red Army is far from satisfactory.' It must be transformed 'into a workers' and peasants' army with proletarian leadership'. In a resolution passed by the ECCI in June of the same year it is stated that 'the task of accomplishing the hegemony of the proletariat involves the party in a struggle to extend the development of the strike movement, to organize and to lead the economic battles of the Chinese proletariat. In combining economic and political struggle, the party must make every effort to develop political strikes, moving towards the organization of a general political strike in all industrial centres or in a number of them.' In another resolution of the ECCI, dated August 1932, the same themes are dwelt upon: 'The hegemony of the proletariat and the victorious development of the revolution can be guaranteed only on condition that the Chinese Communist Party becomes a proletarian party not only in its political line but in its composition and the role played by the workers in all of its leading organs' (Schram and Carrère d'Encausse, op. cit., pp. 243, 245, 246; see also Degras, op. cit., III, p. 135, n.)

27. *Inprecorr* (English edn), Vol. 10, No. 21 (30 April 1930), p. 393, and No. 22 (8 May 1930), p. 408.

28. Schram and Carrère d'Encausse, op. cit., pp. 244–5.

29. Guillermaz, op. cit., p. 197.

30. In Shanghai, Wuhan and Tientsin – cities each of which had several million inhabitants – the Communist organizations numbered, at most 2,000, 1,000 and 500 members respectively (ibid., p. 201).

31. ibid., p. 197.

32. This question deserves a detailed analysis such as it cannot be given here. Practically all studies of the Chinese revolution emphasize the contrast between the predominant role played by the town proletariat in the 1924–7 stage and its almost complete eclipse in the following period between 1927 and 1949. Deutscher, Harold Isaacs and other writers influenced by the Trotskyist point of view – which on this question coincides with that of the Comintern – tend, it seems to me, to exaggerate the role played by the proletariat in the first stage and to explain its eclipse in the second mainly by the effects of the 1927 defeat and the mistakes of 1927–34 (the 'Trotskyist' writers blaming the Comintern and Stalin, the 'Stalinists' blaming the Chinese Communist Party). They draw a highly dubious analogy with the process of the Russian revolution. Deutscher, for example, writes: 'In China the alignment of the social forces broadly resembled the Russian pattern: the country was ablaze with agrarian revolt; but the urban workers were the driving force of the revolution' (*The Unfinished Revolution, 1917–1967*, OUP, London, 1967, p. 82). Lucien Bianco considers that the minority situation of the working class did not debar it *a priori* from constituting '*the* great revolutionary force … the more so since it was concentrated in a small number of industrial centres that were also among the country's leading political centres. (In similar circumstances the workers of Petrograd and Moscow played a more decisive role in 1917 than Russia's tens of millions of muzhiks)' (Bianco, op. cit., p. 83). In my view these analogies are ill-founded. Shanghai was not the political and economic centre of China as Petrograd and Moscow were of Russia. In China there was no working-class nucleus formed in heavy industry like the workers of Petrograd, the Urals, the Ukraine, etc. but only a working class of very recent origin, employed mainly in light industry and transport. China did not possess a structured state organization, in which an overturn at the centre could confer on the proletarian minority power such as the October revolution in Russia conferred on the Bolsheviks when they had become masters of Petrograd. Shanghai and the other towns of the coastline, where the working-class nuclei were mainly concentrated, were more the political and economic centres of imperialist power than the nerve-centres of Chinese society. This was essentially a society without a backbone, as Mao was able to appreciate. The urban proletariat of China represented only 0·5 per cent of this immense, amorphous social body. Even so, the adventuristic policy in the urban centres that was followed by the leaders of the Chinese Communist Party, at the instigation of the Comintern, between 1927 and 1933,

must undoubtedly have aggravated the effect of the terrible bloodletting suffered by the working class after the defeat of 1927. (According to Chinese trade-union reports, about 38,000 trade-union militants perished in that year: 25,000 died in battle and 13,000 were executed. See Guillermaz, op. cit., p. 226.)

33. Speech to Party cadres, 26 May 1943, quoted in Stuart R. Schram, *The Political Thought of Mao Tse-tung*, Pall Mall Press, London, 1963, p. 290. Actually, the Comintern did try to go on interfering in the internal affairs of the Chinese Communist Party, but without success. This is confirmed by the history of the Comintern recently produced by the Institute of Marxism–Leninism in Moscow in the context of the Sino-Soviet conflict (see note 11, p. 3).

34. Thorez, op. cit., Vol. 14, p. 281.

35. Speech of 31 October 1939, in *Soviet Peace Policy: Four Speeches by V. Molotov*, Lawrence and Wishart, London, 1941, pp. 28, 31, 32.

36. ibid., pp. 71–3.

37. André Fontaine brings together the different opinions that continue to prevail regarding this matter, in his *History of the Cold War, 1917–1950*, op. cit., p. 116: 'People are still debating the Soviet Union's real intentions during this period . . .' He considers that 'the two explanations that have been current for twenty years – that Stalin had tried unsuccessfully to come to an agreement with the allies, and that he had long since thrown in his lot with Hitler – are equally debatable'. For my part, until the mystery has been elucidated on the basis of irrefutable documents, I am inclined to think that Stalin's basic 'intention' was to choose the solution that would enable him to remain out of war, at least for as long as possible. This was why the outcome of the diplomatic game of 1939 depended on the path that *Hitler* decided to take.

38. A. Nekrich's book (see note 66, p. 71) undertakes to reveal the causes of the terrible defeats suffered by the Red Army in the first months of the German–Soviet war. This leads the author to consider a whole series of questions, such as the weakening of the Soviet armed forces in consequence of the great purge ordered by Stalin at the end of the 1930s, relations with Germany during the period of the pact, and so on. Nekrich shows no *a priori* enmity to Stalin, but he does not hesitate to bring out the latter's responsibility, basing what he says upon documents, in so far as the censorship enables him to do this at the time the book appeared. At the discussion meeting mentioned in note 66, p. 71 the majority of those taking part supported Nekrich's view, as against Deborin and the other

representatives of the official standpoint. A report of this discussion was circulated 'discreetly' in Moscow, and succeeded in crossing the Soviet frontier. It is included, along with Nekrich's book, in V. Petrov, op. cit. Soon after publication, Nekrich's book attracted the anathema of the Brezhnevite neo-Stalinists, who launched against it a campaign the climax of which was the author's expulsion from the party in 1967. A number of Soviet scholars declared in writing their disapproval of this new blow struck at freedom of expression.

Among other facts showing the Soviet government's desire to prolong the life of the pact with Germany, and make it even more intimate, Nekrich mentions the statement of the Tass Agency on 14 June 1941, indicating that the Soviet government was ready to negotiate the signing of 'a new, closer agreement', and that if negotiations had not yet begun to this effect, it was because the German leaders had proved uncooperative (pp. 200–202). Melnikov's contribution appears on p. 256. Nekrich neither confirms nor refutes Melnikov's statements. He confines himself to mentioning that, during the Hitler–Molotov talks, the Soviet representative rejected the proposal that the USSR should join the Tripartite Pact of Germany, Italy and Japan (p. 148), and says nothing about Molotov's counter-proposal. As Melnikov said, this matter is taboo. It is nevertheless significant that Deborin, spokesman in this discussion of the official standpoint, admitted that Stalin 'placed too much hope in the German–Soviet pact' (p. 251).

39. Nekrich's study shows that the facts of Germany's preparations for an invasion of the USSR were known to the Soviet leaders and to Stalin himself, but were interpreted in a totally mistaken way. The Councillor of the German Embassy in Moscow, Hilger, whom Nekrich quotes, summarized thus his impressions of Stalin's attitude: 'Everything indicated that he thought Hitler was preparing for a game of extortion in which threatening military moves would be followed by sudden demands for economic or even territorial concessions. He seems to have believed that he would be able to negotiate with Hitler over such demands when they were presented' (G. Hilger and Alfred G. Meyer, *The Incompatible Allies*, Macmillan, New York, 1953, p. 330). And, basing himself on the testimony of Soviet military leaders, Nekrich states that this was, indeed, the opinion held by the Red Army High Command, an opinion which, of course, echoed Stalin's own (p. 194).

40. The 'desperate situation' at the beginning of the Soviet–German war was recognized by Stalin in his 'toast to the Russian people' during the

solemn celebration of Victory that was held in the Kremlin on 24 May 1945. 'Our government,' said he, 'made not a few errors; we experienced at moments a desperate situation in 1941–2, when our army was retreating, when there was no other way out. A different people could have said to the government: "You have failed to justify our expectations. Go away. We shall instal another government which will conclude peace with Germany ..." The Russian people, however, did not take this path ... Thanks to it, to the Russian people, for this confidence' (quoted in Deutscher's *Stalin*, p. 465). Stalin might have added: now that we have won the victory we shall study these mistakes. That would have been a Marxist attitude ... But, a quarter of a century later, the study of these mistakes is still a dangerous business, as the Nekrich case has shown.

Nekrich's own conclusion is that, while the pact itself was necessary, Stalin's policy during 1939–41 was wrong. Another historian, Slezkin, who took part in the discussion of Nekrich's book, said: 'The 1939 pact was perhaps inevitable, but it was a crime to base any hopes on this pact, and, above all, to stop the fight against Fascism. And that is what Stalin ordered' (V Petrov, op. cit., p. 258).

41. Speech at the election meeting in the Stalin district of Moscow, 9 February 1946 (in *Speeches by Stalin and Molotov, February, 1946*, 'Soviet News' pamphlet, 1946, p. 4. My italics).

42. A curious anthology could be compiled from the fluctuations in Soviet writing on the character of the Second World War. It was, of course, only after the Twentieth Congress that Stalin's definition of 1946 began to be radically reconsidered. In 1957 the party journal *Kommunist* organized a conference on this subject, a report of which appeared in *Recherches internationales à la lumière du marxisme*, Nos. 9–10, 1958, pp. 9–32. The new official definition will be found in the 1960 version of the *History of the CPSU*, by B. N. Ponomaryov et al. (on p. 557 of the English edn, FLPH, Moscow). In the second part of this book I shall deal with the opportunist hoaxing that characterized Soviet and Communist documents of the 1941–7 period regarding the aims of the imperialist powers in the Second World War.

43. The revolutionary forces could not, of course, confine themselves to this 'very least'. They should have sought to take advantage of the second great universal crisis of the capitalist and imperialist system to create the political and organizational conditions for the socialist revolution, wherever this was possible. The fact that national independence and bourgeois-democratic freedoms were threatened by Fascist aggression gave the revo-

lutionary forces an exceptional historic opportunity to rally and mobilize very wide social circles under their leadership. The policy followed by Stalin and the Comintern did not allow this opportunity to be taken in the first period of the war, while, in the second period, they tried to restrict the action of the revolutionary forces to the 'minimum' mentioned – defence of national independence and bourgeois-democratic freedoms.

44. Degras, op. cit., III, p. 459. In 1936 Dimitrov had written: 'The blow against the Fascist aggressor must be directed with definite purpose and with concentrated force at every moment; the attitude taken towards the aggressor must be different from that taken towards the victims of his attack; any attempt to gloss over the difference between Fascist and non-Fascist countries must be exposed' (1 May 1936; in Dimitrov, *Selected Articles and Speeches*, Lawrence and Wishart, London, 1951, pp. 173–4). This was the position of the Comintern down to the very day of the Soviet–German pact. Thenceforth the Comintern started to 'expose' any attempt to differentiate between aggressor and victim and between Fascist and non-Fascist countries.

45. ECCI Manifesto on 2nd Anniversary of the Russian Revolution, in Degras, op. cit., III, p. 446.

46. J. Koplenig, 'The War and the Collapse of the Second International', in *Communist International* (USA edn), No. 9 (September), 1940, p. 599. The passage quoted subsequently is from p. 595.

47. Deutscher, *Stalin*, pp. 458–9. In support of Deutscher's statement it may be noted, among many similar facts, that the French Communist Party produced and circulated clandestinely 50,000 copies of Molotov's speech of 1939, some passages from which I have quoted, and in which he backed Ribbentrop's 'peace' proposals (*Histoire du PCF (Unir)*, 1, p. 261). At the colloquium of Communist historians of Poland, Yugoslavia and Czechoslovakia which was held in Belgrade in 1966 it was said that the policy imposed by the Comintern on the Communist parties of Europe during the first phase of the Second World War had the practical effect of preventing these parties from taking up the struggle against Fascist aggression (see the report of this colloquium in *Z Pola Walki*, No. 2, 1967).

48. Henri Michel, *Les Mouvements clandestins en Europe*, PUF, Paris, 1965, p. 20.